# Crystalling the Legacy

To my favorite
law student,
says his wife
Heidi
THANKS GARY,
Ron
Lansing

If kept
FALLING OFF

Ron
Lansing

Return. Reflect. Reconnect. | 100 CENTENNIAL CELEBRATION

**THE FOUNDERS**

Judge Matthew Paul Deady
[Chair, University of Oregon
Board of Regents, 1883-1893]

Richard Hopwood Thornton
["Professor-in-Charge"
and Dean, 1883-1903]

Judge John Flint Gantenbein
[Proprietor, Registrar,
Trustee, 1941-1965]

Judge Calvin U. Gantenbein
[Proprietor and Dean, 1903-1919]

Judge J. Hunt Hendrickson
[Proprietor and Dean, 1921-1941]

# *Crystalling the Legacy*

## Stories and Reflections on the Accreditation Era of a Law School
### — 1965 - 1974 —

# Ronald B. Lansing

Northwestern School of Law of Lewis & Clark College, Portland, Oregon

ISBN-13  978-0-9630866-4-8

Library of Congress Control Number:  2010940652

Publisher: Lewis & Clark College

Printed in the U.S.A.
All paper is acid free and meets all ANSI standards for archival quality paper.

1 3 5 7 9 10 8 6 4 2

Gracious support from the following
made this book possible:

James S. Coon

William A. Gaylord

Charles S. Tauman

Raymond F. Thomas


*Sine qua Non*

For:

Helga Peters

Ruth VanWelden

Eugenia Busong

Harvey Lambka

Ruth Hale Canaga

Robert Bertram

W. G. Friedrich

Herbert Umbach

Charles Gromley

John Paulus

and all others who through primary, secondary, college, and law schooling showed me what it takes to be and means to be a teacher.

# CONTENTS

## Photographs

## Illustrations

"Lawyers without history or literature are mechanics, mere working masons; if they possess some knowledge of these, they may venture to call themselves architects."

— Sir Walter Scott

# PREFACE

In the catalogs, bulletins, and handbooks of Northwestern School of Law of Lewis & Clark College and among its many paragraphs, there is tucked away an easily missed item: The school is "accredited by the American Bar Association and the American Association of Law Schools." That's all it says, but that's not all it was. How it came to be accredited is a main sojourn in this book.

The entire history of the school has passed through seven eras.

I. *The Thornton Era, 1893-1903:* The decade in which England scholar Richard Hopwood Thornton and U.S. Federal District Court Judge Matthew Paul Deady founded the school in Portland, Oregon, as the Law Department of the University of Oregon.

II. *The First Gantenbein Era, 1903-1918:* The period leading up to and through World War I during which, in 1915, the university abandoned faculty, students, and location in Portland and Judge Calvin Gantenbein (then dean) assumed private ownership of the Portland school under the name Northwestern College of Law.

III. *The Hendrickson Era, 1919-1941:* The decades of the Roaring Twenties and the Great Depression in which Judge J. Hunt Hendrickson was dean and a proprietor along with Charles R. Spackman and members of the Gantenbein family.

IV. *The Second Gantenbein Era, 1942-1958:* The period covering World War II and the Korean War and their aftermaths in which Judge John Flint Gantenbein (son of Calvin) was Registrar and sole proprietor.

V. *The Merger Era, 1958-1965:* A short period in which the proprietorship was transferred to a corporate trust and eventually merged with an established liberal arts college, thus becoming Northwestern School of Law of Lewis & Clark College.

VI. *The Accreditation Era, 1965-1974:* The decade in which national accreditation was sought from the American Bar Association and the Association of American Law Schools—a period covering four dean regimes.

VII. *Modern Eras, 1974-Present:* The decades following accreditation begin the advance of the school through the multi-dean regimes of Steven Kanter, Arthur LaFrance, James Huffman, Robert Klonoff, and those yet to come.

This writing targets the sixth period, the "Accreditation Era." It began almost a half-century ago as of this publication. It could be the story of any school of any kind coming out of hiding, venturing into wide worlds, seeking eminence, and daring to be great. In the fable of the Phoenix rising from ashes, we are awed by the beauty of the Phoenix. This story is about the ashes.

My career as a law teacher began in that accreditation era, thus making this history a memoir. While the accreditation quest occupied much of our time in the first eight and one-half years of the merged law school, we also had to tend the prime function of education—the development of a strong school experience for those who came to learn. To be sure, the two endeavors were linked, but they were also distinct—a difference but not a disagreement. Accreditors focused on major themes—the *big picture,* so to speak. Educational business, however, involved us in multiple mundane chores, the sum of which present the *real picture* of schooling. In accreditation we were being pushed; in education, we did the pulling—a difference in being "good enough" and being "damn good." In the former, we were judged; in the latter, we judged. It is one thing to comply with goals already fixed and another thing to define goals and fix them. The reader will note that the two quests (accrediting and educating), while on the same track, were nonetheless on different trains. Accordingly, chapters herein will sometimes leave one to board the other—a shift from annals to the little stories of weeks and days.

In both pursuits, we were faced with choices, and those choices involved another distinction. Whether as governed or governor, whether meeting or making the rules, in either case, solving is always a matter of *how to do so.* Alternatives are often between one of two roads—a fork lit by penumbral glow one way and by bright lines the other way, each bearing sign posts that raise these kinds of questions: Should we go toward general principles or precise dictates? Do we follow informal guides or formalized order? Are we to heed situational clues or normative controls? Considerational or canonical standards? Protean/Procrustean means? Qualification/Quantification? Circumstance/Abstraction? All such bifurcating is founded, on the one hand, by concerns for compassion, exception, and equity, or on the other hand, by concern for uniformity, certainty, and predictability. Both are concerned with fairness—one a fair warm-heartedness, the other a fair even-handedness.

Accordingly, throughout these pages, the reader may note, here and there, decision throes torn by the foregoing alternatives. Pressed by the need to collect them in one place, I have indexed them under this heading: "Qualitative Circumstance/ Quantitative Abstraction."

Some cautions to the reader are in order: When the text uses money numbers, the reader is reminded of what those numbers mean in today's inflationary calculations. In general, dollars in that past era, based on Consumer Price Index statistics, are equivalent to five or six times that amount as of this writing. Furthermore, higher education costs have risen considerably higher than that CPI ratio. See, S. Friedman Morgan's *Inflationary Calculator*.

The "Bar" is capitalized whenever used as a proper noun referring to the title of any official or organized body of lawyers but not when merely a descriptive adjective (e.g., "bar exam," "bar member," "bar rules").

The word "Law" is capitalized whenever it refers to the whole jurisprudential concept by which societies seek to organize their governance. Individual rules, statutes, codes, or judicial decisions are "laws" [not capitalized]. This is a helpful distinction between the gestalt and the efforts made to promulgate it. And it should serve as a reminder that there are anarchic, monarchic, totalitarian, and pious societies that do not put rights and justice at the capital of governance.

While the overuse of acronyms borders on criminality, sometimes common use or conservation compels them. Accordingly, the reader will frequently encounter these initials: "*ABA*" [American Bar Association]; "*AALS*" [American Association of Law Schools]; "*SCOLS*" [The Standing Committee on the Operation of the Law School]; "*JFC*" [Judicial Fitness Commission]; and others explained in the text.

Another acronym deserves more attention. During the merger negotiations in 1965, one of the intense issues was what to name this adopted school. Should it continue as "Northwestern" or now be called "Lewis & Clark." Eventually, it was agreed that both designations must survive. The official title finally etched into the Merger Agreement was "Northwestern School of Law of Lewis & Clark College"— a fairly long drink of water that time and use would turn into a sip. Negotiations, certificates, christenings do not have the last word. Common parlance is what names us. Among veteran alumni and heritage family, the law school is still affectionately, "Northwestern." Within the last two decades and at least among the nationwide circles of law schools, law professionals, and journalists, "Lewis & Clark Law School" has become the inevitable version. But back in the Accreditation Era, use and familiarity had not yet worked its transience. Resistance to capsulating the long title was still fresh and strong. "Northwestern School of Law of Lewis & Clark College" was the

appellation used in all correspondence, letterheads, business cards, public announcements, and other documentation. It was an unwieldy mouthful born of compromise in
1965, maintained during the Accreditation Era, and kept revived throughout the last
of the 1900s. Now here in the twenty-first century this author engages in a compromise of his own: To respect the agreed and actually used name in those older times
yet also to relieve these pages of too much ink, I have adopted the acronym "NWLC."

Part of the book title needs explanation. *Webster's Third International Dictionary -
Unabridged* says the verb *crystal* means, *inter alia*, "to cause to take a fixed and definite
form." My definition suggests a great deal more:

> Crystal [kris•tahl] v.t. [Gk.: krystallos, ice] to solidify in clear prisms capable of
> casting light, color, and brilliance.

Throughout the book, as throughout my life, are some of my cartoons and caricatures. They were doodled during faculty business meetings and printed in the
minutes when I was the faculty scribe. They are here as reflections of the times when
sobersides begged for a merry-andrew. Sometimes it is right to find humor in what
troubles us and other times to find trouble in what amuses us.

By way of further caution, I take a lesson from my late friend Terence O'Donnell.
Even though he wrote of history, he always confessed he was not a trained historian.
Likewise, I grant that I have no academic degree or scholarship in the discipline of
history. But I have been rash enough to write and publish historical accounts. Like
so many, I am a follower and consumer of our past. So, I know phony history when
I read it. Call it "candy history"—history packaged to sell its subject by making
"sweet" the people, events, and institutions it promotes. It's often a coffee-table
book that simply aggrandizes. Such loyalist history must tear at the soul of the true
historian. All of which is to say that this book does not engage in that kind of popu-
larizing. It means to be impartial—candid, but not offensive. It tells what truthfully
happened, whether graceful, grim, or gross.

A final caveat: Some readers will have noted in the Epigraph to this book that the
Sir Walter Scott quote is not exactly correct. He originally stated, "A lawyer . . . if **he**
possesses some knowledge . . . **he** may call **him**self architect." I took the liberty of
pronominal patching in order to update the substance of that 19th century wisdom,
for fear that it might be lost in what has become modernly an argument over form
and an avalanche of gender equality within the Bar.

Intellectual study is often characterized as life in an ivory tower—a fair allusion
to its sometimes cloistered existence. The walk through Academe can be isolated.

This book explores those gardens. But the inner workings of anything cannot be fully understood without the context of what lies beyond its walls. And so, chapters herein are interspersed with items of what was going on in the world outside—insights that may give added meaning to what permeated NWLC. Indeed, the 1965-74 years were turbulent times—times of hot and cold war; atomic weaponry and nuclear experiment; political burglary and "dirty tricks;" White House purges and Presidential impeachment; anti-war demonstrations and racial confrontations; women's rights challenges and chauvinist response; massive rioting and law enforcement repercussions; generational gap; drug commerce; use and abuse of land, water, and air; development of lawyer ethics and professionalism; population explosion; assassination. And all of it was electrified by the dynamics of student, feminist, and minority movements for greater recognition and participation in the establishment— all propelled by technological and economic advances in transportation and communication that brought global involvement closer to the sanctuaries of home and campus. Our island had no form without the ocean from which it arose.

In writing both memoir and history, one runs into a fuzzy line that ought to separate the two. Wanderers in the penumbra are the living, like me, who took part in old times. When a memory seems like only yesterday, surely it cannot be antiquated enough to be called "history"; can it? But no matter, for both history and memoir relate old times. Thus does the past come to us from researchers who exhume its fossils or from reminiscers who re-live its days—the difference between tracing backward or carrying forward—digging up or handing down. This author has done both in the writing of this book. I lived the times and carry it forth, and I dug back into documentation—sometimes the reminiscer and sometimes the researcher.

Whether digging or living, however, there were times when I wished I had paid better attention—times when I had neither documentation nor a clear memory. For example, in the summer of 1966 when I first accepted the assignment to teach law, I happened to be seated across a lunch table from one of the Bar's elder statesmen. When he found that I would be teaching at his alma mater (Northwestern College of Law), he lectured me about grand traditions of the school. From under craggy eyebrows, he stared down a boney finger pointed in my direction and spoke of his school and mostly of the judges who were his teachers there. His final admonition to me was something about living up to the legacy.

Attention was given the respect owed to his years, albeit not with the full ear it deserved. It was only later, when researching the school's history, that I learned I had been talking to Abraham Asher, the school's oldest living alumnus. He had enrolled in 1915, the year "Northwestern" first acquired that name. A 1918 graduate class photo now hangs in the halls of NWLC and shows a very young looking Abe Asher and the teachers of whom he had spoken—teachers whose tenures can be traced back to the 1800s. Mr. Asher died at age 87 before I could appreciate the value of what his memoirs might bring. At that table in 1966 I had been in the presence of history—so close to what was so faraway—a heritage he lived and with which I was then about to meld—just as now I hand down a history I lived and with which readers can meld. Such is the nature of heritage: it does not dawn until dusk.

But memoir and piggyback memoir on memoir should carry the usual caveats, especially when fuzzy and without documentation. These annals, basted as they are in reminiscence and seasoned with commentary, make it a recipe where conceit, self-effacement, nostalgia, and hearsay might spoil the broth. So, let me assure the reader that my recall and research have been obedient to care. When verity was at risk, please note my awareness of it, my sincerity in guarding against it, and my candor in admitting that, like all observers, I witnessed much but not all from my parallax view.

Finally, in striving to do both memoir and history, sometimes it may seem that my personal stories and NWLC annals ought not to have become mixed. If that occurs, be kind enough to understand that after forty-four years together, it is no wonder that school and self may have grown into one another.

– *R.L.*

# INTRODUCTION
### *1963-67*

Over half of my life I have been a law professor and sometimes have to remind myself that I used to do other things. I was thirty-one when I first reached out to do law teaching. On January 15, 1963, during a lull in the day's practice of law, I sent a letter expressing my interest in being a part-time instructor at Northwestern College of Law, a night school in downtown Portland. It was presumptuous of me, for I had only been out of law school for about thirty months and was then a young associate in the law offices of Shuler, Sayre, Winfree, and Rankin. My letter went to Judge James W. Crawford, dean of the school, and he replied one day later. While there were no vacancies on the faculty at the present time, he wanted to know what fields of law I was qualified to teach. I wrote back and listed as many as ten specific courses and then had the audacity to conclude with: "and any special courses derived therefrom."

That wide swath fancied myself as a devotee of Law with a nonchalance toward *laws*. It did not matter what laws were taught; what had to be learned was Law itself, and the latter could spring from any of its curricular corners. I favored jurisprudence—a penchant for the whole instead of its parts—what Oliver Wendell Holmes, Jr. characterized as "the seamless web" and the "echoes of the infinite." I confess it was not a good attitude in law practice. In a law world of increasing complexity and specialization, a Law synthesizer becomes a non-conformist.

I never heard back from Judge Crawford nor did I try to resurrect what had been merely a fleeting fancy. Nevertheless, that idle dip fomented a lifetime immersion. Two and one-half years transpired before the taste came again. By this time I

1

was now a partner in the law firm of Bailey, Swink, Haas, and Lansing. I had taken the place of Sid Lezak, whom President Kennedy had appointed U.S. Attorney for Oregon. Sometime in the summer of 1965, Judge John Flint Gantenbein invited me into his chambers after the trial of a case. He said he was Northwestern's Registrar and kept a file of those who had expressed interest in being a part-time law instructor and asked if I was still interested. He summarized the school's history and his lifetime with it—a life span that began as a child at his father's table. In 1915, the father, Calvin, as dean of the University of Oregon Law Department, took over the proprietorship of the downtown Portland law location when the university decided to move its law school to Eugene, Oregon. The son, John Flint, from those days on, fused his life with his father's school, first as a law student and graduate, then as the school's registrar, then one of its owners, then as the sole proprietor. Now here in his chambers, he told me that he had in recent years transferred his proprietorship to a non-profit corporation headed by five trustees: Jack H. Cairns, Jack L. Kennedy, Thomas H. Tongue, Judge Crawford, and himself. He further confided that the Northwestern trustees had been shopping for merger with one of Portland's four main undergraduate schools of higher education: Portland State University, University of Portland, Reed College, and Lewis & Clark College.

The judge said he was not getting younger nor was his part-time faculty. They were venerable and successful judges, lawyers, and teachers. What experience lacks, however, is continuity, he said; their success did not provide succession. He did not want to see his father's school wither. He needed younger teachers who might carry on. "Would you like to do so? I need faculty who will stick around."

As a young lawyer, I was filled with the bite of energy and involved in far too much extra-activity: Portland City Club, Portland Opera Association, Unitarian Fellowship, Oregon State Bar committees, Multnomah County Bar continuing legal education, and other community and neighborhood efforts. Then too, in my law firm I was given the role of business manager. I was also involved in a precedent-setting, land zoning case [*Smith vs. Washington County*, 241 OR 380 (1965)]. That, plus family time with an equally energetic wife beginning her work as a CPA and three children (ages four, five, and eight), inclined me to resist taking on another responsibility.

Those who remember him will attest that Judge Gantenbein had the kindest of faces and a soul to match. He sympathized with my reluctance but said he was simply urging me to update my 1963 application. To such curry and non-commital, I was an easy mark. In a June 29 letter, I renewed my request for an instructorship.

That 1965 re-application, like its 1963 predecessor, bore no immediate fruit. Northwestern got side-tracked. Its trustees became deeply involved in merger negotiations. On September 12, 1965, those involvements culminated in a contract between two pioneer schools in Oregon history. Henceforth, Northwestern College of Law would be known as Northwestern School of Law of Lewis & Clark College—the former tracing its origins to 1883 as the Law department of the University of Oregon and the latter evolving from Albany College founded in 1867.

For the next year, the name was the only ostensible change in the law school's operation. Judge Gantenbein became the part-time interim dean and remained so until a professional educator could be found. The school continued to operate in the Giesy Building in downtown Portland just a few blocks from my office in the Corbett Building. At the surface, the merger for the time being seemed no more than a ripple upon which my re-application was adrift. No one, including me, could see what lay beneath those still waters.

Then, in August 1966, Judge Gantenbein contacted me again to see if I would be able to teach the Code Pleading course at the law school. He said that Lewis & Clark College had appointed him caretaking dean; that a new dean was not yet in place; that the previous Code Pleading teacher, Phil Levin, a prominent appellate lawyer, had died; that the school needed a replacement at once; that I had been picked from my letter of application and résumé.

The fact that Levin had died many months prior indicated that I had not been a first choice nor likely a second or third. While it was not flattering to be a last minute recruit, that was overcome by the honor of serving in a part-time faculty that over eight decades had been the pick of the Oregon bench and bar: supreme court judges, trial judges, national and state legislators, district attorneys, senior law partners, Bar presidents, and distinguished practitioners who had carried and handed down the traditions of what had been called "Northwestern's Living Law." I did not hesitate to accept the Gantenbein offer.

As of 1965-66, part-time instructors were paid a paltry $225 per semester credit hour and $1.00 for each exam graded. At the start of my 1966-67 academic year, the pittance was raised a mite: $400 per semester hour that included exam grading. I was required to teach two nights each week for thirty-two weeks. Each class evening, I spent four hours at the work—three hours of preparation beginning at 6:00 p.m. and one hour of classroom contact beginning at 9:00 p.m. There was no time to come home after my law practice hours. So, I tabled at a downtown restaurant, partaking of bread, notes, and text and managed to stay just twenty pages ahead of the students in the Code Pleading casebook.

Classes were held on the top floors of the three-story Giesy Building at the northeast corner of SW Park and Stark Streets—a structure destined to be razed to make way for downtown Portland development. It was next door to the luxurious, multi-storied, venerable Benson Hotel with its brilliant Crystal Ballroom—a marked contrast to the dingy, dim-lit classroom just walls away. The haunts of the law school were every bit indicative of valid education in vile surroundings, made so by affording opportunity at affordable prices. I was informed that 78 percent of the night students were married, 61 percent of them had two children, and 93 percent had regular daytime jobs. Their average age was 27 years. I was only six years older than that average, and many of them were far older than I.

That nighttime, part time education was my first unique impression in law teaching. The commitment was awesome. An ancient adage in Law study is that Law is a "jealous mistress." For the night law student that mistress or master competes with family and job. Dovetailing those devotions with school discipline was a multi-tasking worthy of wonder.

As their night teacher, I began to feel the crunch myself. By the time I arrived home after a night of teaching, it was 10:30 p.m.—time to peek in on the pillowed and tousled heads of my children already tucked away. None of the foregoing agenda took into account the tedious hours of preparing, evaluating, and grading final semester exams. For all of that, I was paid at the end of the academic year $1,600. But the real "pay" was something hard to put into words. Fascination did not quite express it. It was attraction mingled with a satisfaction that all teachers must get when completing the circle by giving back what was once received.

In the middle of that 1966-67 academic year, a major disruption occurred: the Giesy Building landlord ended the law school's lease. The building was destined for the wrecking ball, which may give some idea of what it was like to have studied there in its waning year.

At the beginning of the second semester we packed boxes of library books, records, class photographs, and eighty-three years of accumulation and shipped them seven miles away to the campus of Lewis & Clark College. Merger on paper had happened eighteen months before; now merger on land took place. Students had to come from downtown (where many worked in the daytime) to spend three evenings each week at the outskirts of Portland on a stately, imposing campus that draped learning in more academic wraps. The new setting caused some departure. There were 248 students at the start of my teaching in the fall semester downtown. When the law classes began in the second semester on the Lewis & Clark campus, only 218 students enrolled. Thirty students had made voluntary withdrawals. It was a matter of concern, and was but the first of many surprises that would take NWLC's journey over many more ramparts in the years to come.

**NIGHT STUDENTS**

Study between classes, mid-day jobs,
family, meals, commute, and sleep

Now that classes were being held on campus, I did my class preparations in the college library. Somewhere about the first week of March 1967, as I was bent over books and a legal pad at a library table, a busy, grey-haired, wiry man sat down opposite me and abruptly asked if I would like to leave the practice of law and make a career as a law professor. I had no idea who he was or what he was talking about. He told me he was the dean of the law school. My immediate reaction was: Who is this crackpot? Did the college have security guards?

It took him awhile to convince me it was no prank. He was George Neff Stevens and was as new to the campus as I was. He had been operating as dean out of his garage at his home in Seattle where he had been the retired Dean of the University of Washington Law School. He had transacted his Northwestern law school business by mailing dictaphone belts to Doris McCroskey, his on-campus secretary at Lewis & Clark College. He had assigned the daily routine of the school to Judge Gantenbein, while he (Stevens) was busy preparing a thirty-seven page evaluation of the law school's operations for the American Bar Association. Now that he and his wife Helen had moved to Portland and classes were being conducted on campus, he had taken full reins.

That one of his teachers did not even know of his nine-month old deanship was not unusual. Throughout much of Northwestern history, the part-time faculty and part-time administration had little liaison. On the priority list of a night school where all levels of the hierarchy including students had other work, teaching was utmost and organization was shortshrift. And so, instructors paid little mind to administration, and administrators paid little mind to instruction. In effect, there was no chain of command. No one was bossed. Meetings, an essential jelling in complex organization, were triflings at Northwestern.

Simple informality would now begin to change. Here now I was met by a full-time, professional educator who was beginning to organize. His question to me was a baby step at the start of learning to walk and then to march together: *Would you like to stop being part-time and become full-time?* It meant: *Would you like to cease being a loose piece in a puzzle and start fitting into the jigs and saws?*

As we sat at that library table, Dean Stevens told me that he had been working on a plan for gaining a status called "accreditation" for the law school. In my naïveté, I had to ask what that meant. He explained that Northwestern, although blessed with a long, deeply rooted, and esteemed heritage, had never sought, in all of its decades, recognition as a training ground for lawyers. The Oregon Supreme Court allowed Northwestern graduates to become lawyers, but virtually none of the other states would do so. To gain that national acceptance the school had to be given credit by the nation's lawyers and by the nation's law educators as represented by two distinct and distinguished organizations: The American Bar Association (ABA) and the American Association of Law Schools (AALS). While these two organizations tried to cooperate with each other, they each had separate notions and guarded powers in accrediting law schools.

In order to gain accreditor approvals, Northwestern had to become part of a recognized undergraduate school of higher learning. The dean waved a hand around the handsome interior of the newly constructed Lewis & Clark Watzek Library, as if to say "first mission accomplished." Northwestern also had to have a full-time dean. His hand went to his chest—second mission accomplished. The next mission was to gather a full-time faculty—career professionals—teachers who made law education their occupational core. And that brought the dean and me full-circle. *Would I like to take on that career change?*

I donned a business-like nonchalance; it hid sheer thrill—an explosion of what I always must have known but never realized. Patience, however, cautioned impulse. Matters had to be weighed. The offer called for me to start in September at a yearly salary of about $12,000 with fringe benefits. As a law partner, I was making considerably more than that. The salary had to be weighed against the salutary. Teaching jobs are for only nine months of the year, broken up by liberal summer and holiday time in which to supplement income as a consultant, arbitrator, or mediator or in which to pursue a goal I had always wanted: research and writing.

On the other side of the scale was the part of teaching that called for evaluating students. Grading student exams and research was deplorable work. Most teachers might concede that they would teach for no pay, were it not for having to make a living and were it not for the agony of telling students, "You are not as good as this student, but you are better than that one;" or "This exam was bad; that one was worse; and that the worst of all." The agony is not just born of sympathy; it springs from selfishness as well. When the student fails to learn, I have failed to teach.

Dean Stevens then put his thumb on the scales—one more item for me to weigh. It was packaged in flattery. I had been doing "outstanding classroom work" and had evinced all of the "raw qualities and motives" of professorship. I don't know how he could have surmised this, for there were no student evaluations at that time and I would not have failed to notice a strange inspector in my classroom. He was not only the dean, he was a huckster. Indeed, a dean, like all leaders, must know how to sell.

After a few more days, I stopped weighing the pro's and con's and succumbed to the foregone. My first, full-time, faculty contract was dated March 21, 1967. As an assistant professor, I would begin in September 1967 at an annual salary of $12,500—the extra $500 was the result of some customary dickering that caps horse-traders with the feel of mutuality.

That summer my wife Jewel and I bought a new home closer to the campus. She had gained her CPA license a couple of years before and was just gaining a taste for politics that would lead her to a career as Multnomah County's elected Auditor, Portland's elected City Auditor, and the Democratic candidate for Oregon State Treasurer. The rest of the family included Annette, who just began kindergarten; Alyse, who was in first grade; and Mark, a fourth grader.

My law partners gave me their best wishes, a send-off dinner, and a desk plaque inscribed "Paul, Don, and Harl." That memento still adorns my desk, where it daily reminds me of a consequence to which I had not given full account: No longer would I do what I would teach. The practice of law would be missed.

Over the years, people have asked what it was like to shift from law practice to law teaching. Indeed, re-tuning was in order. The music of practice was high-strung staccato. In academic gardens, the tone was a low legato—the difference in cadence between a tap dance and a waltz. Oddly enough, for me, the hours were longer at teaching than in practice. So, the real difference in shifting from the one to the other did not lay in a contrast between the two; rather it was a shift within me—in one the obedience of work; in the other the labor of love.

At age 35, the vast majority of my life had been spent in school. I had now embarked on what would become more than 44 years in schooling. In 1967, however, I had no idea that I was making a lifetime home in Academe.

# MID 1960'S: TIME CONTEXT

**1963**: Civil rights uprisings in Alabama. Martin Luther King is arrested. President Kennedy sends 3,000 troops to quell riots.

Telephonic "hotline" directly connects the White House and Kremlin.

Nuclear test ban treaty between U.S., Soviet Union, and Britain is consummated.

President Kennedy is assassinated. Oswald kills Ruby on national television.

Gallon of gas costs about 21 cents.

**1964**: Lyndon Johnson is elected U.S. President.

Warren Commission reports Oswald was lone assassin under no conspiracy.

North Vietnam reportedly attacks a U.S. destroyer in the Gulf of Tonkin. U.S. retaliates with air attacks in North Vietnam.

Congress authorizes the Gulf of Tonkin Resolution escalating U.S. military involvement in Vietnam. Senator Wayne Morse of Oregon is one of two voting opposed.

Martin Luther King wins Nobel Peace Prize.

24th Amendment makes it unconstitutional to tax the right to vote.

Orbiting U.S. unmanned rocket photographs moon surface.

Congress passes National Civil Rights Act.

New musical rock group—The Beatles—make their first appearance in the U.S.

Cassius Clay wins heavyweight boxing championship.

Disco dancing and the "hippy" generation emerge.

**1965**: Civil rights violence, including KKK shootings, erupts at Selma, Alabama. Martin Luther King leads processional of 4,000 from Selma to Montgomery to deliver civil rights petition to state government.

Malcolm X is murdered.

Students demonstrate in D.C. against U.S. bombing of North Vietnam.

North Vietnam rejects peace talks. Soviet Union supports North Vietnam with arms deliveries.

Race riots in Watts (L.A. district) ends in 35 dead, 4,000 arrests, and $40 million property losses.

North Vietnam jet plane shoots down U.S. jets.

President Johnson appoints Abe Fortas to U.S. Supreme Court.

The Beatles give a concert in Portland, Oregon and pronounce it the "most orderly crowd on their national tour."

**1966**: Israeli and Jordan troops battle.

U.S. plane crashes in Spain after releasing four unarmed hydrogen bombs in the countryside.

Unmanned U.S. spaceship lands on the moon.

California elects Ronald Reagan governor.

Color TV sets become popular.

Miniskirts are fashionable.

Gallon of gas costs about 32 cents.

# 1
# THE STEVENS REGIME
*Autumn 1967*

## MOLEHILL TO MOUNTAIN TASKING

Beginning in September 1967, Northwestern School of Law of Lewis & Clark College [NWLC] seated the first full-time faculty in its eighty-three year history. There were five of us including the Dean. Full professors Jack Cairns and Paul Gerhardt had been instructors at Northwestern since the mid-1950s—a combined teaching experience of more than twenty years. Each was a sole practitioner in downtown Portland with long-standing clientele. Their switch to professorial careers would prove to be a difficult shift. Taking a lawyer out of the practice was one thing, but taking the practice out of a lawyer was another thing entirely.

Assistant Professor Ross Runkel, on the other hand, was a recent graduate of the University of Washington law school where George Neff Stevens had been dean. Ross had a teaching career in mind, but I was an experiment. With Jack and Paul as bridges between the old and new and Ross as an academic apprentice, I floated somewhere in between.

Just prior to accepting the deanship with NWLC in the summer of 1966, Stevens at age 68 had been on the faculty of Hastings College of Law, the oldest law school west of the Mississippi River. The Hastings faculty was a pasture for semi-retired, nationally prominent, senior deans and professors of law. Stevens was Director of the Hastings Law Journal. He was hired by NWLC trustees to gain accreditation and was specially suited to that task because he was currently the chairman of an American Bar Association [ABA] committee drafting new law school accreditation standards. Thus, Stevens wore two hats: the head of our school seeking approval and the head of the committee drafting the approvers' rules. That certainly appeared to be an

**FIRST FULL-TIME FACULTY**

Paul Gerhardt and Jack Cairns

[Top, l. to r.]

Ross Runkel, author Lansing, Dean
George Neff Stevens

[Bottom, l. to r.]

advantage to us. But Stevens, as a dean of a law school yet also an inspector of law schools, would be torn between the loose meaning of standards and the strict meeting of standards – a contrast in loyalties between players who must abide rules and referees who must enforce them. It augured for trouble ahead.

AFTER SEVERAL MONTHS OF PUTTING my law office and business in a transferrable condition, notifying organizations of my change of business address, and bidding goodbye, I came to academe and began adjusting to professorial life. Our **makeshift offices** on campus were a couple of houses on Huddleston Lane. Each was a two bedroom residence, vintage post-World War II—relics of the time when that portion of the campus had been a family neighborhood. The four faculty members were put in the old Freeda Hartzfeld home. Runkel and Gerhardt were officed in the two bedrooms; Cairn's office was a small sun room connecting the house to the garage. I was put in the living room, separated by a temporary partition from the faculty secretary—a secretary yet to be hired.

The kitchen was the "faculty lounge," where true to its beginnings, it became a gathering spot around the coffee urn for the cooking of collegiality. Tobacco smoking commonly accompanied those coffee breaks. In 1967, folklore scares were generally understood about smoking: it will "stunt your growth" or "make your hair or teeth fall out;" but its cancerous and other scientifically confirmed invasions were ignorance to the consumer and ignored by the industry. Paul Gerhardt was the only careful one among us. He was fastidious about his health: taking naps, preparing his own carefully dieted meals, and not smoking. Paul had multiple sclerosis—a slowly debilitating disease that affected his eyesight. So, when the four of us gathered, we were marked by our properties in hand: Cairns with his cigar or pipe, Runkel with his pipe, me with a cigarette, and Paul with his magnifying glass—an unhealthy quartet to be sure—but hearty and harnessed together, teaching first-year, fundamental law courses: Jack ensconced in contract law, Paul in property law, Ross in commercial law, and I the tort law teacher. Dean Stevens, secretary Doris McCroskey, and Assistant Dean David Shannon were officed in the former Huddleston residence next door to the faculty house. Shannon was hired in May 1967 to tend to some outside administrative chores and not to teach. He had been a Seattle attorney and, like Runkel, had been a former law student of Dean Stevens at the University of Washington. Shannon's stay was short-lived.

Dean Stevens' multiple files were kept in kitchen cabinets. At the beginning, the law administrators shared their house with some foreign language professors. Russian, German, Japanese, now capped with legalese, made the house a tower of babel.

**NASCENT STAFF**

Registrar Dorothy Cornelius [upper left];
Secretary Doris McCroskey [lower left];
Library and Book Store Tender Virginia
Hughes. [Dave Shannon not pictured.]

Officed with them was the law school's Registrar, Dorothy Cornelius. Dorothy was the second full-time employee in the history of the old, downtown Northwestern law school. The first was Richard Hopwood Thornton, founder of the school and first dean from 1884 to 1903. After his term ended, the school never had a full-time employee until Dorothy was hired in 1956. Her past service to the old school was honored in the 1965 Merger Agreement where she was singled out and given formal tenure. Item 8 read:

> "Lewis & Clark shall continue the employment of Dorothy Cornelius, the recent secretary of the law school, at not less than her present salary until she reaches the age of sixty-five or obtains other employment to her liking."

Our classes were held on the other side of the campus in undergraduate **class-rooms** made vacant by the night. Once literature, economics, biology, history, and such were put to bed, law education took over. Cairns, a pre-law chemistry-major, taught law in the chemistry lab. Law students in some classrooms were made to sit in cramped, arm-tabled chairs. Inasmuch as the study of law called for many open books and papers, it was not unusual to see the floor around those armchairs made into desk tops.

The **law library** (less than 8,000 books) was first stored on the other side of the campus beneath the chapel and music department's organ. Virginia Hughes was the law bookstore operator and caretaker-librarian with guidance from Multnomah County law librarian, Jacqueline Jurkins.

That constituted the maiden roster of NWLC in September 1967.

MY IMMEDIATE TASK AT THE start of the 1967-68 academic year was to learn Civil Procedure—an expanded view of the narrower Code Pleading course I had taught as a part-timer. Civil Procedure would be my fall semester course and Torts my spring semester course. Later on, both courses would be spread over both semesters. Civil Procedure had been Dean Stevens' major field of scholarship. He was nationally known in that field, especially on matters of court venue. It would be good to tap his experience.

In learning the substance of a subject, there also came the task of packaging and dispatching its message. Method was every bit as important to a teacher as content. The difference was the contrast between getting smart and making others so. Most certainly, they aid one another. But, surprisingly, there are professors who are intellectually rich yet pedagogically poor. It has always puzzled me: How can someone be smart enough to know but not smart enough to explain? Can letting loose of the baton be any more difficult than grasping it?

Soon after I was dubbed "law professor," I began to receive invitations to do volunteer, public service for civic, Bar, and government entities. Professors are particularly susceptible to enlistment on task forces, committees, commissions, and panels—all gratuitous work. Presumably, that vulnerability is because professors are seen as scholars. I had the title, but I had not yet earned its value as a scholar. Nevertheless, I was sought. Although there was no desserts, there was, at least, dressing. Lacking

ARMCHAIR EDUCATION, 1967-70

worthiness, I clung to a hope taken from world history: the many instances where, instead of excellence deserving title, it was title that induced excellence.

Accordingly, the first invitation I accepted was service on an ad hoc study of police work for Oregon's Council of Crime and Delinquency. I also soon found myself as a co-editor (with attorney Bernard Jolles) of an Oregon State Bar Continuing Legal Education publication on Damages. Eventually, I also chaired a number of Portland City Club reports and did task force work for the Portland Public Schools.

Sometimes the outside work was not voluntary; sometimes it was an assignment. E.g., On October 25, 1967, just two months after I started as a full-time professor, Dean Stevens gave me the task of **evaluating Oregon State Bar Exam** questions: the ones on Pleading, Evidence, and Torts. Professorial advice to the bar examiners was a new idea instigated by my old boss, Chief Justice William McAllister of the Oregon Supreme Court. All three of the Oregon law schools were asked to participate. Academicians did so grudgingly, and the bar examiners were just as loathe to have professorial oversight.

Criticism from the schools had to do with timing. The exam had been given in July; Bar examiners finished grading the July exam in August. Successful examinees were admitted to law practice in September. Professors were given the exam for critique in October. My analyses needed to be sent to the bar examiners in mid-November, just three weeks away. The short deadline was not the only problem; sequencing was the greater problem. Once exam grading and bar passage were done with, what good is ex post-facto advice? That it was good for future exams was tokenism without clout. The wrinkle would be ironed out years later when the chief justice would bring the bar examiners and academicians together on a more efficient chronology.

All of this outside work was a sample introduction to a category of duty beyond schooling that was expected of professors. "Community service" was the name for it. My new work place was not just a law school; it was a law center. Teaching, publishing, and community service were the criteria for promotion through the ranks of assistant, associate, and full professorship. And they were also the keys to the grant of tenure and salary increment.

To my surprise, I soon learned that neither pedagogy nor scholarship nor service was going to be our foremost task. At the start of the 1967-68 academic year, Dean Stevens called a faculty meeting—the first official convening of law professors in the history of NWLC. Assistant Dean Shannon took the minutes. Stevens' agenda led off with an admonition: We must gain the approval of the national accreditors *at once*.

He left no doubt about his charge toward accreditation. Just seven months before, on January 27, 1967, he had committed himself to a deadline in a thirty-seven page evaluation report to the ABA accreditors, wherein he concluded:

> "...There is reason to be hopeful that this law school will be in complete compliance with all minimum requirements by the middle of the school year 1967-68."

He was staking his reputation and putting his word on the line to national friends, colleagues, and peers. At the time of the report, his self-imposed deadline was just one year away. Four months later, on June 1, 1967, Stevens' written report to the Lewis & Clark trustees had prodded them toward that goal:

> "This ... has been the year [1966-67] of planning. Next year [1967-68] must be the Year of Action."

He had emphasized "Year of Action." And now, three months later in our first faculty meeting, with his self-imposed deadline growing closer, he was punctuating the task again. The dean was anxious and brooked no delay. He wanted provisional ABA approval in just five months! The word "quick" epitomized Stevens' nature—quick as in both "alive" and "swift." Lewis & Clark College was about to learn what it meant to have on campus a rambunctious stray anxious to herd with the nation's professional organization, the herd from whence he came.

At that primal faculty meeting, the dean listed for his new faculty the accreditation labors ahead for the next few months:

> (1) **Obtain a Full-time Professional Law Librarian**: Jacqui Jurkins was a professional, but she was currently the Multnomah County Law Librarian and merely a consultant to NWLC. Virginia Hughes was full-time but was a bookstore operator not a professional librarian.
>
> (2) **Increase the Library Book Count and Quality**: When the school had been in downtown Portland, the students found it handy to use the more complete Multnomah County Law Library at the courthouse just a few blocks away. Now that the school was at the outskirts of Portland, the meager 8,000 volumes in the law school library were "completely inadequate." At least 25,000 volumes were needed. Furthermore, the books were not catalogued, and the coverage was far from complete. Although words and language were essential to lawyering, the library did not have a law dictionary nor an unabridged English dictionary.

(3) **Provide Scholarships and Grants**: We had only about $14,000 for superior and needy students. Federal and state monies for loans were generously provided but were far from enough to satisfy accreditors.

(4) **Raise and Tighten the Admissions Standards**: Twenty-eight percent of the present student body did not have undergraduate college degrees and twelve percent did not meet other minimum standards for admitting applicants to the study of law. The kindly "Gantenbein policy" of previous decades asked for no more than a passing score on a college equivalency test plus an earnest desire. An undergraduate grade point average (UGPA) was not required. The law school had also become a repository for some who had been academically dismissed from other law schools. Northwestern admission policy had simply emulated the Statue of Liberty's immigration standard: "Give me your tired, your poor, your huddled masses, yearning to be" ...lawyers. While Dean Stevens sympathized with the sentiment, he noted that accreditors would see licensing as something quite different from migrating, albeit both sought hopes and dreams.

(5) **Raise the Graduation Standards**: Northwestern's requirements for earning a Bachelor of Law degree demanded successful passage of only 72 credit hours of course study—an accommodation that allowed for a minimum of just nine credit hours each semester for eight semesters (four academic years), which constituted nine classroom contact hours each week (M-W-F, 7 to 10 p.m.). The neat convenience of NWLC's small numbers in class time fell shy of accreditor rules that gave no special dispensation to nighttime education. We had to make the study of law longer.

(6) **Improve Bar Exam Passage**: This was not so much an accreditor *goal* as it was accreditor *evidence*. ABA accreditors used the pass-fail ratings of graduates on state bar exams as a clue to their alma maters' educational service. Over the years, Northwestern had not fared well on comparative bar exam results. In the 1965 Oregon bar exam, Northwestern examinees' passage rate was under 50 percent, while graduates from other schools hovered near 75 percent. Customarily, about two Northwestern graduates out of ten would never pass the Oregon bar exam in three tries, whereas graduates of the other schools would have only one failure out of ten.

(7) **Increase Full-time Faculty Salaries**: ABA accreditation salary standards were generally keyed to the national median of the median

salaries reported at each of the then 130 ABA accredited law schools. Observe: the standard spoke of two different medians: the *median salary* at a given law school and then the *median school* in the ranking of medians of all schools. The list of those schools showed median salaries ranging from approximately $9,000 to $27,000. Across the nation the median law school reported $15,125 as its median salary; that then formed the standard to be met. Fringe benefits were not recorded in those statistics. With a full-time teaching faculty of only four, our median calculations were not too meaningful, albeit comparatively low at about $14,000. Thus began the first of many accreditor guidelines that would use competitive mass as a base for averaging in order to set goals to be reached by those seeking to enter that market. Other such median sizings included: tuition dollars, library book count, student body numbers, faculty numbers, and other market quantums. The use of medians as a gauge for standards would prove to be troublesome and dubious.

(8) **Improve the Depth and Breadth of the Curriculum**: The current course curriculum was lacking in certain particulars. There were too many one-credit hour courses—a traditional accommodation to part-time teachers. There were no elective courses—all four years being structured. There were no seminar classes. As for extra-curricular opportunity, there was no legal aid clinic, no law review, no moot courts, no student body association, and no apprenticing externships.

The foregoing were some of the goals that needed to be reached within the five-month deadline for our application to the ABA for provisional accreditation. Dean Stevens then went on to list still more goals—distant ones for which a detailed plan had to be set now in order to assure accreditors of future compliance. These were the necessities that called for heavy lifting in order to gain permanent accreditation. Commitment would have to come from President John Howard and the college trustees. They would have to promise to:

- Construct a law school building complex
- Commence a daytime law division for full-time students
- Improve the faculty-student ratio
- Increase the full-time faculty size
- Support faculty research and publication
- Encourage national colleagueship and local community service
- Increase the endowment for scholarships, grants and loans

"Construct," "commence," "improve," "increase," "encourage," and "support"— all translated into financial dedication. Current annual student tuition at $500 for each of 230 students produced $115,000 income each year. It was far from enough. Current full and part-time faculty salaries totaled about $60,000. Administrators and staff salaries (including the dean who did not teach) came to about $50,000. Fringe benefits, office supplies and all of the sundries of a typical operating budget put expenses in excess of tuition income. Without endowment monies or a strong program of annual alumni giving, the law school budgets called for deficit spending, which called for the transfer of money from undergraduate college income—a situation that did not set well with certain college personnel.

In January 1967, Dean Stevens had projected deficits of $16,000 in 1966-67 and $78,000 in the current 1967-68 fiscal year. None of that operating budget included payment or future funding for all of the other accreditation tasks before us, not the least of which was the building of facilities, endowment, and library count. For those items, the trustees had previously promised a $2 million fund drive; but as of September 1967 it had not yet been publicly launched. Thus far, the only anticipated developments of non-tuition income were $4,000 in pledges, a ten-year trust fund of undisclosed amount, and an application to fund a professorship in commercial law presented to the Maud Hill Foundation of Minnesota. Needless to say, the funding of a professorial chair at an unaccredited, developing law school seemed premature and naive.

Observe that a $2 million fund drive in 1967 would have an equivalent purchasing power, as of this writing, of roughly $11 million; a $78,000 operating deficit would be equivalent to about $400,000; and a $500 student tuition would maximize at almost $3,000. [See "Preface"]

The dean wound up his address to the new faculty by putting his five month deadline into a more realistic setting. He had told us what had to be done; now he told us of what need not be done. For now, our goal would be to gain meaningful assurances (not fulfillments) for temporary (not permanent) accreditation from the ABA (not AALS). While that took something off of the press of task, it did nothing to ease the stress of time.

IN THE WEEKS FOLLOWING THAT first faculty meeting, certain matters were readily accomplished by the dean and faculty without the need for any significant finance. A quarterly law school "Newsletter" publication was instituted in order to reach pre-law advisors at other colleges and universities and to open communication from the alma mater to its alumni. Fees were charged for admission applications, for acceptance of admission offers, for late registration, and for graduation. A "Planning Guide for the Proposed Law School Building" was drafted and then approved by the college trustees. The appeal to the Hill Family Foundation for a chaired professorship was appended with a second less presumptuous appeal for funding an intensified Legal Writing and Research program.

A student body association was also instituted, as the changing law school got more in step with the way things were done nationally. Our traditionalist dean also felt it significant to encourage and boost the organizing of a **law wives club**. He called it "Wives-in-law." The 230 student body included about ten women thus making a "Law Husbands Club" too paltry, a "Law Spouses Club" too lop-sided, and a "Law Partners Club" too unthinkable for its time. Officers of the new Wives club were identified as, e.g., "Mrs. Bob Smith" or "Mrs. Bill Jones" or "Mrs. Husband Name."

Jacqueline Jurkins was made the full-time **librarian**. Efforts at cataloguing library volumes began. Location of the law library was moved from its music hall location to the basement of the college's new Aubrey Watzek Library Building where space was available to shelve 20,000 books. An appeal was made for book donations to fill that empty shelving.

**Admission standards** were raised by requiring applicants to take the national Law School Admission Test (LSAT) and to have completed at least three successful years of study at a recognized undergraduate college or university. Transfer students had to prove good academic standing at their previous law school. Undergraduate GPA scores were now required.

Graduation standards were raised by requiring ten more course credit hours and eight more weeks of study over the four year span. In line with the national trend, a **Juris Doctor degree** instead of a Bachelor of Law degree would be awarded. Academic scholarship rules were adopted. The academic probation status was tightened.

To improve the percentage of bar exam passage by NWLC graduates, the dean had a pet idea: a **comprehensive exam** to be given to upperclass law students at the start of each academic year. The test would cover all previous law classes taken. The purpose was to inculcate the drilling of constant review, even throughout the summer. Failure to pass the exam required re-taking. The innovation was met by groans from takers and this grader. I voiced my dissent to no avail. I argued that while review was good, more exams to force review were not good. There was already plenty of exam impetus. Going over old turf took time away from new study. The reasons for NWLC's previous unsatisfactory showings were more obvious. The school had simply been too lax at the admissions entry and graduation exit. Tightening requisites at those two portals plus tougher grading in house, followed by early scholastic dismissals, was a simple fix. To be sure, such sternness would take awhile before it could overcome the legacy of Gantenbein leniency.

So, in the fall of 1967 we made some inroads on the outskirts of the chart mapped by accreditors. But the center of accreditation was yet untouched. That core was rooted in significant financial outlay. That commitment would have to come from the Board of Trustees by February 1968 if Stevens timetable was to be honored. Lots of work marred by chaos and catastrophe lay ahead of that attainment.

On October 11, 1967, we had our maiden contact with the accreditor force—a preliminary visit from forward-observer **John Hervey**, advisor of and inspector for the ABA. He was a strict taskmaster and was called "the ABA Accreditor Czar." He stayed for three days and told us what we already knew: we were a long way from our goal. He put it in more drastic terms—something to this effect: "You're nowhere close to being an acceptable law school; on your present course, you will not make it; there are already two law schools in Oregon and six in the Pacific northwest." We would later learn Czar Hervey was given to alarm and harsh statement. Indeed, he was dire, to say the least. Unfortunately, he was also in a position to make himself correct.

In an April 12, 1967 letter, Dean Stevens had formally welcomed me into professorship, calling it a quest that would be "interesting, exciting, and rewarding." Indeed, the concept was beginning with interest and excitement. "Rewarding," on the other hand, would have to wait many more months of carriage. The aches of gestation and the pains of parturition come to mind.

# 1967: TIME CONTEXT

At the Lincoln Memorial, D.C., an estimated 50,000 demonstrate against the Vietnam War.

In New York City, an estimated 700,000 march in support of U.S. soldiers in Vietnam.

Martin Luther King leads an anti-war march in N.Y. City.

U.S. bombers attack Hanoi in North Vietnam.

Civil rights riots break out in Cleveland, Newark, and Detroit.

Muhammad Ali (Cassius Clay), heavyweight boxing champ, found guilty of refusing draft into the military.

Israel and Arab nations engage in six day war.

U.S. has 74 nuclear powered submarines.

Communist China explodes its first hydrogen bomb.

For the first time, a new TV comedy show ("Smothers Brothers") leads the way in making humor out of current political, military, and religious issues.

President Johnson appoints Thurgood Marshall to the U.S. Supreme Court—the first black Court justice.

Oregon passes the Beach Bill, making all of Oregon's coast open to the public.

Dr. Christian Barnard performs first heart plant surgery; patient lives 19 months.

The catch of a 410 pound shark sets a record—landed by a woman.

Price of an average new house is about $14,000.

# 2
# THE STEVENS DEPARTURE
*Winter 1967 - 1968*

## SCHISM

By the end of autumn 1967 the accreditation quest was dragging along at a pace much too slow for our spry dean. He saw no progress from the trustees on the urgency of raising the funds necessary to gain accreditation. The commitment to a building fund had already been officially promised in the 1965 Merger Agreement. Item 12 of that contract read in part:

> "Upon completion in 1967 of the presently projected fund-raising campaign...,
> a separate fund-raising campaign will be... conducted... for the raising of at least
> $500,000 in capital funds for... a new law school building...."

A first fund-raising campaign was supposed to have been completed in 1967; it was not. Plans for a $2 million fund drive for the law school would not be made public until October 1968. Dean Stevens was not impressed. For him, it was far too late with not enough. Coming from two well-funded and stable law schools (the University of Washington and Hastings Law School), he saw things larger and faster. In his January 1967 report he had anticipated a $5 million fund raising campaign in two stages.

As the leader in only one corner of a full house, Stevens could not allow himself to dwell upon all of the problems confronting President John Howard and the trustees. The college was already involved in other building operations. In 1962, the campus was still recovering from the notorious and catastrophic Columbus Day Wind Storm that hit Oregon and destroyed the college biology building and caused other extensive damage throughout the heavily forested campus. A few months before Stevens' arrival on campus, the college gymnasium had been destroyed by fire and funds were being raised for its resurrection. In those same years, the Watzek Library building was in the middle of construction, as was the imposing Agnes Flanagan Chapel. Undergraduate professors were calling for better salaries and benefits. Then came the surprising cancellation of the newly-merged law school's downtown lease. Classrooms, library, and study space for over 200 law students had to be crammed into the college's facilities and financial operations.

In a November 10, 1967, Board of Trustees meeting, it was reported that the undergraduate college was in something of a "financial crisis." And so, questions arose: Could the college reach law school accreditation within the promised time? More critically, could the college afford a law school at all? The balk was not in step with Stevens' momentum. He fired back a written "Progress Report," dated December 8, 1967. It laid down five "alternative roads" toward ABA accreditation "at the earliest possible date." Stevens' first alternative (his preference) called for an application for ABA accreditation in just two more months (February 1968); a day school by August 1969; a $1 million building by August 1969; and an endowment of $500,000.

His second alternative was more aligned with President Howard's time table. It delayed matters one more year: Accreditation application by February 1969; day school and building by August 1970; and an endowment of $500,000.

His third and fourth alternatives painted a picture of retreat. Both dropped any immediate prospect of a day division. One kept the endowment goal, but lowered the building plan; whereas the other kept the building plan and dropped endowment. Stevens probably knew that the third and

**JOHN HOWARD**
President of Lewis & Clark College

fourth choices would be repugnant. No one wanted to cease plans for a day school or to play endowment and building goals against one another. The third and fourth prospects were not real choices; they were there to emphasize the emptiness of a failure to fulfill.

It was the contrast between the first and second alternatives that went to the heart of a rift developing between President Howard and Dean Stevens. The dean felt that the second alternative was brinkmanship and foot-dragging. The president felt the first alternative was unrealistic. But Stevens argued that a February 1969 deadline for accreditation reneged on an assurance made to prospective students. An October 1965 letter to them from President Howard had stated that NWLC would "reach standards of accreditation of the ABA not later than 1967-68," thus qualifying a graduate for admittance to the Bar of any state in the nation. Furthermore, on September 17, 1967, President Howard, just ten months before, had recognized the need for dispatch and reported the consequences of failure were even more drastic than Stevens had outlined; a September 17, 1967, memo from Howard read:

> "...we must meet accreditation standards within two years or the Oregon Supreme Court has suggested our graduates will not be able to take the Oregon bar examination."

Each one of Stevens' four alternatives spread the expense of its goals over a five year projection of deficit spending in the law school budget. Law school operations were going to be a significant strain on college finance during those five years.

It was then that Stevens concluded his report with a "do-it-or-else" choice:

> "A fifth alternative should be kept in mind: a decision to terminate the Merger Agreement, as being in the best interests of both the law school and the college."

Short and abrupt, its finality was more ultimatum than option—more attack than tact. If memory correctly serves me, Stevens' version did not pass muster with the president's screening and, therefore, did not reach the Board of Trustees.

That was among the final straws that prompted Stevens to tender his resignation in the final weeks of December 1967—less than four months after my start as a full-time professor. His letter of resignation promised that he would stay on as dean through the 1967-68 academic year ending on July 1. President Howard quickly fired back with a demand for a more immediate "departure." Stevens must "resign" on February 1, 1968. Stevens labeled it differently for the press: "If you want to put it mildly, I was dismissed."

It was not just the abruptness of Howard's call for resignation that put fat in the fire; it was also the place and the timing that did so. Howard's response to Stevens came in the last week in December 1967 while Stevens was attending the Chicago convention of the American Association of Law Schools [AALS], one of the accrediting agencies. It was the annual gathering of law deans and law professors from all over the nation—scholars and cronies that Stevens had known for decades. Stevens was not one to be

*President—Dean Rift*

silent about what he regarded as an insult. He would not allow his dismissal to be swept under academia's carpet. It soon became a chief piece of gossip and astonishment that traveled throughout the conference—a well heard, unheard of, action. A college president out in the Pacific northwest had fired, of all people, George Neff Stevens. For some, it could easily have been taken as an affront, not just to Stevens, but also to law education in general. As we were to learn in years to come, America's law schools were more than an alliance; their teachers were a collegial society.

Just one year prior, President Howard had not endeared himself to that community when, on November 18, 1966, his letter (likely composed by his financial development staff) made a pitch to the Olin Foundation for law school funding. That letter resorted to unfortunate (some would say "preposterous") descriptions in assessing lawyers, law schools, and the state of legal education:

> "The optimum law school does not exist anywhere. Many, if not most, lawyers are inadequately based in language, literature, and the arts. Few lawyers seem adequately prepared, psychologically or technically, for the changes occurring so rapidly in our society. The Law - - and law schools - - should find more effective approaches to social problems. The legal community need not be so exclusively an instrument for resolving social problems after they occur - - seeming to capitalize on tragedy."

At the time of that statement, Howard had been a college president for just six years with an even more recent role as a leader of and a learner about law schooling. I am certain that, armed with a few more years of association, he would have been the first to see the statement as unwarranted and to wish it had never been put to his pen. Nevertheless, in 1966-67, those descriptions were viewed as a fogged window into legal education and undiplomatic when coming from one who would be coming to those targeted in order to gain entry into their established halls.

Rash presidential and decanal impolity were widening a rift between the two. Back in Portland, Howard's private notice to Stevens of his early discharge was soon followed by the college's public press release of that action before Stevens had an opportunity to respond. On January 4, 1968, both Portland daily newspapers reported that Stevens "submitted his resignation" and then quickly added that Jack H. Cairns "has been named as dean." The simultaneous report of resignation and replacement was an easy clue to the nature of the departure. When the "new" is seated almost in the lap of the "old," it does not take a rocket scientist to read "scooted out" into the so-called "re-seating." Howard was quoted as praising Stevens for "advancements at the law school" in his eighteen month tour as dean. But the abrupt vacancy so quickly filled, undermined the grace in Howard's off-hand courtesy.

The opening news story did not quell appetites. It was news that hungered to know why Stevens resigned. Reporters dug further. Follow-up articles began on January 11, 1968, after interviews with Stevens. Headlines were "Dispute Jars Law School" and "Delay in Lewis & Clark Law School Accreditation Spurs Dispute." Stevens was quoted as saying:

> "The program for accreditation has collapsed.... The law school won't qualify for accreditation.... It may take five years.... They simply can't afford it.... We are turning out lawyers that need an education they aren't getting."

Later, Stevens explained to his faculty that the newspapers had taken the last of those remarks out of context. He meant that the education the students were getting did not meet accreditor standards, not that the education was academically unsound—a distinction sent from the heart but not taken to hearts.

Stevens pinned his disappointment on the college's failure to keep its promises.

> "The delay in accreditation is unfair to students. It means that graduates of the school will not be able to take bar examinations in some other states without going through further law clerk training."

The news articles also quoted one of the law students:

> "Lewis & Clark has misrepresented its intentions to... students who enrolled

with the promise of accreditation before graduation. To a student desiring to practice outside of Oregon, a diploma from an unaccredited law school is a worthless document."

President Howard responded:

"It is possible we will fall behind seven or eight months... [but], we are on schedule for developing the law school.... There is no question we'll get accreditation.... We hope to have the... building ready for occupancy by the fall of 1969.... Accreditation may be earned in 15 months... most likely during the next two years."

In the January 12, 1968, issue of *Pioneer Log*, the college student newspaper, Stevens amplified his views when interviewed by the student editor. The library problem was that while there was now enough money to buy law books, there was no place to put them. "Shelf space in our section [of the Watzek Library] would have to be doubled." Furthermore, ABA requirements urged an annual law school operation budget of at least $400,000 by its third year of operation. "Ours is far below that." Current operating income came largely from tuition money. "Northwestern... has no endowment fund at all." Solicitation of gift money was attempted solely from the same people who had shown unwillingness to support it in the past. If no new money is sought, "there is no real advantage to having merged with Lewis & Clark." A campaign for a slate of new donors was necessary.

Stevens went on to observe that, after the merger had been finalized, the movement to gain accreditation was allowed to slip away.

"The Board of Trustees apparently favors a policy of continuing the drift.... If we weren't prepared to go all out, we shouldn't have said we were. I'm not interested in running a borderline institution."

Stevens then acknowledged the problem confronting his opposition. President Howard and the trustees were trying to balance the woes and placate the differences between two struggling bodies - - the undergraduate liberal arts and sciences college and the new law school. Stevens saw difficulty in gaining even-handedness between the two.

"I'm not sure that both Lewis & Clark and the law school can be properly developed at the same time.... I kind of favor concentrating on the arts school, but that leaves the law school out in the cold...."

Indeed, the law school was already "out in the cold." Prior to the merger, many of the undergraduate faculty had opposed the joinder. They felt that a law school on campus would not only siphon off money from undergraduate study but would also divert attention from the social and educational needs of liberal arts and science learning. Their fears were shaping up.

Wedded, not by heart, but rather by parental matchmaking, the joint faculties were colleagues in name yet strangers in fact. Publicity had been resplendent, but privacy never consummated. It was not a personal thing; it was institutional. When Ross Runkel and I would eat at the college faculty dining room just across the street from our make-do offices, we were always received warmly. But when the conversation drifted toward the merger, a chill came with it. The law school was a new kid on the block—an intruder with something to prove, yet a beggar seeking care and coin.

Perhaps, a more fair breakdown of the undergraduate faculty's reactions to the merger was that *most* were quietly agreeable; *some* were patiently watchful; and a *few* were vigorously resentful. Within that range of silence, neutrality, and vehemence was an uneasiness that belied true merger. Somewhere near that time I attended a meeting of the college faculty and rose to speak upon an issue that I do not now recall, but it had something to do with the law school on campus. It received smatterings of mixed applause and hisses.

News of Stevens' departure and the reasons for doing so were a major low point. At the same time, it was a boost to those who had criticized the merger. When a wall weakens, outside opportunity rushes in. And so, in a January 12, 1968, *Oregonian* article, State Representative Keith Skelton, a lawyer and teacher at Portland State University, urged the State Board of Higher Education to acquire Northwestern and make it a Portland adjunct of the University of Oregon law school. Skelton was quoted as saying:

"It is important to have an accredited [law] school in the metropolitan area.... If Lewis & Clark cannot give the necessary financial support to its law school, it may be appropriate for the board to consider whether to purchase and operate Northwestern as a separate law school...."

Little did Skelton know that his proposal was harkening back to an old event. Five decades before, the University of Oregon abandoned its Portland-based law school, leaving it to become Northwestern College of Law. So, in effect, Skelton was now urging the state university to reverse its fifty-two year old decision and take back the school it had founded eight decades ago. The publicity surrounding the Stevens' departure and the Skelton proposal had one salutary effect: It raised the hackles and then the priorities of the powers-that-be. Like aftershocks of an earthquake, however, the Howard-Stevens crash reverberated throughout the accreditation sojourn and seemed never to subside.

Whether Stevens was or was not a good dean, was not for me a question. He was the one who gave me my start as a law teacher—a career change that has filled the majority of my lifetime. For that, I am grateful, just as I am grateful to President Howard for his role in continuing to mend the gaps between the law school and the campus and the law community. Stevens had been pirated away from Hastings by Howard's promises of action. Both men were imbued with action—vigor that brought them together and then tore them apart—both the better for whatever learning was in it.

But it took time for my gratitude to surface out of that disappointment of yesteryear. Indeed, it was a shocking turn of events. Just eight months before, the dean had led me into a school that he was now leaving. Morale was low, and Stevens knew that. So, just before he left in late January 1968, he took me aside for some memorable soothsaying and avuncular advice. What follows are my words put to what he confided to me across a restaurant table—advice faded in mind but taken to heart:

> Ron, your colleagues, Jack and Paul, are transitions from the pre-existing to the emerging law school. Older and with their law practices still viable, they will likely return one day to more familiar paths – as I now do. But you and Ross are the law school's future. As of now, neither you nor Ross nor I have been here long enough to make this our school. Stick with it. It takes time, but you'll grow into the life. When that happens, don't fall into the trap of academic seclusion. The tendency of professors is to turn away from the outside world and into the cloistered existence of the campus world. Academe has exercise facilities, swim pools, infirmaries, saunas, music halls, theater, landscaped walks, cafeterias, dining halls, bookstores, gift shops, libraries and all things needed for living and repose. Resist the hermitage. Publish. Be public. Extend yourself and join the civic and bar communities. Reach out to other faculties and other schools. Put a face of this faculty upon the national scene. Take part. This is not a monastery; it's a law center with infinite perimeters. And in that reaching out, never forget that, foremost, you're one who teaches and not just one who professes. Explain to those who don't know; don't just converse with those who do. There'll be disappointment in the accreditation struggle, but it'll come eventually, in spite of my effort

*to make it come quicker. When it does, you'll find it easy to rest and let the walls close around. Then will be the time to mark my words.*

Speaking from the experience of nearly forty years in legal education, he had a final piece of advice—again, the substance of which I put to my form:

> *When full and permanent accreditation comes, this school should continue to rise from such roots and gain a rightful place among the treetops. In that high atmosphere, it'll be important then to introspect instead of always measuring the school's advancement by the standards set by others. Don't fall error to elitism—a way of seeing growth by contrasting the lowly to the leviathans. Instead, reflect on these dark times, for this is the base from which the growth should be measured. Your rise should be judged by how well you advance your own principles, not by how far you fall below or exceed the standards of others. There is a difference between making an imitation and making a contribution. Don't copy. Originate.*

Stevens was not able to return to Hastings. Instead, he taught for awhile at the University of New Mexico law school. We corresponded on a few occasions over the years. I looked for him when I became a regular attender at national and regional conferences of lawyers and law educators. But after that restaurant booster, I never saw him again. He ceased to be quick on September 23, 1998. He was almost ninety then.

Out of all of this, for me, one certainty had surfaced: While previously I understood schooling, now I was beginning to understand its business.

# 3
# TROUBLE WITHIN THE ABA
*1967 - 1968*

## HITTING A MOVING TARGET

Our accreditation leader, George Neff Stevens, was now gone. We were asea with no helmsman—no one with savvy about the shoals and currents within the ABA and AALS. Our acting dean, Jack Cairns, was an outstanding lawyer and teacher but was the first to concede his want of background for the duties of doyen on an accreditation course. President Howard and his chief advisor, Assistant to the President John D. Phillips, were also strangers to navigating in law professional and law professorial waters.

When approaching any large organization for favors, it is well to learn its hierarchy—the stairs to be ascended. The ultimate ABA authority was the House of Delegates [the "**House**"] as spearheaded by its Board of Governors [the "**Board**"]. Beneath that authoritative body was the ABA Section of Legal Education and Admissions to the Bar [the "**Section**"]. In 1893, the Section was the first compartment instituted within the ABA. Indeed, the Section was the principal reason why the ABA itself was founded. A formal organization was needed to screen and police those who chose to call themselves "lawyers" and "educators" of lawyers.

The Section was so central to the ABA's existence that some regarded it as a separate and autonomous organization. At the time of our accreditation pursuits, it had hundreds of members. By the time of this writing, the Section had expanded to 7,000 members. Indeed, lawyers had a deep interest in the education and entry of those who sought to join their ranks. **The Advisor** to the Section, John G. Hervey, felt that he was the employee of the Section and not of the ABA. Therefore, he argued that he was not beholden to the ABA Governors. Although the ABA headquarters was in Chicago, the Section records and files were housed in Oklahoma City, where Hervey resided.

The ABA accrediting hierarchy was further layered when the Section created within itself the Council on Legal Education and Admissions to the Bar [**the "Council"**]—a more, manageable eight-man group in the mid-1960s. The Council had preliminary screening powers over applicant law schools. NWLC would make most of its appeals to the Council. George Neff Stevens was one of the eight Council members.

Still another layer was formed. The Council delegated some of its work to its **Committee** on Draft of the Proposed Revised Standards. The Committee's charge was to revamp and codify the accreditation rules. Stevens was chair of that committee. In January 1968, during the waning days of his lame duck deanship at NWLC, he and his Council committee forwarded to the Council and Section leaders the final draft of newly proposed accreditation standards. Although the ABA letterhead still listed him as "Dean" in "Portland, Oregon," his typewritten return address was given as professor at the University of New Mexico School of Law.

Just months before, Stevens had been a seeker of ABA accreditation, now he was among the bestowers. He was out of our search, but not out of our sights. There was wonder to know how his separation from NWLC would play in our efforts. Ironically, while seeking entry through the gate, we had sent packing the lead person designing the lock and keys. If ever there was a scenario for "no admittance," we had embarked upon it.


WHILE WE HAD OUR TROUBLES in-house, little did we realize we were facing a hierarchy that was having its own troubles in-house. There we were, ready to mount the steps of Advisor, Council, Section, Board, and House, when we were apprised that the steps were undergoing repair. ABA Section members were at odds over what accreditation standards should mean. The problem was engendered by the Stevens Committee proposal. It was met with stern attack from the Chicago Bar Association.

The core of the critique went to a very old issue in the fashionings of jurisprudence: How specific should rules be? Are laws to be general principles or precise dictates? How much room should be provided in a standard to allow for adjustment to the particular facts at hand? Should the perimeters of a rule have bright or penumbral borders? Should laws be canons or considerations? Mandatory or precatory? Normative control or situational ethic? How quantitative—how qualitative? No doubt attitudes will vary depending on the consequences for failure to conform. Is the purpose of the rule for criminal penalty, land use privilege, contract obligation, academic grade award, financial loan, license bestowal, membership, or, as here, simply a stamp of recognition?

The Stevens Committee's draft put accreditation standards in broad, general, qualitative terms using amorphous modifiers such as "adequate," "highest and best," "suitable," and "sufficiently strong." The Chicago critics demanded more specificity. Without more precision, they charged, law schools seeking approval would have no notion of expectations. The proposers countered by pointing to specific "Factors" set forth to guide interpretation of the "Standards." Those Factors spelled out in greater quantity the relevant considerations involved in the quality decisions reached. The proposers explained the Factors in this language:

> "The Factors are designed to provide guidance.... Formal compliance with the specific terms of a Factor is not necessarily equivalent to satisfaction of a qualitative requirement, nor is a departure... automatically demonstrative of a qualitative failure."

The critics found this language anathema and wanted to know when quantitative compliance was not satisfactory or when non-compliance was nevertheless qualitative. They wrote:

> "Who, then is to say, in any given case, whether compliance with the 'Factors' is enough - - or failure to comply is not enough - - to satisfy the 'Standards'? Is it the Council?... What test is to guide them?"

Stevens and the proposers justified their approval by observing that "The Standards are and should be a constitution not a statute." In a bit of sarcasm, the Chicago Bar saw the proposed standards-versus-factors as saying to the applicant law school:

> "We will not tell you what to teach. But unless you teach what we approve, which we leave you to guess, you will not be approved."

The Chicago critics then focused on the heart of the difficulty with "constitutional" expression of standards:

> "Such proposals raise, also, the old problem of justice. Lawyers know, if anyone does, that all experience with the administration of power teaches that unless power is required to act according to ascertainable standards, power presently becomes arbitrary and capricious, even self-seeking."

At NWLC, we waited and watched. Memos fired back and forth between the Stevens Committee and the Chicago critics. Hitting a moving target made our aims waver. Issues kept shifting. What began as an argument over specificity of rules or generality of principles became a disagreement about the purpose of rules. Are they to control the governed or the governors? That then evolved into an ago-old contention between individual independence and government regulation. Contrariety within the ABA Section infected the NWLC faculty and prompted our own debates in the kitchen of Hartzfeld house on Huddleston Lane.

Extremists left and right, in forums or kitchens, will carry on such quarrel forever. Once exhaustion ensues, there is seen the need for balance and the need for wisdom of when to do which. Standards should be specific enough to relay what is expected yet general enough to make room for the unexpected. Try as we may to mechanize a complete system of laws to govern all possible situations, there is no escape from the even-handedness of the wise judge of stern compassion, mindful of both the rule aloft and the situation at hand.

MEANWHILE, BACK WITHIN THE ACCREDITOR ranks, controversy continued and would not be resolved until August 1968. That time would be the next scheduled meeting of the ABA Section, where the Stevens Committee proposal, now approved by the Council, would be on the agenda. We would have to wait. But, we did not. Impatience was in the craw of powers-that-be. So, in spite of Dean Stevens' and Advisor Hervey's cautions that we were far from ready, NWLC filed an application for ABA preliminary accreditation in February 1968 just days after the deanship was passed from Stevens to Cairns and while the smoke of the Stevens' firing was still in the air. It was as though the college administration had to make an immediate public showing that Stevens had been wrong. It was impetuous, to be sure. Not only were we not ready, neither were the accreditors. They were in no mood to administer standards they had not yet set.

ACCREDITOR DISTRACTION WAS COMPOUNDED BY still another seething within the ABA: a growing dissatisfaction with John Hervey, the official "Advisor to the Council of the Section." Personnel problems are difficult issues to deal with in-house, and the Hervey problem reached out externally to affect our efforts. His conferences with NWLC went as far back as the negotiations for merger in 1965. His service to the ABA accreditors went back even farther. For over two decades he had been the "hands-on" link and traveler between the accreditors, the accredited, and the hopefuls. He was the inspector of the nation's law schools and, as previously said [see ch. 1] had become in that role, something of a "czar."

I remember having a long discussion with Hervey in my "living room" office. His vast accreditation knowledge was seasoned not just by the standards he was hired to invoke but also by his own interpretations. When long at the helm, the wheel becomes worn to the hands. At age 68 and after two decades as an inspector, he was viewed as a patriarch, and therein was the seed of the problem. Like a magnet, power attracts polar opposites. He had his critics.

We had looked to Hervey to help us with our troubles, but now he was facing his own. According to him, his trouble began when, on October 28, 1967, two months after full-time operations at NWLC, he was beckoned to a so-called "conference" with the President of the ABA. Hervey called it a "confrontation." He was told that he was beyond the ABA retirement age of 68. But Hervey contended that the ABA had no such compulsory retirement age. He was informed that just three days prior to the "confrontation" the ABA Board had passed a compulsory retirement resolution. Hervey argued that his existing tenure "grandfathered" him as an exception to the general resolution. He was then informed that just two days before the "confrontation," the ABA Board passed a special resolution specifically ordering Hervey's retirement on March 1, 1968, and ordered him to transfer all of his records to the ABA central office in Chicago. No new replacement had been appointed. The "retirement" had all of the signs of a discharge. Eventually, he was allowed to phase out his work until the August 1968 Section meeting—the one at which NWLC was making its first plea for accreditation.

Hervey labeled the whole treatment as "despicable," "high-handed," and "sordid." He saw beneath it a "first step being taken by misinformed leaders in the profession to liquidate the Section and to make AALS the exclusive accrediting agency."

That last observation, albeit exaggerated, may have had a slight germ of truth in it. Hervey was a practicing lawyer in Oklahoma City, not a legal educator. He had made criticisms of law schools that did not set well with educators. He wrote that "law instruction was too theoretical," that "insufficient attention was given to insure high ethical standards," that there was "too much moonlighting among full-time teachers and full-time students," and "too much 'me tooism' in legal education and too little experimentation." He criticized the ongoing conflict in law school circles over whether schooling should be "for advocacy or for social engineering." Hervey's departure from the ABA was far more bitter than the Stevens departure from NWLC. For that reason, perhaps our own internal bad publicity may have been unnoticed or trivialized within the ABA ranks. Ashamedly, we hoped so.

And so, that is where our February 1968 bid to the accreditors found itself. Our trouble was met by theirs. Unfortunately, the bestower's troubles did not benefit the bidder. Our first application for accreditation was tabled indefinitely—which is to say "denied."

# 1968: TIME CONTEXT

Vietnamese citizens (estimated 300 to 500 including women and children) massacred by U.S. troops.

President Johnson seeks not to run for a second term.

Martin Luther King is assassinated in Memphis.

Robert Kennedy is assassinated in Los Angeles.

Riots and brutality occur outside the Democratic National Convention in Chicago.

Richard Nixon is elected U.S. President by a narrow margin.

Portland Mayor Ivancie proposes a midnight curfew to counter what he saw as a "hippie invasion."

U.S. explodes an underground H-bomb in Nevada.

CBS-TV Board of Censors strikes controversial portions of the Smothers Brothers Comedy Show script.

Three astronauts orbit Earth for eleven days.

Three astronauts orbit the moon.

The new "*midi*-skirt" fails in its attempt to out-fashion the "*mini*."

Gallon of gas costs 34 cents.

# 4

# THE CAIRNS REGIME: PART ONE

*Spring 1968*

### LIGHT FROM A SMALL WIRE

On February 1, 1968, the day of Dean George Stevens scheduled departure, acting Dean Jack Cairns called a faculty meeting. Stevens did not attend. He had received notice at the end of December of his discharge at the end of January. Having just one month to clean out and re-schedule, he asked me to take his place as a speaker at a mid-January conference at Portland State University. Other appointments also had to be canceled and that included any farewell at a faculty meeting. So, Dean Cairns, Librarian Jacqui Jurkins, Registrar Dorothy Cornelius, Assistant Dean David Shannon, and Professors Paul Gerhardt, Ross Runkel, and this author met in Professor Gerhardt's bedroom office without the previous shepherd. It slowed down the flock. Most of the items on the agenda were given short shrift and tabled for future resolve.

Dean Cairns gave one item on the agenda his personal attention: the **summer bar exam review course** which he operated privately and in which we all taught. He reported that henceforth the course would be taken over by Lewis & Clark College. Although the transfer of ownership did not need ratification, the law faculty nevertheless gave it blessing with one dissent: mine. From private conversations with Dean Stevens and ABA Advisor John Hervey, I was aware that certain members of the ABA Section and Council were not fond of law schools operating courses aimed at coaching exam-takers on how to pass state bar exams. Eventually, in the months ahead the accreditors would formalize their concern in the ABA standards:

> "...neither the law school, nor the university or college of which it is a part, shall conduct instruction in law designed to coach students for bar examination...."
> [Factor VIII, Standards of the ABA for Legal Education, Nov. 1, 1969.]

The rule and the argument in support of it were curious: Higher educators should teach and test but should not teach tests. It demeans tests to train in techniques for passing them. Tests are not for beating; they are for learning. There was something hypocritical about the ABA using bar exam passage ratings as evidence of a law school's worth, yet banning law schools from using a specific course program to boost those ratings. And so, in February 1968, we endorsed a college operated bar review course and thereby created one more obstacle in our path to accreditation.

Only one other item on that February agenda brought action. Students were not taking the new **comprehensive exam** seriously enough, as evidenced by the unsatisfactory grade results on the first attempt at comprehensive examining. [See ch. 1] Again, I dissented when the faculty voted in favor of putting more teeth to the test. Henceforth, failure on the August exam would require a re-taking of the exam at the end of the December holiday season and right before the taking of first semester exams in January. A second failure would threaten academic dismissal. It was an exaction that would prove to be a distraction. Reviewing past courses was taking time away from fresh course study.

Two final items on the agenda were the most pressing yet were given only fleeting attention. No one was anxious to plunge into the issues that had recently engulfed us: accreditation limbo and a dean replacement. Professor Ross Runkel was handed the assignment of preparing "a paragraph which would explain to new students the accreditation status." Students needed an inside report of what they were reading in newspapers. Enrollment following the January Stevens publicity fell twelve percent from 231 in the fall to 204 in the spring. Dean Cairns pinned the loss on the military draft for the Vietnam War.

As for a dean search, acting Dean Cairns said he believed it was "in the interest of the school to delay . . . until matters had quieted down." In short, without Stevens, that first faculty meeting spent time ducking for cover instead of seeking to recover.

SOMETIME IN THE WEEKS FOLLOWING that meeting, the law faculty was surprised to find out that the college administrators had been in the process of submitting our **first application for accreditation** to the ABA Council. Our ignorance was probably just as well, because when we were later informed of the denial (an indefinite tabling as previously reported [see ch. 3]), it saved us the more crushing disappointment that flows from mounting wait.

And so, throughout the spring semester of 1968, NWLC recuperated from the double punch of losing both our dean and our first accreditation try. In those doldrums I found druthers—the opportunity to do what professors should do—research and write. The lead article in the June 1968 issue of the Oregon Law Review was my analysis of the newly enacted Oregon Tort Claims Act: "The King Can Do Wrong!" [47 Or.L.Rev. 357 (1968)]. It was the first law review article published by a NWLC professor. It would be my last law review publication for the next decade. Administration, teaching, Bar, and civic chores kept getting in the way of scholarship. However, during the calm of that spring semester, I did collaborate with Professor Louis L. Williams of DePaul University College of Law in the periodic publication of his *Oregon Officers Law Bulletin*, by sharing some editorial cartooning work with the celebrated cartoonist, Bill Mauldin.

I was also involved in a Portland City Club study on "Racial Justice in Portland," which followed the blueprint laid down by the nationally prominent "Koerner Report." My particular segment focused on discrimination in private clubs. It proved to be the most controversial segment and reached national attention. At home in Oregon it soured certain civic leaders. It was the 1960s, after all—a time when it was the rage to stir the established and make a stew.

The 1968 spring calm also provided time to convince my colleagues to schedule a course in **Jurisprudence**—the philosophies of law. Not since Dean Robert Thornton, the English scholar, who left the school in 1903, had there been a course specifically devoted to the broader theories underlying all of Law. Colleague Runkel needed no persuasion, but colleagues Cairns and Gerhardt were schooled by many years of law practice and were no nonsense, law journeymen. Convincing them would not be "the harvest of low-hanging fruit." In a four-year curriculum encompassing only twenty courses—all fundamental and practical—the inclusion of a general theory course was, in their opinion, like frosting a half-baked cake.

The standoff was broken in favor of a try. This was the approach that won approval: While Jurisprudence may not be for the practical-minded or ABA professionals, having it on the curriculum was very practical in that it appealed to the theory-minded AALS accreditors. One might disagree with the usefulness, but not with the value, of ornament.

Jurisprudence began as a required course for upper-class students. Exactly fifty were enrolled. It would have been better as a seminar limited to no more than fifteen, but we had no elective programming in September 1968.

Persuading the learners in the classroom was the next step. Evening students were not callow, campus youngsters. At age 36, I was not much older than the average age in the class and did not have the advantage of veneration. Their interests were more "how" and "what," not "why." I found my mission to be an oar in the sand. And so, I sought guidance from two experienced Harvard law school professors: Lon Fuller and James Vorenburg. Having corresponded with Fuller, I met with him over coffee at an AALS convention. This jurisprudential scholar put me on the right path and earned a lifetime of my respect. Two of his teaching wisdoms have stuck with me: "show-and-tell is not just kindergarten prudence" and "whimsy lightens a heavy load." His way of putting difficult concepts into tantalizing narrative was a style with which I was in full accord—witness his classic "Case of the Speluncean Explorers," the "Contract Signed on Book Day," the "Case of the Interrupted Whambler," and "The Grudge Informers."

Professor Vorenburg also greatly assisted. He sent me a hard-to-find and battered copy of the famed *Hart and Sacks Jurisprudence* materials. For my Jurisprudence class I assigned Fuller's *Problems of Jurisprudence*. After a heavy dose of studying laws, students came to appreciate something of Law as well. Just as every architect must know the realities of carpentry, every carpenter benefits from seeing architecture.

The course lasted two years—brought down, not by lack of interest, but rather by other demands in the curriculum and in the accreditation pursuit. There was simply no time for indulgences. While Jurisprudence may have been, in fact, the *base* of Law, others saw it as the *frieze*; it had to wait for the building of *columns*. It was replaced in future years, however, by a course called "Law and Society," also taught by me. That too would succumb to the disregard for philosophy courses, which in turn would succumb to the need for them, albeit under still different names like "Legal Method," "Elements of Law," and other such blankets of cover.

THE END OF THE 1968 spring semester put me at my **first graduation ceremony** as a law professor. It was different than my student graduations from grade school, high school, college, and law school—each the end of a chapter and the commencement of another. This time I would not exit or enter portals. This time I would stay back at the gate—satisfied that I had opened it.

That 1968 ceremony was an odd mix of endurance and enjoyment. The endurance was having to sit through a combination of both the college and law school proceedings. It was an all-school ceremony that included the usual speeches and the award of honorary degrees, bachelor degrees in arts and science, and masters degrees in music and education. Last came the award of law degrees. There paraded 465 degree candidates across the stage that day—55 of whom were future lawyers.

But the endurance was overcome by the cheers and tears of joy emanating from the mothers, fathers, grandparents, spouses, sisters, brothers, kin, and kindred who witnessed better than anyone what it all meant; for they were there through all of the ages and stages of their graduate. Endurance and wait were well worth that moment of pride on stage. It was a lesson in patience that the alma mater could well use on its own wait for accreditation.

IN THE CLOSING DAYS OF that spring semester, our **accreditation** sails began to flap again as we edged out of the doldrums. John Hervey, on his last legs as Advisor to the ABA Council of Accreditors, had given us written reasons for why the college's February accreditation attempt had been turned down. His designated shortcomings were matters we already knew: (1) library volume count, (2) median faculty salary, and (3) progress toward a law school building. But those were goals at which to aim. The law faculty, however, was not included in the targeting. The trustees newly appointed Standing Committee on the Operation of the Law School [SCOLS] had taken over and had been at work while the law faculty attended to educating through the spring semester. SCOLS had in mind an immediate second try at ABA accreditation. To that end, Dean Cairns reported in June that "additional books have been ordered to provide for 15,000 volumes, to be shelved in the college library." Then too, the college and SCOLS had hired a new law professor. Wayne Walker was previously on the law faculty of the University of Maryland. With his hire, our median faculty salary had now moved upward to meet current ABA requirements.

SCOLS members felt confident that those steps had taken care of "shortcomings" one and two. The third step, however, needed convincing. College presidents and trustees, new to legal education, did not always appreciate why **separate buildings for the law school** were necessary. Was it not just another "department" like history, economics, business administration, political science, and such? Shouldn't there be exchange between disciplines, as promoted by mixing under the same roof? Why did lawyering deserve separate status and isolation? An ABA consultant report tried to explain the need:

> "[H]igh standards of ethics and trust in the profession required the development of a sense of community in each member of the profession.... The law school experience in which each student spent his student days in a building associating only with other law students was one of the effective ways to build the essential sense of community."

The report went on to say that one unnamed college president, while conceding the importance of the "sense of community," still questioned whether a separate building "was an important means to that end." The Law discipline ought not be cloistered. We were not training monks here. The president's concern served to spotlight a seeming inconsistency in the ABA standards: On the one hand, accreditation required merger with an arts and science institution, yet on the other hand, it commanded a separate place from other disciplines in arts and science. The issue, however, was closed by custom so entrenched that it no longer needed a rationale. Separation began back in the 19th century with Harvard's Christopher Columbus Langdell. It would not go away.

Whatever may have been the **grounds for building**, the ground on which to build was SCOLS's immediate mission in the summer of 1968. Various downtown Portland structures were considered for purchase and renovation. Had it not been for the Portland City Commissioners' decision to tear down the downtown Oregon Journal newspaper building, the law school might have been located in that two-block-long, three-story, riverside building, which was then serving as a parking garage. In its heyday, it had housed a bustling newspaper and is today the Tom McCall Waterfront Park.

The venerate and stately federal post office building, located at the core of downtown Portland, was for sale but was not chosen, partly because it was too small. Today it is the U.S. Pioneer Courthouse—a place large enough for lawyers and judges to apply law, even though it had not been large enough for future lawyers and judges to learn law.

Both of those locales would have returned Northwestern to its downtown Portland origins. Oddly enough, that would not have been the first separation of the law school from its parent. In the first two decades of its life [1884-1915], the law school operated in Portland some one hundred miles from its parent (the University of Oregon) in Eugene. But at NWLC, in 1968, such schism was resisted. The law school should not be allowed to stray. Better location choices were some vacant properties nearer the campus, *e.g.*: a portion of the adjacent Riverview Cemetery or the campus sport center parking lot or the Huddleston Lane frontage where we were temporarily housed.

None of those possibilities were chosen. Instead, the college purchased a six-acre site at the north end of the **Tryon Forest** just one block off of the campus. The forest covered one square mile and was said to be laced with forty miles of trails. Architect Paul Thiry of Seattle envisioned plans at that site for a "cluster-type series of law buildings" in three separate structures.

On hearing that good news, Runkel and I took a lunch hour stroll over to the wooded site. We tromped and kicked our way around trunks, branches, wild ivy, and

**TRYON FOREST SITE**
Interim Dean Jack Cairns and Construction Supervisor Bill Stahl at future law complex location

brush among the sweet sound and fresh smell of forest. I saw a deer trail and fancied it to be a library aisle; I transformed a boulder into an office desk; a rotted stump became a lectern; and fallen leaves were the discarded notes of a scholarly re-draft. All of it was no more than airy silliness born of the joy in outlook.

ARMED WITH THOSE SUMMER FULFILLMENTS, SCOLS anticipated that a **second attempt** at **provisional accreditation** would be made at the ABA Council and Section meetings just two months away in mid-August. But Dean Cairns was not confident about success. The purchase of grounds and architectural plans without committing to a drive for money to build would not be enough. He wrote that ABA willingness to grant provisional accreditation "is problematical."

Cairns was correct. Our second attempt ceased to be problematic and became a real problem. Again the ABA accreditors tabled our effort indefinitely. This time we rationalized that the tabling was merely a postponement, that we were not faulted, that the Council and Section did not give our petition fair attention because they were too pre-occupied with the Hervey "retirement" and the Stevens Committee proposal. Candor, however, should have warned us that the postponement was, indeed, a second denial on account of our failure to back our promises of building, endowment, and day division with a public announcement of a fund drive. Then too, the Council likely noted that we lost two administrators: Assistant Dean Shannon had resigned, and Librarian Jurkins did not renew her contract, albeit she did continue as a library consultant.

The doldrums were back. Our sails fell slack.

Somewhere during that spring and summer of 1968, professors at three different law schools in Ohio, Indiana, and Idaho phoned or wrote me to ask if I was interested in being a candidate to their faculties. It was surprising. I had not put my name into any job search. I was curious to know why they called. Each simply said that I "had been recommended." It could have been Dean Stevens, but more likely it was underground gossip that had begun at the Chicago AALS convention and was spread by news of the failed February accreditation attempt. Wreckage has always been a call for scavenging. The scavenging was made all the more intense because dean vacancies in those troubled campus years were happening with greater frequency. It was not flattering to be treated as salvage.

I turned down the invitations. Our current problems may have fostered discouragement but not abandonment. Like Professor Wallace Stegner, who was then in his waning years as Director of Stanford's Creative Writing Program, I too was a man of place, a transplant from the concrete, railroads, and factories of the Chicago area, where I was born and raised. Now I was firmly rooted in the forests, mountains and shores of Oregon country. Facing my second year as an academic, ambition was no longer a substitute for environment. The quantums of economics could not replace the qualities of life.

Then, too, as a naïve optimist, I looked at our accreditation attempts just as Thomas Alva Edison looked at his thousands of so-called "failures" to make incandescence: They were not failures, he observed; each was a success at learning how to make light glow from a small wire within a bulb.

# 5
# THE CAIRNS REGIME: PART TWO
*1968-1969*

## EUCHRED

At the start of the 1968-69 academic year, the law school roster listed five full-time faculty members (one dean and four professors). The fifth professor, Wayne Walker, was a surprise—a mystery hire. He cropped up suddenly and without formal faculty consultation. Seemingly, President Howard and SCOLS took him as a hasty replacement to show that the Stevens gap was readily plugged. Three staff (bookstore operator, registrar, and secretary), rounded out our full-time personnel.

Five part-time instructors were scheduled to teach that year. There were sixteen other part-timers on-hand for future years. Among them was Judge Robert E. Jones, whose résumé today includes: federal judge, former supreme court justice, and state legislator; a scholastic chair at NWLC honors his name. His credentials are but one example of the caliber of a vast array of sacrificing and dedicated lawyers and judges—all volunteers working at paltry stipend—who had served as the corps and at the core of old Northwestern since 1884.

My year-long course load included Torts, Civil Procedure, and Jurisprudence, plus participation in a faculty-taught Legal Writing and Research course. The 1968-69 curriculum carried only seventeen course offerings for all four class years—all at nighttime—all required. The upcoming fall semester would jam its credit hours into only ten and a-half classroom hours per week (M-W-F, 6:30 - 10:00 p.m.). The paucity, rigidity, and crowding of our course offerings needed fixing.

On October 24, 1968, the ever promised $2 million **fund drive campaign** was finally given public launching in a gala kick-off celebration in the Crystal Room of downtown Portland's venerate Benson Hotel. In 1968, the Crystal Room was the premier place in all of Oregon to host large conference events. There, award-winning architect, Paul Thiry, unveiled his plans for a three building law complex. The library structure would have a highly innovative roof ("hyperbolic parabola," Thiry called it), which allowed for glass, non-support, outer walls and, thus, future expansion. The goal included $1,200,000 for the building complex, $500,000 for endowment, $200,000 for student scholarships, and $100,000 for library. By modern comparison, $2 million does not seem a lot; but, it has the inflationary equivalent of at least $11 million today. [See Preface] The campaign was newsworthy and received both newspaper report and television interviews of President Howard and Dean Cairns. Needless to say, those interviews, designed for promotion, nevertheless resurrected inquiry about the Stevens departure—once hot news, now tepid ten months later, but still good for follow-up journalism.

Completion of the fund drive was projected for "early 1969"—a timetable just three to five months away. One month later, a November 30, 1968, statement reported that twenty-six percent of the goal ($463,000) had already been raised. Most of that attainment were pledges gained privately over many months preceding the October public announcement. "Seed money" it began to be called—money sown to make the garden grow.

In mid-January 1969, gifts and pledges had reached $850,000. President Howard in a January 24, 1969, letter to the ABA Council reported this to be "encouraging progress" and forecast that there would be "no reason why the goals of the Campaign should not be exceeded." Some ABA Council members, however, expressed "doubt... about the progress of the fund-raising drive." They could not see how the ambitious undertaking could be reached in so short a time.

Their lack of confidence may have triggered self-fulfilling prophecy. It came about like this: The January 1969 correspondence between President Howard and the ABA Council had been part of the college's **third application** for accreditation. The timing was unfortunate. The two failures just eleven and five months before made that third try a serious gamble. It was not only too soon, it came in the middle of the fund drive. Therein laid the risk: Losing a third time would dampen donative spirit whereas *gaining* provisional accreditation would boost giving.

ROBERT E. JONES

Charity is extended to the needy. Those in want can be either the dire and hopeless or those with bright promise but not liquidity. So, should the donor be approached with promising or beggared prospects? Potential, not pity, is what motivates the larger handouts. Alms for the downtrodden; largesse for winners. Donation dollars were riding on success with that third accreditation approach.

Apparently, college officials saw no risk. They were confident that provisional accreditation was now certain. Concerning the accreditation goal, President Howard had written on December 13, 1968:

> "The acquisition of an adequate plant is the only remaining ingredient in achieving that objective."

But as foresaid, ABA confidence was not yet earned. Accreditors did not see how it could be done. Their prophecy was backed by their vote. In February 1969, the third application for accreditation was promptly denied by the ABA Council. We were euchred. [In the card game called "Euchre," the taking of three tricks is required in order to win. Denied those three attempts, one is then said to be "euchred."]

Then came the self-fulfilling of prophecy. By June 1969, only $1.4 million had been given or pledged; that was thirty percent shy of the $2 million goal that had been set for completion by "early 1969." By July of 1969, the drive was still short of the mark and was in fact made shorter because preliminary contract bidding made it clear that the proposed building construction would cost $1.5 million ($300,000 more than the anticipated $1.2 million). Thus, realistically the fund drive was for $2.3 million, making the $1.7 million thus far received as of July 1969, $600,000 off of the needed amount.

QUITE APART FROM THE BUILDING fund drive shortfall, a January 31, 1969, letter from Millard H. Ruud, the new ABA Consultant on Legal Education and the replacement for John Hervey, listed a number of **ABA Council concerns** not previously indicated, but now emphasized. Paragraph "3" of the Merger Agreement read: "The law school shall be conducted on a self-sustaining basis." That provision was a bone upon which the accreditors would continue to chew. Our deficit budgeting justified accreditor concern over a "precarious financial situation." Furthermore, the promise of a new law building complex was apparently not going to hide the fact that education was still being conducted in current "facilities [that] leave something to be desired." And finally, they frowned upon a curriculum that offered no elective flexibility and a schedule that packed education into just three evenings each week.

In addition to these expressed concerns, we also faced a library shy of books. Furthermore, our faculty salaries were now below the nation's newest and ever rising median that had passed us by. Then too, there was an unacceptable full-time faculty-student ratio of 1:40. And we had no full-time law librarian, no funds for faculty research support, no day division, and no endowment, and we had not yet replaced our lost dean and were operating with a caretaking dean. All of these were clear signs of naïveté and impetuosity if not arrogance, in our pursuit of premature approval. Nevertheless, undaunted by its most recent turndown, the college quickly began to amass another attempt at ABA recognition.

FOUR DAYS AFTER NOTICE OF the third accreditation denial, the full-time law faculty was called to President Howard's office to lay plans for a **fourth accreditation assault** aimed at the ABA's Section meeting just four months away in August 1969. It was officially the first time that the college brought the law faculty into the organized formulation of the pursuit. To be sure, Dean Stevens had put us on errands, but now for the first time we were given some degree of management. Failing at ABA recognition had one bright aspect; it gained college recognition of its law faculty.

My assignment was called "Development and Promotion Programs." Runkel's was "Strategy." Walker's was "Curricular Goals." Gerhardt's was "Budget and Finance."

We were given just twenty days in which to formulate written "thinking papers" and then report to the President at a February 25, 1969, meeting. John D. Phillips, the President's assistant, was the coordinator. In laying out these assignments, Phillips wrote us on February 6:

> It is understood that you may encounter particular difficulty in developing your "thinking papers"... inasmuch as you are burdened with the responsibilities of grading examinations during this time period. On the other hand,... the development of these materials carries a very high priority..., and we at least hope to have some fairly solid starting points for discussion by February 25.

While Phillips' breakdown of assignments showed analysis, the faculty did not agree with its organization. So, we reorganized. We saw the tasks put before us as a single effort that called for our unity, not our separation. I was asked to prepare a preliminary draft of a united strategy, but I could not because I was serving as an Oregon State Bar volunteer to counsel the 1969 Oregon Legislature, then in assembly at Salem. It was a month-long service and was coupled with night classes to teach and with the grading of about sixty Tort exams, sixty Civil Procedure exams, and twenty-five

Jurisprudence theses. It left me no time to draft a position paper in less than three weeks. Runkel was anxious to take on the task. Having been a law student of Stevens, Runkel, more than anyone, was upset by the Stevens departure and, furthermore, was annoyed by the college's three misses at gaining ABA's graces. Runkel called the college's last attempt a "deplorable" presentation. Now he was pleased that the next attempt was going to emanate from the law faculty.

Within four days following the Phillips' memo and in spite of exam grading, Runkel submitted three strategy papers to the faculty. On February 17 at a kitchen caucus, the faculty arrived at a consensus capsulated by Runkel in a February 21 memo entitled "Accreditation Summary." Mindful of the ABA Section's, in-house troubles [see ch. 4], we had to resolve an opening issue: Which set of ABA standards should we use as a template? Should we pattern our application upon the existing quantitative rules or upon the proposed qualitative guidelines. To be sure, the issue did not have to be an "either-or" proposition, but it did call for emphasis on one or the other. Our consideration of the issue leaned us toward quality more than quantity. We felt that accreditors would feel more flattered to be asked to bestow tribute, not just to note compliance. Meeting bright-line minimums showed a mere desire to stay in bounds. To succeed, we had to exceed. No brinkmanship. Astound, not just conform. Runkel recorded our consensus thus:

> "Technical quantitative compliance with existing factors... will not succeed... Therefore, we must offset our deficiencies... by excelling in areas in which we already meet minimum quantitative requirements."

Then Runkel added, "the Council will likely be unimpressed with crash programs."

In our forthcoming meeting with President Howard and John Phillips, the insinuations of poor timing and hurried choices in the college's past attempts had to be wary of the line between advice and scolding—a thin line that can cross the bounds of tact. Our "Advice" urged the following **fourteen strategy steps**:

**(1)** Let us **not be hasty** about bombarding the Council accreditors with repetitive attempts. We might try for the August 1969 ABA Section and Council meetings but only if we assess fully our readiness. There can be no more failure.

**(2)** The new Council Advisor **Millard Ruud**, should be invited to our campus and embraced as a consultant to us and not just a consultant to the ABA.

**(3)** The **written materials** to the Council should be exemplary and should be given to the inspection team well in advance of arrival.

**(4)** The **fund drive campaign** goals should be fully attained and not just time-predicted.

**(5)** Ground breaking for and **construction of the building** should be well under-way or accomplished and not just promised.

**(6)** A **full-time experienced** dean needs to be in place. Dean Cairns granted that an acting or interim dean would not impress quality-seeking accreditors.

**(7) Faculty research support** should be financed and a faculty secretary hired.

**(8) Library** count should reach a quality 25,000 volumes, not just our minimum quantity of 15,000 volumes, which barely satisfies ABA existing rules.

**(9)** We need to take greater care at **lobbying** our cause, *e.g.*, by contacting Council members informally in advance of formal presentation.

**(10)** We should schedule **four nights** (instead of three) each week for classes, thus giving more room for a flexible (elective) curriculum.

**(11)** As for **bar exam** results, they are results, not causes. Accordingly, we should repair the causes with tighter admissions, grades, and probations.

**(12)** We should institute a student-edited, scholarly periodical—our first stirrings of a **law review** publication—a sure clue of the reach beyond mere quantity minimums.

**(13) Admissions** requirements needed extensive attention. This was a prominent aspect in both the existing and proposed ABA standards. Admissions occupied ten of the sixty pages of the proposed ABA promulgations. Our admissions system was still influenced by Northwestern's former leniency attitude. For example, although we now complied with the ABA rule requiring each applicant to take the national Law School Admission Test (LSAT), we did little to factor the LSAT scores into the admission decision. Often we admitted the applicant before we were furnished the score. Furthermore, we simply required, in keeping with the ABA's existing minimum, that an applicant successfully complete three of the four years of undergraduate study; we did not require an undergraduate degree, a quality step which many other ABA approved law schools were beginning to do. We also recommended the creation of a Faculty Admissions Committee to oversee the process. Our foremost point was: Admission issues should be solely within faculty province without approval from SCOLS and oversight at the presidential level. The quality of admittees was an educational decision for academicians not administrators. Since Dean Stevens' departure, the president's office had taken the reins. That would have to be a matter for future corrections if the accreditors were to be satisfied.

**(14)** In our final strategy point, we strongly urged President Howard to convince the trustees to strike the **self-sustaining clause** from the 1965 Merger Agreement. The ABA would never yield accreditation to an offspring whose parent college would not sustain it. Some did not regard the issue as momentous, because eventually the law school would stand on its own feet and be self-sustaining. Then the tables would turn. Throughout the nation, law schools are "cash cows." Once they become going concerns, they shore up, not lean on their parent college. As far back as the merger negotiations, President Howard foresaw that distant prospect. But, in the meantime, the ABA would not countenance a merger contract where one of the two parties was fiscally on its own. A merger meant what its name implied: union and mutuality.

The strategy points raised in our so-called "thinking paper" were supposed to be "points for discussion;" but as I recall it, not much discussion ensued at our February 25 meeting in the president's office. Our bottom-line was a recommendation to withdraw from the fourth accreditation try in August. We were simply not ready. We were thanked and once again relegated to months of wait-and-see. Although Dean Cairns may have been "in the loop," Gerhardt, Runkel, Walker, and I were left to tend shop.



IT WAS DURING THESE SPRING 1969 months that Ross Runkel and I made the law school's first showing in the nation's family of law educators. We were representatives at the American Association of Law Schools (AALS) Western Conference in Tempe, Arizona, March 1969. It was a first opportunity to witness the vistas beyond our own backyard. If nothing else, I learned a central value of such conferences: Problems are seldom original, and there is therapy in sharing.

In May of 1969, I was chosen as the first executive director of the **Oregon Judicial Fitness Commission** [JFC]—a new state agency assigned the task of investigating complaints against and recommending discipline of Oregon judges. The Commission's chairman, Thomas H. Tongue III, was principally responsible for my appointment. He had been a part-time teacher of evidence law at old Northwestern, was one of the five trustees of the former Northwestern College of Law who signed the Merger agreement, was now a member of SCOLS, and would soon become a justice on the Supreme Court of Oregon. My JFC duties were administrative and investigative and called for occasional visits to county courthouses throughout Oregon. It was a part-time job that took four days a month away from my professorship, but it brought the offices of a state agency to our campus which helped to show accreditors the school's reach into community and professional service. Still, some trustees, accreditors, college administrators, and even law professors were uneasy about such moonlighting.

At the May 1969 faculty meeting, the law faculty recommended its first **professorial promotion**. I was moved up from the rank of assistant professor to associate professor. It was unanimous—four affirmative votes. Professor Walker was not present. I was one of the "yea" [or should I say "yeah!"] votes. It was the only time in NWLC history that a faculty member was permitted to vote his own self-promotion.

Our recently passed Principles of Employment and Tenure was just a scant paragraph or two with little word for procedure and nothing at all about self-promotion. The informality of our "kitchen-business" gave parliamentary order no more courtesy than a passing nod and wink.

Once the thrill of advancement had calmed down, I faced a reality: My promotion was driven more by need than merit. The move from assistant to associate would mean a $1,500 pay raise, thus also raising NWLC's median salary figure to meet accreditation requirements. So, prior to vote on my promotion, my colleagues centered their discussion on median salary upgrade. I remember wishing that they might have given some thought to my values. It was my first inkling of the muddled mix that would trouble the two major tasks that occupied NWLC in that era. We struggled to be both accredited and academic. To be sure, the two tasks had common aims, but sometimes the accreditation carrot would dictate education merit. My promotion in order to promote NWLC, was but one example. The demands would surface again in choosing faculty hires in order to gain numbers and to lower faculty-student ratios. Another example was increasing library book volumes for the sake of accreditor quanity demands.

At that same meeting, we considered four candidates for a full-time faculty position and selected one. The faculty, for the first time, took initiative in professor hiring. The deciding vote, nevertheless, was cast from above. Our selection was rejected by higher authority. Merit was not the question. Numbers was the question. We had no money for hiring another faculty member at this juncture.

THROUGHOUT THE 1969 SPRING SEMESTER, the proposed ABA standards at which we aimed were targets that swung back and forth. Within the ABA Section, Council, and various subcommittees, changes were vigorously asserted but not yet affirmed. For example, Proposed Standard B:3 addressed **faculty size**: "A law school shall maintain a faculty... of suitable size." That was the quality principle to be met. But the accompanying Factor B:3.2, which was supposed to be merely a guide, quantified the principle by stating emphatically that a school could not: "...possibly meet its obligations with fewer than four full-time faculty members."

With five full-time faculty members, we met that minimum "guideline." But then, on May 21, 1969, a special ABA committee, created to review the proposed standards and factors, recommended that the minimum faculty size be six instead of four. Now we fell one short of a threshold that was really just a guideline and, as yet, just a proposed amendment to change a main proposal, neither of which were close to enactment. To add misery to that muddle, the Council then ended up with the following confused change to faculty size:

> "...a minimum of three full-time instructors, and not less than one for each 75 students or major fraction thereof, in addition to a full-time dean and a full-time librarian."

"Guideline ambiguity" is oxymoronic. Numbers and math danced with grammar. Does it call for "a minimum of three" *plus* "one for each 75"; or does it mean "a minimum of three" *or* "one for each 75" *whichever is greater*? In addition to a dean and a librarian and based upon an anticipated student body of 220, did we have to have three or six or anything "suitable"?

Bear in mind that, even if all powers could agree on interpretation, it was just a clarification of the *Council's* proposal. What would the *Section* do with it? And would the Section's word be final? Was the Section autonomous on these matters, or did it take ABA Governors and Delegates approval? Assuming we needed six professors (plus a dean and librarian) then in May of 1969 we were short two professors.

That's when we were hit with another shocking turn of events. Wayne Walker and Ross Runkel had enough. They quit. We were going to need to hire four, not two, full-time faculty members.

Ross's decision was upsetting to me—but not Walker's. Throughout his sole academic year with us, Walker was a shadowy presence. His résumé was studded with all of the right academic "paper": Phi Beta Kappa and Order of the Coif to name a few. But he and I did not simply disagree; we were mutually disagreeable. My reasons were petty at first. He was hired by the college without consultation from the law faculty and hired at an annual salary that was twenty percent higher than mine ($16,000 versus $13,000), even though we were the same age and both 1960 law school graduates. The salary disparity was one of the ugly facts about supply and demand marketing: It is cheaper to maintain existing employees than it is to entice new ones.

But during the course of our troubled 1968-69 academic year, sounder reasons for our misfit developed. Walker was gloomy, and his predictions of failure were a drag on progress. Where Runkel's critiques were constructive, Walker's negativity hung like dead weight on a whine. To be sure, we were in need of a good bedside manner, not sackcloth and ashes. Unfortunately, his despair took Ross with him. Walker resigned after only ten months with us, and Runkel's resignation soon followed. Walker returned east to direct the clinical program at Ohio State University Law School, where he stayed about a year longer than he had stayed with us. Then, as far as I can gather, he abandoned the field of legal education entirely. Runkel, on the other hand, moved to Salem, fifty miles to the south of us, where he joined the Willamette College of Law faculty and there retired after about thirty years. In subsequent years, following his departure, I would have gladly accepted him back into our fold, but detractors more adamant than my persuasion could not forgive his defection.

To make the landscape more desolate, Dean Cairns and Professor Gerhardt had expressed their desire to return to the private practice of law. But when they heard of the Walker and Runkel departures, they promised to stay on for another semester or two. Neither had meant "full-time" to be "forever-time." Their hearts were in lawyering. As former part-time downtown law instructors since the mid-1950s, they had come to campus life to close the remaining gap of merger. After one more academic year, they would have spent three years cementing that closure even while witnessing the widening of the accreditation fault.

The 1969 Graduation Day is a vague memory, and I found no notes of it—maybe because it was rainy and the ceremony was cooped up indoors. The Cascade Mountain Range was not in view—nor was what loomed ahead.

AND SO, AT THE BEGINNING of summer vacation in 1969, I was alone in an empty faculty house. The only other employees on hand were Registrar Cornelius and Secretary McCroskey, who kept busy next door with grade transcripts, admissions, and the chores that never saw an end. In the supplement to the AALS *Directory of Law Teachers*, I was listed as the sole professor at NWLC. Just twenty-two months before, I had entered a school full of the bite of energy with the knowledge that I had found a career home. But now, at my living room desk, I was taken by the wonder that solitude begets. I remember those hollow moments well. The Runkel bedroom was cleared out. The Cairns and Gerhardt chairs were vacant for the summer. Voices were gone. No argument from the kitchen. Even the silence seemed to echo.

When the phone rang, it was louder than ever before. President Howard's secretary invited me to his office. Worried about mass exodus and the intent of his remaining straggler , President Howard asked me if I was a "team player." Those were his words: "team player." I don't remember how I answered. I could be a team player in sports, which are just games, pretense, and play. But in the real world of business and schooling, I knew I was not a corporate or organization man. If that puts me down as a rogue, maverick, or renegade, then so be it—even though I don't fancy those labels either. I saw it this way: A school of fish will dart and turn in unison, each fish seeming to be wired to the whole in instant regimentation to some unseen robotic force. That kind of "schooling" was not for me. I could be loyal, not in the sense of *joining* the school, but rather in the sense of *giving* to it. It's why teachers are given tenure—sanctuary in self.

Back in the president's office, in view of the recent thinning of the "team," I knew what the president really wanted to know: What were my future plans? I remember my exact answer, because it was one of those utterances that, on the way home, one wishes to have better phrased. I assured him that I was "headed nowhere." It was a well-intended affirmation of loyalty, of staying put, of confidence in the school's future—but packaged in a poor choice of words.

On the other hand, perhaps, it was a subliminal moan from somewhere inside. Had I made a good career change? I had to wonder. But teaching was so gratifying and my place in Oregon was so strong that any thought of abandonment was subsumed by vows to make this law school supreme.

# 1969: TIME CONTEXT

Hundreds of thousands in many U.S. cities demonstrate against U.S. involvement in the Vietnam war.

The "Chicago Eight" found not guilty of violating the crime of anti-rioting in the 1968 Chicago demonstrations.

CBS-TV cancels the popular Smothers Brothers show for failure to send advance copy of the show's script for censor scrutiny.

Assassins Sirhan Sirhan and James Earl Ray each sentenced to life imprisonments.

Abe Fortas resigns from the U.S. Supreme Court after questionable dealings with a convicted financier.

President Nixon appoints Warren Burger as Chief Justice of U.S. Supreme Court.

Astronaut Neil Armstrong is first man to walk on the moon.

International inflation and ocean pollution become world-wide concerns.

Santa Barbara oil spill triggers modern concern with ocean pollution.

A purported half million attend the counter culture Woodstock Rock Festival in New York.

The Beatles make their last public appearance together.

Women's trousers and pant suits become fashionable, but still unacceptable for lawyers in Oregon courtrooms.

# 6
# THE WREN REGIME: PART ONE
## *1969-70*

### *FRESH VISTAS*

Late spring of 1969, we hit bottom—a dead halt in pursuit of accreditation. With the departures of Professors Ross Runkel and Wayne Walker, with the prospect of Professors Jack Cairns and Paul Gerhardt doing the same, with the bad publicity of the Stevens firing still ringing in our ears, with a fund drive sputtering to reach its goal, with a three-strike-call by the ABA Council of Legal Education, and with conflicting accreditor guidance, we were not just *at* the well; we had fallen into it. At such descent, the college followed the law faculty's advice [see ch. 5] and withdrew its fourth attempt at an accreditation try at the August 1969 ABA meeting. I regard that fourth effort as another denial—the only difference being, that instead of the ABA calling the refusal, we took a look and called the denial ourselves.

Students came to me with questions and concerns about the future. The school seemed to be leaving them, and they wondered about leaving the school. I tried not to look at despair and told them of a saving grace: From the bottom of a well it may be dark, but from there one does not lose the sense of direction.

While handing out pep talk, I too could have used one. I got it from Judge John Flint Gantenbein who was no stranger to bleak times for his law school. In that summer of 1969, he found me alone in my living room office. It had been a long while since he and I had sat for a talk. In his judge chambers back in 1966 [see "Introduction"] he talked of new beginnings in the law school's future. Now in the living room, he talked of near endings in the law school's past. In 1915, the University of Oregon tried to close the law school in Portland and to open law classes on its main campus some one hundred miles away. Calvin Gantenbein (John Flint's father) refused to allow the end of the school in Portland. As sole proprietor and dean under the new name "Northwestern College of Law," he continued legal education in Portland with essentially the same faculty, the same student body, the same books, the same facilities, the same curriculum and operations.

Dean Calvin died during World War I. The combination of lost leadership and war put legal education on last legs. Northwestern laid down. But somewhere in 1920, the Gantenbein family and a new dean (Judge J. Hunt Hendricksen) got Northwestern back on its feet.

The school's third brush with demise, Judge John Flint told me, was just a little over two decades ago. During World War II, enrollment fell to six or seven students. All three of Oregon's law schools suffered the same loss to the military. It was proposed that the schools should consolidate their enrollments and educations. When that idea failed, continued operations became a defiance of good business sense. Accordingly, the owners decided to end Northwestern. Like his father, Gantenbein refused to allow that. He bought out the other owners, became the sole proprietor, and kept the school open by mortgaging his home and taking a second job in Portland's shipyards.

Then, in the living room, the old proprietor reminded me that NWLC now had more than two hundred students enrolled. He looked knowingly at me with a wink and smile that said two hundred is a long way from six or seven.

From down in the well, his history lesson was the company that misery loves to keep. We began a slow climb. The 1969-70 academic year, was to be a very long chapter in the accreditation era of NWLC.

THE NEW DEAN:

The first step upward began in July 1969. President John Howard informed me that in that month, the law school would welcome a new and permanent dean: Harold G. Wren, a tax law professor from Boston College. At age 47, Hal Wren already had a long career on the law faculties of many universities: Mississippi, Oklahoma, Cornell, Northwestern, California, and New York. That experience was needed, even though the fleeting shadow of a rolling stone does not assure a coming-to-rest. Indeed, Wren was eventually to leave us in the years ahead to become the law dean at Richmond University in Virginia.

Nonetheless, he was, in 1969, a godsend to us. President Howard gave me Wren's Boston College address and urged me to write him. My letter to the new boss did not hide excitement. It relayed the "absolutely wonderful news;" reported "everyone here is thrilled;" and forecasted a future "bound to increase in stature." Following those overtures, I loaded the welcome with a couple of items needing immediate

HAROLD ("HAL") WREN

attention. For one, I had a promising full-time faculty candidate whose career alternatives hinged on a prompt decision from us. For another, we had a number of student applicants whose LSAT scores would not be forthcoming until autumn, but whose future opportunities also needed our quick decisions.

As a final word in the letter, I offered "to stay aboard... if you would be needing my services here this summer." In his return letter, he accepted that offer and added, "We will have a very large amount of administrative work to do." His final words referred to "the great *work* that lies ahead," to which he was "*anxiously* looking *forward*."

It did not take long to learn that those words: "anxiously," "forward," and "work"—genuinely characterized the man. "Exuberance" is another word that comes to mind. His enthusiasm could at times border on impetuous. For example, toward the end of his first year at NWLC, while we were still seeking membership in AALS, he volunteered our school to host the next year's Western Conference of AALS. Fortunately, Texas Tech Law School won the nod.

About the same time, he led the way in creating a "sub-conference" of just the seven Pacific northwest law schools [Oregon, Willamette, Washington, Gonzaga, Idaho, Montana, and NWLC] and urged the inclusion of the British Columbia (Canadian) law schools. He was made the president of that new consortium, which was buoyed along on Wren's energy and lasted no longer than he did.

Nonetheless, our new dean's vigor was exactly what was needed at that point in our history. One of his initial acts in the summer of 1969 was to create a dean's *advisory* board of distinguished Oregon judges and lawyers. He dubbed the group "the Fellows." Some wondered why the trustees' Standing Committee on the Operations of the Law School did not serve the same purpose. But SCOLS was an arm of and thus beholden to the trustees and, therefore, was *supervisory*; whereas the Fellows, aside from the insinuation of being hale and hearty, were *advisory* and served as the stanchion for bench and bar support and the link between the legal and educational professions.

Wren was an active reserve commander in the U.S. Naval Reserve (specializing in the Japanese language). Accordingly, he was aware of the ship-board necessity for maintaining morale. On July 1, when he was first piped aboard the NWLC, he immediately made me "morale officer" and "first mate"—not remarkable since I was the only faculty member on deck. With Cairns and Gerhardt and the students on summer vacation and Wren at times away on naval reserve duty, my crew was just Registrar Dorothy Cornelius, secretary Doris McCroskey, and bookstore clerk Virginia Hughes. Never troubled by the doldrums, I was nevertheless fully concerned about sinking.

In that first conference between the new dean and I, he gave me some advice after looking at my résumé. "Impressive accomplishment here," he said, but then went on to note a deficiency. Like Dean Stevens, he urged me to take a leave of absence in the future (not now) to get an advanced doctorate degree from Yale, Harvard, or such. He said I would have no difficulty being admitted to those schools for a JSD degree. He said it would do me good to get a degree from one of those "big name" schools. My résumé needed "some elitism," is the way he put it. It pained him to say that there was "condescension in academia" and that degrees from "choice schools" speak volumes.

While I had seen little of that snobbery in the practice of law, I had yet to learn of the astounding weight that alma maters carried in the ranks of higher education. In spite of sound advice, I refused to perpetuate pretentiousness. I have found over the years that status seldom stopped me from going where I wanted to go or from gaining what I wanted to get. On the other hand, we are seldom privy to the subtleties of the insidious.

## AUTONOMY AND SUSTENANCE:

Accreditors required that a parent college must not treat its law school as just another department of liberal arts and sciences. Law schools must have a degree of autonomy in their operations—the extent of which was not defined, but was nonetheless concrete in its insistence. As previously mentioned [see ch. 5], the 1965 Merger Agreement stated that the law school shall be "self-sustaining." *Autonomy* and *self-sustaining* would seem to be compatible features, but accreditors found them jarring. The parent college must *sustain* its *autonomous* child, they said. Control of operations and support of operations were different matters. The balance between independence yet nourishment needed delicate interpretation.

That attempt at balance came to fruition on June 2, 1969, when the college trustees amended the 1965 Merger Agreement by adding to the words "self-sustaining" the phrase: "to the fullest extent practicable." That would appease the accreditors. But to appease the liberal arts college, the amendment also added that the law school "shall make every effort to finance its own operations... without drawing upon resources of Lewis & Clark College." Then to reassure the accreditors, the amenders added:

> "[F]or some appreciable period of time, and particularly during the transition period prior to attaining national accreditation..., the law school may nevertheless require assistance from Lewis & Clark,... [which] accepts responsibility to furnish to the law school such supplementary financial assistance as may become necessary...."

Finally, as if to remind all sides of the true spirit of merger, a last passage swung to middle ground and family: "[T]he law school has been merged into and has become and will continue to be an integral part of the college." But no matter how well couched, the new words could not hide the underlying hypocrisy in those who resist regulation from above, yet welcome its subsidy.

On July 18, 1969, the trustees of the old Northwestern College of Law agreed to the amendment. Thus did the two entities merge once again, as the accreditor entities watched silently in the wings. "SCOLS" had been the broker between merger, autonomy, and sustenance.

## SCOLS:

As evident by now, the law school had come to use the acronym (and pronunciation) "SCOLS" for the trustee Standing Committee on the Operation of the Law School. [See ch. 4] Sometimes we called it simply "the Standing Committee." It and its sub-committees loomed large throughout the accreditation era and played a strong part in major policy decisions involving the law school—a role ordinarily played by a law school's dean and faculty. While the law school personnel were in a developing state, SCOLS authority was unquestioned. The new faculty was credentialed, but untested. In the beginning the two worked efficiently, usually by staying out of each other's ways. But as the accreditation pursuit was to become more intense and as the faculty matured, the two entities were destined to get into cross purposes.

## GROUND BREAKING:

Well before Wren's arrival, President Howard and the trustees had taken another forward step; they gave the go ahead to construction of the new law building complex, even though the fund drive was not yet fulfilled. The winning contract bid was $1.5 million (by some tables, the equivalent purchasing power of $8 million today).

Paul Thiry's architectural plan had to serve many purposes. Foremost, it had to house classroom, library, office, study, and lounge facility. Then too, the law structure should complement the forest into which it would now be naturalized. It had to become a denizen, not an intruder.

To their credit, the president and trustees, even though short of money in bank, stuck to their original promises. There would be no cutting back on the original blueprint nor the money to be expended for it. Development Officer Glenn R. Gregg put it this way: "The facility, as planned, could not be responsibly reduced in size and... will never be built for less."

A ceremonious ground breaking was scheduled. Formal and fancy invitations called it a "turning of earth." And so, on Sunday, July 13, 1969, midst the trunks and trillium of the Tryon Forest, there came lemonade, cookies, a college band, speeches, bountiful press coverage, and shovels to turn the earth. Indeed, more than earth was turned. Students, alumni, faculty and friends saw a turn of a new page in the law school's eighty-five year history. It was going to have, for the first time, its own home.

## LIBRARY:

Our future was looking better, but there was to be a lot more ash before we were to rise from it. One of the major shortcomings was the library situation. Our current library book count had grown to about 19,000 in the summer of 1969. The trouble was that the ABA minimums were also growing. Dean Wren predicted we would have about 22,000 by the end of the 1969-70 academic year—enough to reach just the bottom shelf of spiraling requisites. Then too, in the distance was the higher shelf of AALS, the second accreditor of whom we had not taken much account before the Wren regime. AALS required 60,000 books.

Book acquisition was one trouble, but so were the tasks of developing space in which to put them and a system by which to find them. Our consulting librarian, Jacqui Jurkins, now part-time, believed we would have no difficulty reaching the 60,000 goal by the end of the 1970-71 academic year provided the new library building was available for cataloging and shelving.

Jurkins also pointed out major deficiencies in architect Thiry's library plan. For one, there was no dumbwaiter. Three feet of books per day would be arriving at the receiving dock in the library basement, which, without a dumbwaiter, would have to be hand-carried up twenty feet of stairs to the shelves. Readers, who lift meaning out of books on shelves, are oblivious to what librarians endure: the heft in lifting books in boxes. We were a long way from the day when the hardware of dumbwaiters, stairs, and books might be widely replaced by the softer wares of bits, and bytes.

While the building plan called for two large water pool fountains to grace the library entrance outdoors, Jurkins' careful eye noted the absence of drinking fountains indoors. Little, but necessary, oversights were a beginning of costs to be added to the $1.5 million construction contract.

Aside from dumbwaiters and fountains, an even greater library blank would have to be filled before accreditors would even begin to consider our next bid. The absence of a library leader was a glaring defect. A *consulting* librarian was not enough. We had been without a full-time librarian for the past year. Jurkins had left that post in the summer of 1968. Now at the beginning of the 1969-70 academic year, Jurkins, the head librarian at the Multnomah County Law Library, was a main target for reprise.

THE TWO "WALK-ONS":

Our faculty ranks had been decimated by the Walker-Runkel exits and would be further weakened by the forecasted resignations of Cairns and Gerhardt after one more academic year. With lame ducks Cairns and Gerhardt gone for the summer and Dean Wren still in Boston, I was, as aforesaid, the sole professor on duty at the beginning of summer 1969—a time of emptiness. Into that downcast, a couple of fortunes stumbled our way. Bill Williamson and Fred Dow Fagg III dropped by the campus separately and unannounced. I was the lone and surprised greeter. One afternoon Williamson burst into my living room office with a handshake, "hello," and offer: "I'm Billy Williamson. I wanna teach law. I understand you could use someone." Fagg came a week or so later; he was on the same mission, but pursued it more cautiously. The contrast in their approaches was unmistakable—the difference between audacious and circumspect—plain and aplomb. Their names alone were enough to betoken their styles: One called himself "Billy"; the other called himself "Fred Dow III."

In all of my years at employer job interviewing, they were the only two who blatantly initiated the hire. It was as though they knew our plan of recruitment before we did. Aside from surprising, it was flattering, because it reminded me that, in spite of news coverage and reputation, we still had something to sell.

In the "chase of paper" both had impeccable credentials. Billy, a Harvard law graduate, who had clerked for Oregon Supreme Court Justice Hall Lusk, was the chief appellate lawyer in the local, Multnomah County district attorney office. Fred, a Michigan law graduate with an MBA degree from Harvard, was an antitrust law practitioner in southern California.

Billy was a bachelor. Fred and his wife, Judy, were touring the Pacific northwest law schools with the prospect of changing his career. Billy's childhood was inconstant. Fred was the son of a former president of the University of Southern California. Where Billy was venturous, Fred was organized and secure. They were the difference between a desk piled high and a desk glassy clean. They were worlds apart, yet had worlds to offer.

I had long conversations with each of them on their days of arrival. No doubt my assessment was fueled in part by the school's want. But I guarded against needs that just plugged empty spaces; we had to have positive workers. Neither were naysayers; they were coupled in that one critical respect. Both brimmed with optimism about the school's future and affirmed their desire to work for it, to make the Pacific northwest their home, and to be at a beginning. I was sold on attitude and commitment, not paper trail and upbringing—where were they headed, not where had they been. Both saw promise, not doom.

First, they had to be sold before we could buy. Williamson needed no persuasion from me. He had done his homework, knew what he wanted, and where he wanted it. On the other hand, Fagg had other opportunities to weigh. He and I spent an afternoon touring one of our strongest selling points—the beautiful Lewis & Clark campus. I plugged the benefits of teaching, of place, and of growing with a law school that was emerging into the national picture. That afternoon was apparently an important one, for later on, Fred would always say that at the outset he was impressed by the challenge of *making* an organization and not simply *joining* one.

Billy was ready to start anytime we wanted him. Fred was "wait-and-see." The next step was to gain the approvals of President Howard and Dean Wren (who was still in Boston). A phone call with Dean Wren was enough to convince him. Howard took a bit more persuasion inasmuch as all previous faculty hires had been at his and SCOLS' instigation. This was the first time that a professor was involved in the successful recruiting of faculty hires. But the desire for expediency on a hurried expedition was overwhelming. My interviews and assurances and their formal resumés were enough. The two "walk-ons" and their careers were virtually sealed with us on their days of arrival. Indeed, Fred was destined to become the dean of the law school and Billy one of the founders of our

BILL ["BILLY"] WILLIAMSON

environmental law image. Both would play major roles in the accreditation era.

RECRUITING FACULTY:

Now that we had a permanent dean, a building complex underway, a library plan, and the revision of the self-sustaining clause, additional faculty hiring became our primary mission. President Howard and the trustees, for the first time, gave the law faculty authority to do the recruiting. A law librarian and two new professors to replace Jurkins, Runkel, and Walker were needed, plus two more permanent replacements for Cairns and Gerhardt, who planned to leave at year's end. Aside from five replacements, we were empowered to add two new faculty positions for the following academic year in order to meet ABA accreditation standards. Thus, beginning in the summer of 1969, the task before us was to search and find seven new hires. Williamson was hired for the upcoming year, and Fagg was contracted to begin in the following year. That left five empty seats to be filled.

At our first faculty meeting on September 3, 1969, with Cairns and Gerhardt back from the summer and Assistant Professor Williamson as a new face, our energetic new dean presented his list of fifty-seven known faculty candidates! It did not take us long to cross off twenty-four from the list, due to either their or our lack of interest. We divided the rest into sixteen imminent prospects and seventeen September 1970 prospects.

In the weeks following that meeting, our faculty of five, including the dean, interviewed two prospects on campus: William Knudsen and Walter Probert. Knudsen and Probert were experienced professors of law at Wyoming and Florida law schools respectively. Knudsen was a fiery New Yorker with a straight-forward, stand-up gift for delivery, characteristic of the courtroom lawyer he once was and with a range of emotion that could take him from hearty laughter to red-faced anger. He spoke from his heart and his mind and never backed away from doing so. He had been a class-mate of Dean Wren when they were law students at Columbia.

Professor Probert was a nationally known scholar, and that was our attraction to him. His home town was Portland, and that was his attraction to us. Fame on the one hand and coming home on the other, were not the kind of magnetism that had staying power. He wanted to join us on a trial basis. His motive and half-heartedness soon dampened the impression that had initially drawn us to him. He was either too big for our britches or too big for his own.

Knudsen was unanimously approved for a full-time faculty position. He accepted our offer in October 1969, but, like Fagg, could not leave his work until the next academic year. Knudsen would come as a full professor, and Fagg would join as an associate professor.

We scrutinized another interesting faculty prospect: David Frohnmayer, a south-ern Oregon lawyer. The record does not show what became of that interest, but what became of Frohnmayer is well known: He would one day become a professor and dean of the University of Oregon School of Law and then that university's president.

In the last week of December 1969, Dean Wren, Professor Williamson, and I attended the annual AALS conference in San Francisco, with the intention of interviewing a vast number of faculty candidates that the dean had scheduled there. Fred Fagg came up from southern California to join in those interviews even though he was not yet on the payroll.

Aside from an academic program, the annual AALS convention was also a market-place for those interested in law professorships. I was surprised at the vast number of aspirants that descended on that convention in hope of academic careers. For two days, from 9:00 a.m. to 6:00 p.m., we met with prospects. The fertile ground for law schools was a tough competition for candidates. What was billed as a "market-to-meet," came to be labeled by the traders as a "meat market." It made me appreciate how lucky I had been three years before, to be in the right place at the right time to happen into academic life without having to learn lines, rehearse, suit up, and perform in tryouts.

Two of our prospects at the conference fit our needs: J. Alan Jensen, a young tax lawyer with law degrees from the University of Michigan and New York University, and Walter Brown, a retired naval commander in the Judge Advocate General Corps and veteran of World War II and the Korean War. Jensen had gone to law school with Fagg, and Brown's naval background was close to Wren's interests.

There was one other promising candidate that had not appeared on our lists nor had he been scheduled for interviews at the conference. He was one of Wren's last minute "finds." Williamson and I were about to meet him in the most peculiar way. It was night after a day full of parleys. Billy and I were ready to retire in the hotel room we shared, when there came a knocking at the door. It was Dean Wren with his late night recruit. More eager than usual, the dean introduced him as "Robert Jagiello." There, at bedside, Billy and I in pajamas and Jagiello in tie, vest, and coat, had a talk.

When Jagiello left, Wren stayed for a debriefing on his latest prospect. The dean wanted to extend Jagiello an immediate offer. Billy was also excited about him. Indeed, Jagiello had exuded infectious enthusiasm. I too would have probably been enthused had not all three of them used up all of the energy in the room.

Never one to waste time, Wren was so impressed that he offered Jagiello a professorship right there at the convention. I would not have been surprised if the dean had gone directly from our room to Jagiello's room to extend the invitation in those wee morning hours. Jagiello accepted the dean's offer without ever seeing our operations. Indeed, Jagiello must have been a "real find." I was too sleepy to tell.

Candidates Brown and Jensen, on the other hand, were invited to come to Oregon

JAQUELYN ["JACQUI"] JURKINS

for further interviews. On personnel recruitment, the opinions of Cairns and Gerhardt were valuable. No nonsense and tough experience as long-time practitioners may not have motivated them for the ways of the ivory tower, but it was a sound background for assessing people and performance.

Brown and Jensen each spent two day visits on the Lewis & Clark campus in mid-January 1970. They were extended offers as a result of informal consensus—not like today where the approval of a new professor must pass muster under specific rules requiring an eighty percent, formalized faculty vote of those present and voting at a duly called faculty meeting. Brown accepted immediately and Jensen soon followed. Years later they would both leave academic life—J. Alan for a tax law practice in Portland and Walt for a legislative and political career that would eventually lead him to the Socialist Party and its candidate for President of the United States.

In March 1970, Dean Wren lured Jacqui Jurkins back into the fold as an assistant professor of law. She would resume her role in September as the full-time law librarian, a position she had left two years ago after Dean Stevens' departure. Although she had continued to be our consultant throughout that hiatus, gaining her full attention was a major step in satisfying accreditors. Jacqui's appointment as an assistant professor made her the first woman on the law school faculty since its beginning in 1884.

Robert Jagiello's brief role upon our stage can be told in the following chronology of quotes from our faculty minutes in early 1970:

Jan .7, '70:    "Dean then reported on our interviews of faculty prospects in S.F. One of the interviewees, Robert Jagiello was extended a firm offer and did accept. He will be joining us in Sept. 1970..."

Feb.19, '70    "Prof. Jagiello... had prepared a formal proposal for development of a Center for Criminal Justice focused at the law school. The Dean reported that he was quite enthused.... The Dean has turned the proposal over to Grace Kralovec in our Development Office. She has indicated that there is a good prospect for developing funds...."

Feb. 26, '70:  "Grace Kralovic of the Development Office is presently revamping Prof. Jagiello's proposal for a Center for Criminal Justice...."

April 9, '70:  "Prof. Jagiello has written and urges that his course load be reduced. He presently has scheduled five courses: Consumer Law..., Law Enforcement..., Family Law..., Law and Psychiatry..., and Remedies.... In addition, he is one of the clinic coordinators. [Jagiello... also had certain legal writing chores with all of the other faculty.] It was agreed that this was too heavy a load, especially in view of the fact that these are all new courses for Prof. Jagiello [who had never taught law before]. Accordingly,... we will drop Consumer Law...."

May 4, '70:    "Professor Jagiello has decided not to be with us next year.... He has decided that law teaching is not for him."

The Jagiello incident was, in spite of all else, indicative of the times nationally. While he may have been disturbed by us tinkering with his formal proposal, by course overloading, and by our insensitive and superficial cure for it, his reasons for withdrawal lay deeper than that—a hint of the discouragement in many young people of the 1960s. His letter spoke of world-wide "bloodbaths," "effete snobs," "benign neglects," "representatives of mediocrity," and other reasons for world sadness. He withdrew because of "personal conscience" and a "restructuring of his life."

The attitude in that letter was something for which we needed to be watchful in our students' lives and something against which the pursuit of accreditation had to be juxtaposed. Indeed, it was a reminder that outside of our cloistered concerns there was, after all, assassination, war, racial unrest, gender upheaval, pollution, over-population, land abuse, and nuclear threat—all exciting danger for risk-takers, but anguish for bleeding hearts.

I had seen the young man Jagiello once at a very brief, sleepy affirmation, but I felt I knew him better now from his resignation. My April 22 reply letter to him stated: "I share your *weltzschmerz* and personal grief... but am persuaded that education and law improvement is the answer." I wished him "well in your search and reconstruction. If ever I can help, I'll try."


And so, it was time to return to faculty recruitment. President Howard urged us to find one more experienced, senior prospect. Again the dean wasted no time. Within two weeks of Jagiello's exit, Wren hired Dale Broeder, a mature instructor and researcher involved in the famed University of Chicago jury project. No one at the law school, except Wren, had ever seen Broeder.

Thus by the summer of 1970, I had seen the hiring of eight new faculty in the past year. They included, in this order: Wren, Williamson, Fagg, Knudsen, Brown, Jensen, Jurkins, and Broeder. For the forthcoming 1970-71 academic year, the NWLC faculty size would be nine (Cairns and Gerhardt destined to be gone), a cadre large enough to satisfy the accreditors. Our recruitment efforts were over for now—at least we thought so.

## ADMISSIONS:

*The LSAT:* At the beginning of the 1969-70 academic year, we had some doctoring to do on our admissions policy. [See ch. 5, "Admissions"] The ABA accreditation "factor" simply stated that the LSAT "should be required of all applicants for admission to the approved schools." It did not say when that test should be taken and received. So, since 1967, partly as a carry-over from the prior Gantenbein leniency policy, we had been stretching the factor to mean that applicants did not have to have that test score *before* acceptance and enrollment. We had assumed that the purpose of the LSAT (the work of the Educational Testing Service of Princeton, New Jersey) was to create a uniform test throughout the nation's law schools that would provide a central barometer for comparing and analyzing and was not meant to impose uniformity in entrance policies. Accordingly, it would make no difference when the test scores were received, just so long as they were forthcoming. But now we felt the pressure to change our policy in two respects: The LSAT score should be a *precondition to admission*, and should be *suitable for admission*. The test ceased to be just *informational*; it became *conformational*.

*Undergraduate Degree:* At our September 17, 1969, faculty meeting we made another change in our future admissions policy. We required an undergraduate pre-law degree of all student applicants. Professor Cairns argued, however, that a bachelor degree mandate discriminated against older applicants who sought a career change and who at their age would find it awkward to go back to youthful collegiate atmosphere. Accordingly, there were some exceptions made.

It turned out that our requirement of an undergraduate degree was also undermined by statements in the catalog of our parent college. Lewis & Clark College had represented to undergraduate applicants that the college had a six-year program for both a college baccalaureate degree and a juris doctor degree—three years at college then three years of law school, the first year of law dove-tailing as the fourth year of college credit. Thus, students under that program could enter the law school without yet having earned a college degree—contrary to the law school's catalog requiring a degree. We had to get on the same page. Although miffed, we relented.

And so, former leniency sometimes crept back into the admissions process when considering older evening applicants and Lewis & Clark undergrads—two exceptions that would make enforcement of the whole idea lackadaisical.

*UGPA—LSAT Balancing:* For authorized entry into the student body, we also fixed minimum floors on undergraduate grade point average [UGPA] and LSAT score (based on a 4.0 ideal UGPA and an ideal 800 LSAT score in 1969). We did not combine the two scores to arrive at a factored profile number wherein a higher LSAT score might compensate for a lower UGPA and vice-versa. Instead, we insisted that each score must rise to minimum settings of no less than a 2.5 UGPA and a 420 LSAT. It was not wise. An excellent UGPA should tolerate a lower LSAT and vice-versa. But in 1969, we avoided the issue for the time being by choosing instead to be somewhat mild in the enforcement of our new quantifications. After all, in the fall of 1969, we still had open seats and a need for tuitions. So, while on paper NWLC had a tightened policy aimed at pre-law quantifiers, in its heart it still harbored a qualitative practice that let the first year of law study be the admissions predictor.

*Diversity:* We also needed to be more attentive to diversity in our enrollment policy. Racial diversity was a boiling concern in 1969; gender diversity was on the stove but had yet to percolate. Some estimated there were only eight black lawyers in all of Oregon. All were graduates of Northwestern College of Law and included the first black judge and the first black woman judge. Another reckoning sported the fact that Northwestern was the only Oregon school to have ever graduated black lawyers (approximately twenty). If those statistics were wrong, they were not far wrong. And they were nonetheless a sample of how poorly racial diversity had fared in legal education throughout the nation. Growing change in the 1960s included the need for a policy called "affirmative action"—a solution that tasked normative admissions rules. While the U.S. Constitution required state government law schools to afford equality of protection in racial matters, accreditors also required private schools like NWLC to be so sensitive. In seeking to abide accreditor emphasis upon diversification yet also upon strict admission rules, the need for any affirmative action was made to sail between narrow straits. Indeed, our neighboring law school two hundred miles north would find its affirmative action admissions policy under intense scrutiny in the courts of law. Affirmative action in student recruitment was one thing, but quite another in student admissions. While it may be all right to *seek* racial diversity, to let it influence *selecting* admittees created possible problems of reverse discrimination. The case of *DeFunis v. The University of Washington* would reach one day all the way to the Supreme Court of the United States. [See ch. 11, "Racial Affirmative Action"]

*Day Student Division:* Desire from both the college and the accreditors to commence daytime student education augmented our admissions problems. The ABA acknowledged that evening education was an opportunity outlet and a worthwhile necessity—but not without a daytime association. Day students were deemed "full-timers"; whereas evening was a place for "part-timers." The push toward daylight was no imposition; the law faculty was likewise anxious to start a day division. But that commitment meant broadening our admissions and recruitment work. It would not be easy to amass a starting first year, daytime class to an unaccredited school. Day enrollment guesses ranged from ten to thirty. We were destined to be surprised.

STUDENT BODY SIZE:

Accreditors favored large student bodies. In 1969, ABA statistics and studies showed a societal need for more lawyers. Furthermore, a bigger supply of students opened opportunity for a more varied curriculum (increased programs and electives). At the same time, however, accreditors warned of getting too large in student population lest it detract from smaller classes and open-door access to faculty. An optimal student body size of five hundred was suggested for our potential operations. That would mean doubling our current size, a seemingly impossible goal.

Increasing student admissions created a spiraling effect: More students called for more faculty. Accreditors urged a minimum 1:28 faculty-student ratio. "Faculty," we were told, meant on-campus, teaching faculty and ought not include part-timers, non-teaching librarians, and deans. As of September 1969 with five faculty [Dean Wren taught tax], we had about a 1:45 ratio. At the start of next year [September 1970] we expected nine full-time professors and an enrollment of 250 students. That would satisfy the 1:28 ratio. But if we were ever to reach the seemingly impossible 500 optimum, we would have to have a faculty of eighteen—nine more hires, another highly ambitious goal.

The spiraling did not stop there: The more faculty and students, the more staff needed. For example, accreditors urged a faculty secretary for every three professors. We currently had budgeted one secretary for an anticipated eight. And, of course, none of our staff considerations took account of future attention to alumni relations, development, school publications, job placement, student assistance, library assistance, special programs and events, and all of the subtle activities that begin to surface once size becomes a dubious sign of quality.

We later learned that in counting student bodies, an evening student (under a four year program) counted as only three-fourths of a day student (under a three year program). That helped reduce our head counts for ratio purposes. It was this kind of juggling of numbers that occupied a great deal of time in ciphering and re-ciphering of bodies, ratios, dollars, and scores at each step in our progress.

And progress we did, much to our surprise. In spite of bad publicity, NWLC was apparently still an attraction. We started the 1969-70 year with a total enrollment of 220. More gratifying was the fact that our median LSAT score for the first year entering class was 517, compared to a 486 median in previous years.

By March of 1970, we had about 400 inquiries from prospective applicants, compared to only 14 inquiries one year prior. In March-April 1970, we had 75 paid applications: 30 day applicants, 20 evening, and 25 undecided. Those applications included 11 women, 4 minorities, and 23 non-Oregonians from New York to Alaska. By May 1970, paid applications more than doubled (165). As of that time we had admitted for enrollment just 75 of the 165 applications and were flattered by our appeal and proud of our caution. Furthermore, we were beginning to settle into and to put a shine on the ciphers of educational arithmetic.

REVENUE:

No matter what the enterprise—whether profit or non-profit, business or family, public or private, lawful or criminal—beneath transaction lies money, the tickets of exchange. Accreditors were very much aware of our finance. Tickets in the education enterprise came from two sources: customers and donors. Customer payments were labeled "tuition" and "fees."

*Tuition:* In the fall of 1969, the law faculty recommended that next year's tuition be $1,200 for a day student and $750 for an evening student—a projected total cost of $3,600 for three years of day education and $3,000 for four years of evening education. As I recall, it was the first year in which the faculty played a role in initiating a budget proposal for the next year's operations. As a maiden effort, it did not go unchallenged.

In need of more revenue to balance the law school budget, college Vice-President John Phillips and other budget officials felt that the two law tuitions ought to be in parity and, therefore, urged a $900 evening tuition—thus $3,600 over four years. The law faculty argued that night education should be more economical because it was "part-time" in more ways than a simple comparison of three and four years of time. While class-time service might be equalized over three and four years, study rhythm and study opportunity are different at dawn and at dusk. I used the diurnal flower to make the point: folks blossom at sunrise and close at sunset. The twenty-four clock division of available class hours between nighttime (*e.g.,* 6:00 p.m. to 10:00 p.m.) and daytime (*e.g.* 8:00 a.m. to 5:00 p.m.) was a far greater ratio than three to four. Furthermore, the typical meaning of "part-time" presumes "other-time" at job, family, and different responsibilities.

The trouble with the argument favoring lower evening cost was that it also furnished fodder for those who questioned the whole concept of evening schooling and who wished for it to go away. If "part-time" meant less fulfilling than "full-time," how can that justify awarding night students the same doctorate degree as day students?

Those were the issues and debates that surfaced in that fall of 1969. The key that unlocked those issues was in the 1965 Merger Agreement. Its dictates were a conversation stopper. Promises had been made, and the integrity of contract had to be followed. Paragraph 1 of the agreement promised:

> "The express purpose of the merger shall be to provide for the continuation of facilities for evening law school education in Portland, Oregon...."

So much for the existence of evening education. It then went on to promise that night schooling shall be "at a cost which can be afforded by those in need...." Paragraph 4 amplified the foregoing:

> "Fees charged to students in the evening law school shall be lower than the fees charged to day law students...."

Some continued to argue that $750 and $900 were both *lower* evening tuitions than the $1,200 day tuition. But it did not take a wizard to know that "lower" cost had to mean the overall charge for a *complete* education, not just *one year* of that education. Otherwise, *e.g.*, a $1,000 annual evening education might also be "lower" yet after four years end up higher than the day education.

And so, in October 1969, the college trustees and its law school committee [SCOLS] honored their promises and approved an evening tuition of $750 per year as proposed by the law faculty. To balance the law budget, however, they made the school's first day tuition $1,500 per year—a $300 increase over our proposal. The day-evening tuition discrepancy was now made even more stark and thus, guaranteed revival, one day, of its issues.

*Fees:* One month later, college administrators proposed charging law students an annual activity fee to cover use of the gymnasium, swimming pools, tennis courts, squash courts, weight room, interscholastic sports events, theater, concerts, and other extra-curricular, campus activities. The fee was $30 for evening students and $40 for day students. The law faculty felt it was poor business practice, but Dean Wren felt it was a justifiable charge for extra services beyond education. Surprisingly, in January 1970, the law students, both day and evening, voted overwhelmingly in favor of the required activity fee. Apparently, they took more use of the campus fringes than we had thought.

*Donation:* Gift income, another source of money for annual law operations, accounted for about 6.5 percent of annual costs. Operations were mainly supported by student tuition and fees—about 85 percent—an unsatisfactory balance that was producing year end deficits, calling for college support.

Lack of operational gifts was on account of the building fund drive that had hoped to be concluded in the summer of 1969. But as of December 1969, the campaign was still short of its goal. Shortfalls were largely attributed to unforeseen congressional cutbacks—a loss of huge projected federal grants. Then too, unusually high inflation swept the globe and added to the predicted building goal. The drive was chasing a moving target. By April of 1970, we were still short nine percent of what was now needed.

Sometimes potential donations had to be declined because they came with strings attached. The Car Dealers Association suggested a sizable gift, provided the law school conducted an annual seminar conference on a topic familiar to their enterprise. Alcoa Aluminum was willing to give if the law school was willing to specially "service Washington residents" as student admittees.

In the summer of 1970, the fund campaign and the law buildings were near completion—so much so that a permanent donor plaque was commissioned for wall hanging in the new law library. It commemorated the biggest fund drive ever achieved at NWLC. It was a testament to the graciousness of givers, from the gratitude of those given. An informal contest was conducted for a notable quotation to be etched on the plaque above the list of about six hundred donor names. One of Jacqui Jurkins' entries was judged the most appropriate:

> The law wherein as a magic mirror, we see reflected, not only our own lives, but the lives of all men that have been.
>
> - - O. W. Holmes, Jr.

Criticism of the male chauvinism in that wisdom did not arise in 1970 nor, most certainly, would it have been targeted in Holmes' time; nor, perhaps should it be leveled today. Placement of words in history ought to be a reminder of another wise quotation from Lord Bramwell:

> Just because the world gets wiser as it gets older, does not mean that it was foolish before.

In the plaque contest, Professor Williamson's whimsical entry was Marshal Pétain's famous declaration when making a defensive military stand against invaders in World War I: "They shall not pass." Needless to say, it did not pass.

## CURRICULUM:

Much of the foregoing was the attempt to satisfy accreditors of *quantity*: the raising of revenue numbers, the increase of book numbers, the upgrading of enrollment numbers, the addition to faculty numbers, and all other countings. Other necessities, however, had to focus on *quality*: the concerns with good schooling. Along with pedagogy, the heart of the education mission has always been *curriculum*, a word which to early Romans was a sporting term that meant a "racecourse." Indeed, a law school's ultimate bestowal of its Juris Doctor degree comes at the finish of a long course of study and a race for grades sometimes too competitive for its own good.

Ordinarily, today, when asked, "What is your curriculum?"—the first thought turns to the list of course offerings. But our curriculum concerns were a great deal more than a course catalog. Curriculum also meant class and exam schedulings, grading systems, scholastic thresholds for advancement and honors, credit hour minimums, teaching assignments, special program emphases, and other judgment calls about implementation of learning. Curriculum was our front-line business. Buildings, monies, books, faculty, and all other sizings, no matter how essential, were all but feeders to that front.

*Night Calendar:* At the beginning of the 1969-70 academic year, many meetings and many drafts honed the proposed academic calendar for 1970-71. Mostly, we agonized over the evening weekly schedule: Should it be three or four nights per week? In order to provide time for more elective course offerings, as advised by the accreditors, our first calendar drafts scheduled four nights. Northwestern had never before put that kind of demand on its night students. Student reaction was not favorable. In deference to the fact that evening schools were commuter schools, Professor Cairns, once himself a night student at Northwestern, felt that elective opportunity could be squeezed into a three night schedule by starting classes earlier and finishing later.

By the time we reached the ninth draft, a tired faculty voted to continue our three-night schedule. For the sake of resolve, not merit, I did not dissent but did register my preference for four nights.

*Exam Schedule:* Another curriculum proposal, urged by the student council, was to shift first semester exam time from January dates to December dates—thus to make exams before, instead of after, the holiday break. A motive was obvious: If the holidays were to be crowded with homework, it should be faculty grading, not student study.

But because accreditation required a minimum number of sixteen weeks per semester, exams in mid-December meant starting the first semester in late August, before Labor Day. While students may have been willing to accept that trade-off, the faculty was not. The proposal was rejected but would come again and again until realized.

*Faculty Teaching Loads:* Accreditors urged that a law teacher's classroom hours with students (so-called "contact hours") be ideally no more than six hours per week. Annually, that meant a so-called "teaching load" of twelve credit hours. This was not spelled out in the new ABA standards recently put into effect in November 1969, but it was a practice that all law schools were given to understand. Nationally, however, state lawmakers, who had to budget the bill for state higher education, were beginning to see the matter differently. They saw *maximum* classroom teaching of only six hours a week as featherbedding. Some began to propose floors instead of ceilings on teaching hours—minimum instead of maximum standards. Legislators in New York and Illinois proposed laws for their state-supported law schools that mandated a minimum teaching load of at least seven or eight hours per week. In Illinois, it became an issue for party politics—Republicans voting in favor, Democrats against. In New York, Republican Governor Nelson Rockefeller vetoed the legislation as an unwarranted government interference in the domain of higher education.

Opponents of low teaching times took no account of a professor's many hours at classroom preparation, at constant updating of materials, at evaluation of student papers and tests, at student consultation time, and at administrative chores. And none of that took into account the other primary obligations of scholars to do research, writing, publication, and community service. Faculty were not just at a law *school*; they were at a law *center*—a place for lawyers, judges, professors, legislators, executives, and concerned citizens to come together in shaping and maintaining a society of laws.

For two reasons NWLC was not affected by any such state dictates. For one, we were a private school not subject to legislative power over the public purse. For a second reason, our teaching loads were much too large by anyone's standards. For example, concern was expressed for my teaching load as projected in the 1970-71 schedule. With the advent of a day division, my contact hours in Torts, Civil Procedure and Jurisprudence courses would zoom to eight and sometimes eleven per week. A teaching load approaching twenty hours annually far exceeded ABA expectations. There did not seem to be any immediate way out of it, other than to placate the accreditors with the fact that it was temporary and that three of my hours were repeat sessions calling for no additional preparation.

*Grading System:* Our grading system—a legacy from Northwestern College of Law—had evolved into rather peculiar nummerical levels. We used grades ranging from "90" to "50," with "68" and "67" being the difference between satisfactory and unsatisfactory work. Thus, there were forty-one levels instead of the more familiar five levels ["A, B, C, D, F"] or the fifteen levels when plusses and minuses are accorded those letters. Usually, the letter system gravitates to thirteen levels when the plus and minus are dispensed with at the "F" level—it being somewhat officious, if not downright sardonic, to quantify an exam paper as "High-Failure," "Mid-Failure," and "Low-Failure."

We were not the only tinkerers with gradation schemes. Big-name testers also dabbled in ranking levels. The Princeton experts, in charge of LSAT testing originally had an ideal score of 800 that bottomed at 200. In 1982, they changed it to a top of 50 and a 10 bottom. Then in 1991, they changed it to a 180-120 spread.

I liked our forty-one levels [grades 90 - 50]. It made no difference to me what designations were given to those levels. Whether the designations were letters, colors, stars, hieroglyphics, or symbols of any other kind, sooner or later, they would have to be averaged, and that meant transposed into numbers. I preferred the fine tuning of forty gradations or so because it meant that in evaluating exam performance I did not have to stretch or jam my raw scoring into the narrower Procrustean confines of five to thirteen letter boxes, which would then have to be turned back into numbers in order to gain a grade point average [GPA] which, when put into decimals ranging as high as 4.00, would amount to four hundred levels. The whole business of such gradation becomes somewhat brutal when one bears in mind that the grade accorded in most law courses, is based upon a single two or four hour exam taken in each course at the semester's end.

A second reason for preferring multi-levels was that each level was insignificant when contrasted to its near neighbors and did not mean as much in averaging and in prestige. The difference between an "82" and "84" grade in a two hour course, had little effect on averaging when thrown in with all grades over three or four years of law schooling. On the other hand, the difference between "A-" and "B+" carried much greater bragging rights and math effect.

A third reason that I preferred the puzzling "90-50" grade levels was because of the puzzle itself. Exam grades ought to be simply a coded message to the examin-ees as to how well they did in the course. Beyond that private communication and beyond the school's need to know for academic advancement reasons, individual course grades ought to be no one else's business.

Accreditors had no difficulty with our numerical grading system. They knew it was not much different from some leading law schools with similar grade evolutions. While we would do nothing with our grade policy during the accreditation era, there would be distant rumblings from those enamored of the publicly understood "A" for excellence and "F" for failure and of the need of prospective employers and other transcript readers to know how good or bad a student was in a given course (which really meant how good or bad the student was on a single exam). The need of grade transcripts to be communicative was a leftover from the days of grade school report cards to parents.

My view about grading had legitimate critics. As years went by, it was more and more difficult to hang on to the "90-50" system. In later decades, NWLC fell into line with the "A-F-plus-and-minus" standard.

In such tinkering and dabbling, is it any wonder that the specter of "Grades" haunts education?

*Elective versus Required Courses:* For the first time in the law school's history, we pro-vided elective courses for the future 1970-71 curriculum. Seniors were given eight credit hours of choice, which then created the issue of which courses would stay required and which should become optional. And among the optionals, which should be chosen? Was tax law more important than constitutional law? Was the law of evidence less significant than the study of commercial codes? Which was more worthy: Labor Law,

Poverty Law, or Family Law? And, in general, when it comes to knowledge, which is more fundamental to a lawyer's schooling: the laws of crime or business, environment or employment, states or nations, judges or legislators? The comparisons go on and on until this realization comes: The Doctor of Jurisprudence degree is bestowed for mastery of Law's mosaic and not for comparing one tile to another.

The best thing about our discourse was that it made us think about the study of Law. The worst thing about it was that it was ignited by a false premise that taught: What is required is better than what is chosen—like as though arithmetic is better than calculus. That a floor must be built first does not mean that it is higher than the roof. From petty thinking, rivalry rose as teachers angled in defense of their bailiwicks.

*Comprehensive Exam:* A minor curriculum concern was when to schedule the annual comprehensive exam—our annual in-house practice for the bar exam. [See ch. 1] I continued to disparage the whole idea. *Whether* to have such an exam, not *when* to have it, ought to have been the issue. The faculty voted to move the exam from August to December. In pettiness, I abstained from voting on what time to host unwelcome company.

*Scheduling of Holidays:* In order to gain more class time, the faculty voted in favor of scheduling classes on Washington's Birthday (then a national holiday on February 22). Professor Billy Williamson dissented, as

he always did when any celebration was ignored. He might have favored vacations for the birth dates of Millard Fillmore, Rutherford Hayes, and all of the other U.S. presidents, as well. Oddly enough, one year prior to our fall 1969 vote, Congress had already come around to Billy's notions. But much to his displeasure, all of those births would be piled into a single commemoration on the third Monday in February beginning in 1971. President Nixon dubbed it "Presidents Day." The expanded import of that new holiday did not change the faculty's mind, however. There would be no holiday time off for Presidents Day. I, for one, felt certain that the Presidents would have unanimously endorsed our form of "celebration"—one that honored them by studying our country's Law instead of taking time away from it.

## LAW PERIODICAL PROJECT:

An expanded part of any school curriculum are special programs—branches of emphasis in so-called *extra*-curricula work. Dean Wren was particularly fond of "programming." In a fall 1969 memo, he revealed a number of ambitious plans: A Poverty Law project, a Trial Training project, a Continuing Legal Education project, a Para-Legal project, a Drunk Driving Law project, a continuation of Jagiello's Criminal Justice project, a Law Review project, and a Clinical Education project.

Had we tried to instigate all of those endeavors during the 1969-70 year, we would have been pile-thick-and-paper-thin. Most of the projects dissipated the way of smoke. But the latter two caught some of Wren's fire: Law Review and Clinic.

The first stirrings on a prospective law review publication had occurred back in September 1968 during Dean Cairn's administration and one year before Wren's arrival. A self-appointed student committee sought permission to publish a law review. They were not interested in doing a single symposium book. Instead, they recommended a regularly published, scholarly periodical of the traditional kind. They did the homework on price and received two estimates from printers: a maximum of $519 for one issue of 2000-3000 copies. That low price, even for the year 1968, seemed naïve. The students realized that "we cannot expect to receive any financial aid from the school." So, they did not ask for a budget line, rather, they proposed raising the money through the sale of published advertisements or donations from graduates. And there was the rub. Any efforts at fund raising had to be coordinated with the college development office. Publication under college auspices had to pass muster through a chain of command, beginning with the law school faculty and dean and ending with the trustees. A project run by fluctuating student bodies without permanent college personnel to provide advice, stability, and consistency, was fated to bog down in the hierarchy. Nothing came of it.

As soon as Dean Wren arrived on campus in the following academic year, he renewed the effort and pushed for a student-operated, faculty-advised law periodical. A law school needed a forum—a soapbox from which to be heard—a voice that would reach beyond our scholastic cloister. That pedestal was classically a formal, scholarly law publication. Although accreditors did not list "law review" as a necessity, all accredited schools had such publications. Wren knew that it was a hallmark that would catch accreditor fancy. Accordingly, the dean appointed another committee of law students to hammer out some preliminaries. This appointment from within the echelons, unlike student self-anointment, was much more savory to those above.

Typical of his mercurial nature, the dean unwittingly picked for the committee chair a student who had failed legal writing. He rectified his selection by formalizing the qualifications for serving on such a committee. Knowing that the committee would likely evolve into the editorial board once publication was approved, he required that committee members be second or third-year students (not fourth-year seniors) with the top five scholastic grade averages. This gently eliminated his initial chair candidate. The new committee members asked permission to make their own selection of a chair leader. Full knowing that that selection would also become the selection of an editor-in-chief, the faculty approved. The student committee chose second year student Ann Morgenstern from their ranks. Purportedly, they did so because she was the only one of them who did not have a daytime job. But the choice was much wiser than that, as evidenced by the fact that she was destined to become the law school's first magna cum laude graduate and would serve as the founding editor-in-chief for two straight years.

The next step was to decide what kind of law periodical we wanted. On that subject, I recall an impromptu get-together in my living room office in the summer of 1969. Dean Wren, Professor Williamson, and I were conversing with Millard Ruud, the new ABA Advisory Consultant. Ruud had made an unannounced stop on his re-inspection tour of Pacific northwest law schools. Conversation turned to our plan for a new law publication. Having been a founding editor of another law review in my student days, I mentioned that a traditional periodical, broad enough to cover all general law topics, was in order. Ruud, however, suggested that we should specialize. His experience with the nation's law schools told him that it would be hard for us to compete in the general law arena. Uniqueness, he felt, would gain greater attention for an upstart school elbowing its way into the nationwide law review market. Eventually, a general law review might be enticing to authors and readers, but not until our recognition was firmly rooted. It made sense.

In order to put a distinctive face upon the school, Wren was the first to propose the environment as a special field that, as yet, had not received the full attention of legal education. Nationally, there had been heralders making song about this planet's over-population, litter, and misuse of air, water, and land. Since the early 1900s, conservationists had courted the problem without predominant success. Exposing the dangers of pollution reached conception in 1962 when, it is commonly said, Rachel Carson's book, *Silent Spring*, shook the establishment. Later in the 1960s, Congressional enactment of "The Lady Bird Johnson Bill for Beautifying America" and books like Paul Ehrlich's *Population Bomb* were signs of gestation. But the so-called "Environmental Movement" did not gain parturition until now, the beginning of the 1970s, when the National Environment Policy Act [NEPA] and Earth Day demonstrations throughout the nation suddenly burst into full public consciousness and conscience. Our proposed law review was about to burst with it. Professor Billy Williamson voiced a strong second to the dean's proposal. In the weeks ahead, the dean gave Williamson the job of faculty liaison to the student committee. Enthusiasm of Chair Morgenstern and her committee for the topic, sealed the nature of our new publication.

At a September 17, 1969, faculty meeting, Billy asked the faculty for input on a title to be given the new periodical. Should it be "Northwestern Law Review"? That was rejected because of the confusion with that other midwestern law school in Chicago that had titled itself back when it was, indeed, in the northwest part of the U.S. Should it be "Lewis & Clark Law Journal"? That might upset our alumni and the Northwestern trustees in the Merger Agreement. Should it be "Northwestern School of Law of Lewis & Clark College Law Review"? Unwieldy, if not downright preposterous. Instead of the traditional alma mater labeling, should the name reflect its topical specialty and disregard its origins, *e.g.*, "Ecological Law Periodical" or "Environmental Law Quarterly"? Furthermore, I questioned why typical "handles" had to be used. Why attach the traditional "Review" appellation? The contents of law school periodicals had ceased to be just *reviews* in the strict sense of that word. Rather they were often original "views." Why append the word "Journal?" Journals are daily news recordings. Why dangle the word "Quarterly" on a publication that most likely will appear only twice a year. Trade publishers do not title their printings with the obvious. It's not "Time *Magazine*" or "New Yorker *Periodical*" or "Washington Post *Newspaper*" or "Gone with the Wind *Book*."

At the October 2 faculty meeting, after a couple of weeks of private discussions among faculty and editors, Williamson moved and the faculty approved the name, "Environmental Law." It would be the first law school periodical in the nation devoted to ecological concerns, and among the first to use a topical, rather than a parental school title. The launch was the first stroke in sketching our image as the nation's foremost environmental law school.

ANN MORGENSTERN REYNOLDS

The now accepted editorial board went straight to work. They were all evening students: Ann Morgenstern, Jim McClurg, Ken Mistler, and Bob Petersen. They invited second-year evening students to serve as staff researchers and as the likely editorial successors: Gary Abbott, Doug Courson, Kurt Engelstad, Jim Gleeson, Don

Hakala, Jim Hubler, Gary Susak, and Tim Titus. These were the midwives who gave our now nationally-known publication its first spanking.

JOE KERSHNER

They set an April 1970 deadline for publication of the first issue. They collaborated with student editors from other law schools. They sought leading national figures for authors: U.S. Supreme Court Justice William O. Douglas; U.S. Senators Edmund Muskie, Mark Hatfield, and Wayne Morse; and consumer advocate Ralph Nader. They even succeeded in getting the President of the United States to write a short christening foreword to the first issue. Nixon's Foreword would certainly have marked him as an environmentalist. He praised our new periodical as "most heartening and promising . . ., a fresh hope . . ., a constructive effort to answer the summons of the Seventies." He posed a "great question": . . . "shall we surrender to our surroundings or . . . make peace with nature and begin . . . reparations for the damage we have done . . . ." It was doubtful that Nixon or any of his men fully appreciated how the scrutiny and its publicity would instigate a monumental standoff between environmentalists and industrialists and between the proper use and improper abuse of nature.

Second year student, Joe Kershner, was named the Business Manager. He was typical of the evening profile law student—mature, married, family, and job as a certified public accountant. In the mid-1950s, long before our law careers, Joe and I had served as soldiers in the same U. S. Army regiment company in Germany. Our wives were good friends and we socialized. It was awkward to find myself as Joe's professor. His presence in the classroom rows humbled me with reminders that teachers are not superiors, that they are just peers who have gone before, and that arrogance is a nosebleed from being too high and too mighty at the head of the class.

Professor Williamson and student Kershner were given authority to negotiate a printing contract for the first issues of *Environmental Law* at no more than $8,400. "Publication"—our reach to the public— was on its way but was still a babe wrapped in the environment by unaccredited parents and placed on the threshold of modern fostering.

### ENVIRONMENTAL IMAGE:

Professor Billy Williamson saw the scope of environmental study to go well beyond a law publication. He set about to make Lewis & Clark College a center for environmental activity. Sometime in late October or early November 1969, Billy prepared a paper urging the establishment of an "Environmental Law and Research Foundation at Lewis & Clark College." It sought to integrate the sciences and law disciplines in the pursuit of solutions to ecological troubles. The *Environmental Law* publication was merely one of many objectives in that pursuit.

Our parent college likewise took to the environmental path with relish. President Howard and the trustees supported programs and concentrations on air, water, and land studies. Science professors, namely, Paul Ehrlich of Stanford University and Ian McHarg of the University of Pennsylvania, two pioneering environment scholars, were invited to the campus as featured speakers. College trustee Robert Pamplin, of the Georgia-Pacific Corporation, sponsored a $70,000 conference on pollution problems.

At the law school, Professor Williamson offered an elective course on the environment, perhaps the first such law course in the nation. Victor Yannacone, a controversial New York lawyer, was invited to speak at the law school and to write an article for *Environmental Law* . He was currently front-page news. His appearance on campus raised a few eyebrows. He had sued insecticide producers on behalf of all U.S. citizens in a pioneering class action. The total damage claim was thirty billion dollars. That hit intruders in the purse and put a new and confrontational face on the environmental movement. To the troubled 1960s now came another field for polarization—along with war, gender, civil rights, and generational concerns.

One part of Professor Williamson's ambitious proposal was the establishment of a new society of concerned citizens, called the "Environmental Defense Fund." Billy, Portland lawyer Charles Mertens, his wife Betty Mertens, and pediatrician Joe Rand had patterned the idea after the NAACP defense fund and similar plans of other action groups. Its purpose was to take "an activist, positive role" in representing the public interest by engaging in litigation; by "education of committed, environmental advocates"; and by taking "political and legal steps toward reclaiming man's environment." Many of our law students were involved in the Fund's operations. The ideas were new then, commonplace today.

On December 16,1969, the law faculty accepted the proposal and recommended that the Environmental Defense Fund be officed at the law school. Like any engagement, once the veneer of romance wore off, the undercoat of reality surfaced. By housing the Fund, was NWLC identifying with its actions and purpose? What looked rosy in the December holiday season, was given a second look in January. The turn into the new decade of the seventies was cause to take inventory.

At the January 15, 1970, faculty meeting, we re-examined the housing of the Fund. Ordinarily, housing an endeavor did not mean endorsing its actions. However, we had formally accepted the Fund's proposal; and it included a clause urging that "a college and law school should assume leadership in such a program." So, the faculty agreed that the Fund "deserved close attention and delicate handling." Billy argued that precedent was already set. We had previously approved an office for the Oregon's Judicial Fitness Commission in our forthcoming law building. The Commission, of which I was the executive secretary, was active in investigating and recommending sanctions against wayward judges. Billy saw no difference in the disciplining of judges and the penalizing of polluters. His theory was correct, but it overlooked reality. What the JFC did was not questioned; what the Fund would do was contentious.

A week later, Dean Wren assembled the Fellows—his group of alumni, lawyers, judges, and other advisers. They suggested that ties between the law school and the Fund could be maintained, but not without "communications between the various factions." In other words, it would be wise to check with the overseers. Accordingly, Dean Wren met with trustees Robert Pamplin, Sr., of Georgia Pacific Corporation, William Swindells of Willamette Industries, Inc., and Bill Moshofsky, a lawyer with Georgia Pacific.

Pamplin and Moshofsky felt that the Fund could continue on campus so long as the relationship of landlord and tenant was observed—a distancing well-understood in the world of business. They also offered to hold a formal conference between students and Georgia Pacific representatives. The tenant arrangement made the Fund an independent organization with a large student membership (making it educational), with outside lawyer guidance (making it orderly), and with home quarters (making it handy).

The following week, some trustees were still uneasy about any NWLC connection with the Fund. Other trustees felt that, while the rental arrangement was sufficient, there should be some "coordination" with the college—the word "control" would have been more candid. So, they urged that a law professor should be an officer with the Fund in order to provide some guidance on impetuosity and some transition between transient student leadership.

Another week passed, in which a few trustees went on record in "preference" for a clean break with no ties. And so, some adjustments were made. A law professor was chosen president of the Fund, and the name was changed to the "Northwest Environmental Defense Center" (a "Center" sounding more middling and reserved than the war-chest image of a "Fund"). But matters still did not quiet down—perhaps, because Professor Williamson had been the president chosen.

At a February meeting trustees reported that they "do not favor a landlord-tenant relationship with the Environmental Defense Center." Ultimately, however, to their credit and in spite of pressure from beyond, the trustees opened the campus doors for a home for environmental pursuit. The Center was allowed an office and address at the law school, and has remained there ever since with a small full-time staff and many student volunteers, sometimes called "environmental watchdogs" and "kayak crusaders."

Over the years, the Center has been joined by other ecological organizations, such as the Pacific Environmental Advocacy Center, the International Environmental Law Project, the Coalition Advocating Transportation Sensibility, the Environmental Justice Advocates, the Environmental Law Caucus, and the Student Advocates for Business and Environmental Responsibility—all coordinated under the auspices of the law school's Environmental and Natural Resources Law Program. The school also hosts other different associations: The Public Interest Law Project, the Student Animal Legal Defense Fund, the National Center for Animal Law, the National Crime Victim Law Institute, and the Lewis & Clark Legal Clinic.

But in 1969-70, the image of a "law *center*" had not yet permeated the traditional view of what a law *school* was. Within that posture, the nation was still unclear about Law's involvement in environmental study. Land, water, and air carried different connotations. It could mean forest, river, breeze, and fresh wind or, instead lumber, electricity, and jobs. Attention to those meanings led to concern, which led to controversy, which led to divisiveness.

Turning over a stone to expose new ground would be seen by some onlookers as a threat and, hence, a reason to let stones lie. Afterall, we were not an established law school, yet looking to be so. Our scholarly search for the bad in what has been done and the good in what should be done, was at the formation of a mounting storm. Our accreditation mission ran the risk.

## THE CLINIC:

As the delegator of duties, Dean Wren operated under an old work maxim: If you want to get a job done promptly, give it to a busy person. Accordingly, he passed along many of his ideas to Professor Billy Williamson, who thrived on tasking, and to me, who needed to learn the word "no." One of Wren's programs was to start providing indigents with free legal assistance while at the same time providing our students with a valuable learning experience—in other words, opening clinic operations. In 1969, clinics and action groups were not prevalent in the nation's law schools. But Wren knew that practical, "hands-on" learning was a darling among ABA accreditors (a lawyer organization), more so than among AALS accreditors (a teacher organization)—thus reflecting a difference between "professional" and "professorial."

Professor Bill Knudsen was hired to be the faculty director of a clinic, but he would not be available until next September 1970, a year away. Consistent with his nature, the dean not only wanted a clinic, he wanted it *now*. So, Billy was handed the job in the summer of 1969. But when Billy took over the environmental program, the clinic baton was passed to me, even though I was currently saddled with scholarship loans and grants, student petitioning, the legal writing program, the faculty meeting minutes recorder, my JFC work, the Oregon State Bar "Bridging-the-Gap" project, a Portland City Club research study, and certain accreditation errands and chores, not to mention, of course, the main task of teaching at least eight class hours per week.

Professor Cairns had reservations about a student-operated clinic. His hesitancy was over malpractice and the insurance costs. A bit of research and pencil-pushing put those concerns into numbers. Errors and omissions insurance premiums per semester would be $16.00 per student and $36.00 for the supervising attorney. By December 1969, sixteen evening students had enrolled in the spring semester clinic operations. Thus, insurance costs for the students and me came to about $300.

I divided the clinic work into two arenas: externing and interning. Externs would work directly with specified attorneys in rendering legal assistance to indigent clients in the tri-county area. About forty outstanding Oregon practitioners volunteered to supervise in the project; they included future judges, state legislators, and governor of the State of Oregon.

The other half of the program involved student internships posted in a school-operated clinic for the Valley Migrant League—an organization of Hispanic farm workers in the Willamette Valley. Students operated clinic hours each Saturday at the VML office in Yamhill County. Later on in the semester, the VML was anxious for us to do similar staffing in Washington County. The offices at Dayton and Forest Grove were about seventy and forty road miles from our campus. Students were not reimbursed for their pro bono travels. They did receive, however, two credit hours for the spring semester and then another two credit hours for re-enrolling in the summer. It was the first summer semester credit ever offered in the law school's history.

Three students on academic probation sought to enter the clinic program. At the November 20, 1969 faculty meeting, we voted against the enrollment of probationary students in clinic work. Professor Williamson dissented; he felt that failing students are sometimes just bored students yearning for life-lessons instead of book-lessons. Indeed, this was a prime reason why the ABA accreditors looked favorably on clinic opportunity. But that reasoning could not overcome the reality that, once we stepped beyond *learning* law and into the real world of *doing* it, we had to be mindful of the service to the public as well as the education of the student.

As the 1970 summer clinic operations grew closer, I proposed that summer enrollees ought to be excused from taking the comprehensive exam then still scheduled at the beginning of the fall semester. Their summer clinic pre-occupations, which often carried over into the following semester, gave them little time for exam preparation. The fact that I was on record in opposition to the whole concept of comprehensive examining tainted my appeal for special abstentions. I only succeeded in persuading Williamson. Wren, Cairns, and Gerhardt voted against the proposal. The problem was resolved, however, when shortly thereafter the faculty voted to move the exam from August to December for all students.

Many external problems also confronted the initiation of a legal clinic. Beyond our educational confines, issues arose as to the test to be used for indigency, as to the practicing of law without a license, as to the intrusion of a law school into the bailiwicks of outlying municipal communities. In 1969-70, local bar associations, municipal authorities, and local judges were not accustomed to unlicensed students giving legal advice, charging nothing for it, and appearing inside the courtroom bar.

RELATIONSHIPS:

The irony of *union* is that, in order to make it effective, *division* is necessary. Thus does the union of those who tend Law divide into government branches, bar associations, and schools. And within each of those arenas further compartments abound. While making matters efficient, the divisions can also operate to undermine the very unified order it was meant to serve. A segment may begin to focus inward, straining to be independent and alone—the failure of a part to see itself in the whole. A school is particularly susceptible to this monastic problem. Call it the "cloister syndrome."

Accreditors were much aware of the infirmity. The cure was to build relationships. So, the NWLC faculty was called upon to take conscious steps to connect with the Oregon State Bar, the courts, the nation's law schools, the Portland community, our own alumni, our undergraduate college, and, the closest of all, our own student body.

Dean Wren became active in several **Oregon State Bar** committees designed to further legal education of lawyers. An effort was made to get automatic admission of faculty members into the Oregon State Bar without having to take the bar exam. It was an effort resisted by the bar governors. The governors, however, did endorse the idea of allowing our law students to appear and represent certain clients in court. The dean and I also met regularly with the Bar Committee on Continuing Legal Education.

Our relations with the **national law community** also needed tending. Almost nine decades of local Oregon schooling, without care for or recognition by the nation's accreditors, had instilled in old Northwestern a parochial attitude. Accreditors needed more than an assurance; they needed a demonstration of our willingness to be collegial with the nation's professors and professionals. Attendance and participation in ABA and AALS activities were urged. Research and publication of scholarly work were also essential to that peer-to-peer communication. Accordingly, our budget had to facilitate those endeavors by providing for research assistance, leaves of absence, sabbaticals, grants, research materials, and travel expenses. Old Northwestern's single-minded drive toward superior teaching had to make the turn toward scholarship and inter-school togetherness—a steerage not readily cornered.

Accreditors also advised law faculties to engage in **local civic and government activities**. On that front, I chaired some Portland City Club research studies, was a labor arbitrator, wrote newspaper articles, spoke at high schools, and continued as a part-time employee of the newly created Judicial Fitness Commission. [See ch. 5]

As for alumni relations, our alumni association was reorganized with a new constitution and by-laws. Lawyer John Ryan was elected the new president. He was one of those who would spark our alumni to give $185,000 to the building fund drive—the modern inflationary equivalent of almost $1 million. A plaque on a conference room in our future law complex would bear his name. He had been my predecessor as the part-time Tort teacher and was still on our adjunct faculty roles. Ties between alma mater and alums were further linked by a gesture. Back in 1967, NWLC had begun the award of Juris Doctor diplomas instead of Law Bachelor diplomas. Now, here in 1969, it was proposed that all alumni could exchange their previous bachelor degrees

**JOHN RYAN**

for the new doctor degree at a price of $100. The swapping idea was unanimously accepted; however, the fee was unacceptable. The gesture should be a reward, not a revenue measure. Why should the victor of a race have to pay for the trophy awarded? A compromise was reached. A fee of $25 was charged to pay for mailing, printing, and calligraphy.

*Retro-Doctor*

Relations with our own **student body** also needed fixing. The gap there required more than bridging; it demanded removal. It would not be easy; we were still dealing with evening enrollment where most students showed on campus after it had retired for the night. Our customers needed to be brought in-house.

To that end, Dean Wren encouraged the reorganization of the Student Bar Association, the creation of a student newspaper, and the participation of students in certain faculty deliberations. The efforts were up against the preoccupations of daytime and the press of bedtime.

In some respects, the relationship with our **parent college** was, perhaps, the most difficult of all the bridges to cross, even though it had one of the shortest gaps. That's not too astounding when observing that country neighbors are better acquainted than urban tenants living across the hall from one another. The college and law school administrators worked just fine together; it was largely the academicians that did not seem to gel. At our September 10, 1969, faculty meeting, the dean urged the law faculty to increase our "fraternization" (his word) with the undergraduate college faculty by attending their faculty meetings and dining in the Templeton Commons faculty lunchroom. I probably was the one most given to make those connections, albeit my efforts were scattered. I attended some college picnics and faculty meetings and played weekly volleyball with a handful of college staff and faculty. Billy and I would eat often in the college faculty cafeteria, but that would cease once the law school installed its own cafeteria in years to come.

One sore point between our two faculties was the difference in our separate promotion and tenure rules. In November 1969, Dean of the College Faculty, Tony Ostroff, proposed that we amend our rules and bring them more in line with the conditions imposed on college faculty advancement in rank and job stability. The truth of the matter was that essentially we had no rules to amend. We were operating informally with just a scant statement of principles. [See ch. 5] We did not feel the need. Aside from me, no full-time faculty member had stayed on the pan long enough to season or "tenurize." Rather than admit our insufficiency, we dismissed the Ostroff proposal as intermeddling. From both sides, it was not the sort of cement needed to bond relations. Our forthcoming building complex—set in the Tryon Forest and separated from the main campus by two blocks of residential homes—would do nothing to improve connections.

In all, the attention to relationships was like a pendulum rocking back and forth between the ticks of engagement and the tocks of estrangement.

## MEETINGS, MOTIONS, AND MINUTES:

Dean Wren's command style called for an increase in the number of faculty meetings. We met at least once, sometimes twice, every week throughout the 1969-70 academic year. Those meetings were long-lasting—on occasion as long as four hours. The dean's notice of a September 10 meeting began: "I would like to call a *short* meeting with the faculty." It lasted two hours and went through lunch time.

The meetings were held in Professor Gerhardt's bedroom office and were attended by Registrar Dorothy Cornelius, Dean Wren, Professors Cairns, Gerhardt, Williamson, and me. We were a committee-of-the-whole—not large enough to breakdown into squads and platoons.

Previously Dave Shannon, no longer with us, had been the minute-taker. Now that he was gone, Dean Wren insisted on having our faculty meetings recorded by a faculty member. Wren felt that minutes were a main document file that the accrediting inspectors would want to examine. I volunteered to be the faculty scribe—a chore not cherished and gladly passed along to future professors over the next decade. The task was eventually assigned to more serious-minded dean secretaries. Professorial scriveners had tended to malign the solemnity of their task with humor. I confess to having started the minutes down that road when, on the October 16, 1969, minutes, I drew a cartoon, thus turning the chore into an idle amusement. That became a habit, which in turn led to doodling caricatures of my colleagues—a pastime pursued unto this day. On our law school walls is a caricature gallery of all the tenure-tracked, law professors who have haunted this ivory tower—a gallery that began as a way of poking fun into the sobriety of meeting minutes.

Sometimes faculty meetings were also taken up by motions of dubious relevancy. At the October 16, 1969, meeting, I moved in writing that the law faculty go on record "opposing the nomination of Judge Haynesworth to the Supreme Court of the United States" and that "we relay this sentiment to President Nixon, asking him to withdraw... the candidacy." Clement F. Haynesworth, Jr., whose record in civil rights and questionable conflicts of interest while on the bench, was abominable in the minds of some, disappointing in the minds of others, tolerable in others, and doubted by still others. Professor Williamson seconded the motion. Professors Cairns and Gerhardt were opposed but not for political reasons. They saw such positioning as inappropriate law school business. Dean Wren broke the tie. The motion was defeated—as was anticipated and as it should have been. It's just that sometimes it is more satisfying to be substantively righteous, than procedurally right.

At our final faculty meeting of the 1969-70 year, Professor Williamson proposed that we allow an elected student representative to participate and vote on faculty decisions. I moved to table the motion indefinitely. Ordinarily, motions to table are not subject to discussion; but in a meeting population as small as ours, Roberts Rules of Order were not in order. Cairns and Gerhardt favored tabling because they were lame ducks. It was their last NWLC meeting, and they felt that they ought not make decisions affecting a future in which they would not be involved. While I favored giving students a voice, I felt our future faculty members, five of them, should also be given voice on that issue. Eventually, the issue was taken off of the floor and put on the table, where it should have gone in the first place, like food that ought to be savored before wasted or eaten.

I confess I was developing a strong distaste for meetings. No one can deny the necessity for and value in meetings. The very goal of meeting is melding—uniting in common resolve through exchange of individual thought. But that joinder demands reciprocity between a wagging tongue and an open ear. Meetings could save a lot of time if there were more listening and less thinking about what to say next. Oddly enough, however, it was listening that led to my early aversion to faculty meetings. As the scribe, I had to concentrate on and take down what others were saying. I knew the Gregg Shorthand system and had been a summary courts-martial reporter in the U.S. Army in Germany in the mid-1950's. It demanded strong focus on listening. As a daydreamer, concentration was never my strong hand. So, I worked very hard at training myself to hear carefully—a labor interfering with what I wanted to say. Furthermore, a minute-taker must summarize what others meant. Such capsulizing called for stripping away redundancy, posturing, and pontification—a defrocking that bared speech to shameful nudity. Indeed, the job of scrivener was not conducive to an affinity for meetings—where minutes became hours.

It did not help matters, when faculty meetings and their minutes came repeatedly. Almost once each week I would translate my shorthand into a long-hand summation and pass it on to secretary Doris McCroskey who typed it on a stencil. Either she or I would then run it through a mimeograph to make about ten copies. It was a long, inky messy process. An alternative was to jam nine onionskin papers and carbon papers into a typewriter platen. What was needed was a magical machine that could instantly copy any page of print any number of times by simply the push of buttons. The fancy was far too much to be hoped for.

*The Dreaded Mimeograph*

STUDENT PETITIONS:

During the summer of 1969, the dean called a special meeting to consider the petitions of twenty-four students seeking probationary status on account of failing grades. On eleven of the petitions, the dean sought merely faculty endorsement of his action allowing academic probation based on the written record. But as to the remaining thirteen petitioners, he granted hearings before the faculty. Those petitioners appeared personally to argue their cases. Seven of the thirteen were denied continuance in their pursuit of law careers. The hearings lasted two days.

In August and September of the following year, we had a similar number of petitioners; but by that time, we had a faculty of eight and could break into committees. I would be made chair of the "Advancement Committee"—the one in charge of all those petitions. It could have been labeled the "Demotion Committee," but our forward-minded dean felt it more positive to think on the "advancing" side of what was done.

In those days, a student's continuance in law study was decided on *ad hoc*, situational considerations; whereas nowadays the decisions are quantified by bright-lines and numerical rules and handled administratively. Getting "Big" dictates that kind of mechanical regulating, but not without a price. Putting "advancement" in a quantified elimination process shielded the faculty from the face-to-face consequences of grading. This is not to say that teachers should readily alter their standards; but sometimes oral hearings on petitions before the faculty could be enlightening.

Not all student petitions concerned grade failures. Some of them sought to detour other rules. For example, at the start of his final semester, a senior student needed nine more credit hours in order to graduate, but our spring semester made available only eight hours of classes that he had not already taken. Should he have to enroll in another semester just to get one more credit hour? Or should we give him a credit for writing an independent study paper, something never done before at NWLC? Should credit hours mean classroom hours, not paper writing? Should there be teaching involved? He researched and wrote. I advised. He graduated. Thus dawned at NWLC independent, preceptored, writing projects for credit.

Another senior petitioner sought to take a leave of absence during his final semester. He declined to give reasons why. Did he have to give reasons for interrupting his education? Was a petition even necessary? Eventually, he finished his law studies and received our Juris Doctor degree with honors.

An applicant petitioned to be admitted as a first year student even though she had not yet received an undergraduate degree. She was only one semester short of that degree. Just one year prior, she had petitioned on the same grounds, and we had admitted her to the 1969-70 year. But she was unable to attend. Now, she was able and was re-applying to start in the 1970-71 year. But now a degree was required. Did we have to follow the new rule, or should we extend our prior decision? Eventually she became a *magna cum laude* law graduate at NWLC.

Another first-year-law petitioner took a reverse direction. He asked to be allowed to go back and take an undergraduate course at Lewis & Clark College yet have it accepted as credit hours on the law school transcript. His reasons were tactful and diplomatic. But could an undergrad course be counted on a law transcript? He went on to become a United States Ambassador.

Not so tactful was the petition of an upperclass student who sought to re-take just one of the questions on our comprehensive exam rather than having to take the whole exam again, as was required. He had missed seeing the question and that was why he failed the exam. The fact that the missed question was the first question printed on the exam, did not help his case. Nevertheless, should we make an exception to a requirement that was a dubious task in the first place?

An applicant for admission sought to enroll in our anticipated day division as a part-time student, *i.e.*, to take as little as nine credit hours per semester instead of the minimum full load of twelve hours required of day students. He qualified as a night student and was willing to be one, and to graduate in four years, except for the fact that his regular job was at night. Could we relax the ABA rule that day students had to be full-time? Does sun-up or sundown really have anything to do with classroom education?

Draftees returning from serving in the Vietnam War, seeking re-admission to law school, were ordinarily granted the right to resume their education. However, in one ignoble case, NWLC's new admission rules scarred that routine. Back in 1966, one of our students, having completed two years of evening law education at Northwestern, was drafted. But when his tour finished, he re-enlisted as a U.S. Army sergeant. Now almost four years later, he sought re-admittance. His petition was denied because his military service, albeit in war time, went beyond his drafted tour and because now he needed to meet our current admission rules that demanded an undergraduate degree. Our failure to make an exception under unique military circumstances was not what one might call a "shining hour." He threatened to sue under the Soldiers and Sailors Relief Act. The college turned the matter over to its liability insurance company, where it was "taken care of." Thus, the consequences of our actions were shielded from us. We were protected, not by law, but rather by insurance. Such are the contraindications of transforming a risk into a security. Removing the danger of pain can be very dangerous.

Then came a second case that, when juxtaposed against the former case, gave reason for head scratching. Late in the 1969-70 year, an applicant fell short of our new admissions criteria. Ordinarily routine denial would have been in order. But the applicant was related to the founding Gantenbien family—a "legacy" was the term used in higher education. Could we ignore in this situation the kindly and lenient, yet now defunct, Gantenbein admissions policy that had provided so many Northwestern alumni with the gift of opportunity? Cairns needed no coaxing. He was a graduate of Northwestern and had been a beneficiary of that opportunity policy. He also shared co-trusteeship with John Gantenbein under the Merger Agreement. Gerhardt and I were both chosen by Gantenbein as earlier part-time night teachers and felt constrained to side with Cairns. Dean Wren's law school experience made him fully aware of the power of legacy admissions. Professor Billy Williamson, the newcomer, had no such emotional leanings. He stuck to the rules. Permission was granted 4-1.

Thus, the caveat when balancing rules against facts: While mechanical application of laws can blunder on draconian insistency, so too can situational decisions stumble on wayward inconsistency.

## PARTINGS AND CLOSINGS OF YEAR'S END:

I was never a dean or interim dean; but in the summer of 1970, I became a "surrogate dean". From time to time, Dean Wren, an officer in the U.S. Naval Reserve, had to attend sailor commitments. When that happened, I took his place at special occasions. For example, in April 1970, construction at the law school complex in Tryon Forest reached its tallest point. The apex was the fireplace chimney above the Gantenbein Student Lounge. Traditionally, this called for a "Topping-Off Ceremony." Wren was away from Oregon; so, President Howard, an architect, and I climbed a tall ladder to the roof of Gantenbein, hoisted an American flag to the top of the chimney, and made speeches to the gathering masses below. Although the apex had been reached, construction was just a shell. More interior work had to be done. It was on target for opening classes in September, less than five months away.

For the commencement ceremonies in June, Wren was away again on Navy duty. So, I was on the graduation platform in the decanal role for the award of degrees. Law graduates still had to share the pomp and circumstance with college undergraduates. The process was dignified, slow, and lengthy. Under heavy robes, hood, and mortar boards, such "bib and tucker" was a colorful presence—and sweltering. It had totally lost its original function. In medieval European schools, the regalia was meant to fight off the cold and damp of those early stone halls having no furnaces. Now in America, the only time the garb was donned was for an annual hot summer day of sitting and watching endless streams of marches, sermons, edicts, and bestowals. Just another case of an idea ceasing its function, yet sticking around for show.

Following goat paths would not have been so alarming were it not fostered by

**CAMPUS IN CONSTRUCTION**
Bare Bones and Topping Off

the scholarly astute. It mimicked the ironic custom of ancient Greek academicians who, having made an intelligent scientific or mathematical discovery, celebrated by slaughtering a goat upon an altar. The lesson speaks volumes about an educational paradox: The enlightenment from which minds are opened can be the same brilliance from which shadows are cast.

But such cold-hearted critique of rites and regalia ran a poor second to warm-hearted occasion. Ceremony was a well-deserved, proud moment—a "topping-off" on the roof for having reached one's highest point in schooling—an acme that towered far above the faultfinders. This was my third commencement, and I too sensed the nostalgia. This 1970 graduating law class was the first class to begin as freshmen students into the merged Northwestern School of Law of Lewis & Clark College. They and I entered together in the same academic year when the school was still downtown. They were leaving, but I stayed on. One of the cherished notions of graduation is the insistence that it is not an end, but rather a *commencement*—an entrance, not an exit. But for those left behind—the faculty and staff—it was hard to see graduation as a coming. From our lecterns, it was a parting.

One more parting was in store. Although a long time in coming, the exit became fixed when Dean Wren insisted on written reports from each of us on "the full extent of our law practice outside of law school." The accreditors' new standards made it absolutely clear that "moonlighting"—the inordinate time taken away from full-time faculty status—was frowned upon. ABA "Factor VII" put it this way:

> "A full-time teacher... devotes his entire time to teaching and legal scholarship and... has no office or business... outside of teaching, although he may take an occasional case or write an occasional brief."

A certain amount of consulting work was tolerated. Law professors were often sought to handle jobs where detached expertise was called for. My written report to the dean showed that I sometimes served as an arbitrator or mediator and had summertime stints as a *pro-tem* circuit judge.

I also reported my work as executive director of the Oregon Judicial Fitness Commission—a job that averaged about four days a month of my time. [See ch. 5] It would have been awkward for practicing lawyers to investigate, detect, and recommend action on the misconduct of a judge before whom they might have to appear on behalf of clients. So, a professor was a logical choice. Accreditors had no difficulty with that work since the state agency was officed at the law school where my availability to colleagues and students suffered no serious deprival.

Professors Cairns and Gerhardt, however, had different outside endeavors. They never really lost their love for or engagement in lawyering. It was understood at the beginning of the 1969-70 year that they would desist from their academic pursuit. At year end, in order to satisfy the accreditors, they made their partings official with letters of resignation.

On June 4, 1970, at the final faculty meeting of the eventful 1969-70 academic year, the exits of Cairns and Gerhardt did not go unnoticed. My faculty minutes read:

> "Speeches were made. Professor Williamson uncorked the champagne. Professor Lansing toasted, Williamson poured. Dean Wren acclaimed. Cornelius cried. Williamson poured. Gerhardt and Cairns heaved sighs of relief. Williamson poured. There being nothing further to come before the faculty, the meeting was adjourned (hic)...."

The whimsy was simply the refusal to face the solemn moment. Indeed, the Cairns-Gerhardt no-nonsense, straight-to-the-point, plain talk would be a guidance sorely missed. They were two threads that had stitched the past to the future. The Cairns pipe and the Gerhardt magnifying glass should have been bronzed for posterity. Their teaching at the night law school had been for a combined thirty years. They had been a final remnant in the bridge that merged the faculties of two colleges and two historic generations.

I was now, not only the last of the first five full-time law professors, I was also a remnant of a part-time cadre of lawyers who taught at old Northwestern in downtown Portland. Those were vestigial honors that I could pocket over the next four decades.

# 7
# PROVISIONAL PASSAGE
*1969-70*

## TRANSIENT SWAGGER

In spite of departures, the summer of 1970 grew radiant—lit by the torches of approaching home fires, bright new cadre, and shining new faces. Our new law school buildings were about ready for occupancy. Our full-time faculty would double in size. Our first daytime students were set to begin. Our law school Bulletin reported that the "summer of 1970 was one of the most momentous periods in the law school's fascinating history." But one more illumination was needed to make the radiance sparkle—one more momentum to justify calling it "momentous." We had been inching toward it with industry and caution throughout the 1969-70 year. We had fallen short of it four times before.

### FIFTH ACCREDITATION LAUNCHING:

In the first semester of the 1969-70 academic year, we had targeted on our fifth attempt at ABA accreditation. The ABA Council was scheduled to meet in January 1970 at Atlanta, Georgia. Achievement there was an important first step on the ABA stairway. We had stumbled there in all previous tries. Dean Wren was determined not to do so again..

In the summer of 1969, ABA Consultant Millard Ruud, the replacement for ABA Advisor John Hervey, had made an informal visit to our campus and was now scheduled for an official inspection on December 10-12, 1969.

This time the faculty was given greater hand at the reins. I was assigned the job of drafting an itinerary for Ruud's visit. Professor Gerhardt, before his departure, had been given the job of responding to an ABA advance questionnaire that also called for amassing exhibits, such as enrollment counts, admissions statistics, rosters, faculty minutes, budgets, compilations, and documentations of all sorts. The phenomenal thing about Paul Gerhardt was that he made it easy to forget that he labored under a debilitating disease—multiple sclerosis. Diet, exercise, and naps were daily regimens for him. In spite of all that, his willingness to take on work and achieve the task, concealed whatever handicaps were otherwise detectable. He put together a very convincing collection of materials for presentation to the accreditors.

When Ruud arrived, it did not take long for us to discover that this new inspector was a godsend. Aside from being an investigator, he was a worker for both the accreditors and us. When he replaced his predecessor, he changed the title of his office from ABA Advisor to "Consultant." It put his role as more helper than overseer. In his reminiscences, he wrote:

> "The most satisfying aspect of the job was helping a new law school... change its program so that it was eligible for approval."

**MILLARD RUUD**

Where his predecessor had been a practicing lawyer in Oklahoma, Ruud was a law professor at the University of Texas Law School. Accordingly, from Academe's garden he had a gardener's insight into the planting of legal education in professional soil. In reviewing our previous accreditation attempts, he observed the scant amount of faculty involvement. His predecessor, John Hervey, had made it a point to deal at higher echelons. Hervey took most of his time with trustees, alumni leaders, supreme court justices, bar officials, and other prominent citizens, all of whom, to be sure, were outstanding sources for assessing the school's future. But in addition, Ruud, the law professor, wanted to hear more from those closer to education. He was not there just to inspect *school*; he was there to inspect *schooling*. Consequently, he spent far more time with students and professors and urged the hierarchy to give faculty more input.

Then too, unlike Hervey, Ruud was most impressed by Northwestern's long history and rich tradition dating back to 1884—the fifth oldest night law school in the nation and the first in the West. With that kind of heritage, he was surprised to find we were the oldest operating law school that had not yet applied for accreditation and wondered why we had not been accredited long ago. Indeed, it was only because of the good graces of the Oregon Supreme Court that Northwestern graduates were allowed to be lawyers in Oregon. Northwestern College of Law had always been a quiet and complaisant institution in its remote outpost.

Like Northwestern, Ruud was modest and unassuming. His self-effacing character was inconsistent with the airs of those endowed with powers to bestow. He humorously defined his job: "A consultant is someone who looks at your watch and tells you what time it is."

But Millard was not a totally "giving" person; he had a tough streak. Years later, I would experience his stern resolve when I became the Chair of the AALS Tort Section and he had advanced to the AALS Executive Directorship. The Tort Section had voted to bestow its annual Prosser Award on Professor Page Keeton of the University of Texas Law School. As Chair, I ordered and personally paid for a handsome plaque to commemorate the occasion at our annual meeting of all the nation's Tort professors. The plaque cost me about $50—the equivalent sum of about $200 - $250 as of this writing. I submitted an expense claim with AALS headquarters in keeping with past Tort Section practice. It was denied. I insisted. Director Ruud wrote back in no uncertain terms that, if the Tort Section chose to make awards, then the Tort Section members, not the total AALS dues-paying membership, should pay for it. He was right, of course. But, for me, the dilemma was: should I make a beggarly, postage-poor, special assessment of one dime from each of 500 Tort Section professors; or should I just absorb the loss? It was a choice with no alternatives. In the years ahead, I made it a point whenever I saw Page Keeton at conferences to remind him that the Prosser Award came from the Tort Section, not AALS, and the plaque hanging in his office came from me.

When Ruud first came to us in the summer of 1969 and then again in December of that year, he was, like us, relatively new to the law school accreditation business. He had begun his ABA work in October 1968. By the time he died, three decades later, his prominent career with ABA and AALS led him to be known as "Mr. Legal Education."

THE INSPECTION:

Ruud's official inspection visit with us in December 1969 was a great deal different than the John Hervey visit two years before. [See Ch. 2] Ruud had done his homework and, by the time of his arrival, knew as much as we did about our operation.

His prepared itinerary took him to the books as well as to student get-togethers; soirees with dignitaries; huddles with faculty; meetings with President Howard and college administrators; a tour of our new law school complex still under construction; and, of course, dinner with trustees. At that private dinner in a room of the Benson Hotel in downtown Portland, trustee Robert B. Pamplin, Sr., wondered why

**ROBERT B. PAMPLIN, SR.**

the accreditors required that our median faculty salary meet the national median. He felt it was unreasonable to ask entering law schools to make their salaries better than half of the already established schools. It was a good point, but Ruud had an equally good response. In his own words, Ruud answered, "with more confidence than was justified," that this was "a rule designed to test a financial commitment...." In my words it meant: Those who seek to belong must aspire to enter erect at no less than the center gate and not crouched through a basement door. Ruud recalled that Pamplin "accepted the answer with limited grace."

Pamplin was right to question medians, however. Testing merit by medians produces ironies: For one, by the very definition of "median," one-half of the component schools will always be destined to fall short of a median standard. For another the standard will always spiral upward on account of leapfrogging. Once a school jumps from the bottom half to the top half, some other school goes from the top to the bottom; and the median is now higher. Thus, median standards always escalate. And that forces schools to become business competitors instead of academic cooperators in providing legal education to hopefuls. In some ways it is a part of the reason for why costs of higher education have risen far greater than ordinary inflation.

After Ruud's visit, he prepared his written report to the ABA Council. Inspector Hervey's past practice had been to keep his inspection report secret from the law school. He advised his successor to do the same, saying, "It is likely only to create controversy." Ruud found Hervey's advice "curious" and declined to follow it. Thus, he gave Dean Wren a copy of his report to the ABA Council.

The report was candid and spoke glowingly of our progress and potential. It was thorough and journeyed through every nook and cranny of our endeavor, and that included Ruud's reactions to classroom teaching visitations. Unbecoming vanity compels me to relay what he reported to Dean Wren, what Wren told President Howard, and what was published: "Professor Lansing was one of the ten best classroom law teachers in the nation." Flattery, and the conceit that comes with it, were not enough to overcome some genuine humility: On hearing the compliment, I wondered how dim must be the nation's classrooms in order for my small wick to shine.

The pages of Ruud's report took a great amount of time extolling the hard labors of Professor Williamson, the sacrifices of Professors Cairns and Gerhardt, and the value of practical experience furnished by the judges and lawyers serving as adjunct faculty. There was no mistaking the emphasis of Ruud (the law professor) on what he saw to be the primary mission of education. He would not deny the necessity for business and finance, but his report made it clear that those functions were the wheels that carry the load and were neither the load nor the destination. Schooling was the cargo and good lawyers for the public was the mission.

Following Ruud's visit, we felt very optimistic about our chances with the ABA Council members, who were scheduled to meet in less than two months. On December 18, 1969, I wrote George Neff Stevens, our former dean, who was now a visiting professor at Texas Tech Law School and, as far as I knew, was still a member of the ABA Council.

> "The school is really looking up these days. Last week Millard Ruud was here, and we honestly believe we are in the best position we have ever been for accreditation.... Dean Wren is exactly like yourself—full of enthusiasm.... We have begun a clinical program, will be publishing an environmental law periodical this spring, starting a day division in September, and our building will be completed this summer.... [T]he financial, moral and academic commitment is all there.... [Y]our sacrifice was a big turning point in heading us down the right path of legal education."

As reported by Ruud, our major shortcoming was full-time faculty numbers. But soon after Ruud's visit, we signed five new faculty members, as previously reported. [See ch. 6, "Recruiting Faculty"] Their arrivals in September 1970 would add to our accomplishments. We were now feeling confident at having closed the chinks in our wall.

That confidence was given a minor nudge forward when the U.S. Postal Service gave our forthcoming law campus a mailing address of its own. We would be: 10015 S.W. Terwilliger Boulevard." At least we were "accredited" by the mail man.

## Pitch to the ABA Council:

In January 1970, President Howard, Trustee Paul Boley, and Dean Harold Wren went to Atlanta to make our case for provisional accreditation before the ten member ABA Council. A fourth member of that team could be deemed Millard Ruud, who sided with us. Also in our favor was a potential "inside operative"—a new Council member—our hometown Portland lawyer, Richard Nahstoll. He was well-known to members of our trustee Standing Committee on the Operation of the Law School [SCOLS] and to Dean Wren's Fellows. Dick Nahstoll and I had worked together on

**RICHARD NAHSTOLL**

Oregon Bar committees and on a Portland City Club study on racial justice in the city.

The persuasions of a president, trustee, dean, consultant, and Council member were sufficient unto the day. The Council recommended approval. It was a big hurdle—its clearance worthy of applause. But there could be no celebration. Although we had the Council's nod, we still had to pass the Section's vote and then the House ratification. Those two forums would meet at the annual ABA meeting in St. Louis in August.

Like a judge passing on sufficiency and then turning the case over to the jury, the Council simply felt that we were eligible for consideration. Accordingly, we were cautioned not to publicize the Council actions until the Section and House had acted. A reason for the caution was that the multi-member Section was currently engaged in internal politics and maneuvers. Ordinarily, the Section vote would be a conventional endorsement within the committee system. But past routine was not to be trusted in view of present intrigue. From a distance, we were not entirely clear about what was afoot, but we were able to surmise this much: although the Section had moved beyond the "Hervey problem" and had settled the "qualitative-quantitative debate" concerning standards [see ch. 3], new differences centered on the polarity between practitioners and professors. Consultant Ruud had been trying hard to consolidate the efforts of the two accrediting agencies. For example, he wanted the ABA and AALS to conduct joint inspections. But detractors were concerned that ABA accreditation was beginning to be driven by legal educators.

Dean Noble Lee of John Marshall School of Law felt that AALS would take over the ABA Section. Lee was described as a "feisty," political competitor. In August 1969, he had packed the multi-member Section meeting with a chartered plane-load of his supporters. Customarily, candidates for Section officers were designated by an official nominating committee. But in 1969, two of those nominees were defeated by candidates nominated from the floor.

The new Section officers then took steps to have the ten-member Council establish an Accreditation Sub-committee within its ranks. This, of course, would be one more echelon between the Consultant and the Council and, thus, one more hurdle for us to clear. Fortunately, our fifth pitch for approval was made before that new sub-committee could get organized.

And so, that is where we found ourselves in the spring and summer of 1970. We had the Council's and the Consultant's recommendation. But the road to provisional accreditation was still long and detoured and seemed never to end.

## PROVISIONAL ACCREDITATION:

On August 7, 1970, the ABA Section on Legal Education and Admissions to the Bar followed the advice of Consultant Millard Ruud and the ABA Council and recommended to the ABA House of Delegates that Northwestern School of Law of Lewis & Clark College be granted accreditation. On August 12, the House bestowed that accreditation. Our fifth attempt finally succeeded. We entered the list of ABA approved law schools as the 149th school receiving that honor.

It was a long time in coming. Generations of faculty and graduates had long ago proven historic worth and just desserts. At an informal gathering of celebrants, Consultant Ruud emphasized that the ABA's action was more a "recognition," than a "bestowal," which was to say: after some soap and water and scrubbing up, the ABA simply beheld the core of what was always there. NWLC had been the oldest law school in the United States to have ignored seeking accreditation.

The practical side of our new stature was that our graduates could now be licensed in any state of the nation. Accreditation also qualified our students for certain federal money loans and G.I. Bill awards.

On August 13, the day following the ABA House action, President Howard and Dean Wren wasted no time in holding a press conference to make the public announcement. *The Oregonian* and *Oregon Journal* newspapers and Portland's radio and television stations gave it a lot of ink and air time. I was surprised at how much community pride surfaced in our success. We had not been alone. Beneath the blossoming laid civic roots. Portland too was proud. And it was heartening for us to know our city embraced us.

At the press conference, Dean Wren, enthused with the joy that thrilled us all, was quoted as saying, "As of this moment, Northwestern is stepping out into the nation. We are every bit as good a law school as any in the nation." It was an effusion excused by festivity.

Once the occasion had passed, however, reality set in. On the ABA roster of approved law schools there was an asterisk after our name. It called our accreditation"provisional." It meant temporary, conditional, not fixed. Our recognition rested on a lot of incompletion. We were still under a sharp probe. But, still on trial, that scrutiny would benefit us, because it was a word to our college governors and authorities that accreditors were still watching. To our law school team we had added another powerful member: the ABA in the person of Consultant Ruud.

Furthermore, when we had sought ABA trust, we were beggared; now that we had that trust, we were beholden. Gratitude made a much stronger call to succeed than did beseeching.

To be sure, there were more obstacles ahead of us. Consultant Ruud would be making frequent inspections on campus. Permanent ABA accreditation had to be achieved within three years, or it would be taken away. Then, around the next bend, was the second accrediting agency—the American Association of Law Schools (AALS), whose requisites were said to be even more exacting.

Once sobriety took over, we had to concede that our accomplishments were not all that had propelled us. External dynamics had come together nationwide to support our plea to the ABA. A wave of student demand for law study had been mounting for several years. One reason for that increase was the so called "baby boomers"— a surge of offspring born in the late 1940s and early 1950s. For another reason, a re-kindling of feminine solidarity was producing more women applicants. Then too, the troubled 1960s instilled in many an increased awareness that law, instead of war and confrontation, was a better pathway to socio-economic-political solutions.

ABA accreditors took note of societal demands for more legal services. Judge J. Edward Lombard forecasted "the mushrooming requirements for legal manpower." The call for more lawyers ran into a limited supply of law schools. Perhaps for the first time in its history, the ABA took the initiative and urged certain universities to commence a law education. Some schools responded; others did not. Princeton University, for example, declined to open a law school.

Prior to our entry into the family of the accredited, there were only six approved law schools in the whole of the Pacific northwest United States—two in Washington, one in Montana, one in Idaho, and two in Oregon. The cities of New York and Chicago each had just as many law schools as all of the four Pacific northwest states. Law schools in the single state of California were triple the number in those four states. Another accredited school was needed in the northwest to handle the spill of anxious bodies over occupied seats. Yearning customers and limited competitors bode well for schools seeking to get into law business. NWLC was well-positioned in time and place.

Since that day and as of this writing, some seventy more law schools have followed our provisional accreditation. All law schools nationally have operated virtually at full capacity. In short, education is turning out a great many lawyers annually. Along the passage of years since 1970, growing numbers have asked: Are we producing too many lawyers? Have we over-compensated? Fortunately, NWLC's efforts came in 1970 when the pendulum had not yet swung in that direction.

So, near the end of summer of 1970 before embracing the academic year ahead, we had an attitude. In spite of a wisdom that says a dire situation warrants bold steps and a joyous situation calls for stepping gingerly, we were happy and striding with abandon. There was just too much to be glad about. Our first law review issue was published with the promise that our second issue would carry a lead article by U.S. Supreme Court Justice William O. Douglas. The two million dollar fund drive was brought to fruition. Student enrollments reached record highs. For the moment, we were not about to bury present joy beneath omens of what tomorrow might bring.

The surest sign that we had finally been welcomed into the nation's halls was a letter from the dean of Northwestern University School of Law in Chicago. In addition to congratulating us on our accreditation, the dean expressed the possibility of confusion of our two identities. He asked us (with a mix of cavalier and concern) to consider changing our name inasmuch as his school had "temporal priority." Dean Wren wrote back and suggested (with a mix of ribaldry and righteousness) that they might consider changing their name to "Midwestern" inasmuch as we had "spatial priority."

Since the ignominious firing of Dean George Stevens in 1968, we had acquired a certain brazen image among American law schools. I can remember at an AALS conference meeting a professor from another school, who, upon noticing my lapel name tag, remarked, "Oh, I see you are from that *spunky* new school out in Oregon." Indeed, we did not just walk head high and erect; we sauntered and swaggered a bit.

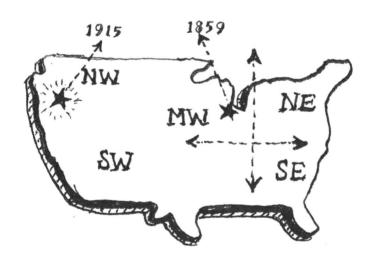

# 1970: TIME CONTEXT

U.S. military invades Cambodia, triggering college demonstrations.

National Guard called out to quell student uprising at Kent State University in Ohio. Four students killed.

Vietnam Peace Talks in Paris show no success.

U.S. troop strength in Vietnam reduced to under 400,000.

President Nixon appoints Harry Blackmun to the U.S. Supreme Court.

U.S. Environmental Protection Agency created.

U.S. population = 85 people per square mile. China = 305 per square mile. India = 655 per square mile. Japan = 1,083 per square mile.

A jury awards the Smothers brothers a $786 million damages award against CBS-TV for breach of contract in canceling their comedy show.

Bomb explodes in Portland City Hall destroying a replica of the Liberty Bell.

American Legion Convention (at which President Nixon was to speak) is scheduled in downtown Portland. To avoid confrontation, an estimated 100,000 anti-war demonstrators are diverted to "Vortex", the first and only government sponsored rock festival.

Alvin Toffler's book title, "Future Shock" opines that the nation is developing a psycho-biological disease from "too much change in too short a time" thus producing "shattering stress."

A man sues U.S. veteran hospital for $500,000 because treatment changed his skin from black to white.

Gas price per gallon 36 cents.

# 8
# LAW CAMPUS
*1970-71*

## A HOME OF OUR OWN

Temporary recognition by the nation's lawyer association was not our only triumph in August 1970. The move into our new building complex was every bit as gratifying. After eighty-six years of shifting between multi-rental locations and then hunkering into spare bedrooms and kitchen of a foster parent, the rambling law school finally settled into a home of its own.

Accreditation status was an intangible. It had content but was without form. It could not be smelled, seen, heard, tasted, or touched. But land and its construct fill the senses. Status gives standing; but home gives a place to stand.

AT 3:00 P.M., SUNDAY, SEPTEMBER 13, 1970, ninety days after completion of construction and two weeks after the start of classes, our new law school structure, Northwestern's first permanent home, at the north perimeter of the Tryon Forest, was dedicated in an elaborate ceremony. President Howard, Dean Wren, ABA Consultant Ruud, and Student Bar President James Hubler gave brief remarks. The keynote address was delivered by Chief Justice Kenneth O'Connell of the Oregon Supreme Court, himself a former law professor for whom I had done some work as a law clerk on the rule against perpetuities. He was not a stirring speaker, but one aspect of his message stuck with me over the years and became a guidon in my writings. He emphasized the need of law schools to reach out to the public with the teachings of law.

The chief justice's message helped to niche my own jumbled notions. Too often scholars huddle within their learned society. They focus inward upon students and

Commerce Building, ca. 1884-1904 (SW Yamhill and 2nd)

First Multnomah County Courthouse,
ca. 1904-1907 (SW Main and 4th)

Second Multnomah County Courthouse,
ca. 1907-1922 (SW Salmon and 4th)

Sherlock Building, ca. 1922-1950 (SW Oak and 3rd)

Giesy Building, ca. 1950-1965
(SW Stark and Park)

**NOMAD SCHOOL**

Northwestern Downtown Portland, Rented Quarters:

colleagues. But in a democracy, law must be understood by its constituents, those who originally sought "to form a more perfect Union... and secure the Blessings of Liberty." Lawyers, judges, and professors needed to reach not just those who caretake the laws but also those who had formed the highest Law of the Land—the People.

At the building dedication, following the speeches, the campus was given leave to speak for itself on a tour through its halls and malls. The grounds around the complex were beautifully landscaped and would become more so once Mother Nature, as gardener, took over the fresh plantings and blended them into the backdrop of the Tryon Forest. Older alumni on that tour witnessed the contrast between these new quarters and their downtown, dingy, rented schoolrooms in the Sherlock and Giesy Buildings. It was a breach wide enough for some of them to wonder if they were still attached. It became over the years a fervent task to convince them that it was still their alma mater. Dressed up in new clothes, she was still that grey-haired, stately dowager lady, rich with the heritage she gave and yet gives.

The smallest building in the complex was the student lounge—a spacious single room, walled on three sides by ceiling-high window glass and covered by one hyperbolic parabola. Circling that ceiling was a massive chandelier with blue shaded lights—a hand-me-down from the college chapel recently remodeled. In later years the lounge became the first piece of architectural plan to succumb to growth. Today it is carved into at least ten offices—its chandelier dismantled—its fireplace tucked within partitioning—aesthetics giving way to function.

The second building contained four classrooms with student seating capacity for 100, 120, 120, and 60 respectively. There were no seminar rooms in the complex because in 1970, there were no seminars in our curriculum. A breezeway outside the

**CHESTER E. McCARTY**

classrooms was covered by a large canopied extension of the roof. That monolithic protrusion gave the building the appearance of a fortification. Inside the "fort," the gray concrete, windowless walls, coupled with the militancy of schooling, soon gave the students "ammo" for dubbing the building the "Normandy Bunkers." Adding to that embattled conception, the words "Chester E. McCarty Classroom Complex" would be attached to the outside wall in later years—a dedication to a generous alumnus. He was a general in the U.S. Air Force Reserve.

The lounge and the classrooms were each dedicated to certain judges instrumental in the law school's recent history. The student lounge building was named the

**CLASSROOMS—NEW & OLD**

Northwestern's Giesy Building (1963)—NWLC's Tryon Campus (1970)

"Gantenbein Lounge," in honor of Judge John Flint Gantenbein. The first classroom was called the "Crawford Classroom," in honor of Judge James W. Crawford. The next three classrooms were dedicated to three Oregon Supreme Court justices: Ralph M. Holman, Arno H. Denecke, and Thomas H. Tongue. Gantenbein, Crawford and Tongue were three of the Northwestern trustees involved in the merger. Holman was one of Northwestern's most distinguished alumni. Crawford was an ex-dean of downtown Northwestern. Tongue, Denecke and Crawford had been teachers at Northwestern. Gantenbein and his father were prime movers and saviors of the school for over a half-century in Northwestern's existence. Four of them had been at one time or another my "boss." Gantenbein hired me as a part-time teacher, and Crawford was then my dean. [See "Introduction"] Denecke was one of the Oregon Supreme Court justices when I clerked there. Tongue hired me as the Executive Secretary of the Oregon Judicial Fitness Commission. All of them played a large part in raising the money for the home we were then touring. That there were others who deserved credit was a pity inherent in the unavoidable singling out of a few from a large team effort.

The third building was the library and the architectural dream. Its roof, composed of ten hyperbolic parabolas, became a showplace for tours by the nation's architects. The outside entry was adorned on each side by fountains and pools. The splendor of that entry warranted a slick front cover photo on the ABA accreditor's 1974 annual publication. The first two photo covers in 1972 and 1973 featured the entryways to the Yale and Chicago law schools. Our law school face was the third to make that cover. Architect Paul Thiry's concept of "preserving the natural flavor of site," as featured by the NWLC complex forest placement, was also featured in the Fall 1970 issue of *American Schools and Universities*, a publication devoted to educational architecture.

The library was named the "Boley Law Library" in honor of lawyer Paul Boley, the first Chair of the Standing Committee on the Operation of the Law School [SCOLS]. His efforts in that role had been monumental throughout our accreditation pursuit.

The Boley building housed more than library. Its north wall was lined with faculty and administrative offices. The dean's office was at the northwest corner. Far down the corridor at the northeast corner was a small faculty lounge. Just beyond that open-ceiling lounge was the immense library area with its rows and rows of study tables and shelves. The pitting of faculty lounge noise and library silence under the same roof would soon become a problem.

The best thing about the new library building was not so much its artificial creation, but rather Thiry's openness to natural creation. The south wall was all glass and the Tryon Forest lay just beyond. That made the south glass one long mural of motion: the passage of birds, squirrels, and deer; the swaying of branches; the flutter of leaves; the turn of seasons; and the change of colors. At night, even the windows shifted to mirrors reflecting rows of books and minds bent in study.

As for me, the dearest spot in the law complex was my island of privacy. My new office was three solid walls and a picture window that overlooked a pool and fountains. Those walls and its door were a privacy truly missed. No longer would I be officed in a living room at the hub of paths and portals to kitchen, bathroom, bedrooms, and outdoors, with my desk as a wayside stopping place on a thorough-fare of comings and goings. Now I had walls to nowhere and a door I could lock shut. Nevertheless, those early living room years had conditioned me to toil in the stir of activity. So, I usually worked in an open-door office. Like so many of our yearnings for freedoms, I wanted the *choice* of privacy more than privacy itself.

Just beyond my door, the freshly built, library expanse was hollow and hungered for books. Our existing volumes, cramped in quarters beneath the college Watzek Library, had to be boxed, transported, and re-shelved for the third time in the last four years. Back in the winter of 1966-67, we had moved 8,000 volumes from the

**FINAL HOME**

The cover of the ABA's annual publication featuring NWLC's fountained courtyard

Giesy Building downtown to a room beneath the college chapel. Later they were boxed and moved again to the Watzek basement. Here, in the summer of 1970, the law library—now about 20,000 volumes—went to its final home with the help of the college buildings and grounds crew, student and professor volunteers, and the coordinating efforts of Librarian Jacqui Jurkins. When all of the volumes were maneuvered into their assigned, decimaled places, there were still rows and rows of naked aisles and shelves—a skeletal rib-cage, ghosted not by decomposing but rather by still gestating.

Of course, it was not just the quantity of books that needed development; quality of the collection was also essential. But having mere bones, we first had to build body from which brain could stem.

By the end of the 1970-71 academic year, with the help of our law alumni association, who took on library development as a pet project, we would increase the volume count to 26,000. Looking ahead, we had to have 60,000 volumes—the number required by AALS, the second accreditor. Three and a half decades later, my third published book would go onto those shelves as a ceremonial number "500,000," the half million mark.

Like the purchase of mail-order shoes, we were about to learn that our new facilities would need some breaking-in. One major shortcoming did not take long to surface; sound was the problem. In some places, voices did not travel where they should and in other places, they traveled where they should not. Classrooms are for hearing, and libraries are for reading. But, in our classroom, talk was mussed and muddled as it clattered along concrete walls, while our library's hyperbolic parabolas wafted talk quite well. It was no mistake that "hyperbole" and "hyperbolic" came from the same Greek origins, meaning "to throw beyond," i.e., to exaggerate. Voices from the faculty lounge, tucked away in a far corner of the library, were an exaggeration much needed in our lecture hall but not in a reading room that begged for silence. As a cure for the classroom, architect Thiry proposed baffling the ceiling and muffling the walls. For the library, some wags proposed the same treatment—baffling and muffling the faculty.

Some found another insufficiency: we had no mock courtroom. Others wondered if that was truly necessary; they argued that formal education in law is incubated in classrooms and libraries and that our clinical education was available, where journey to real, not mock, courtrooms was at hand. But was a law school without a courtroom like a medical school without an operating room or a military academy without a parade ground? So, steps were taken to convert the Crawford Classroom into a court forum appended with jury room and judge chambers. On April 15, 1971, the "Crawford Courtroom," the "Ralph King Jury Room," and the "First National Bank of Oregon Judicial Chambers" would be ceremoniously dedicated.

Those dedications and other building and room titles were eventually re-christened by convenience. In common parlance they became simply "the lounge," "the jury room," "the chambers," "the courtroom, the classroom, and the library." The Gantenbein, Crawford, King, Holman, Denecke, Tongue, and Boley plaques were obscured by their patois and by overgrowth or outgrowth. For the sake of efficiency, not legacy, the courtroom and classrooms simply became "Rooms one, two, three, and four."

Another problem, quick to surface, was the absence of a room sufficient in size to conduct faculty meetings. No longer were we small enough to fit into a "Gerhardt-bedroom" size. We now needed to accommodate as many as twelve occupants. So, for our first eight faculty meetings in the 1970-71 academic year, we had to move to the college campus in the undergraduate Templeton Commons Student Union. The problem was solved when contractors put a finishing touch to the King Jury Room, with its traditional twelve seats. But that room too was destined to be outgrown.

One glaring misconception in the concrete mall was the wheelchair ramp outside the library entry. In 1970, forethought was far ahead of disability laws that would require such accommodation. But where hearts may have been right, design went wrong. The ramp was placed at an angle of degree productive of high velocity coasting. The slope might have been acceptable had it been followed by a long and level stretch for slowdown. But just ten feet from the bottom of that speedway was one of our water pools. Not even broad-shouldered, deliverymen would wheel their heavy loads down that descent without flotation equipment. And if a wheelchair were ever to conquer its roll downward, there was no way, like Sisyphus, it could roll its way back upward.

The ramp problem took only a few days for discovery. When volunteer students and faculty helped to bridge the transfer of those 20,000 books from the college library basement to the new law library, the ramp became a menace. I remember it as a day when my wheelbarrow and I nearly lowered a cargo of U.S. Supreme Court reports across the skids of co-worker bodies, almost baptizing the books in the pond.

In those days the lack of money and maintenance produced a lot of self-help and pitching-in from law teachers and learners. The cold call of such extra tasking was warmed by togetherness.

Librarian Jurkins reported another serious shortcoming: the library was not secure. It had far too many unguarded and highly accessible exits. Two months into the 1970-71 academic year, Jurkins reported twenty-five books were missing from the

**BOXED, WHEELED, AND RAMPED**

Students and professors transplanting law library to new gardens

library shelves. It wasn't just a matter of library *exit*, it was also a matter of easy *entry* into all of the buildings on account of late night open doors.

Some of the students, on the other hand, petitioned the faculty for a more open campus. The petition urged leaving the Gantenbein Student Lounge open twenty-four hours a day. Safe curfew for buildings was not foremost in the minds of our new day students. They had grown up in and were threatened by much bigger safety issues throughout the world. The faculty, on the other hand, as new proprietors, saw the need for property safety and ordered campus security officers to turn down the lights and lock all doors at 11:00 p.m. The law school was learning for the first time in its eighty-six years of tenancy what it was to be a lord of land.

Among the dissatisfactions were a potpourri of minor grumblings. The class-rooms needed wall clocks and morning heat. Complaints of noisy blower fans were countered by complaints of poor ventilation. Shades or drapes were needed on windows. More chairs were needed in the student lounge. Inadequate outdoor lighting. Carpet wrinkling. Potholes in the parking lot. Not the smallest complaint escaped the faculty record: the faculty minutes reported a puzzling "brass-screws flaw." That's all it said—a whimper lost somewhere in time and swallowed by an inundation of other cries.

Many such troubles went away, not by mending, but rather by adaptation. Indeed, not only must the shoe fit the foot, the foot learns to fit the shoe. Campus car parking falls into that category. Like every college in the nation, our new building complex developed an immediate parking problem—more cars than spaces. Decrease the number of cars or increase the number of spaces were obvious solutions and over the years both have been tried.

To some extent, our landscaping plan exacerbated the parking problem. We were enamored of our green surroundings. That led us to sacrifice parking slots for forest. Bill Stahl was the college's building coordinator and overseer. He was adamant in his insistence that parking should be *placed among* the woodlands, not *carved out* of the woodlands—a *park* in the forest, not a park in a lot. The law faculty embraced the concept. Consequently, our car parking wended its way around numerous islands and peninsulas of trees and nature. Unfortunately, over the decades pieces of Stahl's plan have yielded to the saw and asphalt, yet still the parking problem persists. America's love for cars was a pest, immune from eradication. Like vector control, the swarm could neither be shooed nor shunned. We solved by learning to live with the hatch.

To THE SOUTH OF NWLC's new complex was the Tryon Forest, but to the east were a few blocks of private homes that separated us from the main campus. Parking of cars spilled over from our limited lot and into those residential streets. Neighbors complained. Meanwhile, south and west of us, a land developer planned to build a 670-unit housing development in the Tryon Forest. Lucille Beck and other neighbors surrounding the forest organized an opposition.

Accreditors demanded merely a law building. But with that package came a home. We were not just a law school now; we were now in a vicinage and had to learn about neighborliness. We closed ranks with neighbors, stopped student parking on their streets, and joined them at public hearings before the Portland Planning Commission. The Tryon Forest was preserved and has become a permanent, two-mile long, 650 acre, Oregon State Park.

ADAPTING TO OUR NEW BUILDINGS and neighbors were not the only adjustments we had to make. Students, staff, and faculty had to adjust to one another. While as human animals, we all had the same 98.6 body temperature, it was a wonder to know where in our development we had come to need differing room temperatures. Then too, some grew up *with* housekeepers and some *as* housekeepers. Variety wrought problems in togetherness. And so, memos had to regulate individuality. We were admonished to not tamper with the thermostats and to wash our own dishes.

Deportment in the library received special attention from Librarian Jurkins. She proposed rules, some of which were testament to the 1960's "hip" generation—*e.g.*, "no bare chests and feet" and "all students are expected to appear... as they would expect to appear in a courtroom."

We were all under the same roof, just as the accreditors wanted. Amassed, we now had to come together.

OUR NEW QUARTERS ALSO HAD to be properly equipped. Aside from the usual furnishings, new office apparatuses were also considered. For one, the secretaries complained about the overtaxing of the mimeograph machine and its operators. What with five new faces on the faculty, the staff was being deluged with work orders. One solution was student work-study help. Another was the use of modern machinery. Apparently, there was new-fangled equipment that could reproduce a document by instant photography without the need for cutting and inking a stencil. At the September 15, 1970, faculty meeting, the dean reported that a "Xerox" (as it was called) would soon be installed and would change the course of office work. Faculty members would each be provided a key for free copying and would be limited to no more than ten copies per page.

As scribe for the faculty minutes, I avoided use of the Xerox throughout the year and continued to use the mimeograph in making copies of the minutes, partly because more than ten copies were needed, partly because I was reluctant to leap into what might be a passing fad, and mostly because I approached new gadgeteering like a Luddite. I am told that it took me many years to put down the spoon and use the fork.

At our October 13 meeting, Librarian Jurkins reported that another different contraption for office efficiency was in the offing—a thing called "electronic data retrieval." Apparently, the system could store all school and personal files and records in a space the size of a small television console. It could retrieve items from its contents on a telegraphed screen simply by imprinting a code through a typewriter keyboard. It offered the future prospect of also being able to "think"—i.e., to put its stored data together, like premises, and to reach conclusions—in other words, it computed. The contraption was met with mixed reaction ranging from warm "ahs" to lukewarm "uh-huhs" to cold "uh-uhs." Little could anyone see what mammoth changes that machine would make in the way we live.

At the December 1 faculty meeting, Dean Wren surprised us with a third type of machine—prospective dictating equipment. A month and a half later on January 19, 1971, sales representatives from the Gray Dictating Company gave a presentation to the faculty on their Nymatic Dictation System. Two weeks later, at the February 2 meeting, the faculty did some dictating of its own. Professor Walter Brown was assigned to investigate. He went to the best source for knowing whether dictation machinery was needed; he checked with Doris McCroskey, Pauline Kallenbach, and Pollianne Noffke—the law school secretaries. The secretaries were unanimous and adamant in opposition to the purchase. Under the circumstances, the purchase went the way of smoke. Finally, Luddites could claim a victory over machines. The victory was fleeting. In the future, we did acquire dictating machines. But that too was fleeting. The acquisition came too late. The advent of the computer with its e-mail and word processing capabilities made garbage of our new dictating machines while they were still in the moment of digestion.

Such was the speed in development of modern technology—innovation quickly followed by obsolescence. Lesson: Just as wait is late when going too slow, so too, haste is waste when going too fast.


LIKE ALL DELICIOUS PARTAKINGS, THE taste of new buildings whetted the appetite for more. The hunger was not a matter of shortcoming; rather it was a matter of longing. It could only be solved by a fourth building. We needed seminar rooms, more office space for expanding staff and faculty, and a cafeteria where law learning could fuse with breakfast, lunch, dinner, and coffee breaks.

The need for our own law campus eating spot received some resistance from the college in that the college student union had a cafeteria large enough to serve all. ABA Consultant Millard Ruud defended the need to segregate the law school experience, and that included separate dining. Professionalism, he had once argued [*supra* ch. 4], "required the development of a sense of community" that called for students to spend their "days in a building associating only with other law students."

This was a rare instance in which I disagreed with Millard. To be *professional*, yes; but to be *isolated*, no. Association with fields of study beyond the law discipline was essential to the lawyer's full understanding of who and what Law serves. Professionalism ought not retire inward upon its own. Rather, Law is that one discipline whose wings spread over all arts, sciences, businesses, trades, and walks of life. Consorting with those other disciplines is a must. This is not to say that a separate law school cafeteria was a bad idea. It was a good idea, but only because the separation was foisted upon us by our distance from the college campus. In short, the reason for the separate cafeteria, was to make it handy, not to make it secluded.

Professor Bill Williamson took the idea of togetherness, repast, and partaking one step further. Ever festive, he suggested the need for a pub. Unlike the undergraduate school, we had an *adult* student body—one that would benefit by consorting in a relaxed atmosphere at the end of a day's or evening's education. What Billy began as merely a whim, gained serious attention. Accordingly, he moved that the law school acquire a beer license from the Oregon Liquor Control Commission. The faculty vote was a tie, which called for Dean Wren to cast the tiebreaker. Needless to say deans, by virtue of their office, would take a sober look at such an issue. There would be no saloon at this time. To placate the losers, the faculty Building and Grounds Committee was charged with further study of the matter. Whereupon in committee, it went the way of passing caprice—a fancy that fell but one vote short of rankling trustees and accreditors.


FOREMOST IN THE EARLY SIGNS for a needed fourth building was the wish for faculty seclusion—yet another sign of the sway between the dynamics of separation and joinder. While our professors tried to gain a good rapport with students, faculty offices immediately facing the student library study area was a proximity that proved too handy. We wanted to be accessible to students without being made a member in their study groups. Professors needed a separate research, reading, and meeting area. After all, comfort lies somewhere between extremes: not too small or too large, too cold or too hot, too soft or too hard. Even Goldilocks knew that.

And so, on the doorstep of our new quarters, we stood in awe but by no means in fulfillment. We were still challenged by temporary status, unfinished housing, and visions still cast in years of dreams ahead.

# 9
# THE WREN REGIME: PART TWO
## *1970-71*

### *TENDING HOUSE*

Just as NWLC was now temporarily accredited, so too were the accreditors now temporarily content. We took the calm as an opportunity to tend house. Attention to schooling and students was, after all, our primary mission. Achieving the badges of national recognition and building place were but off-shoots of that purpose. Still, it did seem as though the tailing of accreditation was wagging educational doggedness. Our opening of the 1970-71 academic year faced major change in-house. We had new status, new building, new faculty, new day students, and new horizons; but into those new bottles was decanted old school wine.

NEW FACULTY ROSTER AND SYSTEM:

On August 31, 1970, at the first faculty meeting of the year, the old guard (Wren, Williamson, Jurkins, and I) prepared to welcome five new members but only three showed up: Professors Bill Knudsen, Walt Brown, and Fred Fagg. Professor Alan Jensen had not yet arrived on campus. Potential faculty member Dale Broeder [see ch. 6, "Recruiting Faculty"], for unknown second thoughts, had decided to back out of his commitment to join us. This was the same faculty seat that we had earlier filled with Robert Jagiello, who also accepted and then withdrew. The faculty had never participated in the entry or exit of Broeder. Except for a momentary blip upon our roster radar, the faculty had never seen him.

Dean Wren wasted no time in dividing administrative chores and assigning them to committees. We were large enough now to become more systemized. Williamson

**FIVE NEW PROFESSORS—(1970)**

Clockwise from upper left: Bill Knudsen, Walt Brown, Jim Lenoir, Fred Fagg III, and J. Alan Jensen

was made chair of the Curriculum Committee, Knudsen was chair of the Faculty Appointments Committee, Brown chair of Building and Grounds, Fagg chair of Student Job Placement, Jensen chair of Scholarships and Awards, and Jurkins, of course, head of the Library Committee. I was appointed chair of Admissions and Advancement—the job of moving students into, out of, and through schooling. Brown and Williamson were assigned to my committee, just as I was assigned to the Appointments and Scholarships Committees.

### STUDENT REPRESENTATIVES AND VOTING POWER:

The first decision to come before the new faculty was Williamson's motion that had been tabled at the final meeting of the previous academic year [see ch 6, "Meetings, . . ."]: Should two student representatives (one each from the Day-Evening division) be given a voice and a vote at faculty meetings? I amended it to provide the students a voice but no vote. It seemed to me the faculty was not large enough yet to absorb so big a student block. To give votes to those who were in transit on the road of schooling and who sought to be educated and not to educate, was to give too much in that stage of our development. We currently had eight potential faculty votes; to allow two more student votes would be to give students a twenty percent voting block. Oddly enough, the faculty vote on my amendment was illustrative: it was a 3 - 3 tie (Fagg, Jurkins, and I in favor; Williamson, Knudsen, and Brown opposed; Jensen in absentia). Dean Wren cast the tie-breaker in favor of allowing the students two votes. Fagg and I then voted in favor of the main motion, conceding that the benefits of student input outweighed the risk of student power. Jurkins, however, continued her opposition. She would become known as our "Great Dissenter."

One-vote margins were often cast in our small membership of that era. In their wake, always came the agony of post mortem. Would students have been given a twenty percent vote in faculty meetings if Broeder had not reneged in joining us? Would students have had their vote if the decision to allow it had been tabled once again to the next faculty meeting after Jensen's arrival? What would be the impact of two student votes in such close decision-making? Indeed, taking to the road of representative democracy was destined to mean squeezing through the ruts of tight voting.

## THE JAGIELLO-BROEDER-LENOIR CHAIR:

At the September 9 meeting, we went from ten to eleven voters. Professor James Lenoir was a surprise addition. The vacancy left by Broeder's doorstep departure created an immediate need to fill the gap before accreditors became uneasy. Lenoir was taken aboard by Dean Wren and President Howard without any formal faculty interviews or consideration. Lenoir was a veteran, with over thirty years of professional service at numerous law schools. During World War II, he had been Chief Counsel for the U.S. Office of Price Administration [the famed "OPA"]. His hiring satisfied the college trustees and President Howard's desire for more experienced faculty. The feeling was that, while our faculty profile was keen, it was also raw. Wren and Knudsen were the only two with backgrounds at other campuses and, thus, seasoned in the protocols and decorums of higher education.

Lenoir lasted through the semester. His exit was not surprising in view of his hasty entry—a stopgap appointment. He knew that we struggled financially and that the low student sign-up for his speciality courses did not warrant his expense. Then too, as an aging law teacher, there must have been the uneasy feeling that comes with being retired in unfamiliar and energetic surroundings. In the minutes of his final faculty meeting on January 19, 1971, he was given the finest compliment that can be accorded a teacher from his peers, albeit younger colleagues. The minutes state, "He has taught us all."

Lenoir's resignation renewed our efforts in filling that troubled seat. Indeed, it was a wonder to know if the Jagiello-Broeder-Lenoir chair was jinxed.

## FACULTY RECRUITING:

We no sooner had welcomed our new 1970-71 law professors than we went to work in search of next year's professors. President Howard had assured the ABA accreditors that three new full-time faculty would be added in 1971-72. With the departure of Lenoir that meant our mission would be to find four. Professors Knudsen, Fagg, and I were made the recruiters. We had these mandates imposed: The college hierarchy wanted us to find at least one senior for a full professor slot and one "middle-salaried" type for an associate professor slot. The goal expressly given us was to gain "steadying influence and seasoned minds." It was not just a mission; it was a message to our young and spirited law faculty.

Accordingly, the first recommended candidate was Harold S. Bloomenthal, currently a full professor at Wyoming University, with law degrees from Duke and Yale and the author of several books and articles. He was interviewed on campus during the Thanksgiving vacation. In the week following that visit, without a meeting, Dean Wren got a faculty *consensus* approval on hiring Bloomenthal through individual telephone calls. It was disturbing. The procedure was contrary to what we had assured the ABA accreditors. We represented that the hiring of law professors required faculty unanimity "at a meeting." At the December 1 faculty meeting, Wren apologized for the telephone vote and offered as an excuse the need for immediacy: Bloomenthal was considering other employment. He assured that in the future a faculty vote at a duly called meeting would be followed. It would be a promise hard to keep in the accelerated pace of a competition that often called for spontaneity.

The Wren assurance and the faculty discontent were hard to explain in the face of what happened next. At that same December 1 faculty meeting, with the dust of difference barely settled, the faculty gave our delegates to the December AALS Conference "meat market" in Chicago, the carte blanche authority to extend immediate hiring offers to promising candidates found there. As we knew from our experience one year before [see ch. 6, "Recruiting Faculty"], that annual convention was traditionally a seething marketplace for recruiters and aspirants. To be in contention, we had to be swift. It was Wren's way, and he may have been right.

Our delegates were Dean Wren, Professors Knudsen, Brown, and Jensen, and student Terry Rahmsdorff. They reportedly screened or interviewed over seventy-eight prospects and extended several offers, two of whom eventually accepted: Jerome O. Hughey and James L. Bross. Along with Hal Bloomenthal, three of the four positions for the forthcoming 1971-72 academic year were now filled: president and trustee approval were virtually certain. None of the three had received a unanimous vote at a faculty meeting, as had been the procedure represented to the accreditors.

Hughey took the "middle-salaried," associate professor seat—a halfway spot for inculcating the faculty with supposedly "seasoned" and "steadying" influence. He was a teacher in California at Southwestern University Law School, an institution that had received temporary accreditation at the same time as us. He had been a member of the professional staff at the Rand Corporation "think-tank" and had a background with many publisher companies. Bross was an assistant professor find, with some experience in a Washington D.C. federal agency.

The fourth seat, another assistant professorship, was eventually filled in the spring of 1971 by Douglas K. Newell. Newell was a sole law practitioner in Southern California. Where Bloomenthal had been a prior colleague of Knudsen at Wyoming and Hughey had been an acquaintance of Fagg in southern California, Newell had been Williamson's roommate at Harvard Law School. Bross was the only one of the four who had come to us without an inside track.

Out of that batch of four, Newell was the only one (and, indeed, the first one in the history of the law school) to have gone through the hiring process represented to the ABA. He gained faculty appointment at a faculty meeting by a unanimous faculty vote. He was also the only one who would become a long-lasting NWLC professor. Bloomenthal would leave after one year to go into private law practice in Denver. Bross would leave in 1977 for an eventual law professorship in Georgia. Hughey resigned after a formal investigation by a college committee appointed by President Howard, a committee on which I served. The departure was labeled "uneasy circumstances"—a hushed euphemism that modernly, in a more candid society, would be called "harassment." He departed in 1974-75 and ended up at an Illinois law school, later to die reportedly in an automobile crash.

Newell took the seat abandoned by Jagiello, Broeder, and Lenoir. Decades later, the seat turned into a "chair"—the law school's first endowed faculty position—the Edmund O. Belsheim Chair. The aisle chair next to the exit for hasty departure, ceased to be jinxed. Its loyal occupant has been seated on the NWLC faculty for almost four decades as of this writing.

With the signing of Newell, the law school's first Faculty Recruitment Committee mission was accomplished. Its chairman, Professor Knudsen, then went to our nation's capital to orally argue a habeas corpus case before the Supreme Court of the United States—a ribbon that all lawyers dream of wearing. In later years, he showed his versatility before audiences. From appearances before students in the classroom and an appearance before the Supreme Court, he went on to perform on stage in the cast of George Kaufman's play, *You Can't Take It With You.*

**STAFF PERSONNEL:**

One other find was recruited to our cadre. Mary Ann Normandin was *"quasi*-faculty status" under the title of "Assistant *to the* Dean" rather than "Assistant Dean" as was her predecessor, Dave Shannon. She could not be an Assistant Dean because she had no law degree. Dean Wren, the naval officer, ever attentive to command protocol, changed the title by the simple insertion of the preposition "to." An *Assistant Dean* was an official dean grade; whereas, one who *assists* the dean was a staff position. Like in the military, ranking was important decorum. Fine distinction in the use of words was also characteristic of lawyering. But while there was a difference in *wording*; when it came to *working*, the aid rendered by a "dean" or an "assistant" was the same. And that made the whole of it rather silly for a place of higher education.

MARY ANN NORMANDIN

By whatever title, Normandin became a work horse whose influence and participation at our meetings was a faculty equivalent short of vote only. She was in charge of fund-raising, job placement, publications, student recruiting, social events, and alumni relations—positions now headed by six people. On top of those law school duties, she was required to spend one day a week in the college development office.

Dorothy Cornelius, the law school's first employee ever, continued to serve as Registrar. She was tenured as an employee under the 1965 Merger Agreement. [See ch. 1] That she could not be fired was an unnecessary clause. Her position was secured by tireless and efficient work without complaint and by over fifteen years of attachment, beginning when the school was Northwestern College of Law still downtown. In future years the law school would establish the Cornelius Honor Society for law students who exemplified Dorothy's commitment to and hard work for the school. Her matriarchal presence in our halls was a daily reminder of heritage.

Once the academic year got into full swing, complaints surfaced from the secretarial staff—three pairs of hands elbow deep in paperwork. Secretaries McCroskey, Kallenbach, and Noffke urged the need for six more clerks to handle the burgeoning output from library, law review, clinic, placement, development, and, of course, eight or nine faculty members. With the potential of four more faculty in the following fall semester of 1971-72, the problem of overwork, for the moment acute, was headed toward chronic. Increasing the clerical budget would have to be the long-range solution, but student troops on work study monies was the short-term relief.

Secretarial resignation was inevitable. Pauline Kallenbach retired in the year ahead. I had brought her from the Oregon State Civil Service System when I moved the Judicial Fitness Commission [JFC] from the downtown State Office Building to our campus. She worked one day a week as a state employee and four days a week on a law school salary. She left in order to return to Brownsville, Oregon, where she and her husband were editors of the *Brownsville Times* newspaper.

I then hired Betty Lou Johnson for the JFC work and the law school accepted her for the remainder of her forty-hour week. That replacement became a union of a different order. I fancied myself in the dubious role of matchmaker. Secretary Johnson and Professor Knudsen courted and contracted as wife and husband. It was good to see that in the dry soil of paper, flowers could grow.

STUDENT ENROLLMENT:

Faculty and staff were not our only growing bodies. True to accreditor warnings, yet to our surprise, our 1970-71 entering freshmen class far exceeded our budget projection. We had anticipated only 60 enrollees in our new day division; we got almost twice that many—117. Evening "one-L's" numbered 79. In November 1970, we counted a total student body of 319, whereas we had planned for only about 250. First year enrollees constituted over sixty percent of our total consumers. The new day enrollees were already well over one-third of our students. We were still principally an evening law school, but with the first step into daylight, we were well on the way to changing that domination.

Our full-time faculty-student ratio jumped from a planned 1:35 to a realized 1:40. Neither proportion met standards. Four new professors for the forthcoming 1971-1972 academic year would be reinforcements; but they would undoubtably be met by an incoming class greater in size than this year. Granting reductions for graduated seniors and drop-outs, swelling numbers of hopefuls were nonetheless an onslaught that surpassed the ability of ratios to keep up with components. The saving grace was that we were not alone; we were in step with national statistics. Across the country, the 1970 law student enrollment rose to 82,000, a twenty percent increase over the previous year. First year students (34,500) constituted forty-two percent of that national enrollment!

The number of women enrollees had been steadily rising over my five years as a law professor. In 1970, one of every five first-year entrants into the nation's law schools was a woman; but at NWLC, that ratio was only one of every eleven. Over the many decades of Northwestern's existence, the school became known for educating a greater percent of women lawyers than other law schools. NWLC was losing that distinction in 1970—not that we were falling back, rather others were pushed forward. To rectify, we organized a weekend seminar for "Careers in Law For Women." It was an event that may not seem innovative today, but was unique in 1970. Attendance was so large that we had to make an eleventh hour transfer of the program and its 120 women attendees to a bigger classroom. That number of aspirants was a clue to past denial and future fulfillment. Three to four decades later, NWLC male-female student body enrollment would be essentially equal; and in some years, the school would admit entering first year classes or would graduate senior classes with more women than men.

In 1970, NWLC's flood of student enrollment, male and female, was a dramatic turn of events from just twenty-five years before when Northwestern College of Law almost closed down with less than a dozen students. Without owner John Flint Gantenbein's devotion to service instead of business and his refusal to cease his father's school, enrollment would never have reached the September 1970 pinnacle of 319. And that climb was but a foothill to the mountain yet to come.

## BAR EXAM RESULTS

With bestowal, building, and burgeoning to our credit, we had "come up" and, alas, were due for comeuppance. On September 27, *The Oregonian* newspaper punctured our ascent by reporting the Oregon State Bar exam results. NWLC's showing was bad, very bad, the worst in the school's recent history and the worst by comparison to all of the other schools. Two hundred twenty-two [222] examinees had taken the test; 160 passed—for a success rate of 72 percent. NWLC success rate was 51 percent—49 NWLC takers, 25 passers. Our neighboring law school to the south (Willamette) had a 97 percent passage rate. A four-column, banner-headline paraded the results. To make matters worse, the article did not stop at simply posting results, it probed for reasons why Portland's local law school had performed so poorly:

> "Is there something inherently inferior about either the students, faculty, curriculum, plant, library, or teaching methods at Northwestern?"

We were more concerned about the publicity than about the poor success rate. The test results were not surprising. Our thirty-five, first time exam takers (fourteen were repeaters) had enrolled as freshmen in the summer of 1966 while the school was still located in downtown Portland. In the middle of their first year, they had to make the disruptive transfer to new quarters south of town, where they were taught in chemistry labs and narrow-desked armchairs with a law library stored in basement shelves. In their second year, they endured another upheaval in administration when their dean was publicly fired. By the end of their third year, their school had failed four times at the promise of gaining accreditation, two full-time professors had resigned, and the resignations of two more were on the horizon. Toward the beginning of their fourth year, with more than half of their original classmates gone, their school faltered at the brink of demise. And at the end of their fourth year, they graduated from a school still unaccredited—contrary to expectations. Then too, as is the case with virtually all evening students, achieving success on test scores was a superficial trial that had to be shared with other tasks—their day labor and family responsibility.

Since that 1970 low point, the annual success rate of NWLC takers on bar exams in Oregon and other states has risen steadily to well above average. Even more gratifying has been a more astute policy of the media. No longer does the press adopt the sport-page mentality of reporting a school's "won-lost" record on licensing exams. The serious business of legal education is not to be likened to an interscholastic athletic competition—no more so than hospitals should be compared by the percentages of cures; nor religions ranked by the number of converts; nor newspapers by the inches of advertising ink.

Be that as it may, following *The Oregonian* article and by the end of the first semester of the 1970-71 academic year, attrition took its toll. Ten percent of the first year class (about twenty students) chose not to continue their studies.

## INTRA-COLLEGE FISCAL MATTERS:

*Overhead and College Business Office:* Even though our move to the Tryon Forest was an estrangement from the college by distance, the merger grew tighter fiscally. The virtual elimination of the self-sustaining clause in the Merger Agreement had been the first step in mingling. [See ch. 6, "Autonomy . . . "] Now, at the beginning of the 1970-71 year, the keeping of separate bank accounts also ceased. The handling of all monies transferred to the College Business Office. Henceforth, that office would collect all tuition, fees, gifts, and other income and disburse all expense payments— while, of course, keeping law school and college monies in separate accounts.

No one criticized the new fiscal arrangement. But beneath the mere accounting, some of the new law colleagues were uneasy about the power that strings with the purse. The business office and its managers would begin to take a hand in administering our budget, which would lead to auditing our expenditures, and then to overseeing our performance. For instance, Bill Malinson, the college business manager argued that our current surplus income from over-enrollment of the entering class should transfer to the college's coffers instead of being carried over as income to next year's law school budget.

The more encompassing issue, however, focused on an imposed payment to the college from the law school for a share in operations costs of the whole institution. The new line item account was called "Overhead." In previous years, that obligation had been minimized by the college inasmuch as the law school had been operating on a deficit. Now that the law school had a surplus income, college business managers levied a fixed sum of overhead payment at $32,400 to our current 1970-71 law school budget. That sum amounted to the tuition income of about twenty of our new, over-enrolled day students. From our vantage point, it seemed that the new "Overhead" dictate was just a way of tapping into our surplus income. We knew, however, that it was right for us to pay our share of the use of college services and facilities so long as the share was fair and our use was common. So, for the immediate time, whatever might have been gained in debate over fairness and commonality was a difference too negligible to justify extended debate. Petty argument yielded to paltry portion.

But once the overhead item gained some congeniality, the business office rushed in to revise the sum for the next academic year. It was far more than double the amount—$75,000! The charge would be over thirteen percent of our projected income for 1971-72. That turned annoyance into rancor. The amount was based on a formula keyed to our income. Some colleagues argued that percentage of income was an unfair taxation. That position was an old one in our nation's society: There should not be *income* tax; there should be *expense* taxation (*e.g.* sales and use taxes). The richer one becomes does not justify having to pay progressively more for the same considerations bestowed equally on all—so said some colleagues. But even if "Over-head" were likened to a price tag, rental, service charge, or other costs, that would be an exaction more typical of customer relations than of family teamwork—so said other colleagues. The cross-currents put "merger" at forks instead of confluence.

Having been with the law school ever since its adoption by Lewis & Clark, I had witnessed a slightly different picture than my new colleagues. I was there when the law school was "poorly" and was pleased to have the college subsidize our yearly deficits. To that end, we welcomed our financial dependence on the parent school. But now, here in 1970-71, we saw the beginnings of sound and firm monetary footing and, thus, were anxious to have independence and self-sustenance restored. That was a knee-jerk reaction, which soon succumbed to something more equitable. So, while we still disagreed with calculating overhead on a portion of income, we proposed paying the law school's share of common expenses based on comparative student body sizes. In searching for expenses that were shared by both schools, we found that the law school was already paying its way for many budget line-item costs, such as our own groundskeeping, building maintenance, financial development, student union, bookstore, library, and personnel salaries. On the other hand, there were other services provided us by the college for which we were not paying, such as the president's office, athletic facilities, parking at the upper campus, security, and now the services of the college business office. The business office's arbitrary percent decrees had begun the overhead issue on the wrong foot. It would take over a decade of wrangling to get in step with what today is a budget item called "common services." For the time being, however, in 1970-71, rather than going through the tedium of a line-by-line item search, the law school was willing to take the business office's $75,000 dictate as a liveable estimate of what expense-sharing would be.

Once again, the overhead issue settled down. But once again, the college business office picked the healing scab. The managers wanted to go back and charge the law school for the college's fiscal support over the five years since the merger. Those prior financings, it was said, were "advances," now in arrears, not gifts to be forgiven.

The whole debacle was resurrected. Late in the 1970-71 academic year, the law school squared off on the three foregoing fiscal sore spots: What should be done about the law school's surplus income, the past subsidizations, and the payment of retroactive overhead.

Paul Boley, chair of the Standing Committee on the Operation of the Law School [SCOLS], came to the rescue. ABA Consultant Millard Ruud also gave a hand. Boley gained president Howard's verbal assurances that henceforth law school surpluses would carry over to subsequent law school budget years, that previous college subsidy of law school deficits would not be an indebtedness, and that overhead charges for past years would be forgiven.

Those assurances would have been a relief were it not for the fact that they were merely verbal. The presidential position needed to be formalized. In June 1971, Professor Fagg took the initiative and drafted a letter for Boley's signature. Boley signed and delivered it to Howard. It confirmed Howard's oral commitments; but, at the same time, it implied our acceptance of the annual overhead expense and the gauge by which it was fixed.

**PAUL BOLEY**

Although our percent of income contribution to the college pool was relatively small at first, it was, nevertheless, a camel's nose under our budget flaps. In future years, the revenue multipliers (percent and revenue numbers) would creep upward. Consequently, the overhead product would eventually reach appropriations well above one million dollars annually. With it, discontent in the law faculty would grow broad and deep. Dollar merging was doing more to separate than to merge.

We were headstrong but had to draw in our horns somewhat when in 1971 Millard Ruud sat us down to explain that, at other colleges and universities, law school overhead charges were customary and considerable. Law schools, with their higher tuitions, bigger course enrollments, larger faculty-student ratios, and more united professional alumni, were cash cows for the whole of higher education. Nonetheless, at this stage in our development, we felt that parental demands were stunting our adolescent growth.

*Arts and Sciences, Faculty Salaries:* From that self-center, we took little notice of the faculty at the college of arts and sciences, who had their own misgivings. A sizeable number of undergraduate professors looked over our shoulder and saw stark fiscal contrasts. Disparity was the trigger and our pay scale was their target. Instead of the college business office, the law faculty now felt the barbs of discontent from a different quarter of the campus.

College professors prepared a November 2, 1970, report that urged President Howard and the trustees to make significant upgrades in undergraduate faculty salaries. They documented "steady deterioration" of their salaries in recent years with an accompanying decline in morale. Their statistics showed discrepancies in salary advances compared to other Pacific northwest private, liberal arts colleges and universities.

At the law school, there was support and no disagreement until the report went on to make other comparisons:

> "A Lewis & Clark... teacher of law is paid on the average close to $5,000 per year more than a Lewis & Clark College teacher."

The report documented that, over the last two academic years, compensation for full professors of law gained at a 12 percent rate, whereas undergraduate professors gained at only 4.4 percent. Throughout the report, disparities between law and college faculty pay were emphasized.

We at the law school were put between the rock of sympathy and the hard place of defense. The college teachers' appeal for higher recompense was deserved, but we feared that trustees might also read it as a denigration of law teachers' higher money scale. Narrowing the gap of disparity might prompt the upgrade of undergraduate salaries by curbing law faculty advances in both bodies and pay. Furthermore, in the face of current demands for overhead and pooling, trustees might eye law school surpluses as a source for raising undergraduate salaries. We could not remain silent. Nine days after the college professor report, we presented our 1971-72 law budget to

SCOLS. Attached to it was our November 11 response to the undergrad professors' appeal. We were defensive.

As I recall it, Dean Wren and Professor Knudsen sketched the initial draft, Professor Fagg dug out statistics and other documentation, and I edited and assembled the final report. It began with our case for more law faculty positions and for higher pay increases. We projected a potential student enrollment of 435 in the upcoming 1971-72 academic year—compared to our current population of about 320. Then we pulled out the accreditation card. By ABA accreditation standards we should have at least five new full-time faculty and an $18,800 salary median. And that would be but a baby step in reaching preferred faculty-student ratios. Further down the road, the other accrediting agency, the American Association of Law Schools (AALS), with its more stringent standards, would call for at least ten more full-time faculty based on current enrollment projections. Our immediate proposal for 1971-72 was based on three new professor additions plus the Lenoir replacement.

And so, what with new hires plus existing salary upgrades, the law budget for 1971-72 proposed a total academic salary pool of $224,000. That was an $80,000 (55 percent) jump over the current 1970-71 fiscal year. Indeed, our total operating budget proposal (including non-academic salaries and other expenses) showed a whopping 40 percent increase—from the current $389,000 to the proposed $547,000.

Those increments (especially the salary rise) would fuel the fire of the college professors' complaints about unfair discrepancy. As distasteful and awkward as it was, our written response had to deal with those anticipated reactions. We began by emphasizing that we "support the efforts of the undergraduate faculty to upgrade its salary structure." But we had to remind of the inescapable dictates of the market place:

> "Traditionally, there has been, and necessarily must be, a wide differential between undergraduate faculty salary levels and that of law schools. The opportunities available to law faculty as alternatives to teaching and indeed within the teaching profession itself, require a higher scale of compensation to successfully compete for legal scholars."

Accreditor guidelines were quoted:

> "It is not feasible to tie law school salaries to a university-wide level." [AALS Guidelines]

> "A law school cannot hope to attract and retain a competent faculty... unless it...

takes fully into account... that law teachers are qualified... for other careers in the legal profession." [ABA Guidelines]

As convincing as that may have been, it nevertheless led some to question the "fair" in fair market value.

At our November 17 meeting, Dean Wren reported that President Howard endorsed our proposed budget fully, which meant that there would be little change when passing trustee muster. The undergraduate professors did not fare as well. Our arguments had done much to explain discrepancy but did little to bridge the gap of divisiveness. The law school was still the new kid on the block with a snotty-nose and now eating from a silver spoon.

In the wake of that debacle, I found myself trying to placate both faculties. I had been with Lewis & Clark College now for almost five years, most of which were in daily contact with the college campus. In those years, I had hobnobbed with undergraduate teachers in meetings, dinings, picnics, volleyball, and other gardens. There was a period in which I was the lone law professor, and my company was in conversation with literature, philosophy, music, chemistry, mathematics, history, astronomy, sociology, and other disciplines. So, it grieved me to see woundings between Law on the one hand and Arts and Science on the other. Like all of nature's open wounds, healing would go from cut to scab to scar, leaving only a seam from which to rue the splitting of education.

## ADMISSIONS APPLICATIONS:

One year ago, our admission policy [see ch. 6, "Admissions"] saw value in allowing the first year of law study to be a far better gauge of a student's potential than LSAT and UGPA scores. As long as we were not silly in our threshold leniency, as long as we were strenuous and firm in our first year grading, and as long as there were empty chairs, a bit of the Gantenbein tender heart continued, and we gave borderline applicants a chance to prove their worth in a trial period.

But that was one year ago. Now in the fall of 1970, for the first time we no longer had empty seats. As previously reported in this chapter, our student enrollment was now over-abundant. Pre-law prediction had to be a necessity, not just a nicety. We had to choose from within a circle of the papered promising and could not chance at borderlines.

Across the nation law schools experienced continuing, phenomenal growth in the number of aspirants interested in law study. Administrators of the nationwide

Law School Admissions Test [LSAT] had predicted a record-breaking 75,000 takers during the forthcoming 1970-71 year. The prediction was short of the mark by 40,000. As of March 1971, 115,000 had taken the test for admission into the 1971-72 academic year.

As of mid-December 1970, we had received 53 applications for first year enrollment in September 1971. That was 38 more than in the previous year at the same time. In mid-March 1971, there were 386 applications, 317 more than at the same time a year before. We also had received about 2,750 inquiries. The profusion gave NWLC trouble it never had before—problems that fell on me, chair of the 1970-71 faculty Admissions Committee—the first such committee in the law school's history.

Two problems were wrought by the numbers at our door: *prediction* and *selection*. As for prediction, we had little previous statistics or logistics to give us aim. Past data was no longer a reliable indicator on how many hopefuls would ascend the steps of inquiry, application, offer, acceptance, and deposit, and then show up at our door. Experience from other parts of the country was little help because the surge had undermined prophecy at other schools as well. Dean Wren gave the trustees a target of 120 first-year day and 120 first-year evening enrollees with fifteen percent attrition (dropouts) before the start of the second semester. Wren (ever the optimist) would have been the first to confess doubt in forecasting but the last to concede the futility in trying.

As for the *selection* problem, in previous years, it was essentially the applicant who selected us. If an applicant (having borderline LSAT and UPGA scores) wanted us, that was, by and large, enough to give him or her an open seat. But now, not only did we not have openings for the infirm, we did not have enough for all of the confirmed. What had been a borderline applicant's freedom of purchase, now became NWLC's pick of able purchasers.

Prolonged scrutiny of each promising candidate file was beyond time and affordable personnel. A threshold screening device was needed. My correspondence showed that schools were now using factoring systems based on scholastic tests—formulas that weighed LSAT scores and undergraduate grades together. The idea is commonplace today; but in 1970, factoring was just beginning a fresh usefulness. Accordingly, at an October 1970 faculty meeting I proposed the use of a factoring guideline that balanced an applicant's undergraduate grade point average [UGPA] at 75 percent and the LSAT score at 25 percent—thus, the formula: 300 UGPA + LSAT = Factor number. *E.g.* 300 [3.2 UGPA] + 600 LSAT = 1,560 Factor. If a factor number was 1,350 or higher, the registrar could automatically accept. If below 1,000, the registrar could automatically reject. Any factor in the range of 1,000 - 1,349 was placed on a standby list for faculty committee scrutiny if quotas were not met by automatic acceptance.

My colleagues raised many questions: Was too much weight given to the UGPA score? Aren't undergraduate schools disparate in academics or in their giving of grades? Recognizing that evening applicants tended to be older and removed from the routine of academic testing, should the impact of the LSAT score be lower for them? Doesn't a quantitative screening system preclude consideration of the values of racial, gender and cultural diversity in law education and in the law profession? These were all legitimate critiques of the effort to quantify quality.

Professor Fagg objected to the whole idea of fusing UGPA and LSAT into one factor. He moved to amend the factoring proposal to provide an automatic rejection of any applicant whose LSAT number fell below 475 or whose UPGA fell below 2.0 regardless of the conjoining score. That amendment was aligned with past practice [see ch. 6, "Admissions"]. In critique of Fagg's proposal, an applicant could demonstrate perfection with an ideal LSAT score of (what was then) 800 or with an undergrad report card of straight "A's" [UGPA of 4.0] yet be mandatorily denied entry if the adjunct score was below Fagg's prescribed minimum. To which Fagg argued that, likewise, under the main motion's factoring formula, an applicant could have an absolutely abysmal LSAT score or an unsatisfactory UGPA score yet be allowed entry by the formula's mandate if the companion score was high enough.

If the two scores were going to be factored, some felt the LSAT was a better predictor of law school success. Others felt that my emphasis on the UGPA was correct. Both scores had clue but faults as well. It all came down to sums instead of souls.

The debate at the October meeting was prolonged. After whirling in dizzy math and hypothetic spins, the whole matter was tabled. Then at the November 24 faculty meeting, my original motion specifying the quantitative factoring formula with its extra UGPA weight was adopted without discussion or dissent. Concerns with undergraduate grading disparity, evening school dispensation, diversity of peoples, and a wretched showing on either the LSAT or the UGPA, were all left to qualitative scrutiny of each individual case in the 1000-1349 standby "maybe land." The debate had been a good lesson for why tabling was good medicine for the maladies of meeting—two aspirin and a bed on which lawyerly pride could get a good-night's sleep and a chance to think about what mattered later instead of what to say next.

As of May 2, 1971, I reported to the faculty that we had closed the first-year day division to any further applications for the 1971-72 academic year and that we would soon do so with the evening division applications. Our offers of enrollment had already received money deposits of acceptance from about 70 day applicants and 60 evening applicants. We still had 139 day and 75 evening offers awaiting acceptance of our offers. We had far outreached ourselves and were headed for mammoth trouble if all of the depositors plus all of the offerees, were to enroll in August. Our capacity was a maximum of 120 in each division. New at the game of decanting admissions bottles, I was desperately afraid we were going to spill over. So, I put out a notice to the outstanding offerees that seats were limited and that our prior offers were now conditioned on a first-come-first-serve basis. Fingers were crossed in the wish that all we had wished would not wish us.

STUDENT RECRUITMENT:
Overwhelmed by the gathering at our gate, we had little thought of going beyond our walls to enlist more. Student recruiting was far from mind at the start of the 1970-71 year. Once the thrill of abundance wore down, however, we took greater concern with the need to compete. Didn't we want so-called "top finds"—those with intelligent, heterogeneous, symbiotic, synergistic potential?

Accordingly, Assistant to the Dean Normandin, organized the "Career in Law for Women" symposium, previously reported. Dean Wren and Normandin also made trips to distant recruitment fairs and to pre-law advisor conferences. They reported that our strongest lures proved to be our Oregon and Pacific Northwest location, our environmental program, and our new status and fresh outlook among law schools. Normandin revised our lifeless catalog and prepared posters all with a bent toward eye-catching candy.

An affirmative hand was taken with the recruitment of students of diverse racial and cultural backgrounds. That brand of recruitment reached its farthest extent when in April 1971, we sought admission of a particular Native-American from the Warm Springs tribes in Central Oregon. He was interviewed by the whole faculty and urged to apply for admission even though he had only two years of undergraduate study, had not taken an LSAT exam, and was discharged from the U.S. Army as "undesirable" because he refused to go to Vietnam. On the other hand, he had served as counsel to hundreds of soldiers, was an assistant to the late Senator Robert Kennedy, and was also targeted for admission at other law schools, *e.g.*, Harvard and George Washington law schools. We lost that recruitment effort. But his case and the times in which we lived were typical of the struggle to unite, but not to homogenize—not a melting pot, but a rainbow with distinct colors arched together. It was also typical of a dubious bending of rules that would later become a constitutional issue.

## FINANCIAL AID:

In recruiting, we were sorely hampered by shortcomings in our 1969-1970 financial aid package—a paltry $19,000 available for student scholarships and grant monies. With the help of our alumni, financial aid to students reached $65,000 in mid-January 1971. It was still far from enough. That pool was substantially loan monies and little gratis money for scholarships. Also, far from adequate, were our work-study dollars—payment to students for work for the school or other non-profit organizations.

In September 1970 we got a check from Farmers Insurance Group for use as loan monies for law student aid. But instead, President Howard diverted the dollars to the mathematics and business administration departments of the college. In an October 14, 1970 letter to Farmers, he explained: "Additional financial assistance for law school students is not required during the current academic year." Disturbing as it was to us, it would have been even more so were it not for the fact that the gift, after all, had been garnered by the good graces of Howard in the first place.

## NADER AND DOUGLAS VISITS:

In November 1970, the college brought Ralph Nader to the campus to speak to the undergraduate and law student bodies. He was then on the rise as a nationally prominent activist watchdogging government and business intrusions into the interests of consumers. He was touring the nation's campuses in pursuit of an idea and sought to capitalize on the current wave of student energy and opposition to war, racial injustice, gender discrimination, and now his foe, consumer abusers. He saw our focus on the environment as still another connection to his consumer interests. He urged his so-called "Nader Raiders" to organize into student public interest research groups—"SPIRGs," he called them. They were to be consumer activist chapters funded by college administered student fees.

A few weeks before coming to the Lewis & Clark campus, Nader had addressed a student throng at the University of Oregon in Eugene on the SPIRG proposal. There, his idea was well-received, so much so that the University of Oregon became the first place in the nation to embrace the concept and to establish a chapter funded by mandatory student fees, calling itself "OSPIRG." When he brought the idea to our campus, the student body at Lewis & Clark was willing, but our college officials declined for fear that it was not legitimate for a private organization to jeopardize its charity standing by collecting fees for "politicizing."

Like the NEDC office at Lewis & Clark and like other environmental programs, OSPIRG would become another bed of controversy in an age where the young-enthused and the old-established would find more contention than comfort in one another.

Soon after the Nader stopover, confrontation was further fed by another visitor to our campus. The law school alumni association sponsored the appearance of William O. Douglas, Associate Justice of the Supreme Court of the United States. On December 22, 1970, he spoke to an audience of over 1,000 at the college student union building—his topic: "The Future of Environmental Law." An ardent conservationist who had written numerous books on the subject, he applauded our school for having led the way in renewing the struggle for conserving nature under the modern banner of "environmental movement."

When President Franklin D. Roosevelt appointed him to the Court in 1939, Douglas, at age 40, was the youngest justice to ever serve on that distinguished bench. When he retired from the Court, five years after the visit to our campus, he would have served longer (almost thirty-seven years) than any other United States justice in history. Three U.S. Presidents (FDR, Harry Truman, and Lyndon Johnson) had considered making Douglas their vice-presidential running mate.

Aside from his affinity for a school with his mutual concern for nature, there were other reasons that induced him to float his stick in an obscure eddy far from eastern currents and from rapids in the nation's capital. He had made his home in our backyard - - the wilderness areas of the Washington Cascade and Oregon Wallowa mountain ranges. In the spirit of former President Theodore Roosevelt, he was foremost an outdoorsman and adventurer, who described wilderness as "paradise... some far-off place of mystery" and wrote that without adventure, one "stays tethered by strings of doubt."

Another inducement for the Douglas visit was that his recent wife came from the Portland area. At age 72, he had entered this, his fourth marriage. Her years were nearly one-third of his. That difference in the "mix of winter and spring" was just one of many reasons to ignite his detractors. Indeed, his controversial stands in favor of civil rights, racial integration, and preservation of the wilderness, made him many critics. His article published in *Playboy* magazine did not help matters. Richard Posner, now a federal circuit judge, reportedly described Douglas as "a compulsive womanizer, a heavy drinker, a terrible husband,... uncollegial" and given to frequent unwarranted absences from the Court.

Prior to the Douglas appearance, President Howard reported to our law faculty that he had letters from influential people opposing that appearance and recommended that we write those objectors and explain why Douglas was afforded our dais. The reason why seemed so obvious that any explanation would likely fall upon ears not given to listen. Need anyone be told that he was one of our nation's nine final interpreters of law and that NWLC was a place of learning, not just a place for listening to the music already in us.

Nader and Douglas were on the same course. Both challenged established citadels—the only difference being that one was on the outside of the walls and the other was ensconced within. Not only did we give them our soapbox, we also gave them our press. Both published articles in *Environmental Law*. With that one-two punch of liberals, is it any wonder that our upstart law school received new attention—or should I say "tension." As President Howard suggested, diplomacy was now need to bring together the education of dreamers with those who make dreams possible.

On the evening before his speech, Justice Douglas met privately with our law faculty at Dean Wren's home. Douglas had been a law professor at Columbia and Yale and was, therefore, relaxed in academic company. In my private chat with him, I found a kindred spirit. We talked of backpacking in the same wilderness areas and shared familiarity with the switchbacks, scree-scrambles, stream-crossings, wildflowers, snowfields, glaciers, crampons, ice-axes, and nights in the alpine and timberline around Douglas's Goose Prairie home in the central Washington's Goat Rocks country, an area triangulated by Mount Rainier, Mount Adams, and Mount St. Helens. Our exchange of tales took us to hideaways in those central Cascades—places such as Dutch Miller Gap, Snoqualmie Pass, Snowgrass Flats, and the Enchantment Lakes. For those brief moments, over libations at the fireside of the Wren home, a U.S. Supreme Court Justice and a young law teacher, on separate trails, joined to hike together. I shall always remember it that way.

## DEVELOPMENT:

Although our two million dollar building fund was finished, we were still on money-raising ways. The money-raising office was changed from "Financial Affairs" to "Development." Our Development Office was captained by the yeoman efforts of Assistant to the Dean Normandin. We received $10,000 in gifts during the first two months of the 1970-71 academic year. Certain donors put up the carrot of $300,000 in matching funds as an incentive challenge to other prospective donors. Milton Pearl, Director of the national Public Land Law Review Commission, gave his library of environmental books in appreciation of the school's mission in that direction. Grant proposals were extended to thirteen national and local foundations.

Oregon judges had contributed thousands of dollars to the creation of the "James W. Crawford Courtroom." As aforesaid [see ch. 8], the courtroom was ceremoniously dedicated in April 1971. The newly created Oregon Court of Appeals christened it with official oral arguments in three cases. In the decades since that time, the courtroom and its "Crawford" title have had to yield to partitioning, remodeling, and other transition. It was fascinating to see how money developed buildings yet then to watch how those buildings develop. The line of exchange began with the architects, followed by the developers, then the builders, and then the consecrators—all to be finally capped by the dwellers, who make of it what they will.

## FACULTY MEETINGS:

Our 1970-71 faculty meetings continued to be long and frequent. Dean Wren scheduled us to meet once a week at Tuesday noon. There were fifteen such regular meetings in the first semester—ranging in length from 75 to 165 minutes—an average time of about two hours. I know because in my second year as minutes-scribe, I decided to record starting and ending times—my subtle way of grousing about how "the taking of minutes" had become the taking of hours.

*Minutes of Hours*

*Voting Power:* At the start of the year, professors with the power of vote at faculty meetings were Brown, Fagg, Jensen,

Jurkins, Knudsen, Lenoir, Williamson and me—eight votes. As presider, Dean Wren would not vote except to break ties. Registrar Cornelius and Assistant to the Dean Normandin had voice, but not vote, at the meetings. In addition and as said earlier, the faculty had given the student body a two-seat voting delegation by the narrow vote of 4-3 with one absentee. Donn Beck and David Moore were the first two students to represent that body. Both were upperclass evening students. Freshman law students, day or evening, were too fresh to be chosen. Starting in the spring semester, the students began playing musical chairs with their two-seat delegation. Various students pop up in the faculty minutes as surrogates (without any apparent credentials): *e.g.*, Jim Benham, Jim Gleeson, Sherry Smith, and Gary Sund. Benham had somehow found his way to a student seat in the faculty meetings, albeit a freshman day student. A few of the faculty were beginning to wonder about our lackadaisical concern with credentials. Nowhere was it written that representatives or their surrogates had to be elected or somehow formalized.

*Confidentiality:* Once student representation was constituted, only then did the faculty begin to agonize over the potential difficulties. Once the need for credentials was satisfied, there dawned a need for privacy. Certain sensitive matters deserved concealment. Should students be excluded from presence on "delicate" agenda items? At the September 29 meeting, Dean Wren appointed the two student representatives, Professor Knudsen, and me to make a list of what matters deserved confidentiality. That group was unable to agree. At the October 27 meeting, Knudsen moved to exclude student delegates from attending agenda items concerning:

> "probation, scholarships and awards, admissions, graduation of students, disciplinary action under the Honor Code, similar matters relating to individual students, and faculty personnel matters."

That placed two issues on the floor: First, should student representatives be barred under any circumstances? And second, if so, under what circumstance? Discussion was long, involved, and began a series of parliamentary doings that wended a convoluted course hard to follow over the next four meetings. It would become a key series of events that would set NWLC on track eventually leading to one of its hallmarks.

At the November 3 meeting, Knudsen amended his tabled motion to add still more confidential issues to his list. Students should also be excluded from agenda items concerning:

> "...grades, promotion, suspension, dismissal,... and matters of a similar confidential

nature relating to individual members of the faculty or individuals under consideration as faculty members."

Student representatives wondered if there was anything left on the agenda to which they could attend. Knudsen's amendment went on to say that the "foregoing restrictions apply only to individual cases" and not to policy or rule-making. That then, raised a third issue: Who would decide whether the item dealt with a sensitive "individual case" or simply with "policy." Knudsen proposed that the professors, not the student representatives, should make that decision. That then created a fourth issue: Should students be excluded from voting on whether they should be excluded on a specific vote. Furthermore, under common law precedent, doesn't a decision on each *individual case* become the making of *policy*.

After considerable debate and some juggling, the Knudsen motion passed. But only a week later (November 10), a motion passed to resurrect the whole confidentiality issue.

Upon reconsideration, Professor Williamson conceded to the Knudsen list of confidential areas, but sought to change the consequences. He moved to amend by providing that instead of excluding students from participating, they should simply be admonished "to refrain from breaching confidentiality."

The tangle of parliamentary maneuvering thickened. Some pointed out that the Williamson motion was not an amendment, but rather a contradiction of the Knudsen motion and was, therefore, out of Roberts Rules of Order. Even though that procedural point of order was not debatable, it got lost in prolonged debate.

From there, discussion got sidetracked and spread to broader issues of barring any voter (whether student or professor) who had a personal interest or bias on a given issue and affording anyone affected (e.g., even a prospective student) a right to exclude any voter with such bias. Eventually, the whole of it was tabled "until student representatives could get a student body vote on this whole area."

One week later (November 24), the students returned with a counter message from Student Bar President Jim Hubler and other officers. The message was adamant: The student delegates to the faculty were elected to represent the student body; their pronouncements are theoretically the views of that body; accordingly, no referendum of the student body needed to be taken.

Nothing more appears in the record as to confidentiality at meetings. Its motions and amends were scattered somewhere upon a very large table of offerings. Nothing official was ever needed because no confidentiality incidents ever arose that could not be reconciled by trust and tact instead of rule. The whole issue simply vanished into that netherland where more issues lie undecided than decided and where this lesson is learned: Trying to anticipate every conceivable troublespot in a plan and then to put a solution ahead of the problem—an answer before the question—is pushing instead of pulling on a rope. It's why there must be a judiciary as well as a legislature.

The student participation discussions, however convoluted, were nevertheless a demonstration of the lengths to which that 1970 faculty was willing to go to sort out the extent of student involvement in law school education business.

In the early 1970s, established schools of higher education were experiencing upheaval and evolution with regard to the younger generation and, thus, were given to resistance. But NWLC was not established on the national scene and was in a state of complete makeover. At such a moment in time, a developing organization, some would say, "is more susceptible," while others would say, "is more receptive" to new ideas.

Student voice and vote at NWLC faculty meetings was conceived, perhaps serendipitously, at that 1970 inception. Today, in a great many law schools, student representation in educational business matters is still quite minimal, while at NWLC, students have voice and vote on matters of budget, curriculum, student admissions, faculty recruiting, faculty hiring, and more. That four-decade old concept has become so routine that it is hard to imagine a time when it needed innovating. It is one of the lessons the study of history teaches: What to some may seem old-fashioned may be to others shocking surprise.

*The Length and Frequency of Meeting:* When Dean Wren did not allow my minutes to be distributed to the student body, the student delegates began preparing and distributing their own unofficial, meeting synopses. At first their minutes fell in step with the meanderings of the meeting—both quite verbose in quoting professors verbatim. But after two publications, the expense of mimeographing so many pages got too dear in time and fees. So, the editors reduced their minutes to just one page. With regrets couched in chiding, their report offered, "At the risk of offending various faculty members who at times hold sway in meetings," faculty comments would be eliminated.

In the same spirit, Professor Williamson at the October 27 faculty meeting produced a written motion to shorten meetings to one hour and fifteen minutes. It proposed that any agenda items not reached by that time "be deferred to the next meeting." He gave as reasons: "to conserve" valuable faculty and student time and "to expedite the business of faculty meetings now all too much taken up by trivia." That the motion was introduced by one of its offenders, was largely a reason for its passage—Fagg, Jurkins and I dissenting. I could not disagree with the idea of shorter meetings but voted against the motion because of its naïveté. Once again the wisdom of Gibran rang true: "Who shall command the skylark not to sing?"

Henceforth, the meetings were to last no longer than fifteen minutes past one hour. The current meeting (in which the motion was passed) lasted two hours. In the Spring semester, seven meetings were over two hours long, one lasting more than four hours. To test the heart of an edict, one should first take the pulse of its probable practice.

*Punctuality of Meetings:* A final effort at "clocking" likewise did not stand the test of reality. The penultimate meeting of the academic year (May 20, 1971) was typically delayed waiting for tardy members and a quorum. When we finally did get started, Professor Knudsen, having been at NWLC now for one full year, moved to start meetings at their scheduled time. He did not care so much about how long meetings lasted or how frequently they occurred, just so long as they began as advertised. The motion passed 4-0—the four new faculty members (Brown, Fagg, Jensen and Knudsen) in favor. The student representatives were absent on account of exam time. Jurkins, Williamson, and myself abstained because, while valuing the sentiment, we saw the motion as "motionless." Classic procedure dictates that it is a quorum, not the clock, that starts meetings. But our new faculty members recognized that sometimes motions, while not wise, can, nevertheless, be a word to the wise.

## STRUCTURING THE HIERARCHY:

From time to time, every sock drawer needs re-sorting, a desk top needs straightening, a file cabinet re-filing, a bulletin board re-posting. Indeed, every order will come to disorder, then to re-order, and so on. For strange reasons, as Robert Frost put it, "Something there is that does not love a wall, that wants it down."

And so it was with our hierarchy in the fall of 1970. It needed reorganizing— a sorting out of what was to be done, and who was to do it. Scattered beyond the faculty entity, were the presidential office, the trustees' Standing Committee on the Operation of the Law School, the Board of Directors of the Alumni Association, the Board of Visitors (a new name for Wren's "Fellows"), the Development Council (a new group to spearhead all fund raising), the Student Bar Association, and the "Northwestern Advisory Board" (a new name for the forebearers—the original five trustees of the merged Northwestern College of Law.)

In October 1970, Dean Wren, the naval commander, saw the need to redefine and re-arrange the structure of those boards, associations, committees, offices, councils, *et cetera*. Wren aimed at streamlining and reducing parts. To do so, he ran contrary to reduction by instigating an addition; he created the Sub-Committee on the Restructuring of the Law School Operations.

I was made one of the five Subcommittee members along with lawyer Walt Pendergrass (chair), U.S. Attorney Sid Lezak, law alumni president John Ryan, and Northwestern trustee Jack Kennedy. Why I was chosen has always puzzled me. Organizing and organization were not among my appetites. While I was not prone to drift far from the herd, I was rogue enough to shun corrales, love roving, and detest roping.

Fortunately, my fellow committeemen were savvy enough to see our task as merely treatment of what one member called, "organizational hypochondria." They quickly streamlined the streamlining by confessing ignorance and bowing to the needs of the reorganizer. Some members wrote:

"I cannot comment on the Board of Visitors as I do not understand it."

"I do not envision the Student Bar having a part in this particular structure."

"I don't know how the Alumni Board functions and therefore do not feel I can comment intelligently upon its placement in the scheme of things."

Our work did not last long. Reorganization was approved with few suggestions. While, of course, it was good for all to know who was to do what and who could boss whom, the major value of re-structuring was simply the act itself, no matter what new structure emerged. It was simply good to tidy up the sock drawer every once in a while.

## CURRICULUM:

As previously mentioned [see ch. 6, "Curriculum"], the word "curriculum" comes from the Latin noun meaning *racecourse* or the verb meaning *to run*. It is the pace to which students are put and the path on which they are routed—the core of what school is all about. Buildings, meetings, faculties, recruitments, enrollments, visiting dignitaries, finance, reorganization, and, yes, accreditation itself are all beholden to the course and momentum of that race.

Two curricula issues, carryovers from the previous year, continued to trouble me: (1) our bar review course and (2) our comprehensive exam. Both had been aimed at improving our passage rate in state bar exams but, in my opinion, the first was inappropriate and the second feckless.

*Bar Review Course:* At our first meeting on August 31, 1970, I moved to transfer to

Paul Gerhardt the law school's ownership and operation of the summertime bar review course —a program of study designed to help law graduates pass the state bar exam. Two reasons were compelling: (1) The ABA accreditors frowned upon law school control of such courses, and (2) Gerhardt assured us that he would faithfully continue the review. Eighteen months ago, the faculty had approved a bar review operated by NWLC [see ch. 4], but now the motion to put the review in private hands was passed with near unanimous affirmation—Jurkins dissenting. Henceforth, our only involvement in the bar review course was as landlord, charging Gerhardt $200 rent for use of a law campus classroom. Later on in the semester, the bar review once again came up in our agenda when college business manager, Bill Malinson, urged us to charge Gerhardt a higher rent. We declined to do so.

And so, without any ostensible hitch, the bar course continued on the same schedule, at the same place, with the same cadre, and under the same format, the only difference being the passing of unseen strings of ownership. The accreditors were now satisfied.

*Comprehensive Exam:* At the beginning of the 1970-71 academic year, I moved once again to rid us of the "comp exam" [see ch. 1 and ch. 4], which required upperclass students to take an annual, all-day test covering all courses thus far taken and mimicking the Oregon State Bar Exam. The composite grade received was entered in the student's transcript and incorporated into the student's grade point average. I felt it was an unnecessary reconnoitering of accumulated lessons. But incumbent colleagues were still not convinced; and the four new faculty members, unfamiliar with the practice, were willing to give it continued trial.

The annual comp test was scheduled for September 2, the same day as freshman orientation. It had been moved back to the start of the academic year, when the previous December scheduling proved to be bad timing. [see ch. 6, "Curriculum"] Professors were given a November 1 deadline to finish their grading. Once those two months passed, the faculty had its fill. The timing of the exam, not its lack of merit, was the key to its demise. It was a test that could not find home in the calendar. Librarian Jurkins moved to abolish the exam and, by unanimous vote, the three-year experiment with comp testing came to good riddance. Ever since that time students have been more content, faculty have been less taxed, and bar results have been better.

*Grade Deadlines:* An important aspect of curricular planning was the business of grading exams. One feature of the grading process plagued us at a series of meetings in the 1970-71 academic year: the deadline for when professors had to finish grading. Grade deadlines were a shopworn issue in the nation's law schools. When to get grades to the students was an issue that seesawed between students anxious to plan their futures and teachers anxious to remain sane. The task of grading as many as, e.g., 120 three-hour essay exams, was tedious and boring. The tedium warranted rest; the boredom induced procrastination.

Another repercussion in the grade report timing was money. Upperclass students desiring to drop out of school in the spring semester were not allowed a refund of their spring semester tuition if that dropout decision was later than four weeks into that semester. Thus, if poor grades played a part in that decision, grades later than four weeks could be costly.

In 1970-71, we were still scheduling first semester exams after the December holiday season and right up to the start of the second semester beginning in late January. Exams would end on Friday, and classes would begin on Monday. Accordingly, at the December 8 faculty meeting, as chair of the Advancement Committee, I moved that all grades should be turned over to Registrar Cornelius no later than February 23—a deadline designed to speed up the grading process and get the grades posted within the tuition-refundable period.

Professor Fagg moved to amend the deadline to March 10—a two week extension beyond tuition refund. Practically all of my colleagues were graduates of large eastern law schools (what Fagg called the "big-hitters") where their fall grades were traditionally forthcoming no sooner than mid-spring semester. It would not be the last time that we took lessons from the traditions of the eastern establishment. Fagg's proposal passed against my lone dissent.

The annual problem of mid-year slow grades could be eased if we would schedule the fall exams before, instead of after, the holiday season. That solution finally came to dawning. At our March 2, 1971 meeting, the faculty finally agreed, after many years of student petitions, to hold fall semester final exams before the December holidays. Beginning in the next academic year, no longer would exams be held in January after the break. No more would exams hamper holidays for students; from then on, exams would vex the vacations of teachers.

*Grade Posting:* Linked with the "deadline" issue, but nonetheless a separate consideration, was the problem of allowing a professor to post exam grades as soon as that grading was completed. The practice had always been that all grades should be posted simultaneously by the registrar because piecemeal postings put undue pressure and, perhaps, embarrassment on those whose grading was unfinished. At the January 19 meeting, I moved to allow postings whenever the individual professor chose to do so. The motion passed—Brown, Fagg, and Jurkins dissenting.

At the March 2 meeting (while I was absent), a motion to reconsider and to require that all grades be posted at the same time and not scattered by separate post-ings was entertained. Surprisingly, it was the student representatives who so moved, and that was enough to ensure its passage. Apparently the majority of students did not want anxiety to be inched out in parcels; they wanted the shock to be dealt from a single report card in one envelope in one swift angst.

*The Williamson Curriculum Report:* As chair of the Curriculum Committee, Professor Bill Williamson dug deep into many issues. His diligence produced a report sixty-one pages long with over twenty proposed motions. Aside from being a planner, Billy was prolix. So lengthy were his considerations that a special weekend retreat was scheduled in early December just for curriculum discussion. Originally scheduled for a distant place, the retreat did not take us far. We stayed entrenched in an all-day session at the law school.

The many agenda items were capped off with Billy's assemblage of some final motions that might best be called "fancies." For the first, he got upon a soap box and took law schools to task by labeling them with "blind adherence to shopworn case methods, casebooks, and Socratic teaching," indicating that they "turn off the social idealism of modern youth" and are wedded "to stifling techniques merely because they are convenient and familiar." His tirade urged innovation "new and viable educa-tion," and non-acceptance of "the status of just another law school."

For Billy, ranting was not enough; there had to be something done about it. Talk without action was a running motor running nowhere. Motion needed doing, action—a motion. And so, he moved. He proposed that his show of colors be made a "rule." After a long period of head-scratching, the movement was tabled indefinitely, not because it idled in neutral, but rather because it ran out of gas—just as Billy knew it would.

His ideas could range from the sublime (witness environmental law) to the downright mischievous (witness the following): It seems a bottle of his vintage wine was missing from the faculty refrigerator; so he moved to instruct campus security guards to search all offices, desk drawers, and lockers for the merchandise. That proposition was rescued from its sweeping invasion of privacy by consigning it to the slow death of "further investigation and report." The report, like the wine itself, is still aging somewhere.

In spite of the oblivion to which his two previous fancies were assigned, William-son kept on firing. The two maneuvers may have been a calculated ploy to make his final effort more plausible by comparison. His last proposal re-raised the issue of canceling classes for George Washington's birthday on February 22 (now President's Day). That proposal had been defeated previously by the 1969-70 faculty. [See ch. 6,

"Scheduling Holidays"] This time it passed without a hitch. For many years, the law school would have another holiday. Likely, this new holiday owed its existence to a softening of the way by Billy's two whimsical vanguards—an educational whine and a missing bottle of wine.

*Elective Courses:* The 1970-71 curriculum racecourse ran us back into the fork between elective-versus-required classes. The small experiment with senior students one year ago [see ch. 6, "Electives"] showed a need for expanding our optional studies. Our course offerings needed more opportunity for a student's motivational pursuit. That meant more elective subjects, which meant freeing up more time slots on our weekly calendar, which meant fewer required courses.

The faculty Curriculum Committee proposal for cutting next year's required courses was vast. Only eight classes had to be taken: Civil Procedure, Constitutional Law, Contracts, Criminal Law, Evidence, Legal Writing and Research, Property Law, and Torts—a total of about 34 credit hours out of the 84 hours required to graduate, thus leaving 50 hours for individual choice. That was a huge departure from past practice.

Ordinarily subject offerings in the curriculum were matters strictly within the province of a school's faculty. But our choice of elective courses drew attention of the trustees' Standing Committee on the Operation of the Law School [SCOLS], whose members were mostly lawyers and judges. Their legal education in decades past had been strictly regimented, keyed to basic fundamentals of law. They were either not yet attuned to the specialization that had infiltrated legal practice, or they were so deeply involved in their own specialty that they saw it as an optimum and everything else as optional. Absolutely essential to a lawyer's understanding, they said, were the courses above mentioned plus Business Organizations (Corporations and Partner-ships), Commercial Law (sales and negotiable instruments), Secured Transactions, Taxation, Administrative Law, Remedies, Wills and Trusts, and others designated for testing on the Oregon Bar Exam, which, they said, gave reason enough to mandate them on the student dance card. Accordingly, SCOLS' preferred list of required courses numbered about 60 credit hours, leaving only 20 hours for electives.

At our December 8, 1970, meeting, the faculty persisted in affording greater flex-ibility to student motivations. Accordingly, the faculty accepted its own curriculum committee's more permissive course plan. At the January 19, 1971 faculty meeting Professor Knudsen, the faculty's delegate to SCOLS, reported that key members of SCOLS were "disturbed." For example, General Chet McCarty, a practicing lawyer and major general in the U.S. Air Force Reserve, was particularly desirous of mandat-ing Taxation, Wills and Trusts, and Conflicts. And so it went, as individuals, one by one, came forth with their notions of required law.

Dean Wren urged the need to prepare a "well-organized statement" in defense of the faculty plan to be delivered at a forthcoming meeting of SCOLS. Compromise was reached and a line was drawn between courses "imposed" and "chosed." But that left a disgruntled faculty: Why did we have to seek SCOLS' acceptance of a faculty action that was strictly curricular business. That, in turn, triggered the beginning of a mounting discontent with the general scheme of things.

The advent of student electives brought about a third and bottom level in the status of a course offering. Now that students could opt for a course, they could kill it. In the course called Future Interests, students could learn the mysteries of the Rule against Perpetuities with its puzzling "fertile octogenarian" and "unborn widow" situations. But those lures were not enough to keep it alive. Because it did not gain enough choosers to justify offering the course, its status moved from *mandatory* to *optional* to *cancelled*.

*Summer School:* We also tried to expand our academic year to include summer classes. Starting in the summer of 1971, NWLC was temporarily scheduled to offer the first summer school session in its history. Fifty-five of our current students were interested in enrollment—most of whom were evening students seeking to shorten their law education. It did not happen. Instituting a perennial summer semester would take more thought.

## STUDENT PETITIONS:

Absent draconian enforcement, every decree will waiver on occasion. Faculty meeting agendas throughout the 1970-71 year continued to be peppered with individual student petitions seeking to bend a rule. Dispensations concerned dismissals, probations, graduations, re-admissions, promotions, schedules, disciplines, absences, tuitions, fees, course transfers, division transfers, school transfers, credit hours, semester residency, and all of the host of strays in and out of the labyrinth through which meanders the paper chase.

For example, at the December 15 meeting, student Jane Weiner petitioned to be given extra time in taking her final exams and to be allowed to answer by oral dictation into a recording machine. Such relaxing of order would be unique to say the least. Law school exams were fixed time and typically written. But, without dissent, the faculty granted Jane's petition, giving her "all the time she needed." She passed her exams with flying colors, graduated, and went on to become the lead counsel in Multnomah County's juvenile justice system. Jane was quadriplegic. Having little to no use of her limbs, she conquered all of law's obstacles and was one of the most exceptional and most determined people I have ever met—making us realize that we had not made her *an exception* to our goals; on the contrary, her abilities were exceptional and goals to be emulated.

It had not been easy for the impaired in the early 1970s to convince the justice system or law schools that they could do the skills necessary for lawyering. Jane Weiner was one of many who set precedent far in advance of the Americans with Disabilities Act, which now mandates accommodations for the so-called "disabled." NWLC has enrolled and graduated the blind, the deaf, the chaired, and others, who have proven the misfit word "disabled" to be nothing more than "abled differently."

Another petitioner—a senior due to graduate—sought the award of a Juris Doctor degree from our law school even though he already had one from Hastings Law School in San Francisco. He got his Hastings law degree in 1949 but went into business instead of lawyering. Two decades later, he was allowed entry into our law studies in order to refresh his knowledge of law. But the "brush-up" saw him finish four complete academic years. Perfect attendance, class preparation, and success on all exams put him in complete compliance with all the requirements for our degree. The question was: Should a former degree—almost twenty years before—deny him a second accolade? We could think of no good answer against it. He became the first lawyer in the nation, perhaps, with two Doctor of Jurisprudence degrees.

An April 1970 petition was a joint plea of two students—husband and wife. It was a strange request and a strange outcome. They urged the faculty to allow them to take their final exams in late August instead of the customary time in early June. Gone from memory and the record are the reasons why. Suffice it to say that in the minds of the faculty the reasons given were not critical. But in the minds of the couple the reasons must have been critical because, when the faculty denied the petition, they quit—deserting nearly a full year of law study and their once chosen law careers.

All such petitioning had to funnel through the Faculty Advancement Committee—Williamson, Brown, and me, as chair. The committee was not empowered to grant or deny the requests; we simply held hearings and made recommendations to the faculty as a whole. But with the increasing number of both students and rules, the waiver pleas were beginning to fill agendas and to try patience. Faculty and its committee were burdened with a lot of work that some would label "administrative" and not "academic." Professors needed to devote their time to writing and teaching and educational policy, not to daily application of general rules to special situations. Rules were made to control circumstances in a uniform, constant manner.

The concern was legitimate but had to guard against aloofness—policy making that declines to face the ramifications of the policy made. Those who do not stoop to witness their ideas at work, are left with theory bereft of reality—an altogether too frequent criticism of the ivory tower. Carried to extreme, the danger in launching principles without facing implementation is bureaucracy from which hypocrisy may grow.

STUDENT BODY PROFILE:

Throughout the nation, 1970 was a year in a time of great student unrest. It meant confrontation with anything authoritative, including faculties. Sometimes the confrontations could end in mere defiance but sometimes in devastation. Just a few months before in Ohio, four student protestors were shot and killed by National Guard on the Kent State campus.

The world beyond NWLC was invading our cloistered walls. Racial and gender civil rights were being aggressively pursued. Our nation was at war on two fronts—violent conflict in Vietnam and saber rattling with the Soviet Union. Those ominous warnings together with the crackle of atomic annihilation and, on the horizon, the clouds of shady dealings from the White House, were not a bright forecast for young people at the doorway of going out into lifelong careers. All of it fostered student preoccupation with or distraction by the noise beyond. Like all graduate schools in the "Seventies," we were heir to lingering undergraduate activism from the "Sixties."

Back east, student protest was having its effect. Princeton suspended classes so that students could campaign during the 1970 elections. At New York University Law School a partial tuition refund was proposed for the period in which the law school was closed during disorder. But at the University of Wisconsin Law School, the dean proposed an opposite financial effect; imposition of a $100 added fee on all students in order to recompense campus property losses due to disorder.

A black woman law dean at Howard University set the record for the shortest deanship in law school history. Upset, on the one hand, by her students who were more interested in demonstration than education and, on the other hand, by her college president's disciplining those students without her consultation, she resigned after less than two months on the job.

When the American Legion military veterans held their 1970 national convention in Portland, Oregon, our town became a target for Vietnam War protesters. Demonstrations spread tentacles onto our college campus resulting in noticeable student involvement during that convention and its prelude.

Activism also reached the law school's machinery. The faculty was bombarded with student petitions of a sort different from personal concerns. One plea, signed by one-third of the student body (mostly first year, day students) protested the building of fifty more parking spaces in our campus lot. The sprawl was called typical "parking lot encroachment." Another plea sought school support for a "Consumer League." Another called for all professors to be present in the Gantenbein Student Lounge on

Mondays and Wednesdays to socialize with the students and their social concerns. Another asserted the need for scheduling two time slots each semester when classes could be cancelled for two hours in order to hold *en masse* student body sessions, town hall style. Another plea argued that the Gantenbein Lounge should be kept open twenty-four hours a day. Another pushed for a two-day rest period between the end of the first semester and the start of the second. Traditionally, the law school had always ended the fall semester and commenced the spring semester without hiatus. As previously stated, that matter was solved when we moved the fall exam period to December before the holidays.

Trouble was also created in the alleged unequal handling of operations between the day and evening divisions. Most notable was the rule that did not allow night students to opt into daytime hour courses, although a day student could enroll in night classes. Disparity in tuitions was the reason. Day tuition for three years totaled higher than evening tuition for four years. Therefore, an evening student paid less for the same course offered in the day.

Another item that disturbed the evening students was the newly imposed infirmary fee. The new daytime students were making an increasing use of that college medical facility. Law student visits to the infirmary at night, when it was often closed, were seldom if ever. Nevertheless, the college now charged all law students an additional infirmary fee of $3.00 per semester. And so, the evening students protested.

No doubt the day student profile was contrary to our night student. The latter was traditionally older with a spouse, maybe kids, and a job or social and civic outlets cultivated long before return to an academic campus pursuit. Accordingly, the evening student was a worker whose attention span at school was filled and left no room for anything other than study and the desire to make a living at the practice of law. Where the night student wanted to know "what?" and "how?", the day student needed to know "why?" Where the night student wanted to harness the horse and do plowing, the day student wanted to ride the horse and do crusading.

Differences between the two bodies reached the point where the first year day class took steps to form its own separate student bar association. Near the end of the 1970-71 year, Sherry Smith was elected the student body leader replacing Jim Hubler, and thus became the first woman student president in the law school's history. It was another harbinger of the times.

Sherry saw the schism forming in her constituency. She sought to close the gap and to allay the ineffectiveness of a student body divided. In the past, the student body had not wanted a "faculty adviser" out of concern that faculty input would unduly influence student affairs. But Sherry felt that much of the day-evening divisiveness was the lack of input from their own common thread—i.e., the school, as personified

**NIGHT AND DAY**

Divisions in the Gantenbein Lounge

by the faculty. Accordingly, she asked me to serve as a link on account of "your sense of fairness." Influenced by flattery, I accepted and was thanked for "taking on yet another extracurricular activity." Indeed, it was a sign-up on my already filled dance card for the next academic year—a year when the day division would soar beyond the evening enrollment and when faculty size would also grow by fifty percent. Closing a stationary gap was one thing; trying to span a gap while it was widening would be quite another.

Finding commonality between day and night students was the key, and there was one area that held promise. Evening students had launched the *Environmental Law* periodical and the *Northwest Environmental Defense Center*. It was uncharacteristic of the night profile—an extracurricular pursuit in a controversial arena that had not been at the forefront of the "Sixties." But now in the "Seventies," our day students warmed to the pursuit. On that common ground, like at dusk and dawn, a synergy was born of the ideals of day and the no-nonsense of night.

PROGRAMS AND PRIORITIES:

Ever the instigator, Dean Wren, continued his penchant for taking on new vistas. He was, to say the most, a patient listener to a sales pitch and, to say the least, a compulsive buyer.

At the September 15, 1970, faculty meeting he proposed that we commence an educational program for para-professionals, to be taught at Portland Community College. At the September 22 meeting, he invited a scoutmaster to make a presentation for our sponsoring a troop of Explorer Boy Scouts. At the September 27 meeting, a spokesman from the Columbia Regional Association of Governments [CRAG]—a federally induced amalgamation of local municipalities—came to us with a promise of $5,000 of funding to help in developing public housing in our area. In December, the dean reported that we would be doing a workshop for high school administrators on "Due Process of Law."

In January, the dean sought to elbow our way into a study being done in our own backyard by the National Conference of State Trial Judges. The local Multnomah County Circuit Court judicial system had gained national attention for streamlining its docket so that cases from filing to trial could take the short time of just six months, whereas scheduling in some metropolitan areas was taking as long as four to six years. Wren wanted our school to have a hand in that phenomenal difference.

The mounting list of project proposals prompted the faculty to create a Program Priorities Committee chaired by Professor Fagg. All projects were to be passed along to him (essentially a committee of one), for weighing each proposal in the context of all, with attention to our limited resources and to prioritizing. "More-patience-less-impulse," was the faculty directive.

It did not stop the dean—the reserve naval officer to whom lying-in-port was anathema and full-steam-ahead was standing orders. In April of 1971, we were committed to host a convention of all law students in Pacific Northwest law schools.

Near the end of the 1970-71 academic year, Dean Wren's exuberance got the best of him. He supported an annual one-day seminar proposed by the so-called "Defense Research Institute." The seminar program insisted on compulsory attendance of senior students and cancellation of all classes to allow all other students the option of attending. The dean was under the impression that the Institute was connected to the U.S. Department of Defense. When I informed him that it was an organization of tort defense lawyers and liability insurers, he blushingly reversed engines and "made aft."

## GRADUATION DAY 1971:

June 13, 1971, was graduation day—my fourth as a law professor. As in all of those years, the ceremony was a joinder of law and college graduates. What had previously been a stir within the law faculty on why there were not two separate ceremonies was now becoming an agitation. In the next two years, the agitation would boil.

The 1971 graduation was the first in the law school's eighty-eight year history in which an honorary scholastic degree was authorized. One student was so praised. The maiden *magna cum laude* degree was bestowed on maiden Ann Morgenstern, editor-in-chief of our maiden *Environmental Law* publication for two straight, seminal years.

"Graduation," some say, is the end of school examination; whereas others prefer to call it "Commencement"—the start of new practice. But in law careers, the truth is that it is neither an end of examination nor the start of practice. One more piece of jigsaw in the puzzle lies between a doctor of jurisprudence and a professional—the ominous "bar exam."

## PASSING THE BAR:

As evidenced by two separate accrediting agencies (ABA and AALS), there was a noticeable separation between law professors and law professionals. Although linked by their chosen Law discipline, educators and practitioners from time to time on certain matters stood off from one another. It was not a *break* in relations—just a disjunction. But it crept into attitudes.

The distancing had never occurred to me when I was in the practice of law, but I gradually sensed it after a few years as a full-time faculty member. Our accreditation pursuit with the ABA furnished some environs for it, but I felt it more distinctly in our dealings with the Oregon State Bar. Millard Ruud and professors in other states throughout the nation told me that the division and the attitudes that came with it were not peculiar to Oregon.

Professor Williamson and I were the only two Oregon Bar members at that time. Brown, Fagg, Jensen, Knudsen, and Wren all came from out-of-state and had no previous involvement in the local professional scene. It would not get any better when next year's professors (Bloomenthal, Bross, Hughey, and Newell) would show up from places beyond the Pacific northwest. They were all strangers to Oregon and its lawyering society.

Nowhere was the separation more distinct than at that gauntlet where graduates who had been honored by their school had yet to run their worth through the profession, that is to say, to "pass the bar." From some educators' standpoint, the bar exam was deemed an affront to their three or four years of teaching, testing, and certifying their students with an academic degree. From some lawyers' standpoint, a law school diploma as a carte blanche entry into bar practice, would be a rude snub of the profession's prerogative in deciding its own membership. Such effronteries, in a few, became a downright unfriendly disregard of one another.

NWLC was in the unique position of having to pay particular attention to that divisiveness, because our two pursued accreditors came from those adverse camps. Both accreditors were inclined to use bar exam passage rates as a barometer on alma maters. The *professional* association [ABA] made the ability to pass the profession's licensing test a major gauge on a school's worth, while the *professorial* association [AALS] shared only a mild interest in such measurement.

The Supreme Court of Oregon was the final overseer above the Bar and the schools. The judiciary was constitutionally in charge of who was allowed to appear within the sanctum beyond the "bar"— that courtroom divider that separated spectating from adjudicating. Back in the mid-1960s, Chief Justice William McAllister (my old boss when I clerked at the Oregon Supreme Court a decade before) took a strong interest in educators and bar examiners getting together on the licensing of lawyers. So, he established OCLAB [the Oregon Council on Legal Admittance to the Bar] composed of the deans of the three Oregon law schools, faculty representatives, the nine Oregon State Bar Examiners, and a liaison from the Oregon Bar Board of Governors. The Chief Justice would preside. Dean Wren and I served on that Council.

**WILLIAM MCALLISTER**

Out of those initial OCLAB meetings grew two innovations: (1) A Bridging-the-Gap education program for new bar admittees, in which I was made coordinator; and (2) a refinement of the chronological steps involved in preparation of the bar exam. Under the current sequence, professors of the three Oregon law school were called on to critique the Bar exam questions after the examinees had taken the test, after the examiners had graded the test, and after the Supreme Court had admitted the successful exam takers to the Bar. [See ch. 1] For years academicians had complained that critiques at that late stage were feckless. They wanted to evaluate before the exam was even given. A compromise was reached that made neither faction happy. The critiques would be allowed after the exam was taken but before it was graded.

Some academicians would continue to argue that a law degree ought to be a good enough credential to justify competence to practice law or to argue for bar exam questions designed by professors, as is the case in many other states. The bar officers, on the other hand, countered with the notion that a true bar exam should not be just another schoolhouse test. Bar scrutiny, they argued, fosters a dutiful concern within the profession about the ability of new lawyers and about the uniformity of law schooling itself.

The contest of attitudes had much to do with that tired, old wheeze about theory and practice being at odds, when, in fact, nothing could be more theoretical than practice and nothing more practical than theory in the application of laws to facts. It was an opposition no more opposed than the two ends of the same rope.

And so it was and still is, that the profession stood guard at the exit gate from law schools. Likewise, the ABA also posted guard at the entry gate of law schools into accreditation. Likewise, the AALS posted its own guard at that accrediting gate. Likewise, the bench, in the form of supreme courts, also patrolled those entries. Thus, at both ends of schooling, ABA, AALS, state Bars, and the judiciary operate separately on who shall be a finished product for lawyering.

## ACCREDITATION RE-VISITED:

Having gained the temporary good graces of the ABA, we had taken much of the 1970-71 academic year as time off from accreditation pursuit. I took some of that time to prepare for and to climb the 11,000 foot Mount Hood. It was arduous at dizzying heights in rarefied oxygen, calling for ice axe, crampons, and roping up while skirting a sulfuric crater along the hogback and through the chute to reach the top. At the summit, we took rest and champagne, but only small sips, for as the climb leader warned, we were two miles high and undone. As all stair climbers know, while it may be more toilsome to ascend stairs, there is far more danger in facing the risks of coming down them.

That reminder was also there for NWLC at the close of the 1970-71 year. We had been catnapping and sipping at what was merely momentary. We had yet to prove ourselves to watchful audiences beyond the cloister. The temporary nod given from one in the audience was just a smattering of applause and still a long way from ovation. We were at one of several summits facing the risks of coming down.

# 1971: TIME CONTEXT

Vietnam War spreads to Laos.

Lieutenant William Calley and others in the chain of command are tried, found guilty and sentenced for the homicides at the My Lai massacre.

N.Y. Times and Washington Post publish the Pentagon Papers, a history of U.S. secret activity leading to Vietnam involvement—leaked to the press by Daniel Ellsburg.

Some polls show 60 percent of Americans oppose the war.

White House "plumbers unit" (whose mission was to plug leaks) burglarizes psychiatrist office to get patient Ellsburg's files.

Twenty-sixth Amendment to the U.S. Constitution lowers voting age to 18.

U.S. Supreme Court finds school busing for desegregating legal.

President Nixon appoints Lewis Powell and William Rehnquist to U.S. Supreme Court.

U.S. explodes an underground hydrogen bomb in Alaska.

Many are killed when police storm the Attica Penitentiary in New York to quell a prison uprising.

Cigarette ads are banned on U.S. television and radio.

D.B. Cooper skyjacks a flight to Portland, parachuting with $200,000, and disappears forever.

# 10
# THE WREN-FAGG REGIME: PART ONE
## *1971-72*

### *GROWING OR WANDERING*

W e could have coasted on the momentum of the momentous 1969-70 and 1970-71 academic years, but we did not. The shifts and shakes, slides and quakes of growing kept things volatile. An aging night institution was still adapting to its recent daylight hours, its fresh cadre, its spic and span quarters, and its re-birth among law schools.

Blisters come with new boots, and the rub is forecasting. How does one plan a new future from an outdated past? Four new professors made a fifty percent increase in faculty size—a sizeable block in faculty votes. Ahead of us, however, was the task of adding another block of new professors. It would be the largest faculty gain in the school's history, then or now.

Shine on the new complex still gleamed when plans for a fourth building developed. Before the year got underway, the current operating budget was labeled "clearly inadequate" and sorely in need of "immediate and radical revision." Plans for a summer school were on a yo-yo that spun between startup and shutdown. The newest law library book count (approximately 28,000) was still far short of what it took to be a satisfactory research laboratory. The faculty needed more staff support. Electives, grades, tests, teacher loads, semester hours, the balance between day and night classroom credits, and other curricular matters were mounting concerns. Our student body organization was torn by differing day and night profiles. And student learning was vexed by a world outside full of troubles storming at the walls of Academe.

Pushing and pulling on those attentions was our desire to please the tentative trust given us by the nation's lawyers [ABA] and to gain the trust of the nation's law teachers [AALS]. And to top it off, our cup was brimming over; the pour of applications to study law with us was so large that filling without spilling became a prediction based on guess, not gauge.

Just a little over a year ago, we could not see in shadows; now suddenly we seemed blinded by brightness.

## ADMINISTRATION:

Dean Wren's administrative style had always favored the idea of exposing each professor to all aspects of school *business*, as distinct from school *academics*. He believed in a strong faculty and its committee system of administration. It was a feature of our law school operations that has come through the decades—a faculty-operated school. Wren regularly rotated each professor through the chairs of each committee: budget, curriculum, advancement, financial aid, placement, building, admissions, and others that arose from time to time. In that way, he had hoped, in his words, "to alleviate the under-administered state of the law school."

I recoiled at the word "under-administered." From the first day of my full-time teaching four years before, my time seemed a case of *over*-administration at the expense of academic ventures. While business boiled, scholarship simmered on a back burner. Accreditation was a fascinating kitchen but not without a longing eye on that back burner.

Then, in the summer before the 1971-72 year, Dean Wren changed his organizational outlook when he noted a "disproportionate number of administrative problems requiring a great deal of faculty time." The new approach involved a lot more "middle-management." He began the change with a new "Associate Dean" position. Then, at mid-year, we would hire an "Assistant Dean" with principle duties concerning student affairs. Near the end of the year, we would take on a second assistant dean with duties in academic affairs. There would also be an "Administrative Assistant to the Dean," which was one of those upgrades in name only; secretary Doris McCroskey continued in her same work but now under the new title. In keeping with military rank, the new Associate Dean would be immediately beneath the Dean and would supervise the assistant deans and administer to the faculty committees.

Wren and Professor Fred Fagg III had worked together that summer to lay out the reorganization. The hand of Fred, the MBA graduate and son of a former university president, was a heavy imprint on the new approach. Wren appointed Fred to the new Associate Dean office. It was the start of Fred's second year at NWLC.

As one of his first functions in the new role, Associate Dean Fagg prepared for the college trustees a set of detailed written profiles of the separate functions of the law school Dean, Associate Dean, Assistant Dean, Registrar, Administrative Assistant to the Dean, Law Librarian, Assistant Law Librarian, and Bookstore Manager. The Associate Dean's own written profile made it very clear his office was second-in-command and charged with "formulating..., supervising..., presiding..., developing..., directing..., controlling..., ex-officiating..., conducting... assisting" in virtually every aspect of law school business. The catch-all clause in the profile summed it up: the Associate Dean "coordinates the implementation of all policies, programs, plans, and activities of the law school." Its apparent thrust did not go unnoticed by a faculty longing to be unbridled yet keeping hands on the reins.

Strangely, the reorganization did not include an independent law school development officer—a money raiser. Mary Ann Normandin had been our sole link to the College Development Office and its supervisor, Glenn Gregg. But President Howard took her away as his official "Advisor to the President." It left us with no immediate dollar developer.

Pressed by President Howard, the "dean team regime," as some called it, now pushed for even greater direct involvement of SCOLS in our faculty work. That trustee standing committee was originally created by trustee resolution dated October 6, 1966, and was composed of trustees, supreme court justices, trial judges, senior law partners, law alumni, five old Northwestern trustees, journalists, bank presidents, industrialists, corporate entrepreneurs, one faculty representative, and two law students. [See ch. 6, "SCOLS"] Chair of SCOLS was lawyer Paul Boley, who proved to be of immeasurable assistance in the accreditation pursuit. SCOLS was intended to be the front-line operator of law school business. As the faculty would grow in size and experience, the notion was that SCOLS would gradually retire as an operations entity and would resort to being simply a body of overseers.

By 1971, the transition of operations from SCOLS to faculty had been subtly underway. But in the 1971 new structuring of the law school administration, SCOLS involvement was revitalized. At mid-year William Swindells, Sr., took over as the new chairman of SCOLS. He then appointed certain members to work in liaison with our faculty committees. Oregon Supreme Court Justice Ralph Holman, law alumni president John Ryan, lawyers Bob Gilley and John Jaqua, and Boley were assigned to work with the faculty budget committee. To the faculty Curriculum Committee, Swindells designated Oregon Supreme Court Judge Arno Denecke, U.S. Attorney Sid Lezak, U.S. Air Force Reserve General Chet McCarty, and tax lawyer David

WILLIAM SWINDELLS, SR.

Patullo. To the faculty Admissions Committees, Swindells appointed Justice Holman and lawyers Lofton Tatum and Robert C. Wall. Liaison was intended to be a courtesy and advisory only. But law professors, especially the newer ones, saw it as patronizing, micro-managing, and insulting. If the chance of linking SCOLS and faculty in operational labors had any thought of leaving the ground, it was a hope doomed never to fly.

In other aspects of the accreditation pursuit, the support of SCOLS individuals was profound. But as potential participants in professorial tasks, they were the first to see frustration. Jobbing was not the best use of their clout. I think it was SCOLS member John Ryan who told me that, as a so-called "higher-up" on the management scale, he "felt like Keneshaw Mountain Landis [a one-time Commissioner of Major League Baseball] trying to advise Babe Ruth how to bat."

Accreditors wanted career educators in charge of law schooling—full knowing, however, that educators needed backers. Such assurances come from community leaders—people out-front with wherewithal and trust. The faculty was to make the case for needed goals, but trustees and SCOLS had to give the needed assurances. Bestowal does not just go to those who *have promised*; it also goes to those who *have promise*.

## THE NEW ASSOCIATE DEAN:

Associate Dean Fred Fagg took to his new position with a passion. No one would have labeled it usurpation or ambition. It was more like a ravenous appetite. I witnessed that passion on the first day we met in the summer of 1969 as we strolled the college campus. [See ch. 6, "Walk-ons"] Raised at the knee of a university-president father, Fred was destined for an administrative role in education. He and I would have occasion to differ on economic-political issues but not on how to school lawyers.

For me, good administrators were not a problem, but I do not speak for all of my colleagues. Some saw administrators as authoritarians who ought to be minimalized and contained. Indeed a thin line separates an administrator from an autocrat—a distinction between those who *manage* an idea and those who *mandate* an idea—the difference between a talent organizer and a control freak—those who manage control and those who seize it.

Fred's imprint on administration began at once. On August 29, 1971, he presided over a specially called faculty meeting, which Professor Jim Bross, the new faculty secretary and minute-taker, called "Armageddon" on account of Fred's dire forecasting. The new Associate Dean pointed out great conflicts in our future budgetary plans. The current budget was "clearly inadequate;" the library was a "major disability;" the paucity of secretarial help was "critical;" "significant dollar increases" were needed for our periodical publication, our development plans, and our building maintenance.

All twelve full-time professors were present at that meeting, including the four new arrivals: Bloomenthal, Hughey, Newell, and Bross. And there were student representatives present as well—five of them. For all of those new faces, fresh at the threshold of new career choices, Armageddon was not the brightest entry into a new year, nor did it make its messenger gleam. Those of us who had been around during the last several years (Registrar Cornelius, Assistant to the Dean McCroskey, Professor Williamson and myself) were accustomed to bleak alarms. But the four newest faces grew long, and I made it a point to do some private counseling.

**FOUR NEW PROFESSORS (1971)**
Clockwise from upper left: Hal Bloomenthal, Doug Newell, Jim Bross, Jerry Hughey.

At the September 29 faculty meeting, Fred was more explicit about operational change. He detailed his procedures for money procurement and tracking expenses. Operational functions once performed by faculty committees would now be performed by "individual directors." Committees would continue to develop policy. Hierarchal graphs and flow charts were distributed. The Associate Dean would henceforth chair the Budget and Faculty Appointments Committees and would be ex-officio at all other committees.

As the law school's fiscal overseer, Associate Dean Fagg admonished on more thrifty use of paper and other office supplies. He also announced that in the future, all formal requests to the college business office for expense reimbursements would require, not only the Dean's signature, but would also require the Associate Dean's signature. The purse was being shifted and its strings double-knotted. As always, sulking followed exhortation.

The September 29 meeting grew long and necessitated a motion to table all remaining items on the agenda. It passed. The minutes of new faculty secretary Bross labeled the reorganizational discussion, "Heavy with *Wordly* Cares." It could have been a typographical error but was most likely Bross's whimsy, which had begun to show itself . His minutes ended with a fancied proposal for building "a suitable rack for the many hats of the Associate Dean."

I had handed Assistant Professor Bross the baton of minute-taker, a duty for which I had humbly volunteered as a veteran but which now, like hazing, was assigned to the faculty rookie. Boredom in the role caused both of us to season the minutes with caprice—the antidote for tedium. Where my attempts had been cartoons, his were literary allusion. For instance, upon the Dean's return from a trustee meeting seeking a revised budget, Bross could not resist: "All hail the brave dean's return from battle either carrying his budget or lying on it." Bross tagged faculty get-togethers as "Bound to Meet;" Development programs as "Beat the Mounds;" and Admissions standards as "Metes and Bounds." In comment about the length of faculty meetings, Bross wrote that Professor Alan Jensen (our resident cross-country exerciser) "runs the marathon faster than we meet one." In speaking of graduation ceremony, Bross suggested that instead of the usual mortarboard caps, there should be a beanie with a propeller "affixed to deflect hot air flow from speeches." Indeed, the air at professorial altitudes was rarified—an oxygen deprival that infected the counting of minutes with giddy accounting.

Whimsy was at first a good-natured reaction to Fred's management style. But once acceptance played out, and so too whimsy, resistance followed. One such defiance occurred in the spring of 1972, when the Multnomah County District Attorney office sought to take on some of our students as summertime clerks. But the

D.A. had no money to pay them, so he suggested that the law school should give the clerks academic credit on their law school transcripts as consideration for the service. At the March 12 faculty meeting, Professor Knudson so moved. But Deans Wren and Fagg were opposed unless school supervision was involved. Furthermore, Fagg insisted that the student clerks would have to pay summer tuition dollars for the school supervision. But Knudsen said he would be glad to supervise for no pay. To which, Fagg observed, that the student payment was consideration for the education and the credit hours bestowed. Schools are not in the business of welfare education, he argued, and could not afford, nor would accreditors condone, running that business without pay.

But Knudsen contended that while students did not expect *to be paid* for their pro bono work neither did they expect *to pay* for it. But, said Fagg, it would not be fair to other students who had to pay tuition for their credit hours.

Whereupon, the matter was tabled and referred to me, as clinic director, for study and report. Then, at the April 19, 1972 faculty meeting, I recommended that two hours of credit, tuition free, be awarded for school supervised summer clinic work at any public agency.

From there, discussion went back to where we had started—a battle swinging to and fro between charitable, then educational, then business motives. The associate dean continued to argue against giving away free credit hours. It struck him as the charitable support of government—a situation that ought to be the other way around.

That prompted Professor Williamson to widen, not to shrink, the scope of the motion. He moved to include students doing gratis law work for private businesses as well as public agencies.

After more heated discussion, the amendment carried and the main motion as thus amended passed. Henceforth, student *pro bono* work in summer law offices (public or private) would be given law school course credit. Fagg then (in something of a pique) moved that, likewise, tuition should not be charged for any law school clinic work whatsoever, whether summer, spring, winter, or fall, whether public, private, or *school* service. The motion failed, but it further focused the issue.

In retrospect, the pro and con of the issue were sides for legitimate debate. It was a seminal encounter, that would be shared by many law schools over the decades, thus making it a matter of national concern. Accreditors saw externships as a danger that would turn law schools back into the old practice of "Reading law" (i.e., apprenticing) as a way of becoming a lawyer. It led to tighter accreditation rules and the spread of independent funding groups like the "Public Interest Law Project" [PILP].

Unfortunately, our treatment of the issue in Spring 1972 had been tainted with the issue of authority as tempered by the sting of audacity.

## ENROLLMENT:

On the opening day of September 1971, we enrolled about 490 law students. We had conservatively budgeted for only 370. While we had saved leeway for a larger number, we had no idea that there would be 120 more than anticipated and 170 more than the previous year. Almost half of the enrollees were first-year entering students—120 day and 120 evening. As many as 40 of the evening "first years" had applied for the day division but settled for night school after the day seats filled. There had been well over 550 applications for admission to our entering class; thus, more than 300 were turned away at our gates because we were full, not because they were unacceptable. The numbers were phenomenal when considering that just two years before we had a school enrollment of just 220 including approximately 85 first years with virtually no one barred at the gate because of crowding.

Our current 240 first year matriculators numbered more than any school in the Pacific northwest. The other two law schools in Oregon (Willamette University and the University of Oregon) enrolled about 140 each. Stanford Law School in California entered 165. But to put numbers in perspective, Harvard on the east coast (traditionally, one of the nation's largest enrollers) took in a first year class [560] larger than all three Oregon law schools put together and larger than NWLC's entire student body.

## FACULTY-STUDENT RATIO:

Student body size was not the only enlargement at NWLC; our full-time faculty also grew. Professors increased from eight to twelve. Consequently, the ratio of students per faculty member did not worsen. It continued to hover at about 40:1. Even when accreditors allowed part-time instructors and evening students to be infused at smaller equivalencies, the reconfiguration produced a proportion still larger than the preferred rate of around 25:1.

We were relieved when ABA Consultant Millard Ruud told us that accreditors were not terribly concerned about our student-faculty ratio. All over the nation, the ratios in legal education were being swamped by student numbers. The undermining of ratios, we were told, was always instigated by rising student bodies outracing professor numbers leaving the latter to catch up. Our promise of more faculty hires was sufficient to satisfy.

But the manipulating of per capitas was more than just math. The adjusting called for some policy decisions. What did we seek? Did we want lower or larger class sizes? How large could a law faculty be and yet be collegial? Did we want to be a big or small law school? Breadth or depth? What would make us different? What made us better?

Those decisions were new to us. They were mentioned but never deliberated. We were too busy with imminence to be concerned with eminence. Growth was at hand and plotted our course. The choice was whether to diet or to binge. Eventually, as with all addiction, it was indulgence that kept growing until one day we would happen to note that obsession had made the decision for us.

## BUDGETING SURPLUS INCOME:

Oliver Wendell Holmes, Jr. said, "Life is painting a picture, not doing a sum." He was frowning upon the penchant of some to measure life's values by numbers—quantifying instead of qualifying. Having said as much, no organization should discount the "counting house." There, measure is in dollars placed in sheets, charts, graphs, ledgers, columns, line items, accounts, journals, budgets, and all other ways in which money talks.

The flood of enrollment made the prior year's projections for our current 1971-72 budget a shambles on both incoming and outgoing money. We gained about $100,000 in unanticipated net income, which included $63,000 in extra tuition, fees, and book purchases and $23,500 in surplus carryover from our previous 1970-71 under-estimated income. All of that windfall amounted to a seventeen percent increase over our $570,000 budget projections. The $100,000 unanticipated income would be the inflationary equivalent of about $550,000 today. If that same seventeen percent surplus over budget were to happen modernly in our current operating budgets, the equivalency would be almost a $4,000,000 surplus. Witness the spell cast by numbers.

Of course, our income excess was by no means profit. We could admit of none. A charitable school is a non-profit organization. The surplus had to be rectified by expenditure and educational lay-away. Instead, increased students meant increased service to be provided. Accordingly, our current operating budget of $570,000 was revised to expenses of $675,000 (present and future).

Just as burgeoning enrollment and its consequent elevation of income and expense had upset our current budgeting, so too it promised to wreak havoc on next year's predictions as well. The 1972-73 proposed budget had to balance and had to be on President Howard's desk by November 1971. Unfortunately, it was a deadline imposed far sooner than previous years and far too early for us to know how much service (to "paint a picture") and how many bodies and dollars (to "do a sum") would be under our charge ten months later.

SCOLS shared faculty concerns with how to meet and balance the rising expense of educating so many. President Howard saw that concern and addressed it at a September 24, 1971, meeting of SCOLS. He said that SCOLS and the faculty should "not be concerned with the amount to be raised for capital development." We should "concentrate on building an outstanding law school." The same notion was applied to the price tag called "tuition." He emphasized the importance of that bifurcation of functions—the separation of incoming returns and outgoing services. But that was not an easy disengagement. Turning out a good product, ignites the raising of money, and money in return is the catalyst for a good product. Nevertheless, Howard wanted SCOLS and faculty to focus on good educational service, leaving the job of where the money would come from to the Board of Trustees and college developers where fiscal and academic pursuits would be balanced.

Although well-said, it was not well-practiced. How could the law faculty separate what we sought to deliver from what would be received? In contract law, the exchange of one value for another is called "consideration"—a word derived from Latin for being *considerate* in the give and take of trade. That one office would regard only one-half of the exchange while a different office saw to the other half, was not only inconsiderate, it was quite improbable. Mutual promises, like ying-yang, were wedded by *quid pro quo*.

## TUITION:

The president's attempt to part duties came to focus on the matter of tuition. How much should it be? About the first week of November, our 1972-73 proposed budget was submitted to President Howard by Deans Wren and Fagg without prior faculty consultation. It was our first one million dollar budget—a whopping $325,000 increase over our current revised budget of $675,000. It called for annual tuition raises of $300 for day and $150 for evening, making day tuition $1,900 and evening tuition $950. That would be a total package of $5,700 for three years of day education and $3,800 for four years of evening education. We were told that President Howard had approved those dollar amounts.

At the November 17 faculty meeting, Dean Wren sought faculty approval of the proposed budget. Needless to say, the faculty was upset about the lack of input prior to submission to Howard. Professor Doug Newell was particularly critical. This was Doug's first semester on the faculty and among his first challenges of upper management—a scrutiny that would become his watch.

I moved to table a vote on faculty approval because of no opportunity to digest the momentous considerations in a budget that was fifty percent larger than our current budget. Wren, the presider, hastened to explain that prior consultation with the faculty was made impossible by recent developments and time considerations. Time was still pressing he said. He had to have faculty endorsement before taking the proposal to SCOLS. The non-debatable, debated motion to table was defeated and the Wren-Fagg-Howard budget was approved, by a disgruntled faculty.

The next step was to pass the budget through SCOLS at its mid-December 1971 meeting. There, it met serious concern. After the faculty endorsement, President Howard had amended the evening raise on tuition to equal the day raise in dollars; i.e., both hikes should be $300, thus, making the annual evening tuition $1,100. That jump for night students brought major dissent at the SCOLS meeting. The previous annual tuitions of day and night had always been a 2:1 ratio. Thus, each year night students would pay half as much as day students. Howard's jump changed that ratio. Furthermore, his evening tuition raise would add up to $1,200 over four years of schooling, whereas the day tuition raise would total only $900 over three years. The $300 night tuition raise would constitute a 37.5 percent raise while the $300 day tuition would be a 19 percent raise.

On the evening tuition issue, two contingents within the twenty SCOLS members developed. One contingent, opposing the president's amendment, was composed of the five former trustees of old Northwestern College of Law plus the president of the law school alumni association; the chair of the law school's Board of Visitors; the president of the law school student bar association; and me, the law faculty representative. These nine were largely lawyers and judges with ties to the old Northwestern downtown Portland law school. The other contingent supporting the Howard tuition amendment, was eleven members of the college's Board of Trustees, whose eyes were on finance trends nationally.

Both proponents and opponents cited the 1965 Merger Agreement for their positions. Items 1 and 4 stated:

"1. [T]he express purpose of the merger shall be to provide for the continuation of... evening law school... at a cost which can be afforded by those in need...."

"4. [F]ees charged to student in the evening law school shall be lower than the fees charged to day law students...."

Proponents of the Howard raise jump pointed out that the Merger Agreement was not violated because night-timers would still be paying $800 less per year than day-timers and $1,300 less over their four and three year respective terms.

Opponents suggested that the proponents were missing the spirit of the Merger clauses which were designed to afford opportunity to those less privileged or unable to apply themselves to law study during business or family hours. Opponents juxtaposed the proposed $1,100 evening tuition against the $330 evening tuition at the time of the Merger signing in 1965. That would be greater than a 300 percent increase in just seven years—an escalation exceeding the bounds of "a cost which can be afforded by those in need."

Proponents observed, however, that affordability is a vague condition open to debate about what consumer marketing could bear. As for that market, President Howard offered the fact that "our evening division now has the lowest tuition [at $800] in the United States."

SCOLS approved the proposed 1972-73 law school operating budget, as amended by President Howard, but not without misgiving. In submitting the proposal to the Board of Trustees there were written majority and minority positions.

The Board of Trustees approved the law school budget after a small re-tooling. The evening tuition would be $1,000. That was a raise of $200, a figure set between Howard's $300 proposal and the faculty approved $150 proposal. It was a minor fix. But, the compromise set a precedent—a kernel from which a field could grow. The former 2:1 ratio (i.e., evening raises 50 percent of day raises) would no longer be a limitation. Tuition raises, viewed as percentages, were now permitted to be higher for night vis-a-vis day education.

FEES:

Pay for higher education was more than just tuition. Aside from the cost of books, there were, in those days, a number of "fees" tacked on. The law school charged each student (day and evening) a $15.00 annual fee for mimeographing. There was also a $2.50 fee for the Student Bar Association. The college made the day students pay a $50.00 "activity fee" for use of the college student union, gym, track, tennis courts, swimming pools, theater, and other facilities and events—for which the evening students paid only $15.00. There was also a "building fee" of $30.00 (day) and $20.00 (evening). Distinguishing the services, expenditures, and other purposes underlying "fees" from those underlying "tuition" was a maneuver about as puzzling as drawing the line between mud and wet dirt. For that reason, the practice of tagging on fees to tuition instead of including them in tuition, was in subsequent years curtailed. But pulling out fees, as every gardener know, was about as permanent as weeding. Fees have a way of re-seeding.

SCHOLARSHIPS AND LOANS:

Curiously and unlike other businesses, schools simultaneously counter their charges for education with efforts to alleviate those charges. At that relief, NWLC was weak in those early years. Less than four percent of our student body were given scholarship monies. All recipients were day students. Loan monies were likewise limited to day students. A $50,000 fund drive for scholarships was instituted. Today, forty percent of our students (day and evening) have some form of financial aid to offset charges.

CAPITAL DEVELOPMENT:

Other money development problems loomed. Now in just its second year, our building complex needed a new fourth building to house offices, cafeteria, bookstore, seminar rooms, and a faculty lounge and reading room. Professors Williamson and Newell began development of a master plan. First steps necessary were to raise capital money; but, as aforesaid, according to President Howard, building development was a matter for the Board of Trustees and college development office. Nevertheless, according to the law faculty, building an "outstanding law school" education included both buildings and the money to build them.

Another capital development was needed for a library that was sorely remiss. We had about 25,500 volumes as of November 1971. The count went to about 28,500 as of March 1972. At that rate, the growth was far short of reaching a 60,000 AALS requirement. While a previous $50,000 fundraiser goal for library was reached in December 1971, it would likely add only 5,000 volumes at most. Our library shelf capacity had a potential for a mere 44,000 volumes. Students seating capacity in the library was only 140, far short of the AALS gauge requiring seats at 65 percent of the existing student body, which meant a 320 seating capacity.

President Howard promised a $5 million capital fund drive for both buildings and library. Faculty hoorahs soon turned hisses at learning that the fund drive would be spread over eight years throughout the 1970s. All money-raising (aside from tuition and fees) came under the direction of Glenn Gregg, the college development officer. The law school did not have its own development officer. That remote arrangement, combined with Howard's eight-year time-line, caused law professors to question how attentive college developers would be to our immediate needs. Those concerns brought President Howard to visit the law school to urge the faculty once again not to worry about money-raising. Build a sound operation and capital will come, was his message. It was reassuring—but puzzling too. As disciples of law, trained to explore every corner of suspicion and to take charge of solving problems, it was difficult, if not downright impossible, to be simply pawns confined to one column; lawyers had a need to be immersed in the whole board game.

Associate Dean Fred Fagg saw the frustration and tried to mend the gap between faculty concerns and college development. As chair of the faculty budget committee and one who had worked closely with President Howard on our capital development, Fred wrote the faculty and assured that "the College had made a commitment to a superior law school." He knew, however, that promise was not enough, so he tried to provide some detail. He reported that preliminary groundwork had been taken on building plans "so that the law school will be prepared for the *serendipity* of a building donor." The word "serendipity" made me frown; it connoted stumbling on good fortune. It prompted me to write, "I trust that our discovery of a building donor will not be 'serendipitous;' rather, it should be a well-planned, active pursuit." To be sure, I was picking at words, but the thought that the development drive might be on automatic pilot waiting for a tailwind to happen, was the very lack of aggression that bothered the faculty. There should be nothing "serendipitous" about a goal that needed doing.

Law professors were not left out of the entire development picture. While they were not to be developers, they were encouraged to be "developees." At the January 12, 1972 faculty meeting, Dean Wren urged each law professor to make annual donations to the capital drive. It was important to be able to represent to potential givers that the faculty had pledged unanimous support. Associate Dean Fagg took it one step further. He moved that all professors be *required to donate*. Wren's *request* had found no quarrel, but Fagg's *demand* ran into serious qualms. Majority vote should not frisk minority pocketbooks, was the complaint. "Commanding a gift" is an oxymoron. Where's the charity in debt payment?

A motion to table Fred's motion carried. He did not give up. He then urged that every professor give Dean Wren a monetary pledge in writing and reaffirmed that "only a unanimous support would produce the desired public relations value." His attempt to salvage slivers of success from the shards of defeat, was dogged.

## FUTURE ADMISSIONS:

As aforesaid [see ch. 9, "Admissions"], the rapid ascent in numbers of those interested in a law education put all law schools at enormous heights that were especially dizzy for those of us who tried to soar on fledgling wings. The rise showed no signs of leveling off. As of December 1971, the expected number of aspirants taking the Law School Admissions Test [LSAT] was 137,500, a twenty percent increase over the previous year. The 145 ABA accredited law schools had a maximum capacity that could handle only 36,000 beginning law students. Crunching demand funneled into pinched supply. The jam made competitive business—customers against customers and shops against shops, the former for few-seat quantity, the latter for high-test quality. It definitely changed the hospitality of old Northwestern—the school that had been a haven willing to take on all customers. Gone were the days of open doors—not because it was questionable, but rather because it was out of the question.

Work on admissions to the 1972-73 academic year had begun before the start of the 1971-72 year. At an August 28, 1971 faculty meeting, we set a goal of 120 first-year day and 80 first-year evening enrollees for the 1972-73 year. We had few clues as to how to reach those goals twelve months later. Having withstood the surge in 1970-71, we had only that one year of experience upon which to draw—enough to caution us, but not enough to give us reliable predictors. How many would inquire? How many should we seek to recruit? How many would apply? How many should we offer admission? How many would commit to acceptance with a money deposit? How many would show and enroll on opening day?

As of December 1971, inquiries from prospective applicants doubled the number made in the previous December. Applications to enter also grew and exceeded twice the number twelve months before. It was an omen of what was to come, and it made us hesitant about extending offers of acceptance. As of January 12, 1972, we had not yet made any offers to applicants and were not ready to do so in the near future.

We lagged because we could not agree on an appropriate factor level for automatic sending of admissions offers. Professor Jerry Hughey, now chair of the faculty Admissions Committee, recommended continuance of the factoring system initiated in my chairmanship one year before. That system weighted grade point average [UGPA minus the decimal] at triple the number and then added the LSAT score to arrive at a *factor* number. Hughey's proposal raised the threshold on automatic admissions offers from a 1,350 factor to a 1,500 factor. He wanted a "slowdown approach," and a curtailment of automatic offers, thus favoring more time spent on individual file scrutiny of letters of recommendation, extracurricular activity, writing ability, motivation, diversity of culture and experience, and any other qualitative values.

It was reasonable, but I wondered if it made sense. Was the added time expended, time we could spend? If we did not strike quickly, would we lose competitively? Associate Dean Fagg also favored biding time, but for reasons different from Professor Hughey. Fagg wanted time for involvement of and consultation with SCOLS. Input from that committee of overseers should be encouraged, he said. At first, the faculty was reluctant to delay any longer on getting offers of admission to applicants. Nevertheless, for the sake of in-house diplomacy, we opted to wait and see what SCOLS had to say

At its January 25 meeting, SCOLS members were given to understand that they had a "hand" in admissions procedure—something more than mere assistance. As reported earlier herein, that was when Chairman Swindells appointed the SCOLS sub-committee to work with the faculty Admissions Committee. The question was: who was assisting whom? Was the faculty looking for advice, consensus, or authorization from SCOLS?

The two entities were kept "familial" by being kept apart, each informing the other from distance and arriving at a "passage" in between. The admission factor issue was a good example of how that passage worked. At the January 25 meeting of SCOLS the members were told that the faculty proposed automatic admissions at a factor of 1,200 or higher—a number never previously mentioned anywhere. The faculty had not settled on any number but was entertaining a 1,500 automatic-admissions level. Under the impression of faculty advice, SCOLS consensus accepted the 1,200 factor.

Then, one week later, at a February 2 faculty meeting, Hughey made a radical departure from his previous proposal of 1,500 and now inexplicably recommended the 1,200 factor countenanced by SCOLS. It was a complete about-face from Hughey's previous emphasis on more time and scrutiny and was also a significant reduction of the 1,350 factor used in the previous year.

The faculty and its Admissions Committee dilly-dallied for a month over the 1,500 or 1,350 or 1,200 gates. The upshot, as in all procrastination, was that the mere press of time became the decider. The buildup of a growing stack of application files, stalled on the law school desk, begged for streamlining. At the March 2 , 1972, faculty meeting, the professors decided that 1,250 would be the level for automatic admissions for day applicants and 1,200 for evening applicants. Finally, we began to send out offers of acceptance with less than six months remaining until the opening day of 1972-73 classes.

We now had to wait on the applicants that we had kept waiting. By the last week of March, we were waiting still. Anxiety was the price being paid for our delays. Would we fall short of our goal? Would we have anybody in our first year class?

That fear was overcome by the incredible demand for legal education. Surprisingly, in April, the pendulum swung the other way. The fear of an empty cup was supplanted by the fear of spilling over. At the May 3 faculty meeting, Associate Dean Fagg had alarming news, painted as "disaster" and "catastrophe." Acceptances of our first-year admission offers were a huge overflow in prospective day division enrollment.

Professor Bross, as faculty minutes-taker, billed Fagg as "still surviving member of the Admissions Committee." Bross himself had been a member of that committee. Chair Hughey was not in attendance—nor was he present at faculty meetings for

"IT'S THE DEAN. HE WONDERS IF YOU WOULD MIND OPENING THE DOOR LONG ENOUGH FOR HIS ADMISSION."

the rest of the academic year. Apparently, the Admissions Committee had disbanded under the impression that its work was done, or "done in." It was far from done, however. The overflow of acceptance was the same problem we had in the previous year. Only this time it was much worse. We seemed to have learned nothing from our prior predicament.

Our total applications for day enrollment had come to 855, for which we only had 120 seats. Thus, more than seven applicants vied for each seat, where less than three had contested in the previous year. In order to arrive at 120 day neophytes on opening day, we had launched 243 offers for acceptance. ABA consultant Millard Ruud had advised us that we could expect no more than fifty percent acceptance. But in fact, as of May 3 acceptance deposits were running at seventy-six percent. It was flattering but disconcerting to know that more wanted us than we or the ABA had imagined.

We were further advised that, of the 180 day acceptors thus far, we could expect about thirteen percent "no-shows," therefore ending up with about 157 first year day students in 120 seats. And that was not the end of it. There were still about 60 day offers yet outstanding! The crunch was more than just students sitting on each others laps, the over-subscription promised to tax "all" of our resources and mess with ratio balances, library use, budget, and other accreditation demands.

As for solutions, the deans were at odds. Fagg recommended revoking the outstanding offers. Wren strenuously opposed reneging and stressed the adverse publicity and hard feelings that would result. One way or the other, the offerees needed to be informed about potentially crowded conditions so that their future plans could be made accordingly. Dean Wren was urged to phone the 60 offerees to explain the situation and to notify them of options: changing to evening division enrollment or simply not accepting the day offer.

Commiseration then ensued on the "undesirability of all options" and on the "magnitude of errors that had brought the school into the predicament." Casting blame instead of forming solutions is a common, knee-jerk reaction. Once problem solving took hold, it led to concern with the pawning off of over-subscription to the evening division. Since the beginning of the academic year we had targeted the ideal first-year evening enrollment at no more than 80. Thus far we already had about 60 paid acceptors of night school. To steer another 60 day offerees plus the 37 estimated over-subscribed day depositors to the evening hours would simply cast almost 100 refugees from one place to another and might be an unfair mix of full- time students with part-time students.

Discussion was so extended that the May 3 meeting was postponed until the following morning. At that new day, the faculty finally passed a motion to have Dean Wren make the 60 phone calls, leaving the extent of options and disclosures to his discretion and persuasion. The record is empty on whether the dean actually made all of those calls. Suffice it to say, that our final count in the 1972-73 academic year showed our goal of seating 200 neophytes, set twelve months before, became 230 faces in seats—but no one in laps.

## FACULTY HIRING:

Early in the 1971-72 academic years and in anticipation of the 1972-73 year, we were authorized to hire six new full-time law professors. Then, at mid-year, Professor Hal Bloomenthal announced that he would return to the practice of law at the end of the year. He had been the highest paid teacher in the history of the law school as of that time. But that salary could not compete with the compensation offered him by a law firm in Colorado.

Soon after, Librarian Jacqui Jurkins also decided to leave her professorship in mid-year. She had been operating both our library and the Multnomah County Law Library. Accreditors were not pleased to have a librarian who was not full-time. Dean Wren had to make her choose. She opted to stay in to her former position as Head Law Librarian for the county—a post that she still holds as of this writing. And so, at the start of our second semester, we were suddenly without a law librarian—a serious loss in our accreditation pursuit.

Those resignations added two more empty spots on the faculty. We now needed to find eight new professors for the start of the next academic year. By the end of the current year, the faculty would dwindle to ten; three months later at the start of 1972-73, the faculty would have to be eighteen, almost double in size. Throughout the 1971-72 year, the search was not just a large order; it was gigantic, the biggest in the law school's history, then or now.

Fagg's efficiency went immediately to work. He laid out a written plan for our quest. He was a firm believer in getting the horse and the cart in the right order—anticipate and get a solution before the problem arises—a bit different from Dean Wren's take-on-the-problem, then decide what to do with it. Normative versus circumstantial attitude—a difference between the *civil law* legislative and *common law* judicial approaches to problem solving.

At the September 29, 1971, faculty meeting, Fred moved adoption of his "Hiring Procedures." They required: (1) a "personal on-campus interview" of a candidate; (2) a "unanimous vote" of acceptance; and (3) no right of vote to any professor or student representative who "did not interview or have personal knowledge of the prospect."

Against Fred's dissent, the third requisite was stricken by amendment. A second amendment was also approved against Fred's protest. It substituted the words "general consensus" for the words "unanimous vote." The faculty did not want a blackball system. Some of Fred's central provisions having been gutted, he withdrew his original motion as so amended. Parliamentarians wondered if the mover could withdraw his motion once it was amended. Professor Knudsen tried to waylay any discussion on that parliamentary point by simply making the amended motion his own and re-introducing it. But the parliamentarians wondered if it was proper to re-activate a motion at the same meeting in which it had been rendered inert. Then, the whole matter was put in limbo when a motion to table was passed. Now, everyone saved face.

One month later at the October 20 meeting, Fred presented new "Hiring Procedures." His plan took into account "two different places" for recruitment: Hiring might take place at either the annual AALS Convention or on-campus. Hiring at AALS could be done by a *unanimous* vote of the recruiters attending and interviewing (including one vote for the two student representatives). Hiring on-campus required a formal eighty percent vote of those attending a faculty meeting with a quorum of ten. At that point, the parliamentarians wondered to know if passage of such a motion required a super-majority vote. Was it legitimate for a simple majority [e.g., 6 of 10] to require an 80 percent vote on a future issue? Can a mere majority empower a minority with a veto? *E.g.*, can 6 of 10 give 3 of 10 a right to defeat, when 4 of 10 did not agree to do so? And is the reverse allowed: Having created an 80 percent rule, can a simple majority undo it? And finally, even if a simple majority can do all those things, should it do so? Such parliamentary sojourns were all quite puzzling, yet intriguing. It was what lawyers do.

But lawyers don't just anticipate problems, they also solve them. So back at that October 1971 meeting, someone finally said, "Let's take the vote on the motion and see if it makes any difference." Fortunately, Fred's Hiring Procedures, including the 80 percent rule, were adopted without dissent. The simple majority versus super majority issue disappeared in unanimity. It was an example of that judicial approach previously mentioned: The bridge may need crossing but not until you come to it.

To adopt a plan and then to follow it, however, were two different matters. Would the weather betray the forecast? How much of Fred's plan was honored does not appear of record. Our on-campus and AALS recruiting went underground, because of expressed concern about confidentiality—an issue unresolved in the previous year when we sought to address it without a specific need to do so. [See ch. 9, "Faculty Meetings . . . Confidentiality"] Now we had a case for it. Professor Newell moved and we agreed that all discussion and votes on candidates should be done in seclusion at unrecorded sessions and not at official faculty meetings held in our open courtroom. In the words and whimsy of Professor Bross, an open forum might inhibit "the free exchange of slanders."

From such closed caucus, the names of hires just pop up in the record as fait d'accomplis—bottomlines in minutes and memos here and there that simply mention in passing the names of the chosen eight. In the probable order of hiring, they were: Edmund O. Belsheim, James M. Dente, Bernard F. Vail, Robert L. Myers, Edward J. Brunet, Leonard DuBoff, William C. Snouffer and Jay Folberg.

Absent a record and trusting my memory, many of them did not enter along the path carved by the adopted "Hiring Procedures." Sometimes there may have been no on-campus or AALS interview or no duly called faculty meeting or quorum or no formalized voting. Sometimes the hire simply sprang from consensus or the sense of what was likely consent taken from silence. The press of time and the beckoning of accreditation drove us beyond the call for the dainty and mincing steps in planning. The enthusiasm of Dean Wren, for one, never saw a border at which to slow down.

Ed Belsheim was our number one catch and eminent windfall. At age 67, he was well along in his career as a law teacher and had been a Rhodes Scholar, the Dean of the University of Nebraska Law School, and the author of leading volumes on law document forms. Contrary to the privacy policy previously adopted, his terms for accepting employment were openly reported at the February 2, 1972 regular faculty meeting. He wanted a three-year contract and allowance to teach the Trusts and Estates and the Business Organizations courses. Consideration of his candidacy took no more than reading his credentials. I moved that we hire him under his terms without further ado. The vote was unanimous, preordained, and public. President Howard had already given his "go ahead." It was not a vote to offer him a position; rather we accepted his offer. We were the find, not the finder. As far as I can tell, that was the fourth time that the Portland law school in its entire history did not initiate the search. Back in 1883, Richard Hopwood Thornton, an eastern scholar, not only *found* the law school, he *founded* the law school. Then too, back in 1969, Fagg and Williamson came uninvited.

Ed Belsheim did not disappoint. He was 88 years old when he retired from teaching. His tenure at NWLC lasted over twenty years, longer than any law school with which he had ever been attached. He so endeared himself to his students that alumni donations after his retirement established NWLC's first endowed faculty chair—the Edmund O. Belsheim professorship.

Acceptance of Belsheim was soon followed by Jim Dente's acceptance of our offer. Jim was also an experienced law teacher, having taught for many years. He was currently at the University of Wyoming Law School. Professor Knudsen had been Jim's colleague at that school and that was the connection for his entry into NWLC, where he would be a Torts teacher along with myself. Out of the eight appointments, Dente and Belsheim were the only two hired as *full* professors of law.

Vail and Myers were hired as associate professors—the middle level in the academic caste system. That position was given them on account of their longevities in the field of law. Bob Myers had been practicing law in Portland for almost twenty years—a law partner in the firm of Shuler Sayre Winfree and Rankin. Bob's associate professor status made me uncomfortable, because I had once been his understudy and now he would be the subordinate. After a one year clerkship on Oregon's Supreme Court, I had entered his law firm as a lowly associate. Bob, as a junior partner, was instrumental in ushering and introducing me to Portland business communities, various social law groups, and the courthouse. He also gave me apprentice lessons about the back streets and alleys never traveled in the ivory halls of schooling and high judiciary. I did not last long in the Shuler firm. It was not a match-made-in-heaven. The firm was nationally recognized as having a corner in the Pacific northwest on legal endorsement in the municipal bonding business. I had a penchant for unprofitably small cases and pedestrian idealism. It was not conducive to no-nonsense, big business. I went on to become a partner in another law firm [see ch. 1] followed by teaching at NWLC, where, starting in the forthcoming 1972-73 year, I was to be a full professor of law—a superior rank to Bob's starting associate professorship. I was now a hirer and ahead of one who once had hired and headed me. It was awkward for both of us.

Bernie Vail, then a law professor at the University of Georgia, had made the acquaintance of our Professor Hughey. Bernie was, perhaps, the only one of record whose path followed exactly our adopted hiring procedure. He was interviewed on campus in the fall semester. Then in the spring semester, he received an eighty percent vote, by a quorum of at least ten at a duly called faculty meeting.

We hired four younger candidates at the assistant professor rank (the lowest tenure-tracked level). Jay Folberg and Bill Snouffer, like Myers, were local Portland lawyers. Snouffer and our Professor Williamson had been colleagues together in the Multnomah County District Attorney office. Jay was on the other side of the criminal fence - - a criminal defense lawyer with a background in legal aid work. Aside from teaching classes, they were hired specifically to be joint managers of our clinical program. Snouffer was to handle the criminal and Folberg the civil aspects of the clinic. Our lame duck, Professor Bloomenthal, was currently the clinic organizer having tentatively taken the chores from Knudsen, who had taken them from me. The clinical program still needed some permanent founding. After many years of service from both of them, Jay would eventually become the dean of the University of San Francisco Law School, and Bill would be robed as an Oregon Circuit Court judge.

The hiring of Len DuBoff had to skirt many of Fagg's hiring requisites. As I recall it, the vigor of Dean Wren, the blessings of President Howard, and the tact of Associate Dean Fagg combined to make an emergency decision to hire a much needed legal writing teacher—Jurkins now gone. DuBoff's credentials and hiring were extraordinary considering the circumstances: As a chemistry major prior to his law studies, he was permanently blinded and impaired by an explosion in a chemistry experiment. He, accompanied by his wife Mary Ann and Alex (a seeing-eye golden retriever), would join us to teach writing and research—an assignment heavily dependent on reading papers. Not only did he (with assistance from Mary Ann) handle that attention to the printed page, he also established himself as an expert in the curricular field of Law and the Arts—including the fine arts, that arm of the arts given to visual appreciation. His 1975 book on Arts and Law was reported as the first book published by a NWLC professor; but it was not. The first published book was authored by Richard Hopwood Thornton, the Portland law school's first professor of law. He wrote a book on Commercial Law in the 1890s. Since the DuBoff book until the present day, over fifty books have been published by NWLC professors.

Ed Brunet was the final choice for an assistant professorship. That eighth seat had been offered first to two other candidates. Both offerees had strung us along in tandem with a series of non-committals. Finally, at a March 1, 1971 faculty meeting, we decided to go to a third choice. We invited Ed (studying for his masters of law degree at the University of Virginia) to the campus for an interview. The process was hurried, ending in a streamlined vote, offer, and acceptance. Ed has never given reason to regret the confidence so hastily bestowed nor has he ever lost composure at being third-in-line. On the contrary, he has gone on to be one of NWLC's most prolific published authors and endeared teachers and is currently seated in the Henry Casey Scholarship Chair.

## STAFF HIRING:

The largest faculty recruitment in the history of NWLC, then or now, was for a brief time made even larger. A ninth position was created. It was largely administrative, not instructive, albeit the candidate was allowed to teach a seminar elective and thus given a professorship. It developed quickly, ended just as quickly, and happened like this:

In the fall semester the workload on Associate Dean Fagg had grown to the point of a needed Assistant Dean. It made some minds ponder whether work grows *on* the worker or *from* the worker. Dean Wren first offered the Assistant Dean post to Ross Runkel, who had left NWLC two and one-half years before and had gone to Willamette College of Law, fifty miles down the road. Ironically, about the same time, Ross mailed me an invitation to be a candidate for Willamette's law dean. Our two "thanks-but-no-thanks" return letters passed each other as ships in the night.

Then, in the December 14, 1971, faculty minutes, the name Tom Niebergall was incidentally mentioned for the first time as the new Assistant Dean. Nowhere does it show how or by whom he came to be hired. The faculty was not involved, although I recall that somewhere in the fall of 1971, I was asked by Wren or Fagg what I thought of Tom inasmuch as my wife, Jewel, and I had known Tom and his wife, Molly, ever since our law student days together. I would have spoken highly of him, and that was the last I heard of the matter until being surprised and elated by his hire in December.

Tom was spirited away from a managerial post in the law department at the Georgia-Pacific Corporation several miles away from us. Tom began his Assistant Dean contract on January 1, 1972. He lasted nine days before being coaxed back to Georgia Pacific. When asked about his reasons for departure, he said simply "personal reasons." Among those reasons, there had to be the shock received when Tom had stepped out of a *well-run*, recognized *business* and into our *running*, unrecognized *"busy-ness."*

The position of "Assistant Dean" was swiftly refilled by Ann Kendrick. But Ann was not a lawyer; and so, at the February 2, 1972, faculty meeting, an issue was made of that title. As previously encountered with the Mary Ann Normandin title in 1970-71 [see ch. 9, "Staff Personnel"], Ann could not be a law school dean, and, therefore, had to be "Assistant *to the* Dean." Some wag carried the grammar even further; suggesting that, insofar as we now had two deans, that she had to be "Assistant to the *Deans*" or "Assistant to the *Associate* Dean." The penchant for parsing speech was just fun and fancy by a tired faculty. But one might well have asked why it was required that a law dean must have a law degree when a justice on the United States Supreme Court does not need to have a diploma from a grade school, let alone a degree from a law school.

Losing lawyer Niebergall and gaining non-lawyer Kendrick, meant that we lost a ninth potential faculty addition. It changed our faculty-student ratio two points from a prospective 1:34 to 1:36. Tweaking, toying and tinkering with ratio ciphers was not the same fun and fancy as parsing titles. Faculty-student ratios were dead-serious maneuvering in the race for accreditation.

Whatever may have been lost by having an "Assistant to the Dean" as opposed to an "Assistant Dean," was a loss immediately transformed into a huge gain. Ann Kendrick was another of those serendipitous lifts that time and again had boosted us. With a masters degree in theology and past service in the U.S. Diplomatic Corps, Ann was currently chair of a college philosophy department. She was also a former nun.

As an independent and forward-thinker, Ann took over work instead of allowing work to take over. At NWLC, she shaped her role into someone there for students along their way - - their recruitment, their financial aid, their counseling, their job placement, and their alumni ties. Much of her time was spent away from the campus, selling the law school to undergraduates and to prospective employees. In spite of those absences from home as our field representative—our John the Baptist and harbinger—she nurtured and was the cord between the school and student. No matter how parsed, Ann was "Assistant Alma Mater."

ANN KENDRICK

The Kendrick appointment began the rise of staff hiring—an ascension that would join the rise of faculty, students, and facilities. Expansion in one part triggers the others and so on until there comes the full circle. An enlarged student body called for more teachers, which made need of more staff support and administration, causing more building, making room for more students. This grey-haired, 87 year old Portland law school had to stop and ask: Was she moving into or out of control? Were her circles upward or idling? Spirals or eddies? Were we growing or wandering?

# 11
# THE WREN-FAGG
# REGIME: PART TWO
*1971-72*

## *SCHOOLING*

W hile immense *growth* was a major involvement for the law faculty in the 1971-72 academic year, *education* itself also took our time. The job of clothiers is two-fold: tailoring and designing. The tailor fits clothes to a growing body; the designer makes clothes smart. So, while growing and fitting, students and teachers at NWLC also struggled at dressing up—getting smart.

### STUDENT BODY UNREST:

The fresh day division (now including first and second year students) exposed NWLC to the carry-over of student activism from the 1960s—a decade that hatched hot war, cold war, assassination, drugs, nuclear fear, oppression of civil rights, Presidential shenanigans, demonstrations, confrontations, and civil disobedience. The situation affected the business of schooling in many ways.

A happening on the campus of our parent college might have been considered dramatic were it not typical of higher education in those times. On April 25, 1972, a large meeting of Lewis & Clark undergraduate students met in the student union cafeteria and voted in favor of stands to be taken by the college on the Vietnam War. They wanted amnesty for draft dodgers and elimination of military recruiting on campus. Their demands also called for a day of cancelled classes as a demonstration of faculty-student unity on the positions taken. They were prepared to stay through the night in the cafeteria. Some forty-five students also proposed to "take over" the Manor House (college administrative headquarters) until their protests were met.

President Howard reacted to the student warnings with warnings of his own. He told the protestors that the college would file criminal charges for breaking and entering and reportedly stated, "By my oath, I will suspend you!"

A special meeting of the undergrad faculty was called the next morning. About seventy professors (including myself) attended. Many voiced the concern that Howard had acted too harshly and had not followed guidelines previously adopted by the faculty on how to handle cases of student unrest. The president conceded that he had responded hastily and under the pressure of the moment. Such conciliatory notes were a good start. But, like most hurried sessions called to calm down, it merely stirred up.

Students were also present at the meeting—they having been invited by Dean of Faculty John Brown. According to minutes taken by Secretary to the Faculty Edith Smith, President Howard argued that the students should be excluded, that "with students presence, every member of the faculty feels an unusual pressure." To which, one professor asked Howard why he "didn't ask the faculty if they felt pressured." Another professor added, "The presence of the president was exerting as much pressure on the faculty as was the students." As I recall it, President Howard then called those remarks "impertinence." Indeed, "pressure" began to define the meeting. A vote was then taken on whether to remove the students. It passed by a 34 to 30 head count, and the students were asked to leave, which they did without disruption.

Discussion then centered on whether the faculty should accept the student petition for cancellation of classes. President Howard said that professors had a contract obligation to conduct scheduled classes even if students should strike and only one of them showed up for schooling.

Some professors felt that even though teachers had to hold class, they could devote the class time to the issues raised by the student protests. Dean Brown replied that faculty contracts meant that classroom lessons should accord with the course description represented in the catalog. Others, however, favored the notion of *carpe diem*; there was nothing wrong in seizing the moment and turning it into a learning experience. The origin of the word "college" meant *society*. Learning to adjust within that society was itself a lesson for those preparing for the society beyond cloister.

Discussion on the point continued for the rest of the morning. Lunch hour loomed. Motions were tabled. Dean Brown ruled that classes would not be cancelled. A motion to reconvene after lunch died for lack of a second. No more appears of record. The points of students, faculty, deans, and president had been made and simply talked out.

Student Involvement in Education:

At the law school, however, student activism steered a different course. Law students had a few more years of maturity and had chosen law process, instead of disobedience, as a way to succeed. When warranted, confrontation and protest might sometimes be first steps in opening the door of a problem; but in a democracy, it had to be lawful entry that solved the problem. And a first lesson of law practice was to seek the right venue, the best forum for achieving. If you want a good car, you go to a car dealer, not a junk yard. If you want relief from pain, you go to a hospital, not a saloon. If you want to stop a war, don't get your school mixed up with the warmongers. Those were the lessons of Law. But in the 1960s, when the right forum was paying no mind, a frustrated new generation tried to make their own venue. That may not have been ideal, but it was real. And while ideality was principle that ought to be chased, reality was fact that had to be faced.

And so, our law students activism on campus was addressed to in-house leaders about in-house, not worldly, concerns. Law deans and faculty were showered with student urgings about their law education, some of which could have been called "demands," were they not deftly put with lawyerly aplomb. One petition to us proposed using students as teachers to conduct special seminars. One student was bold enough to assert that he could teach Dean Wren's income tax course. From such immodest proposals, the faculty was able to glean a modicum of good; we authorized the use of senior students as teaching aides to assist in the legal writing and research program. From that grew a student tutorial program in other subjects.

And there were other student proposals. In response to promptings from prison inmates, students proposed that we send student teachers to the Oregon State Penitentiary in Salem to teach a course in criminal law and criminal appellate practice, especially post-conviction review. Professor Knudsen (as a clinical director) and I (as one who had once represented all of the inmates in their petition against the warden for certain cruel and unusual punishment) were assigned the task of exploring whether the proposal showed promise. We did and found it didn't.

Another student plea argued for formal **student evaluations of professors** at the end of each semester. The student position was a *tu quoque* argument: Professors grade students, so shouldn't students grade professors? Today, student evaluations of their teachers are commonplace throughout higher education, but in 1971 the practice was far from customary. Teachers were reluctant about giving judgment to those still learning what to judge. Professor Newell noted that grading the graders was counter productive and that students would not understand the value of a teacher until years after schooling.

Professor Walt Brown was not opposed to student evaluations in general, but emphasized that they should be given limited use. There was nothing wrong with them being used as a message of advice among students in choosing their electives. Nor was there anything wrong in professors using them in order to hone their personal skills. But a third possible use would be wrong, Brown said. In keeping with Newell's observations, it would be unfortunate if they were to be used by the faculty or school authorities in deciding momentous personnel matters such as promotion, tenure, job security, or salary.

Others then noted that even if Professor Brown's limited use was formally adopted, student evaluations would be a camel's nose under the hierarchal tent; i.e., the value as peer advice and as teacher feedback would nevertheless evolve eventually into consideration by authorities.

A motion to adopt formalized student evaluations of a course and its teacher was affirmed by faculty vote. The uses to be made of such evaluations were left to another day. Today, as forewarned, they have come to be used routinely in deliberations on promotion, tenure, and merit pay raises.

Of course, it did not take faculty authorization to allow a student to vent critique of a teacher. Humans evaluate and will do so without permission. "Who shall command the skylark not to sing?" One fiery memo to Dean Wren had this to say about one of our part-time instructors: It charged the instructor with classes cut short, classes cancelled, classes taught by substitutes from his law firm, classes adjourned to taverns. Allegedly, the instructor ruled out any final exam or final paper and had no basis upon which to assign a final grade except for class performance, of which there was little opportunity.

To be sure, the alleged conduct, if true, was remiss and not typical of our usual part-time teachers, who were later to be called "adjunct professors" and whose commitment to education throughout NWLC history has always been dedicated even in view of the lowly pay given them. As a consequence of the memo, control of part-time instruction was taken from the faculty Curriculum Committee and given to Associate Dean Fagg, urging him to give greater attention to the hiring and monitoring of instructors. The newly adopted, formalized, and regularly conducted student evaluations would be helpful in that regard.

Other student complaints ranged from whining to constructive critique. In the gripe department, claims bordered on paranoia. A day student wanted to know why the Standing Committee on the Operation of the Law School [SCOLS] had "an overwhelming philosophical prejudice" against the day law school. It seemed to this claimant that SCOLS members thought day students were "playboys" and evening students were "Horatio Algers." Judge Mercedes Deiz, a Northwestern College of

Law graduate and a SCOLS member, was surprised and wanted to hear from day students as to why and where they had gained such a perception.

A college administration decision involving the "law dorm" may have triggered that particular student's perception: One wing of the college student dormitories had been set aside for our new daytime law students. At the end of the 1971-72 fall semester, we were informed the wing would be closed to law students in the next academic year. Henceforth, all law students would have to live off-campus. Day law boarders were incensed, and our law faculty was disturbed by a decision made without law school consultation. At the January 12, 1972, faculty meeting, we voted "to take a stand" and authorized new Dean Niebergall "to carry on the fight." The end of Niebergall's nine-day term in office pulled our fighter out of the ring and brought an end to the fight before it had begun. The aftermath was the day law student's aggrieved assessment of the college hierarchy, for which SCOLS took the brunt.

In general, the perception, true or not, stemmed from a gap, prevalent nationwide. On one brink were elders with attachments and established ways. On the other brink, was a younger generation with detachment and fresh ways. Clouded by dark and distance, it was hard to see across.

INTERNAL STUDENT BODY TROUBLES:

But most student body uneasiness at NWLC in 1971-72 did not focus on professors, college, or SCOLS, or the world scene. Rather, quarrel turned inward upon itself—trouble within student ranks. It began in the previous year with the start of a day division that had now become effusive. In speaking of the day and night *divisions*, the word "division" was taking on a meaning not intended. Divisiveness erupted in many places.

At the January 25, 1972, SCOLS meeting, the law school student representative, John Wittmayer (now an Oregon Circuit Court judge), requested that the student body should be represented at SCOLS by two delegates—one for each division, night and day. He reported that the day division no longer regarded itself as part of the existing student government and was organizing itself separately; the evening division had no objection to that secession.

Ann Morgenstem, first editor-in-chief of our law review periodical, had foreseen the coming dissidence. In a May 1971 memo to Dean Wren just before her graduation, she wrote,

> "The greatest problem the law review will face next year will be the integration of day and night students... Because of the discord in the student bar, we must guard against a similar upheaval in the law review."

Dean Wren tried to head off the schism with a foil: He would allow the segregation so long as there was integration. The day division could have its separate organization but then the officers of both student bodies (day and evening) would have to join in a composite board that would elect a single chair leader with whom the law school administration could transact. Day division leaders were not receptive to the dean's plan.

As the faculty representative to the student bar, I was unable to calm the approaching storm. It was like trying to stop rain with a stick. What was needed was a mediator who was neither student nor faculty. The need was among the reasons for creating the new Assistant Dean position [see ch. 10, "Staff Hiring"], whose duties would include being an "Ombudsman"—a word that in the 1960s had gained popularity across the nation and had worked its way into English dictionaries, from a Swedish government office set up to counsel, console, compromise, or otherwise solve constituent complaints. Accordingly, the new word and office fit the turbulence of the 1960s in America. But Niebergall as ombudsman did not last long, and Ann Kendrick as "ombudswoman" came too late.

The first sign of disintegration within the student bar came with the demise of the *Nightowl*, the student body newspaper edited by Student Bar President Sherry Smith. It was replaced at mid-year 1971-72 with the *Weekly Law School News*, which after several issues betrayed its title by coming out bi-weekly. Unlike its extensive predecessor, the *Weekly* was a sketchy pamphlet hurriedly assembled and limited by school administrators to one mimeographed page into which a beleaguered student editor was forced to cram minimums of what students needed to know about happenings in their school.

The next repercussion concerned the anticipated Honor Code. The Student Bar Association was given the threefold task of (1) drafting a code of ethical rules against cheating and other violation of campus policy, (2) describing the procedure under which such alleged transgressions should be decided, and (3) prescribing authorized punishment.

Many students objected to promulgating a student honor code. Their reasons were mixed. Some felt a written codification of substance, procedure, and remedy was not necessary. Honesty on exams, written papers, and other school reports and respect for property were well understood without formalization and written edicts. As for process and punishment, fairness could be left to *ad hoc* determinations by trusted authorities. Underlying those reasons and in the minds of some, there was an attitude in those days against student bodies cooperating with the establishment in any way to create rules regulating their moral energy. A January 24, 1972, memorandum from a student Honor Committee put it this way:

"[D]ue to the diverse backgrounds and attitudes of our student body, the basic question of how far a code should extend into a student's own personal, moral, and ethical sphere may have such a wide range of answers that no written code could adequately represent the sentiments of the entire student population."

So, the student Honor Committee's first step, before drafting any proposed code, was to take a vote to see if students favored such a code. Only sixteen percent of the students voted. Therefore, as predetermined by the Honor Committee, because the balloting was less than a majority of the student body, the vote was deemed to be a rejection of any student honor code. In other words, no vote was the same as a "no" vote and meant no code. Accordingly, the Honor Committee was dissolved and no further student action was taken.

The faculty was amazed and dismayed at what was viewed as student apathy. Students pointed out that many law schools had no student honor code; they used Harvard Law School as an example. Whenever I heard an argument supported by the precedent of what is done at leading law schools, my heart sank. I longed for the day when a Harvard might use *our* flag as *its* guidon. Ranking was repugnant elitism to those who had to look upward through the levels; but to those above, ranking was simply honest condescension. We had to climb; they would not stoop.

In the April 19, 1972, faculty meeting student representatives inquired as to what was to be done with reported cheating on exams. Professor Knudsen was "extremely distressed" and voiced no sympathy for student concerns about the lack of a remedy that the students were suppose to have supplied. Professor Newell, a Harvard graduate, felt the faculty did not need an honor code to punish cheating. Dean Wren was anxious to have a written code. So he presented for faculty vote an ABA honor code draft. What the students did by apathy, the faculty did by postponement; it tabled the dean's proposal.

A formal Honor Code was not adopted until 1975. It took a case of exam cheating to instigate it. Without a formal procedure in place, the faculty had to quickly fashion proceedings and then find guilt, and expel. Complaint about that makeshift, common law process was followed by NWLC's first honor code.

Early in 1972, another critical student body vote arose—one that was not so easy to duck. Student leaders scrapped the existing student body constitution and then put it back up to vote along with two other alternative proposals. Passage of a new constitution required a two-thirds student body vote. Getting a student body of 500 ambitious advocates to agree by a super-majority on one of three choices, was the stuff of which self-defeat was pre-ordained. A January 1972 student body meeting on the issue was "scantily attended." At a February election, only 82 votes were cast. A second opportunity to vote on the three constitutions was scheduled in March and brought no different result. The coup de grace occurred in mid-spring semester when all of the student body officers resigned.

Some argued that insofar as the existing constitution had been wasted before the election, the defeat of all three constitutions left the student body with no constitution at all. Others argued that the existing constitution was still viable because it was not within the power of student leaders to dissolve a constitution. But, argued opponents, the failure of students subsequently to give it a two-thirds support meant the student body had junked it.

Still others observed that, as a practical matter, it really didn't make any difference whether there was or was not an existing constitution, because it had been abandoned by all of its officers and by the overwhelming number of non-voters. In short, without followers, it had no body. A constitution does not constitute its constituency; rather, it is the constituency that constitutes its constitution. It is people who form "union,... justice,... tranquility,... defense,... welfare,... and... posterity." Without followers, a statement of principles is simply paper. I sided with that marvelous lesson in constitutional government: To be successful, a constitution is not just encased in books, it is carried in hearts.

Another trouble with internal student body dissidence was the continuing problem of knowing who exactly were the student representatives with credentials to participate in faculty committees and at full faculty meetings. [See ch. 9, "Faculty Meetings"] Students were entitled two votes at such meetings—one each from the day and the evening divisions. At the first faculty meetings of the year, when we were still meeting in the jury room, there were as many as five students present and always day students inasmuch as our meetings were held in the daytime. An evening student representative did not begin to show until the second semester. It was not too far into the fall semester when faculty secretary Bross stopped counting and simply recorded "sundry students present." Without duly elected student agents, we were developing student spectators. The numbers made the jury room tight quarters. So, we moved faculty meetings into the adjoining Crawford Courtroom. That simply made the audience larger. Nowhere in the record does it show any official faculty action authorizing open meetings. It simply evolved from the casual curiosity of students and the nonchalance of the faculty. It was tolerated, democratic, popular, honest, kind—and given time, unworkable.

Spectators were flattering to some professors and annoying to others. Audience would occasionally move beyond mere spectating. Highly opinionated activists were hard pressed to simply watch. From the gallery might come a moan, sigh, clapping, outburst, or a frantic waving of a hand to which our presider, Dean Wren, would sometimes give recognition to speak. It was a reflex action—a classroom teacher syndrome.

As audience without authorized voice became more vocal, faculty with authorized voice grew more silent. We had a slowly developing experiment that was rapidly developing into an issue—town hall democracy in need of a republic. A damn good education but poor business.

Now that the student body was leaderless, without an association, and with dubious representation in faculty meetings, some concerned students met with Dean Wren in May 1972. The students "complained of a lack of identification with the school." That lack was blamed on the need for better faculty-student relations. The dean reported to the faculty a definite morale problem. Professor Newell felt the problem would resolve itself with the increase of faculty numbers next year; a better ratio would develop more opportunity for student-faculty contact. Accordingly, he moved to table further discussion about "morale identification" problems. But no one wanted to second that motion.

I suggested that posting faculty office hours for student consultation might alleviate some of the problem. Newell objected. Professor Walt Brown suggested assigning students to each professor—a sort of "big brother" system to promote identification with the school. Fagg and I objected. Professor Fagg suggested more faculty-student get-togethers—from which came audible moans.

It was clear that the law professors were not equipped to solve identification problems. Dean Wren resorted to a final "fail-safe" solution: He referred the matter to the Faculty Student Affairs Committee. Existence of such a committee was news to most everyone. Perhaps, the Dean meant Ann Kendrick, our ombudswoman.

Eventually, a Student Affairs Committee would be constituted under chairmanship of Professor Bernie Vail, but not until Ann had tended to matters. She met with students near the end of the 1971-72 year. The student turnout for Ann was much larger than at the Dean's May conference. Her report to the faculty put a slightly rosier hue to student morale. Indeed, there were complaints, but they focused on older and smaller gripes, *e.g.* library noise, late grade reporting, parking, and other grievances. Although grumblings, they were also clues to a dormant body becoming attentive and constructive instead of depressed and withdrawn. Contrary to supposition, complaint is a sign of life. Pain identifies.

On one of ABA Consultant Millard Ruud's visits to our campus that year, I informed him of our student body turmoils and expressed my concern with how that might affect accreditation. He recognized that student body relationship was an important part of ABA investigations. But after listening to some of the foregoing unrest, he winked and smiled and said something along the lines of "join the crowd; welcome aboard; par for the course; a sign of the times." Not pestilence, just pester.

Throughout the nation, educators and schools were experiencing the same student disgust, disruption, and despondency. Ruud assured us that we were simply in the wake of unrest, not the cause of it. He was even more encouraging when he went on to say that we had done decidedly better on student relations than other more established schools. Considering that NWLC was still green and struggling with organization, we had done remarkably well at keeping campus peace. The gap between the typical evening student and the modern day student, he said, was to be expected. If his flattery exceeded its desert, it was welcome nevertheless.

Like the ache in being told that you cannot fly, there followed delight in learning that no one can. I felt sad at taking joy from others in worse condition than us. But that guilt was relieved by learning that my pettiness was so commonplace that there was a word for it: schadenfreude. So goes the maneuvering in which the mind makes its own comfort.

CURRICULUM:

When it comes to dressing up, getting smart, and educating, as emphasized before, curriculum along with pedagogy was at the core. Three new curricular issues drew particular attention in the 1971-72 school year: (1) Should we become involved in moot court competition with other schools across the nation? (2) Should we schedule course subjects that cross law study with other fields of knowledge—so-called interdisciplinary courses? (3) Should first year students be required to take an introductory course concerning the philosophies of law—an *over*view of what *under*lies? All of those questions called for moving NWLC out of its vocational closet.

Now that temporary accreditation had moved us into ABA recognition, we received an invitation to participate in the national interscholastic moot court contest. In 1971-72, there was virtually only one such nation-wide competition. Today, that competition has become the "granddaddy" for a whole host of differing contests, and NWLC engages in many such scholastic tourneys. But in 1971-72 we took part in none.

I was anxious for us to join the fray. In my law student days at Willamette College of Law, my classmates won the national championship. It built school spirit, and I was eager to see it happen at NWLC. But the faculty saw it otherwise. We had homework and did not choose to go out and play. Ambition was one thing; readiness was another. We stayed indoors.

A course called "Law and Psychiatry" was proposed. Such interdisciplinary courses were just beginning to be popular: *e.g.* Law and Medicine, Law and Economics, Law and Sociology, Law and Literature, Law and History, and Law and Accounting. The trend did not go without its detractors. They argued that Law was its own discipline, and law schools should limit themselves to teaching only the ethical principles, rules, and skills of that internal structure. Legal education should not go too far into the game of policy-making. Lawyers ought to concern themselves with the rules and ethics by which the policy game must be played without themselves, as lawyers, playing the game. Lawyers, like referees, should ensure that the fighters are playing by the rules, but should not throw punches. Socio-economic-political policy ought to be left to other educators. So said the detractors.

The trouble with that attitude, said other educators, was that it was monastic tunnel-vision hooded from a periphery of what a lawyer is called upon to see and do. A lawyer is not just a referee; a lawyer must at times be a fighter. Advocates don't just deal with legal issues; they must deal with factual issues. They are not just officers of the laws; they are voices for their clients. The lawyer needs to know the socio-economic-political-scientific realities of other disciplines, especially when those actualities engage with law rules or principles. That inter-disciplinary knowledge then becomes reasons for honing laws and connecting them to life itself. So said the proponents of the Law and Psychiatry course now offered to NWLC.

Both the inter-disciplinary and intra-disciplinary approaches to legal education could be overdone. Like ever so many debates, the victory of wisdom is not won by extremism. Resolve is not always a black-or-white, either-or solution. Where both sides have something to offer, the value of eclectic selection is not middling, not mild, not a compromise, not the gray-area in between on a spectrum. The correct spectrum is not from far left to far right; it is from bad to good, from dumb to smart, from unfair to just. The extremists, the idealogs, the fanatics, the obsessed are all at the same end of that line, no matter what extreme philosophy they espouse. They are all bad, dumb, and unfair. The top of the mountain is not middle ground; the top is the only place from which to see all sides.

As for the Law and Psychiatry course, some on the faculty were enthusiastic, some were amenable, some were reluctant, and some were opposed. But a majority were willing to experiment. In the 1972-73 course curriculum, NWLC would offer a Law and Psychiatry course taught by psychiatrist Dr. Daniel Voiss. We even went one step further; we offered a Law and Medicine course taught by Dr. Stanley Welborn.

Voiss had no law degree. Welborn had added to his medical degree a law degree from NWLC just a few years prior. Although those two experiments did not last long, today inter-disciplinary courses have prevailed at NWLC.

Well before the Law and Psychiatry course, I had taught a Law and Society class. It was not the same as an inter-disciplinary course. It was a re-positioning and re-naming of my previous Jurisprudence course. [See ch. 4] Designed as a legal methods overview with a mix of legal history and philosophy, Law and Society had been scheduled as a required first-year subject, set to give entering students a look at Law's gestalt— forest instead of trees. I labored at the belief that students from their birth into Law should understand their chosen enterprise philosophically and not just vocationally. Law was more than a trade; it was a calling.

The 1971-72 faculty was not convinced. Professor Bross would be teaching an upperclass elective in Jurisprudence. That was all the philosophy that opting students needed in one concentration. The rest of it they could get pervasively. Faculty time and numbers were limited. That attitude caused me to wonder aloud why we crown students after three or four years of education with a Doctor of "Jurisprudence" degree. But my taunt was unproductive. The Law and Society course was discarded by a narrow vote. The wounds were not fatal. After pouting for a few days, I moved some jurisprudence lessons into the cracks of my six-hour Torts course. That was my uneasy concession to the notion that philosophy should be nutrient for plantings, but not a plant itself.

And so, in 1971-72, we considered including national contests, other fields of learning, and a greater focus on law philosophy. We shunned the first, sampled the second, and shrunk from the last. Indeed, our curriculum was stepping gingerly.

## CLINIC PROGRAM:

Long before the rise of schools of law, candidates for law careers prepared by a method called "reading law," *i.e.* serving as an apprentice to a law practitioner. Once law schools were firmly established in the twentieth century, bar organizations insisted on a law school degree. Thus, tutelage by clerking became passé as an entry into lawyering.

But in-the-field practice as a schooling within law schools did not lose its appeal. Law practice within the educational curriculum first took the form of on-campus interviews by law students dealing directly with real persons and their real problems. It was called "clinical operations."

The first clinical operations began in 1931 at Duke University. It did not catch on. It was not until 1947 that the University of Tennessee began the second such operation. By the end of the 1950s, only twenty-five law schools had clinical education. At that point, the idea stalled.

Then late in the 1960s the surface of legal education rippled again with the notion that in-the-field practice could augment in-the-classroom theory. By our 1971-72 academic year, the ripples had become waves. The catalyst was a 1968 Ford Foundation decision to donate millions of dollars of seed money to the Council of Legal Education and Professional Responsibility [CLEPR]—a fund to coax law schools into sound clinical programs. That in turn sparked the interests of the ABA, an organization who by its lawyer constituency was keyed to practical learning. AALS, our other accreditor and an organization of academicians, while supportive, was not as assertive. Unfortunately, "street-smarts" along side of "book smarts" smacked of competition, when in truth it begged for complement.

By 1970 the number of law schools with clinical programs had grown to eighty. By 1971, it took no genius for us to see that, while clinical programming was not a command, neither was it much of a choice. The ripples that had become waves were now a surge. With CLEPR money as a carrot and ABA accreditation as a stick, we lobbied President Howard and the Board of Trustees for a more ambitious and intensified clinical pursuit.

Our efforts had begun slowly. As previously reported [see ch. 6, "Clinic"], clinical education began with me as the provisional director in the 1969-70 academic year. In 1970-71, Professor Knudsen took over the clinical directorship with assists from Professor Williamson and myself. Like me, Knudsen was a temporary fit for one year while we readied for a permanent clinical leader.

Now here in 1971-72, Professor Hal Bloomenthal arrived and became that fixed director. At least, that was the plan. But circumstances drew Knudsen back into clinical operations when Bloomenthal tendered his resignation at mid-year for a departure at the end of the academic year. Knudsen took co-directorship while Bloomenthal, lamed by no future here, ducked—but not before he and Knudsen spelled out their ambitious clinical plan. They proposed a clinical budget for 1972-73 that called for two office rentals, one in downtown Portland and another in downtown Oregon City. Salaries for a so-called "clinical lawyer" and three secretaries were also included. Most of all, salaries for, not one, but two professorial directors were listed. Additional expenses included utilities, furniture, books, phones, travel, litigation costs, insurance, and other sundries. It was no longer to be viewed as simply a program within the curriculum, it was to be a full-fledged "clinic"—permanent law offices, off-campus, for indigent clientele, with regular business hours, people at desks, typewriters, telephones, waiting rooms, and case files ready for counsel and student courtroom advocacy. The proposal would cost the college $100,000—almost one-sixth of our total law school budget proposed for the 1972-73 year.

CLEPR promised to offset some of our expense with $40,000 of seed money. But that support was fixed for only one year with merely a prospect for years thereafter. From 1969 through 1973, CLEPR had made grants to over one hundred law school clinics. Could that last forever? As beachcombers we had to be wary of tides. High tidings that bring income also build expenses—costs that can be left high and dry by receding seeders. Nevertheless, NWLC went forward with its ambitious clinic plans.

Accordingly, a main task in our clinic efforts was to find permanent leadership. As aforesaid, we shored up stability in that position by finding, not one, but two leaders: Jay Folberg and Bill Snouffer. [See ch. 10, "Faculty Hiring"] Late in the 1971-72 year we began looking for another hire to fill the "clinic lawyer" spot and for office places near city cores and courts. Those searches produced possibilities but no recruit or rentals. It would have to wait and be primary business in the 1972-73 year when the Folberg-Snouffer directors could put the crawling clinic on its feet.

At the same time that CLEPR money launched our clinics, it also insinuated itself into curricular decision-making. CLEPR officials were pleased to see Bloomenthal's proposal for a "clinic semester." Under the proposal, not only did the clinic take one-sixth of our budget size, it also took one-sixth of our semester size. One of our six (day) semesters was to be set aside exclusively for clinic enrollment. That special semester would include six credit hours of required classroom courses keyed to courtroom practice, plus a minimum of twenty hours per week in clinic field work, the latter worth four credit hours. Only a few credit hours were to be elective. No one could enroll in the clinic semester without having first completed certain designated courses.

The proposal met CLEPR's approval and inducement and was adopted by the faculty but not without some professorial frowns. The semester ran counter to the faculty's position in favor of more flexible elective course study. Hackles were also raised about CLEPR's outside intrusion into traditional aspects of faculty domain.

While a lame duck, Professor Bloomenthal had pinpointed another subtle issue where he felt we might be at odds with CLEPR. Clinical education had two goals. On the one hand, a clinic provided service to the public; while on the other, a clinic was a schooling for students. At a glance, fulfillment of the two seemed to work in synergy. But could they work contrary to one another? Is the citizen need served by help from those still learning? Is learning served by needy cases of little educational value? To what extent could citizens serve schooling while school served citizens?

Bloomenthal wrote, "While we are interested in performing a service function, this function must be secondary... We must have cases which... have educational value and... are within our students' capabilities." CLEPR, on the other hand, saw things differently. CLEPR policy viewed the primary purpose of clinics to be legal assistance to the impoverished and education as secondary. Money grants from CLEPR were keyed to that priority. Thus, CLEPR insisted that student capability had to be sound and had to be delivered on all cases regardless of educational value.

It was a difference that could be overcome, but not without balanced supervision. The marriage of schooling and practicing could be wed by academic and lawyerly monitoring of students work. It would take *professorial* respect for public service and *professional* regard for theory. The deferences would take time for adapting.

Having adopted an ambitious clinic plan for balancing practice and theory, and including a curriculum studded by a jeweled "clinical semester," that was when we were jolted by Bloomenthal's tendered resignation.

## SUMMER SCHOOL:

NWLC had never offered summer schooling in its eighty-nine year history. We had attempted to do so in the summer of 1971; but when only fifty-five students promised to enroll, we abandoned the project because that was not enough to cover expenses. [See ch. 9, "Summer School"]

We tried again for a 1972 summer semester. Now that we had ABA auspices, our summer course had more promise of success, inasmuch as students from other law schools could now transfer our course credits to their home school transcripts. Visitation could also enrich our image nationwide. Sharing a unified summer program for both day and evening students might also do something to improve the divisiveness and morale in our student body. Furthermore, enrollment in two summer semesters might shorten an evening education to just three years.

Finally, summer schooling made higher education a year-round, instead of a seasonal enterprise. Many criticized schooling for its summer hiatus. Summer cessation was born in a once-agricultural society where children and young bodies were needed in the fields. Now that modern economy had become more industrial, technological, and business oriented, and rural life more mechanized, the reason for replacing summer education with field work had ceased while the tradition persisted.

As for my druthers, summertime formal education has never held personal appeal. I did do a few years of summer teaching on a small scale at Stanford and other law schools for the American Academy of Judicial Education, but vowed never to do so again. I fancied that the human mind was deciduous. Like the drop of leaves in autumn, the drop of formal training in summer is a time for the roots and limbs of the brain to restore. Learning is an inhalation—a constant taking in. It needs time to exhale. Vacation was more than just an idle pastime for *recreation*. It was time for *re-creation*. "Working in the fields" was liberating.


Our efforts at establishing summer learning at NWLC were indicative of the volatile nature of the 1971-72 academic year. Like a yo-yo, the fate of summer education spun up and down. It got underway in early September 1971 with a faculty committee of Professors Brown, Jensen, Williamson, a student representative, and, of course, Associate Dean Fagg. I was listed as a "sometimes" participant. The committee faced an urgent deadline. A decision on fiscal viability had to be made before the end of October.

At the end of September, Dean Fagg reported that the operation would likely suffer a $17,000 net loss. It would take seventy-five enrollees to break even and that many sign-ups could not be predicted. That cast the spin downward and seemingly put an end to the matter.

But at the October 20 faculty meeting, the yo-yo spun back up. Summer school was resurrected when student Bill Valentic had taken upon himself to conduct a student poll wherein eighty-three students "committed themselves to potential enrollment."

Faculty members focused, however, on the words "potential" and "commitment" calling them oxymoronic. So, a motion was made to adopt a summer program but conditioned on at least seventy-five students ready to pay a $50 deposit as an advance on enrollment. Not even that financial commitment, however, was enough to satisfy faculty concerns. The motion was defeated, sending the yo-yo downward.

Shortly after the October deadline had come and gone, Associate Dean Fagg (the Contracts teacher) sought to nail down student commitment. He moved to institute a summer school if seventy-five students or more signed promissory notes formally binding themselves to pay full summer tuition. At a November 3 faculty meeting Fred's motion passed and the summer school plan climbed upward.

At a December 1 faculty meeting, the string snagged. This time the problem was whether summer classes should be scheduled at night or day or both. Professor Williamson opted in favor of daylight. Associate Dean Fagg hoped that some evening classes could be mixed into the schedule. Student Terry Rahmsdorff doubted that a daytime program could survive because even day students had to work during the summer. Fagg doubted that an all-evening program could be sound. I doubted whether a mixed day/night program could properly allocate credit hours under unsettled ABA accreditation rules. ABA Consultant Millard Ruud, who happened to be in attendance at this meeting during his inspection rounds, tried to explain an indefinite ABA rule situation. Unable "to devise a sound program which would serve student needs at this time," the faculty voted to junk any 1972 summer schooling, day or night. So, as of mid-year 1971-72, the spin spun down. Contrary to gravity, however, the yo-yo teaches this: Whatever goes down will come up.

At our February 16, 1972, faculty meeting, students Valentic and Hemphill proposed a summer school balanced budget of $25,000 showing no financial loss. It presumed night classes and $400 tuition for a full enrollment of six credit hours of class study by 50 students, plus an average of $200 tuition for 25 part-time enrollees. Associate Dean Fagg moved adoption of a summer school roughly based upon the student terms. The motion carried subject to their being 75 full and part-time enrollees as detailed in the proposal. The yo-yo rebounded.

At the next meeting on March 1, the faculty was informed that administrators had set a deadline of only one more week for enrollment of 75. Full-time enrollment of six credit hours called for a $50 deposit plus a $350 promissory note for the remaining tuition. The short deadline and the cash and note commitment virtually sealed the death of the summertime classes. When March 8 rolled around, the conditions were not met. Summer school spun to the bottom.

At the March 12 meeting, Fagg reported approximately 65 full and part-time students had registered, thus producing about $20,000 in cash and binding promise. That amount would pay all expenses except for $5,000 owed to the college for summer "overhead." The college share had been budgeted at $7,000—twenty-eight percent of the summer enterprise.

Professor Knudsen observed that students at other law schools would pick up much of the difference once publicity flyers were sent. Then too, the overhead obligation was soft; it was, after all, just a debt from child to parent—an in-house charge that ought to be carried on credit. Accordingly, Fagg moved once again to operate a summer school. The motion carried once again, and once again summer school climbed the string.

College administrators, however, demanded assurance that a summer program would be "completely self-supportive" before it could be authorized. The college wanted cash, no credit. The parent having spoken, a last minute deadline was invoked. In the days following the March 12 faculty meeting, the student *Law News* cast a final plea to the student body: "Today is the last day to sign up." It reported that summer schooling was just 13 commitments shy. "If you are on the borderline, please sign up today!" Spin slowed downward midst desperate cries.

But hope rose higher than dire pleas—so much so that plans were made. A summer curriculum was outlined, and teachers were aligned. Six courses were planned [Trial Practice, Federal Practice, Juvenile Law, Property Transactions, Family Law, and Environmental Law] to be taught respectively by Judge Robert E. Jones,

Professor Knudsen, lawyer William Schultz, Professor Vail, lawyer Ira Gottlieb, and Professor Williamson.

Like a photo finish, no one breathed in the wait-and-see if summer school could climb the last inch. Then, in the first week of June 1972, the yo-yo was finally and firmly in fist. NWLC opened its doors to the first summer semester in its history. It has never wound down since the bobbing in that seminal year.

## TESTING AND GRADING:

Throughout most schooling—whether primary, secondary, or higher education—there looms the scoring and ranking of student performance. In law schools, the grade etched on the written transcript in each course was typically the grade given in a single final exam. Four months of a semester's assignments, study and learning were evaluated on one written test in the last few hours of the course. Making the course grade the final exam grade was initiated somewhere in history in order to de-emphasize testing by reducing its incessancy; constant quizzing put too much accent on tests.

But the one-time exam had a contrary effect. It accentuated instead of minimizing testing. Solitary final exam scores were used to bestow *laude* degrees, to assign coveted law review editorships, to entice law career hirings, and to justify academic probations or dismissals. They developed into contest more than test—a crucial game filled with a range of exhilaration, rivalry, and dread. Is it any wonder then that honing the testing-grading process was riddled with a host of tangential problems:

*The "90-to-50" Grade System:* Among those problems was the concern for uniformity. Were all graders on the same page? Each year's crop of new professors and part-time instructors had to be informed about the necessities for team consistency in applying the grading standards. Understanding our "90-50" grade structure was essential to fair ranking. The grade of "78" for example, had to mean the same thing to all evaluators. Was that possible?

First semester grading efforts evidenced that the new teachers, conditioned throughout their own schooling by the "A-to-F" grade designations, were puzzled by NWLC's "90-to-50" gradations. [See ch. 6, "Grading Scheme"] So, Dean Wren called for a February 28 "sack-lunch" meeting of full and part-time teachers to discuss testing and grading and asked me to lead that discussion. It went well except for the fact that little of the time was spent on *how* the system worked, and most of the time went to *why* it had to work that way. The take-over of the "A-to-F" tradition was just a matter of time. A few more years of new cadre would do it. Traditional grades would not completely solve the uniformity problem, but its simplicity and commonality might help.

*Anonymous Grading:* Within my experience, it had always been the practice at NWLC to have students identified by assigned numbers on their test answers. Thus, professors were not to know student identities when evaluating exams. But nowhere was this written; nowhere was anonymity made mandatory. Consequently, some of our professors began to invade that secrecy. Name identification was needed, they said, because they wanted to average into the final exam grade an evaluation on attendance, preparedness, research, or homework.

The lack of required anonymity upset the activist student body. They suspected conscious or subliminal favoritism or discrimination. Oddly enough, it was not a suspicion that would have occurred to them during their primary, secondary, and undergrad schoolings where, in that day and age anonymous grading was virtually unheard of. But once exposed to law school anonymity in grading on crucially important final exams, they now recoiled when their non-identity was threatened. At stake was not just privacy for its own sake; at stake was honorary degrees, editorships, jobs, yea, their very law careers. Accordingly a few students implored the faculty to make anonymity compulsory in grading of any kind, whether final exams or written theses.

ABA accreditation standards did not address the issue. So, our faculty took no action on the petition other than to counsel professors and part-time instructors on the custom of identity secrecy when grading exams. Following that disposition, disappointed students promised that a petition would be circulated among the student body demanding mandatory anonymous grading. The promise did not materialize. But anonymity in testing was an issue that persisted, and it would move in a few years from resistance to insistence to existence.

*Dean's List:* Unlike the report of those with "academic difficulties," a Dean's List was a publication each semester of the names of those students whose semester grade averages put them in the top ten percent of their classmates. It was popular at other law schools. As chair of the Advancement Committee, I had to relay a committee recommendation to institute a Dean's List. As a voting member, I argued against it. The faculty voted to publish the list as an experiment but to reconsider its future in the future. The future proved it had none.

*Testing Seniors:* Some senior students raised another secondary issue. They petitioned the faculty to cancel all exam taking for graduating students in their final semester.

After a moment of astonishment, the professors gave the petition the courtesy of vote and the disdain of denial.

*Grade Deadlines:* Grades and grading also locked us into the annual discussion of two different deadlines: (1) When shall be the last day for professors to turn in their grades to the registrar? And (2) Should there be a single date at which all grades would be simultaneously conveyed to the students? [See ch. 9, "Grade Deadlines"] These were especially problems for fall semester exams. Now that those exams were scheduled prior to the holiday season, the Advancement Committee felt that teachers had more free time to do grading and, therefore, recommended February 7 as a deadline for reporting to the registrar and February 14 as a deadline for reporting to the students. Dean Wren urged even earlier dates. He recommended a day in January because he had already promised the students January deadlines.

Once again, Associate Dean Fagg pleaded for more time. Once again, some students argued to allow piecemeal posting of grades, thus to put some pressure on tardy graders. And once again, the deadlines were extended to a late February date for finished grading and a uniform date for posting.

As a final plea, some student wag suggested that, when referring to grades, professors should refrain from using the downright cruel word "*dead*line."

*Student Graders:* While my foregoing ambivalence about grades suggests an opposition to testing, that would be a misguided impression. There were, of course, very good reasons for evaluating student performance. Students do need to know how they are doing. Classmate comparison is certainly a way of conveying that. But the danger is that gradating goes beyond a need to know and becomes a contest as grades evolve into a driving force instead of a passenger along for the drive. Grading was a good thing so long as it was a learning experience—a *means* of education, not a *goal* of educating. You don't learn in order to be an "A+"; you are an "A+" because you learned.

As a teacher, I personally learned a great deal from grading. So much so that after enough experience with it, I felt it was being wasted on me. If it was a good learning device, why haven't we offered it to learners? I was not alone in the observation. Professor Knudsen had explored the idea in the previous academic year. At our December 8, 1970, faculty meeting, he had proposed the authorized use of supervised student graders. He produced a student poll showing nearly seventy-five percent student approval of student graders on exams. Some professors were quick to point out that the poll was taken from a mere twelve percent sampling of the student body.

On the matter of polling, in 1957 a national poll of students had shown opposition to student graders, but then in the late 1960s a similar national poll showed no student aversion. Student attitude in the short span of that decade had done an about face—all in keep with a 1960s evolving generation wary of established order.

ABA Consultant Ruud reported that ABA accreditors had no problem with the use of student graders who were diligently supervised by the course professor. Likewise, Michael Cardozo, Executive Director of the American Association of Law Schools, reported that AALS had "no official objection." But Cardozo hastened to opine personally that the practice "was not in the best traditions of legal education." That was the lay of things—no dark, but no sunshine either. It was enough to table Knudsen's motion until the next meeting. The delay and mulling were long enough to lead Bill to withdraw his motion authorizing graders.

Now here, over a year later in the spring of 1972, I resurrected the idea on my own. I took it upon myself, without a faculty vote, to seek $1,421 in work study monies from the 1972-73 proposed budget to pay for student graders. My impetuosity was born of impending calamity. I had over 250 students enrolled in three classes—Torts (day and evening) and Evidence (day). That would mean an annual 500 exams to grade—there being two exams per student over those two-semester courses. I calculated that the grading would entail over 700 hours of grade time. If I spent forty hours a week at grading (quite apart from other academic duties), it would take almost nine weeks each semester to do that work—one half of the academic year! With the help and supervision of three student graders, the four of us could complete the job in three weeks in each semester. Rough calculation—to be sure. But, rough labors to warrant it.

As there was no recorded rule against it, I felt I needed no faculty authorization to use student graders. I suggested that my work with the students would be an experiment upon which we all could draw. The 1972-73 budget proposal was approved with my expense item along for the ride.

I used scholarly upperclass student graders who had excelled on my Torts and Evidence exams. Over the years, they included Michael Corn, Richard Cremer, Brent Crook, Bruce Crocker, Peter Dehlinger, Carl Gaul, Fred Kerley, Maureen Leonard, Jack Lundeen, Katherine O'Neill, Tom Sand, Stewart Teicher, John Thomas, Thane Tiensen, Mary Trieber, Nelson Walker, Theresa Welch, Susan Whitney, and Daryl Wilson. [If I have omitted anyone, I deeply regret my poor record and failing memory and beg forgiveness.]

Seven years later, the experiment would cease. In spite of what I saw as success, some of my colleagues were still uneasy with the idea and were bothered by my aggression in initiating it. Then too, my having to supervise, consult, and double-check the process was almost as time-consuming as my previous plod alone with it.

As far as I know, no one at NWLC has ever used graders again nor has there ever been a rule promulgated against it. It remains a shame that the grading process is wasted on those to whom it has become an infernal, but necessary, drudge. In 1991, Rutgers Law Journal published my article entitled, "The Agonies of Exam Grading." It's a story of a fictional professor whose mournful cries echo through the halls and hollows of late-night grading.

But enough! Soon the groaner's ache in the back can become another's pain in the neck.

ENVIRONMENTAL LAW:

During the 1971-72 year, our law review periodical under Editor-in-Chief Gary Abbott, published its *third* and *fourth* issues. The editorial board were all evening students who had seen service in the two previous founding years. Amazingly, *Environmental Law* was receiving numerous, unsolicited manuscripts from across the nation—more offerings than could be published. From the experience of being a founding editor of another law review when I was a law student, I was surprised to see the extent of early unsolicited attention given our fledgling publication. Older, more popular, and well established law reviews of the east could count on unsolicited zeal for personal byline recognition in their renown pages. But what was it that enticed authors to the new-found pages of an unknown law review of a temporarily accredited school in the far Pacific northwest? It could not be personal ambition; it had to be genuine concern. An avenue had been opened for those with real care for our planet instead of the desire to impress their peers.

Those same deep concerns were also evidenced at the other end of the media pipeline. Many readers and libraries signed for continuing subscriptions at $6.00 per year. With that, our conduit to the nation was well on its way to paying for itself.

In the summer of 1971, *Environmental Law* received its first appellate court mention in the case of *State v. House*. [260 Or. 138, 143] Oregon Supreme Court Justice Thomas H. Tongue, cited volume 1, page 278 of *Environmental Law* as research authority. Oddly enough *House* was a homicide case and the text had nothing to do with our environment. Nevertheless, the citation became a milepost for *when* it was, not for *what* it was. It was a first. We celebrated with a champagne toast in the foyer of our law library.

There were other small *Environmental Law* accomplishments in 1971. A professor at the University of Puget Sound was using our law review as an assigned text in his college class. We also took accomplishment from rivalry; contest came from the University of California Law School at Berkeley (Boalt Hall). They began their *Ecological Law Quarterly*. Competition was flattering and challenging. We were being followed by a well established and worthy rival. Therein lies the irony of competition:

its challenges pull forward while pushed from behind. And therein lies the puzzle for Law: Enliven the challenge with success but somehow keep both the forward and the followers lively.

The law periodical was just the jewel in our environmental crown. There was more. A number of environmental elective courses began to pepper the curriculum. Likewise, the Northwest Environmental Defense Center [NEDC], the law school tenant, was pursuing demands upon the established order. NWLC also received a $30,800 grant from the U.S. Department of Health, Education, and Welfare [HEW] for our environmental program. Spearheaded by the law review, the program was putting a face on the school.

When back in the summer of 1969, Dean Wren, ABA Consultant Ruud, Professor Williamson, and I had met in my living room office on Huddleston Lane [see ch. 6, "Law Periodical Project"] to give NWLC's periodical an environmental focus, controversial issues unearthed by ecological study were not yet prominent. We were then in uncharted territory. But since then, politics and economics have mapped battlefields. Issues were drawn and sides taken. Critics called environmental study "environmentalism" and researchers became "environmentalists." Contest pitted environment against atomic energy, lumbering, industry, jobs, mining, the automobile, whaling, waste disposal, ranching, farming, irrigating, dam building and other uses or abuses of land, air, and water. NWLC tried to stay at center in those arenas in order to balance preservation and use of nature. But in a time of upheaval, equilibrium was difficult. By 1972, "divisiveness," not balance, became the key word.

## RACIAL AFFIRMATIVE ACTION:

The U.S. Supreme Court's renowned decision in *Brown v. Topeka Board of Education*, was issued in 1954. It triggered a vast movement of change away from centuries-old, racial discrimination in education as well as in other walks of life. The movement expanded slowly, however. It wasn't until the mid-1960s that the ABA took a formal position in favor of equal opportunity in law education. In 1971-72, invidious racial discrimination was still an open attitude in some private law schools—a lingering legacy from a day just a little over a century before when people owned people. ABA Consultant Ruud told the story of a Mississippi law college trustee whose "face had a look of shock and dismay... when informed that the ABA would not tolerate... exclusion of blacks."

Back in 1968, I had a similar experience as a member of a Portland City Club research study in "Racial Justice in Portland." [See ch. 4] The project was broken into parts concerning discrimination in the usual areas of housing, employment, law enforcement, and education. The committee added a fifth, less customary category "private clubs." I was assigned the job of writing the latter section. It was the most controversial in that it reached a lair of discrimination that was most personal and intimate: social association. Some of what I wrote was picked up and quoted on news wires and received national attention. The quote was:

> "There are myriad clubs, lodges, fraternities, orders, and other private social institutions in the city, be their ostensible purpose athletic, educational, religious, mystic, civic, or business, which are nevertheless socially oriented. All too many of these groups follow racist policies and practices. There are quota systems, exclusionary clauses, "blackballs," and other forms of *de facto* discrimination... Such systematic exclusion is not only insidious, worst of all it is infectious. It infects its members, and its members are often community leaders—the same men who educate, who provide housing, who employ, who govern."

Fraternal organizations reacted strongly to that language. Like Consultant Ruud, I was confronted by indignant club members. One of them put his freedom in this way: "Simply because we want to be with our kind that does not mean that we are prejudiced against them!" Such was the language and the logic of those days. "Them, those, and they" were the convenient pronouns that denied prejudice while putting "us" here and "them" there.

It is difficult for us today to fully realize the open and accepted resistance to racial mixing that was afoot in the early 1970s. Modernly, anathema to integrating is not outspoken. But what is invidious can also be insidious. Once ethnic prejudice works its way into a social fabric, it's an undetected parasite feeding on the blanket of indifference—a subliminal discrimination that is the hardest of all to disinfect. *E.g.*, in NWLC's mid-1960s applications for admission, we were not asking applicants to identify their race or ethnicity, but we did ask them to send two photos. It was a carry-over from decades of practice. Why? What did photography have to do with allowing entrance through our doors? No one could answer, because no one asked and, if asked, no one knew. Then one day an admissions application came and gently unmasked our subliminal indifference. Where the form asked for submission of "two permanent photographs," the applicant pasted two photos of his car. After all, it did not say "portrait" photos. Beneath the photos the applicant penned something to this effect: "These are black and white photos; did you need to have color photography showing other colors like brown, red, yellow?" Not only was it humor, it was poignant. It made us think, and think was all it took. Thereafter, we continued to ask for portraits but gave the option of submitting them after our offer of admission, not before.

The history of Northwestern College of Law in downtown Portland showed no official or patent incidents with racial or ethnic bias. But if the insidious and latent experiences at other schools of higher education were any indication, then perhaps Northwestern in earlier times might have been just as vulnerable as any of those others in earlier times. *E.g.*, law fraternities nationally and at Northwestern had practiced invidious discrimination while under the roofs of their home schools.

And so, by the mid-1960s, past and present racial suppression and *de jure* and *de facto* denial of equal protection were everywhere recognized as a problem. But exposure was one thing and solution was another. An immediate answer was to give the suppressed a boost under the name: "affirmative action."

At first, there were no notable complaints with affirmative action policies, largely because there were still empty places available to take care of most all qualified applicants. But burgeoning numbers at the turn of the decade into the 1970s had filled law seat vacancies and left qualified aspirants outside school doors. The resulting competition made the racial credential a dubious criterion in the minds of some.

At the start of our 1971-72 academic year, an obvious wrinkle in affirmative action surfaced. In Seattle, some two hundred miles from our law campus, the *DeFunis* trial was scheduled. [See ch. 6, "Diversity"] Marco DeFunis, a law admissions applicant, had filed suit against the State of Washington's law school, challenging its affirmative action policy as an unconstitutional denial of equal protection of laws. He argued that he was barred from admission on account of his white color, inasmuch as minority group applicants with credentials less than his own were admitted ahead of him—the sole difference between his and their files being racial.

ABA Consultant Ruud was called to testify in that September Seattle trial. On his way back to ABA's Chicago headquarters, he stopped in Portland to notify us of this new counter development. Ruud's warning put us far ahead of the publicity that the *DeFunis* case was destined to arouse nationally.

Higher education efforts to boost admissions opportunity to the deprived had developed a snag. The snag moved beyond a mere "development" and threatened to become an impasse when the U.S. Supreme Court agreed to hear the *DeFunis* case and to pass judgment on the new issue called "reverse discrimination." The pending pronouncement of the nation's highest judicial tribunal would cause all government schools of higher education to walk on the egg shells of threatened law suits.

That threat did not directly pertain to a private school like us. Constitutional equal protection and due process were mandates to public institutions, not individual enterprise. But indirectly, private schools were significantly affected. What the Court would say about affirmative action, would undoubtedly be guidelines for the U.S. Department of Health, Education, and Welfare [HEW]. That agency was empowered to give financial aid to students of all schools—public or private provided the schools met certain conditions, among which was no racial discrimination. If NWLC wished to continue partaking in that dole, we would be obliged to comply with what the Court would order. Whether by carrot or prod, all schools of higher education were wrapped in alert.

At NWLC, more than admissions, recruitment, and financial aid were involved. We were in a status of provisional accreditation. That then involved pleasing accreditors as well as HEW. HEW gave its financial aid to only "recognized institutions," and that meant *accredited* schools. That in turn meant that those agencies who gave accreditation had to be inspected and investigated by HEW every five years. HEW assigned that job to its Advisory Committee on Institutional Quality and Integrity [ACIQI].

And so, while NWLC was being accredited by ABA and AALS, those accreditors were being "accredited" by ACIQI, who were under auspices of HEW. That chain of "acronism" would have to answer to Congressional delegations and Presidential on-lookers, who had to abide what the Supreme Court would say about proper and improper considerations of race when recruiting and admitting students for enrollment.

DeFunis contended that it was unconstitutional to fight racial discrimination with racial discrimination. Schools cannot reverse the forward movement of a wrong by countering the wrong with more of the same. No matter how good its intentions, reverse discrimination is invidious.

To which, the proponents of affirmative action argued that their way was not "reverse." Rather it was a *forward* attempt. When a runner has been unfairly hobbled in a race and thus handicapped by lost ground; removing the hobbles is not alone a fair remedy; the handicap—which is to say, the lost ground—must also be removed by moving the "lost" runners forward, which is not the same as putting the front runners in reverse. As every firefighter or vaccinator knows, to stop spread or contagion, back-fires or inoculation of disease must sometimes be used.

Waiting for the Court to focus issues, and give solutions would prove to be a frustrating seven year vigil. The constitutional issue was a lot more complicated than it at first seemed. The Court needed time to sort matters out. The "out" was handed to them when Marco DeFunis was admitted to another law school. Thus, he no longer sought his remedy of admission to the defendant law school. The case was now moot, and the Court removed it from the docket.

Although the *DeFunis* case was dead, the issue was very much alive in the admissions halls of all schools of higher education. The pins and needles of wait still tingled with what the Court might do one day with affirmative action. Seven years would have to pass before the Court would speak again on the constitutional "cans" and "cannots" in selecting and recruiting students. The allegations arose this time in medical schooling, where an applicant claimed denial of equal protection when his desire to be a doctor was rejected on account of his white race. *Bakke v. Regents of California*, 438 U.S. 265 (1978).

But that case and its progeny were much too late for our immediate needs in 1971-72. We and our accreditors had to know to what extent our admissions and recruiting actions could affirmatively consider racial profiles. Could we legitimately create a *racial quota system* for acceptances? Could we legitimately take into account the need of the law profession and the public to have *racial role-models*? Could we legitimately attempt to *rectify centuries of racial suppression* by boosting? Could we legitimately consider the educational values in having *racial integration and cultural diversity* among student peers?

Future judicial decisions would tell us that only the latter diversity-in-education purpose was constitutional. It was not invidious for schools to consider sound education when admitting and recruiting students. Education in general is served by exposing peers to mixed cultural difference. But education, the essence of schooling, is not there to service an individual's personal opportunity or societal wants beyond learning itself. Accordingly, racial quota systems, role-modeling, and rectifying past wrongs would one day be declared reverse discrimination and unconstitutional. But in 1971-72 and for the next seven years, we, like most schools, were careful to not let any form of racial consideration enter our formal admissions and recruiting process—not even educational integration. Ostensibly, we wore blinders.

Just as the blind-fold hides the view, so too does it shield the peek. I would not consider color or culture when casting my vote for an applicant's entry into NWLC. But, I do recall being *mindful* of the need for racial minority lawyers in minority communities and in the law profession. I also was *mindful* of how past systematic suppression was an infection that, left untreated, would continue to fester long after the suppression had been checked. Was being *mindful* of such inescapable truths the same as *considering* them in candidate selection? It was a predicament—much like not thinking of people locked in chains when deciding what to do with the keys.

## FEMINIST MOVEMENT:

Past oppression and invidious discrimination also infected gender. Northwestern College of Law, as a low-tuition, open admission, nighttime law school in downtown Portland, had been a small isle in a sea of oppression for women who fought for career opportunity. One such woman aspirant has told her story many times. In 1962, Betty Roberts decided to get a doctorate degree in political science and made the trip to the University of Oregon at Eugene in order to apply for admission. She was interviewed by the head of the political science department, who told her, in no uncertain terms, that as a homemaker and a woman of her age, she was not acceptable. Oregon taxpayer money could not be wasted on someone whose employment was not promising and whose "career prospects were far too short."

Back home in Portland, she did not give up. She went to Northwestern, where the registrar, Judge John Flint Gantenbein, without hesitation, simply said, "School starts in two weeks; see you there." The judge had done the same thing for women many times, including his wife Alice. As a wedding present back in the early 1940s, he enrolled his wife as a first-year law student.

Betty got her law degree, passed the Bar exam, practiced law, and eventually became an elected state representative and senator in the Oregon legislature, was appointed one of the first judges on the new Oregon Court of Appeals, and finally was seated on the Supreme Court of Oregon. Justice Betty Roberts, a NWLC graduate whose "career prospects were far too short," was the first woman in the history of Oregon to serve on that high tribunal.

What put her on the road to those honors could not be described as *"affirmative* action." At the University of Oregon, it was *"negative* action." At Northwestern, it was simply Gantenbein's *"standard* action." Justice Roberts had followed the paths of three other Northwestern alumnae. Mary Jane Spurlin, a 1924 graduate, was Oregon's first woman judge. Jean Lewis, a 1938 graduate, was Oregon's first, woman Circuit Court judge. Mercedes Deiz, a 1959 graduate, overcame two barriers: she was the first woman, black judge in the history of Oregon.

Although women enrollees throughout the country were still a paltry minority in 1971-72, their feminine enthusiasm whipped up a lot of male backlash. The reaction was often and open and gave new meaning to an old and dormant word: "chauvinism." At NWLC, our student body president was Sherry Smith, the first woman in the school's history to surface in that position. She was also the editor of *Night Owl*, the student newsletter. Her prominence and assertiveness aroused certain male quarters. One such reactionist wrote Dean Wren and called her doings "damn nonsense." The writer went on to color her in Annie Oakley metaphor: she "shoots from broad hips in shotgun fashion, seeking only an ink blood bath;... a feminist Don Quixote who rides side-saddle through her classes." The tirade reached back to a seventeenth century quote when it likened her to "...an ugly, old-maid courted by incapacity." So went the name-calling and vitriol of those days. Today, that backlash has disappeared in open ground—yet still sulks in hidden (sometimes chilling) corners.

The biggest hurdle for women lawyers in those times was not schools. The biggest hurdle was employment after schooling was all over. Caroline's Stoel's story is an example. She graduated from an eastern law school in the 1930s with top academic

## JUDICIAL ALUMNAE

First women judges in Oregon: [top l. to r.]: Mercedes Deiz, Betty Roberts, Mary Jane Spurlin; [lower left]: Jean Lewis; and student scion.

honors. She and her husband Tom (also a law graduate) came to Oregon because Tom had been hired by a leading law firm in Portland. When Caroline sought to get a job in the same firm, she was not only rejected, she was told not to practice law in Oregon because it might create a conflict of interest with her husband's law work. So, top graduate Caroline never did practice law. Instead, she went on to be a noted historian and college professor. Beyond mere job rejection, female prospects faced an impasse that could stifle entire law careers.

By the 1970s, however, what women law students and women lawyers lacked in numbers and clout was countered by the vigor of their movement. They confronted teachers, schools, bar associations, and law firms. They even took their aggression to law school accreditors. For instance, in 1971, AALS adopted a position stating that law schools should *"firmly expect"* no discrimination against women from employers recruiting law students on law campuses. *Expectation*, no matter how firm, was not sufficient, said the feminists. AALS accreditors should *require* that law schools must *insist* that recruiters have a *strongly stated policy* against gender discrimination. Mandatory, not precatory, language was called for.

The war against invidious discrimination in the early 1970s was no longer a time of hope; it was a time of pursuit. That activism put a lot of dander up. Change has never been a darling of establishment, and our law faculty had to deal with it. Still distant was the issue of sexual orientation. One day far ahead, gays and lesbians would be following the same route in challenging suppression.

## ACCREDITATION:

Although surrounded by in-house attention to enrollment, environmental curriculum, hiring, finance, building, electives, clinical study, confidentiality, testing, grading, student activity, summer schooling, integration, and more, our main look had to be outward—our entry beyond and into the national family of recognized law schools. That meant we had to please. Some would have called that focus a "diversion," because it engaged us in compliance instead of venture. We were anxious to excel and not just adapt. But, it was the desire for accreditation that had sparked NWLC. We were not yet fully accredited and had to be wary about not letting our flame consume that spark. So the headstrong law faculty had to discipline itself to the lesson learned in the transitions from infancy to youth to adolescence to maturity: Independence cannot be asserted without first being dependent.

To please ABA Consultant Ruud, we thought it best to begin accreditation overtures with the other accreditor—AALS. This would allow the dual accreditors to work together—a coordination that Ruud urged upon leaders in both houses. Accordingly,

Dean Wren aimed to gain permanent accreditation from both AALS and ABA in the middle of the next 1972-73 academic year.

During the 1971-72 year, we readied ourselves for and entertained three separate visitations by ABA Consultant Ruud. Assistant to the Dean Doris McCroskey was assigned the job of coordinator and compiler of a lengthy ABA questionnaire to which most of the faculty submitted data. When she was done, the text of the report was one hundred pages, to which twenty-four exhibits were attached and included our printed catalog, handbook, student-faculty directory, building blue prints, sample copies of the "Night Owl" (student newspaper), the alumni "Bulletin," and faculty meeting minutes. It was an inky mimeographed tome in multitude copies that begged for technology yet to be. All of it sorted out and storied the life of a school—what we were, what we had become, and what we were to be—a task wrapped in ropes of statistic and knotted with hopes of acceptance.

In February 1972, Dean Wren went to New Orleans to report to the ABA Council. He was steered to the Council's new "Accreditation Sub-committee." [See ch. 7, "Pitch to ABA Council"] The sub-committee was another echelon for us to convince—indicia of an ageless phenomenon in commerce: Just as small yearns to get bigger, big then needs to get smaller.

At the Accreditation Sub-Committee, Wren faced its chairman, none other than George Neff Stevens, Wren's predecessor dean at NWLC. The record does show President Howard making that trip. No doubt it was fair to say that Stevens and Howard were not likely on the best of terms. The question was: Would Stevens help with our toll across the bridge or be a troll beneath it? Stevens had departed NWLC under harsh circumstances; and, concerning our accreditation, had been quoted in the press to say in no uncertain terms, "They aren't going to get it."

While a Stevens' grudge was certainly grounds for ponder, such pique and pettiness were not in Stevens' make-up. In later years, he would confide to me (in mixed metaphor, if my notes are correctly recorded) that he had deliberately "put the burr in the Lewis & Clark trustees' saddle" at the risk of "sandpapering the lion's tail." [See ch. 3] There had been method in his call for urgent action because he thought highly of NWLC's prospects. Even after his departure, he maintained a strong interest in the future of NWLC—a law school he had a modest hand in promoting. He looked back and saw accomplishment, not defeat. For example, in a flattering letter he told me, "You are one of my prize recruits to law school teaching." That expressed a dynamic that motivates educators. They are vicarious partakers who take joy in the success of their students, colleagues, and schools. Stevens was not in education to deny others in order to allay his piques; rather he was dedicated to boost others toward their peaks. Genuine teachers pass, not covet, the baton.

After his visit with the ABA Accreditation Subcommittee, Dean Wren reported that Dean Stevens was more helpful than hurtful. Stevens offered the constructive advice that our most glaring issue was the lack of a law librarian, a serious remiss in our accreditation goal. Wren assured the Committee that the problem would be taken care of shortly. Back in Portland, the law professors were puzzled to know how.

Another troubling issue on the accreditation path was handed us in the middle of the 1971-72 year. Nationwide student disobedience, confrontation, trespass, and perceived promiscuous activity bothered a certain contingent of ABA leaders. They were particularly troubled about this new generation seeking law careers. So, they pressed law schools for help in screening out undesirable aspirants who had unethical backgrounds. Ordinarily, state bar examiners were the scrutinizers of moral character when law graduates applied for membership in a bar organization. Admission to law school did not entail any intense investigation into character. Now the ABA was urging law schools to conduct detailed ethical checks prior to law education and to cooperate with state bar organizations in revealing any dishonorable happenings in an applicant's past. The ABA contingent argued that in-depth inquiry should happen sooner than later for aspirants who ought to know in advance whether their past would bar them from their future as a lawyer in a particular state. A specially invoked ABA committee gave precise steps for how that cooperation would be conducted. It involved written questionnaires, tests, interviews, and personal recommendations.

The ABA Council, our immediate accrediting entity, approved the concept "in principle." It had yet to receive section approval. Law schools, by and large, did not want the job. Educators felt that schools should not pre-judge a soul. Learning law and its ethical base is not just for the moral. It's needed by the amoral and applies to any kind of schooling. Nels Peterson, a NWLC alumnus and a member of our Board of Visitors, took the criticism to a stronger level. He called the Council's endorsed report, "a most horrendous document,... a chilling effect on First Amendment rights,... the specter of a police state,... the repression of those who feel that change is necessary,... a trend toward an establishment of an elite group to the practice of law."

Other law schools were circulating a petition to the ABA hierarchy to resist the Council's position. At our May 17, 1972, faculty meeting, Professor Knudsen urged us to join the petitioners. Practically all of our professors, including myself, were in favor. But Dean Wren urged caution; more thought was needed, he said. We had a burden that other schools did not have to carry. We were provisional. As such, we sought offerings from the very entity we might now antagonize. Accordingly, discussion was postponed. At the June 6 meeting, Knudsen attempted to re-open the discussion with a motion to resist our involvement in moral fitness investigation of admissions applicants. The motion was tabled until sometime in the next academic year when our ABA accreditation may have solidified into permanency—a more stable soapbox on which to stand. Alas, it was another case for the wisdom of the mind wizening the heart. In the meantime, our response to the issue was to ignore it. That seemed to work, because within the ABA the concept was never instituted. It was typical in an era where knee-jerk ideas could go quickly limp.

## END OF THE YEAR:

Clocks and calendars tell us that all days are twenty-four hours and all weeks are seven days. But the mind tells us otherwise. Some days are longer than their hours, and some weeks fly by faster than their days. The clock and calendar had definitely slowed down for the 1971-72 academic year as shown by the length of these last two chapters. But even the far-reached is eventually taken. In Academe, the end is capped by commencing.

Our commencement ceremony in June 1972 conferred thirty-seven Doctor of Jurisprudence degrees. There would never again be a class of seniors that small at NWLC. They were the last exclusively evening graduates. Since 1886, the school had always bestowed its diplomas on only students of the night. Next year, the 1973 graduation would infuse day seniors as well.

The 1972 law graduates began their schooling in September 1968 with about sixty-five enrollees. Only fifty-seven percent of that class finished. They and their alma mater had come over a lot of peaks and into a lot of bottoms in their school's struggle to get accredited.

The graduation was still an all-school ceremony. The push for a separate law ceremony was growing stronger but so was its resistance. That resistance was intertwined with a contest over the school's name. Should it be titled "Lewis & Clark *University*" instead of Lewis & Clark *College?*" By dictionary definition, "college" denotes an integrated, undivided campus of arts and science departments, whereas "university" recognizes diverse and distinct disciplinary schools. We were undoubtedly a university but still embraced the tradition of college. Opponents of the "college" title saw that the school had changed. Evolution taught that once tails were lost, it was time to come down from the trees. On the other hand, others saw no harm in homage born of respect for the vestigial tail. Most others said, "It's just a name. Get over it." But once denotation of words was resolved, there was still connotation to deal with. Is a residence a "house" or a "home"? Is there a difference between a "donkey" and a "jackass"? Is a sheepskin calligraphy better called a "diploma" or a "degree"? Does the degree read better if it comes from a "University" or a "College"? Would Shakespeare's "Rose" have smelled so sweet if it had been named "succotash"?

Unceremoniously, yet still an honor, the end of the year was also culminated by faculty promotions. Assistant Professor Bill Williamson was made an associate professor, and Associate Professors Fred Fagg and I were made "full" professors. I had been with NWLC for six years. Now that I was "filled," I felt no differently than when I supposedly "assisted" or merely "associated."

Graduation and promotion were both overtures to future promise. Indeed, the future of the law school itself was also promising. We were ending on an upnote in spite of a rather volatile year. Full accreditation was on the visible horizon. Reach was there before us, and we were confident of grasp in the next academic year.

Then came a shock—yet another setback. In the summer of 1972, Dean Wren resigned.

# 12

# THE QUESTS FOR PERMANENCY

*Fall 1972*

## ONE DOWN, TWO TO GO

From the start of the year, "permanency" was our task on two separate fronts: ABA accreditation and the deanship. At our July 13, 1972, faculty meeting, matters seemed normal. Dean Hal Wren informed us that in the future he would be sitting in on each of the professors' classes as part of his decanal duties. Nothing was said about renouncing his duties. It was to be his last meeting at NWLC. One week later, the faculty was informed that Dean Wren had resigned. It was sudden and unexpected. He had left to become the dean of the University of Richmond law school in his native Virginia. Later, he would also serve as the dean of Brandeis School of Law at Louisville University in Kentucky.

Assistant to the Dean Ann Kendrick was assigned the duty of arranging a "suitable farewell." She set August 15 as a date for that event, but Professor Bross's August 19 faculty minutes reported: "Wren was unable to attend his own farewell party because of excess emotion." In later years, his son Geoffrey wrote me that the "accreditation process caused Dad a lot of stress." The stress, however, had been endured by his conviction that "nothing could stop the school from becoming the best in the northwest."

In conversing with Hal over the years at conventions and by phone, he always expressed his deep sorrow at leaving NWLC. He told me that his time in Portland was "the best in my legal career and I wish that I had stayed." Granted that Hal's superlatives had to be tempered by his boundless optimism and energy, nevertheless I saw sincerity in his regrets. Indeed, he sought to return to the Pacific northwest just two years after his departure from here and did so in still later years. Hal had been our dean for three academic years. He came to us at an ebb-time, when his buoyancy was uplifting. The Wren regime saw the building of the law school's first permanent home, first daytime education, and first successful step in accreditation.

Since the beginning of the law school on the Lewis & Clark campus just six years before, the full-time faculty had been led by three different deans and now a fourth interim dean was needed. "Permanency" was hardly the label to describe our decanal office. Like our ABA accreditation status, our deans were turning out to be temporary. Trustees were vitally concerned about the instability and the publicity. It did not vouch well for a school to be seen getting its fourth dean over a six-year period. We needed an anchor in our seafaring and a captain that would stay topside. We most certainly did not need any more public attention to another filling of that post. Sentiment strongly favored sliding someone quickly into position with little fanfare. Some felt an "in-house" dean would best fill that purpose.

## THE FIRST FACULTY DEAN SEARCH:

At the July 31 faculty meeting, Associate Dean Fred Fagg III informed us that President Howard had appointed him interim dean. He said that President Howard first offered him the job of permanent dean, but he refused for two reasons: For one, he was not sure he wanted the job; and for another, he felt that the law school needed someone with credentials equal to Hal Wren's experience. Some might have suspected his first reason, but all affirmed his second reason. Whatever the reasons, the faculty, like Fred, favored a search, even though that would slow us down in our accreditation push.

Our full-time faculty at that time included eight new professors, [see ch. 10, "Faculty Hiring"] all of whom had either made a career change or had pulled up stakes at distant parts of the nation in order to join this promising new law school venture. It had to be a troubled moment upon entering to pass by their lead recruiter exiting. Not the most hearty welcome, to be sure.

Interim Dean Fagg recommended that a committee be formed to conduct the search—a committee that included law professor members. The proposal must have had a half-hearted approval from President Howard. Both a committee search and law faculty involvement was something new. Our three previous deans and now our acting dean had all been college administrative decrees. There was no full-time faculty when George Neff Stevens was hired; Jack Cairns was an interim dean whose seniority and old Northwestern trustee status sealed the spot; Wren was appointed by President Howard without formal faculty input (the faculty at that time being for the most part just me).

A full-fledge dean search inculcating law professors was a stepping stone to

**EIGHT NEW PROFESSORS (1972)**

Clockwise from upper left: Ed Belsheim, Jim Dente, Len DuBoff, Jay Folberg,
Bill Snouffer, Bernie Vail, Bob Myers, and (center) Ed Brunet.

what would become future searches conducted exclusively by the law faculty. Faculty involvement was not so much innovative as it was necessary. No sane candidate for a law deanship would deign to try leading a cadre of headstrong law teachers without first having near unanimous approval from them. Our interim dean knew this. Our president was learning.

Membership on the 1972 seminal Dean Search Committee, as recommended by Interim Dean Fagg, was composed of college trustees (William Swindells and Paul Boley), law alumni (Justice Ralph Holman and Judge Philip Roth), and four law professors (Knudsen, Williamson, Jensen, and myself). President Howard added two more college trustees (Robert Pamplin and Chester McCarty), and one more law professor (Belsheim). It was then pointed out that Item 7(b) of the Merger Agreement called for old Northwestern Trustee representation "on the Search and Selection Committee for a full-time Dean and full-time faculty." Accordingly, Justice Thomas Tongue and Judge John Flint Gantenbein were added. Two law students were also added—Don Lloyd from the day division and Karen Creason from the evening division; they were destined to be our first two *summa cum laude* graduates. Their addition made a total of fifteen members,—sixteen when President Howard, of course, was included. It was unwieldy in size, yet focused in aim.

Acting Dean Fagg suggested that I should be the chair of that Search Committee. But that was not about to happen. A professor was not going to lead such a high-powered assembly. Trustee Swindells was made chairman.

The Law Dean Search Committee's maiden gathering met informally in late July 1972. It did not take long before the focus became somewhat blurred. Members were invited to express their opinions on whether a search was necessary and, if so, how it should proceed. I penned some notes on the commentary that ensued. Law alumni President Roth said that he and the alumni were "impressed with Fagg." On the other hand, Tongue announced that someone other than Fagg would "be his selection."

Boley was concerned that hiring another national figure, who (like Stevens and Wren) might become a third resignation in just six years, and that "would give us a bad name." He felt that Fred Fagg had been an outstanding administrator and the "community was sold on him." But he granted that two things worked against Fred's candidacy: he was young in age (less than forty years) and young in experience (just two years as a legal educator).

Belsheim warned that we were going to find it difficult to do an "outside" search in view of our current, tentative accreditation status. As a former law school dean, he ventured that our permanent dean would have to come from within our current faculty. Likely as not, the only interested internal candidate was Fred.

President Howard revealed that he had already offered Fred the permanent post, but it was Fred's idea to organize a national search. A hesitant committee then agreed to go along with Fred's and the law faculty's request, provided the search would be "short and discreet." Strong emphasis was placed on both words. "Short" meant hurried, and "discreet" meant hushed. Committee work had to have a deadline for completion and no public announcement. Inquire but do not be subject to inquiry. "Quick-and-quiet" was the guidon repeatedly stressed.

Discussion then centered on the abilities we needed in a dean. Swindells, the business man, said the dean "must be a developer—one who could establish rapport in the community." Roth, the trial judge, said the dean should have "experience in the practice of law" and only "lastly a scholar." Faculty members, on the other hand, emphasized that legal scholarship was important. Students Lloyd and Creason felt the dean needs "experience and contacts with national legal education." Former Northwestern trustee Tongue urged that we should be "looking for someone with leanings toward evening education." We were blind-folded with hands on the elephant.

Wishful touchings went on for awhile until President Howard brought us back on his track: We already had a templet in the form of his front runner. The job was to find someone whose qualifications could surpass the interim appointee. "We should be done with searching and have our man no later that the start of 1973." That finish line was just five months away.

If it was the faculty that wanted the search, then the faculty should conduct it. That was the next step taken. So, the trustees changed its "Search Committee" title to "Selection Committee" and then still later began to call itself the "Dean Review Committee." The labeling served to clearly define separate functions. The faculty would *search* and the Review Committee would *review* and *select* from what the faculty found.

It would be the first faculty dean search, but it was on the short leash of one semester and in the tight fit of secrecy. We were to simply probe and find—quick-and-quiet—what was out there—without making contact. If there was any selecting to do, then the interviewing and scrutinizing of candidates would fall upon the Review Committee, not the faculty.

Following the Review Committee meeting, the law professors got together in late August 1972. Fagg recused himself. Again, I made some rough notes. We began with the awareness that one contingent of our college family "strongly favor the incumbent acting dean and see further search as useless." Where Fred had predicted that the search was "bound to be a long and arduous one," the faculty sided with President Howard in observing that "a prolonged search can be harmful what with accreditation on the pan and continuity of development being imperative." A long and involved pursuit might also be "harmful in the way of opening old wounds and starting new ones." Accordingly, the faculty was determined to conduct a thorough national search even though short and clandestine.

The faculty then created a Dean Search Committee that included all five law professors on the Dean Review (Selection) Committee and the addition of volunteer professors Hughey and Vail. I was made "spokesman" of faculty input from the Search Committee to the Review Committee. As spokesman, I was instructed to carry this preface to the Review Committee: The faculty's desire to have a national search was "in no way intended to disparage the competent man we now have;" we simply wanted to inspect candidates, not to reject a candidate. A few professors cautioned me to relay the preface as a consensus not a unanimity.

The "spokesman" job was initially fashioned to be no more than a messenger between faculty and the Review Committee—a function made necessary because our acting dean was an active candidate. But "spokesman" evolved into a chairmanship, which meant a lot more than just an intermediary. At the same time that I was saddled with leading a dean search, I also had agreed to serve on a citizens task force for the Portland Public Schools to study its financial difficulties. Oddly enough, those two entries into administrating academics took a lot of time away from academics itself.

When I called a first meeting of the faculty Dean Search Committee, it was agreed that our first step would be to contact contacts. "Contacts" were quidnuncs, those within legal education whose ears were tuned to the nation's professorial gossip. They were not candidates; they were snoops who might know of candidates. There are always such newsmongers. And so, we began the discreet look for matchmakers who would be discreet in putting us together with those discreetly looking for deanships. Indeed, it was a game of hide and seek at both ends.

We made a list of potential contacts and then assigned specific professors to tap those sources—based on how well a professor knew the contact. I was assigned to talk to the most logical choice, Millard Ruud. Belsheim was to consult with his old friend, Professor Myers McDougall at Yale. Williamson was to phone Professor Albert Sacks at Harvard. Jensen would seek the confidence of Professor Frank Newman at California-Berkeley. Knudsen would connect with Professor Walter Gellhorn at Columbia. Hughey was linked to Professor Willard Reese at Columbia, and Vail to Lindsay Cowan at Case Western. President Howard himself pitched in and volunteered to reach Professor Jeff Fordham at Pennsylvania. And there were other probes. Many others. Our rain of probes was so intense that the probability of puncture increased. Covert operation sprung leaks made into rivers by intrigue.

The first sign that we may have blown our cover came when we began to receive unsolicited letters from dean aspirants. It was exactly what the Review Committee did not want. How were we to deal with those letters when to do so would be contrary to our instructions about not connecting directly with candidates? For example, one letter, dated as early as August 17, ended up on my desk. It began: "It has come to my attention that Dean Wren has resigned.... I suppose there is no delicate way for me to inquire as to whether or not my name can be placed in consideration...."

I responded politely with a letter explaining that our search was not yet organized and ending with a typical off-hand remark: If there were any questions, "please do not hesitate to contact me." Like many curtesies, it was a thoughtful, but unthinking, cordiality that did not mean what it said. It violated the prime directive placed on us. Quickly squeezing through the narrow channels of quiet inquiry was not going to be easy.

Many of the unsolicited résumés were typically padded "paper chase." For example, one aspirant boasted over forty published law "articles," itemized five published "books," and ten book reviews. He was my age (40 years) and had been teaching law for just one year more than me. That's about one publication every six weeks. I was envious and dubious at the same time. Like all too many résumés, it exemplified the vast array of publisher avenues available to academicians, which in turn spread proliferation far beyond significance.

The faculty Search Committee worked throughout the fall semester, getting a list of "possibles" from our contacts, narrowing the list to "likelies," and further paring the "likelies" to a handful of what we called "approachables"—the latter were those we would like to contact directly. To do that, the Review (Selection) Committee's permission was necessary.

I met with William Swindells and Paul Boley at the Arlington Club and with President Howard several times. They were a triumvirate of leaders highly instrumental in our accreditation efforts. They wanted progress reports on the faculty search; I wanted authorization to phone the "approachables." The faculty needed to know if these interesting finalists shared our interest. I told them we were competing nationally with eight other law schools openly seeking to fill dean vacancies. Those vacancies evidenced how stressful were dean occupations in those trouble-ridden times. We had to let the market know that we were in the competition and had to find out if there were any buyers for what we had to sell. I emphasized that the faculty was ambivalent in our ability to compete with eight other schools. While there was comfort in knowing we were not alone in the hunt, there was also frustration in contesting with an arm tied behind our back. Swindells, Boley, and Howard consented to taking the issue to the Dean Review Committee at its next meeting in early December.

Meanwhile, at a November 22 meeting, the faculty Search Committee was having second thoughts on the approachment issue. Did we really want to spend any more time in pursuit of candidates? It was Professor Belsheim who sought to put an end to our business. He called our in-house candidate a "known quantity" whose biggest virtue was that he "had the eye and ear of the president." As an ex-law dean himself, Belsheim knew how important it was that "a university president and his deans have rapport." Knudsen and Jensen were amenable to Belsheim's view, but Williamson and Hughey wanted to continue explorations. As long as there was significant disagreement, I felt we should continue with the mission assigned us. And so we did.

When the matter was taken up at the December meeting of the Dean Review Committee, Alumni President Roth, Justice Holman, trustee Swindells, and SCOLS member Chester McCarty all favored taking an immediate vote on selecting Fred Fagg as dean. I urged the committee to let us plumb the market one step further by phoning four prospects named on our list. When President Howard surprisingly suggested a fifth individual for contacting, committee permission was granted. The allowance, however, was conditioned on discovery of "interest, not suitability." In other words, we were not to conduct an interview probing candidate credentials or to extend an invitation to a hiring process or to otherwise do anything other than finding out the extent of interest in our dean vacancy. The arm behind our back was loosened but not freed. It was not the way to horse-trade. "We don't want to know about your horse; we don't want your horse; we just want to know if your horse is up for sale."

*Coy Recruiting*

We had just one month to finish our work. The Review Committee was scheduled to meet in the first week of January 1973 where it would vote on whether to select Fagg or to interview further candidates for suitability. It was now the holiday season. Professors were away from their desks. Contacting the five "approachables" took some time in "phone tagging." This was not the day of modern telephonic voice mailing or e-mails. Phone messages requesting returned calls, prepared by secretaries, were left on the absent recipient's desk. I have in my files seven such return call messages from one of the prospects—each responding to my messages on his desk.

I phoned four of the five and President Howard talked to the fifth. Four immediately expressed no interest in being a dean anytime, anywhere, or anyhow. As one of them put it, he was more interested in being a "scholar and an educator" as opposed to being "an administrator of the education business." At a well-established law school, management from a dean's office is well-manned, organized, and routine, leaving the dean time for scholarship. The so-called "academic dean" was much more suited there. At a growing school such as ours, a dean had to be a developer and business manager.

The fifth "approachable" expressed a tentative interest. He promised to meet with us and give a definite answer at the AALS Convention in New York City in the last week of December. We scheduled a coffee at the Waldorf Astoria. It was not going to be a phone call like the others. As one can well imagine, that personal conversation took on more the posture of an interview as it tiptoed back and forth across the line that was supposed to limit us to do no more than test the man's appetite as opposed to taste his worth. Whatever might have been a betrayal of the line drawn, the upshot of that conference was mutual "no interest."

From our dean search work, I witnessed four different categorical attitudes within the nation's professors about leadership: (1) the *covetous* [those who want to lead]; (2) the *cooperative* [those who don't want to lead yet support those who do]; (3) the *critic* [those who don't want to lead but contest those who do]; (4) the *curmudgeon* [those who don't want to lead or be led or have anything to do with any business that needs leading]. The fallacy of such stereotyping is, I suspect, that we have all found ourselves at one time or another in each of those categories.

Indicative of the curmudgeon category was a January 16, 1973 memorandum to the law faculty from Professor Bill Williamson. The memo was startling (to say the least) and scathing (to say the most). It came at a time when the patience of the president and the trustee Review Selection Committee was near end. The Review Committee had pushed its scheduled meeting ahead to the last week of January to coincide with a SCOLS meeting. Billy began his three-page memo with this observation: "It seems that a selection will be made by no impetus other than default: the inability to come up with a reasonable alternative to the existing candidate." He then urged that there was, however, a "reasonable alternative to installing the acting dean as dean." His alternative was "no dean at all!" His reasons followed:

> "There is a feeling of misgiving and mistrust towards the existing candidate.... I fear that we would lose extremely competent people on our faculty if we selected Professor Fagg.... We pride ourselves as a faculty run school. With Professor Fagg as dean, we would still need to involve ourselves in a number of administrative duties, simply because of the existing mistrust. There is no reason why these administrative duties cannot be handled by the faculty directly, since they are being handled by the faculty directly anyway...."

He went on to elaborate how our budget, our enrollment policies, our academic advancement of students, and our curriculum are all presently steered by faculty committees. As for spokesman and figureheads in fund development, student relations, community relations, college liaison, and such, he felt that specific professors could be assigned on an *ad hoc* basis.

> "If it is necessary for there to be a focal person as the signatory of our correspondence, then I would suggest we have a Chairman of the Faculty, which position would rotate among us on a six-month basis."

He finally recognized the difficulties and admitted what he called "the very real problem of advancing such a radical proposal to the president of the college, SCOLS, the Board of Trustees, and the American Bar Association." Indeed, those where high hurdles—so tall that Billy might well have readied himself with crutches, for assuredly he was about to break both legs in attempting the clearances. He had titled his memo "A Modest Proposal." It was about as modest as Jonathan Swift's original 1729 essay by the same name that called for eating the children of the poor Irish. But just like Swift, rogue Billy had mischief in him. He himself ended up calling his modesty "radical"—not a word to be used if persuasion was truly sought. Still, there is purpose in those who toy. Billy's hyperbole tried to lay another stone in building a faculty-run law school—dean or no dean.

On the wisdom of faculty-operated schooling, there is this to ponder: Support for that notion grew out of a small cadre, close-knit, and focused on the unifying goal of accreditation. Only time would tell whether "faculty-operated" could survive the days after we would reach our goal, become larger, and fragment into inevitable factions.

As for Bill's innovation, at a faculty get-together his proposal did not get togetherness. It was a bird bereft of wings on which to fly. At a point in our fledgling development when we were trying to make way on others' agendas and not our own, we had to have a leader, a single voice, someone with whom outsiders could deal because some issues cannot be negotiated by assembly and parliamentary rules of order. We were at crucial powwows in our accreditation pursuit and needed a tribal head. The faculty voted to recommend Fred for that leadership. Needless to say, it was not unanimous, but nearly so.

The Dean Review Committee met at the law school on January 30, 1973, at 3:30 p.m. That was immediately followed by a SCOLS meeting at 4:00 p.m. No record could be found of those two back-to-back sessions, but the conclusion reached was foregone. I attended both meetings. Discussion at the Review Committee was "cut" (we had less than thirty minutes of allocated time) and was "dry" (Williamson made no fuss). SCOLS consideration of the Review Committee's recommendation was likewise cut and dry. Those two approvals were then approved by a phone canvassing of the college Board of Trustees on February 1. Fred Fagg III effectively became the law school's permanent dean. Technically, his appointment was not made official until February 6 at a duly called trustee board meeting. He was the seventh dean in the school's eighty-eight year history. His rise from professor to associate dean to interim dean to dean, took just thirty months.

Williamson's earlier memo had predicted that "a number of our people will not guarantee that they will remain if Fred is selected dean." After Fred's selection, not one was lost; all remained—including Billy.

The hurried maneuvers in cloaking Fred as dean were complicated by yet another simultaneous goal—ABA unconditional acceptance.

## ABA ACCREDITATION:

In the summer of 1972, the faculty was faced with this preliminary question: In view of a dean search, do we want to abandon our previously set time table for application to the ABA and AALS accreditors? Dean Wren had scheduled us for those attainments by the end of the forthcoming fall semester—just five months away. At the July 31, 1972 faculty meeting, it was agreed that we had to "pull out the stops" and go for at least the ABA permanent status. Our three-year provisional status would expire at the end of the current academic year. The last opportunity for making a pitch for permanency would be at the winter ABA meetings in Cleveland in February 1973. Thus, preparation for full ABA accreditation would be on-going all through the dean search. Indeed, the two quests were wedded. ABA Consultant Ruud had assured us that Wren's departure would not jeopardize our application for ABA full accreditation provided a permanent dean was in place. On the other hand, getting an outside candidate for our dean vacancy was hampered by not first becoming fully accredited. No accreditation without a dean, and no dean without accreditation. Those dilemminous pursuits made the fall of 1972 energetic, to say the least.

Consultant Ruud advised us that between now and February there would have to be three major repairs: (1) a permanent dean; (2) a raise in faculty salaries to meet rising ABA school medians; (3) library enhancement in leadership and book count. Other matters needed attention but nothing that could not be handled by mere promulgation; *e.g.*, we should devise written policies concerning sabbaticals and research assistance. Promulgation also included a formalized "mission statement." ABA insisted on this customary composition vowing goals and principles under which individuals are transformed into a unified entity. I have always had an uneasy attitude about mission statements. I had no argument with "missions," it was the "statement" of them that troubled me. Trying to formalize what many strive to do is a joinder that leads to either vague abstractions or digression from the mission itself. Sometimes more angst and attention goes into the promulgation than into the fulfillment. When talk is cheap, work ought to dominate words. A recipe does not a pudding make; proof of the pudding is, indeed, in the pot.

As for increasing salaries and library count, those issues boiled down to money, and money simmered down to promises as embodied in a trustee approved budget for the following 1973–74 academic year. That prospective budget would be the commitment to fiscal ends that the ABA was looking for. But money had to do more than talk; it had to deliver. That meant we also had to show the ABA some evidence of keeping budgetary promises. The evidence would have to be some "cash on the barrel head"—some strong delivery of gifts in the 1972-73 year.

All of those tasks, including the dean search, had to be jammed into a time frame that fit the agendas of others. The ABA House of Delegates was set to meet on February 12, 1973. That was the final body who would or would not bestow permanent accreditation. Preceding that session we would first have to gain the recommendation of the ABA Section and Council and before that the Council's Accreditation Committee. The latter would meet on or about February 2. Before all of that, we would also have to achieve a favorable Inspection Report from Consultant Ruud. He was scheduled to be on campus making his official investigation on October 31 through November 2.

Aside from those ABA echelons, the law faculty had our own hierarchy to please. Ultimately, the Lewis & Clark Board of Trustees would have to give final approval of our budget, our dean selection, and our fiscal plans. Every step toward the trustees had to take into account presidential and SCOLS good graces, which meant a lot of accommodations timed to SCOLS and trustee meeting dates.

In late summer 1972, Interim Dean Fagg laid out task divisions and time lines. As a plan, it was well-designed. But, like mission statements, saying is only as strong as doing. "Doing" jumped out of the blocks at the start of the 1972-73 year. Acceleration was felt mainly in the Dean Search and Budget Committees. I was on the Budget Committee as well as "spokesman" for the dean search. Professor Knudsen was chairman of the Budget Committee. The interim dean took a heavy ex officio role in budget matters. There was no time for procrastinating.

As for income development, our previous 1971-72 academic year left us in good stead with $140,000 surplus income. From the look of things, we were going to be having another surplus of $110,000 for the current 1972-73 year. Gift income for the current year began to break records. At mid-year, Grace Kralovec, our liaison with the college development office reported gifts of $120,000. By years end, we had total gift dollars of $284,000. The trustees authorized another $2,000,000 capital fund drive for the law school, albeit without a kickoff date.

As for budgeting, we finished our 1973-74 projections in time for Ruud's October-November inspection. The faculty proposed a budget predicting expenditures of $1,276,000—an amount more than double our actual expenses paid just one year before in 1971-72. The 1973-74 proposal included $62,000 for increasing faculty salaries to bring us in line with median salaries in ABA approved schools.

As for the library, our current revised budget for 1972-73 called for $224,000 for the purchase of enough books to meet ABA minimums, but still short of AALS minimums. As of mid-year, the library had a count of 41,400 volumes—almost a 12,000 increase (30 percent) in just six months. In 1972, computerization and microfilm-microfiche storage were not yet taken into account in the measure of library size. Therefore, shelf-space was a crucial consideration in proving commitment to library growth. We now had shelving space for 90,000 books.

Still a sore point in our library picture was the absence of a professional law librarian at the helm. We had trouble finding one. When we found one, we had trouble keeping her. So, if we could not *find* or *keep* one, we decided to *make* one. Professor Walt Brown took on the task of becoming that expert. He enrolled in library science courses at the University of Oregon in Eugene—a city one hundred miles from our campus. He made that trip while still teaching classes in Portland. No one doubted the ability of Walt (a Mensa) to master the science and gain his certificate in that area of library expertise, but there was pause about a neophyte leading a complex research center.

By the end of October, we were ready for Ruud's on-campus inspection. His three days with us included three faculty get-togethers, various classroom visits, library scrutiny, presidential and decanal conferences, and sit-downs with students, staff, alumni, and trustees.

I remember a confidential coffee time with Millard at the airport after his visit while awaiting his flight home. He wanted my report on the dean search and my summary of the law school's progress as I had witnessed it over the last six years. Those preliminaries brought us to his main concern: the upshot of the Howard-Stevens debacle ending with the Stevens discharge five years ago—an incident made public and a gossip throughout the AALS Convention in the last week of 1967. [See ch. 3] Many in the AALS organization had been astounded by that happening. As the last remaining professor from those bygone years, my perspective on what made that schism would help to explain it—so I was told. Millard went on to say that some were still riled or at least puzzled by it. Why did it happen, and what possessed the president to do it? Millard was direct: The accreditors needed to know (in his words) "the timber" of the college president who would be leading the school that they were being asked to accredit.

In keep with his turn of phrase, I said that President John Howard was "solid, Oregon Douglas Fir." Those were my notes penned in my office following the meeting. I told Millard that Howard was committed to the law school. His pride and reputation were on the line inasmuch as he had fought for the merger in the first place. Success was his to prove. Furthermore, I would have assured Millard that what Stevens foresaw as necessary was now fully done or being done by Howard. The division between the two men was nothing more than a matter of calendaring. Both had the same direction; one wanted it *now*, as promised in law school publications; the other had contingents of an entire college to deal with—not the least of which were trustees and some undergraduate professors who wondered about the cost of this new adoption. The schism, therefore, was simply the case of two strong-willed and decent men conflicting over *when* to act—one with experience as to what accreditors could endorse and the other with attention to what his college could be led to endorse.

Ruud asked me to pen those thoughts in a note—something he could take with him on the plane. He said he needed to be able to cite a frank assessment from someone close to the situation when it happened. He promised to quote it anonymously. He knew the issue would certainly arise with the AALS accreditors and might arise also in the ABA process insofar as Stevens was still active on the ABA Council's Accreditation Committee.

I have no knowledge of the use to which my notation was put. But it is true that

Millard's diplomacy would need shoring from one who had served with Stevens in his NWLC days and who had also witnessed the sincerity of a parent in fostering an adopted child.

Having satisfied Millard's query, I was curious. Why was this employee of the ABA so concerned about what bothered AALS? He seemed to make AALS his business when it was not. Was there something I didn't know? He dismissed my curiosity by simply saying that he hoped one day to make ABA and AALS work together instead of duplicating their efforts. Something in his response told me to press it no further. We would learn later what brewed there.

Before Ruud left, he told the faculty he was pleased by his inspection. Based upon his glowing account of what he witnessed, we felt confident about sailing into ABA permanency, so much so that we decided to test the AALS waters as well. Thus, we made overtures at the AALS conference in New York City in the last week of 1972. President Howard attended and spoke to the AALS membership section, assuring them of Lewis & Clark College's dedication to its law school. Those authorities were pleased to make the acquaintance and the measure of the Lewis & Clark president. Consequently, they were encouraging about our chances, except that they felt we were premature. They advised us to wait and to apply after our dean office was filled and after acceptance into ABA halls.

Postponement was expected, for we simply wanted to know where we stood with the AALS leaders. We also knew that we did not have our own trustees' approval. Oddly enough, some on our Board of Trustees still needed convincing that AALS membership was necessary. But the president's visit with AALS went a long way to clearing the air about the past and arranging our goals for the future. We re-focused on the ABA.

As aforesaid, the ABA meetings in Cleveland in February were times of reckoning that brought the completion of our dean selection to an end just days before those meetings began. Fred Fagg III was placed at the helm unofficially on February 1 and officially on February 6. The meetings began on February 2. That converging of two pursuit finishes caused a crunch of numerous last-minute preparations. The chain of meetings began with the ABA Accreditation Committee, then the Council, then the Section of Legal Education, and finally the House of Delegates, the ultimate "dubber."

Among all of the documents in the our final package, two items were cardinal: a February 1, 1973, letter from President Howard and Ruud's Inspection Report on his three day visitation. In the Howard letter, Committee members found what they were looking for in the college's strength of commitment to legal education. Howard wrote that the college was dedicated to allocation of "its resources to... upgrade its present excellent faculty" and to creation of "a superb research facility in its law library." In addition to those two major concerns, Howard added support for other endeavors, such as clinical education, inter-disciplinary courses, continuing legal education programs, and evening classes.

Consultant Ruud's 25-page report was especially glowing on all fronts dealing with administration, faculty, library, curriculum, admissions, placement, and physical facilities. His report alluded to a troubled past now buried in understanding and ended with this observation:

> "The law school... has come a long way in the last seven years, especially in the last 3 ½ years. While there were times *in the earlier years* when there were doubts about the capacity of the school to acquire the *necessary resources and doubts in the leadership* that quality legal education needed to cost that much, there was throughout the aspiration in the leadership... that the program should be one that the college and the community could be proud.... Substantial credit rightfully belongs to President Howard, Dean Wren, Dean Fagg, and a *devoted faculty....*" [Emphasis added]

His reference to early "doubts," "leadership," and "devoted faculty" were the only subtle ties that I saw in his twenty-five pages that might have had any bearing on our confidential talk during his visit back at the end of October. To be sure, there were many considerations that had to go into the Accreditation Committee's final decision, but the Ruud report and Howard's letter were undoubtedly clinchers.

On February 10, the Committee took the baton of commendation from Ruud, made it a recommendation, and handed it off to the Council, who passed a "re-recommend" directly on to the House. On February 12, 1973, the ABA House of Delegates bestowed permanent accreditation.

Celebration was in order but momentarily on pause. Somewhere in the relay, the Section had been skipped. The baton of recommendation went directly from the Council to the House. We were concerned. But why bother? The House had ruled. Wasn't that an end of it? Why look into the mouth of a gift horse? The concern, however, would not go away. For lawyers, process was critical. Many times before, we had been led to water and not allowed to drink. The Section of Legal Education and Admissions to the Bar was the largest and most authoritative arm of the ABA. As previously reported [see ch. 3], its function could be traced to the origin of the ABA itself in the 1880s. It was the Section that created the Council and demanded its reports. Some considered the Section autonomous. Indeed, the grant of temporary accreditation to NWLC back in August 1970 [see ch. 7, "Provisional Accreditation"] had passed muster with the Section. To bypass it now was trouble.

Concern was moving toward anxiety, when suddenly there came relief. In the interim since granting our provisional accreditation, politics within the ABA had made a hierarchal change. Section 9, Article VI of the new ABA Section by-laws had been amended one year before our current plea for permanence. It read:

> "The Council shall have plenary authority... to recommend to the House of Delegates... full approval of a law school... without first referring... approval to the Section...."

The weight of caution was lifted. Grave expectations vanished. We could celebrate. Our Valentine's Day 1973 faculty meeting agenda listed:

1. Report on Accreditation Status
2. Toasting
3. Consideration of Millard Ruud as Honorary Faculty Member
4. Toasting
5. Toasting
6. Toasting

But when the last glass hoisted came down, one more cork was yet to be pulled. Saved on a rack in the accreditation cellar was a full flagon tagged with a note saying, "Save for AALS."

Two down, one to go.

# 1972: TIME CONTEXT

Police arrest five who were burglarizing Democratic National Headquarters in Watergate office building. Republicans and Attorney General John Mitchell deny involvement.

Alabama Governor George Wallace shot and paralyzed.

Arab terrorists kill eleven Israeli Olympic athletes in Munich, Germany.

Nixon-Agnew re-elected over Democrat George McGovern in landslide victory.

Military draft system replaced by all-volunteer military.

Women's Equal Rights Amendment to U.S. Constitution passes Congress but will fail to gain three-quarters State ratification.

U.S. astronauts stay on the moon for over three days.

Gas price per gallon 55 cents.

First time a foreign-made car (Volkswagon "Beetle") becomes the most popular car sold.

A stone age tribe (the Tasadays) are found living in caves in Philippine jungles.

# 13

# THE FAGG REGIME: PART ONE

*1972-73*

## IN-HOUSE ISSUES

While dean search and ABA accreditation had taken a great deal of faculty time and energy in the fall semester of 1972-73, other in-house issues co-existed to challenge us throughout that academic year. One such issue area developed out of our growing environmental law image.

### ENVIRONMENTAL LAW:

Concern with the environment continued to expand in the nation and especially in Oregon. As previously reported First Lady, Lady Bird Johnson, had established herself in the mid-1960s as a prominent campaigner for what she called "the Beautification of America." Her agenda was a gentle form of attention to our planet. It called for planting flowers, banishing billboards, and anti-littering. In an enactment called the "Lady Bird Bill," Congress used $325 million to beautify federal highways. That kind of reform did not ruffle business spirits, but it did open doorways to more aggressive, intrusive action. Federal enactments like NEPA [see ch. 6 "Law Periodical Project"] and subsequent legislation beyond cleaning roads went to cleaning air and water and protecting endangered species.

Oregon was not to be outdone. On July 2, 1971, the Oregon legislature had enacted "The Bottle Bill"—an anti-litter measure that was the first state statute in the United States to require a few pennies deposit on the recycling of certain beverage bottles and cans. The idea brought enormous resistance from processors and retailers as its precedent spread across the nation. Other Oregon enactments established land use planning by government regulation. A 1967 statute made the full length of Oregon's ocean beach boundary a public easement. Another Oregon law outlawed the sale of cans with detachable, metal pull-tab openers. The 1971 "Bicycle Bill" earmarked one percent of Oregon transportation revenue to the development of cycle paths. All such measures began to paint Oregon as "pro-environment." NWLC's curriculum and law review publication were swatches on that canvas.

Force begets resistance. College trustees and the SCOLS Budget Sub-Committee were beginning to question the law school's periodical publication. In the spring of 1973, Paul Boley and other members of the sub-committee wondered whether a more general law review should be published and whether the title "Environmental Law" should be eliminated. The sub-committee suggested that ecological articles could continue to be published but felt that a broader scope would open the publication to more kinds of scholarly discussion. The faculty ignored the recommendation. It would come again, a bit more forcibly, in the next academic year.

## SALARY RAISES:

Accreditors had always been after us to increase the dollars in our faculty salary pools (one each for full, associate, and assistant professors). But, as for salary contracts of individual professors within those ranks, that was left to in-house discretion. That parceling involved the dean's office and faculty in an age-old business issue that pitted merit reward against seniority increment.

In the beginning, our line-item budgeting openly displayed individual contract amounts. When our faculty size was smaller, it had not been a problem. But now we had seventeen noses to get out of joint—a lot more comparisons to incite envy. The huff was not so much *why-I-deserve-more-than-another*; it was *why-does-the-other-deserve-more-than-me?*

A reflective memo from new professor Ed Brunet made a case for why merit raises were better because ability was more important than durability, and incentive more valuable than longetity. But he was virtually alone in his position at that time.

Another factor that influenced salary increment was the ubiquitous force called "market." As every employer knows, external market competition creates major difficulties in balancing and adjusting internal salary structures. NWLC's faculty hiring spree had joined with the nation's law offices and law schools on the same mission—a competition that drove entry salaries upward. Consequently, in order to hire and hold, we sometimes had to pay a new professor more than was being paid an existing, peer professor. Established faculty complained that their roots in Portland tethered them to restricted bargaining positions, more so than those with a free rein in the employee market.

Salary raising was also aggravated by having a new dean—young and a peer. Deans were field officers at the front line of setting salary contracts. Our previous deans had been older, experienced, and avuncular—seniors much easier to abide as paymasters. Dean Fred, who had come from within the ranks, was smart enough to know that he needed to consult on pay alignments. When a merit raise might surpass a senior, Fred would sometimes confer with me (as the senior faculty member in residence and as chair of the Promotion and Tenure Committees). More often, he sought the experience of Professor Belsheim, a former law dean.

Eventually, salary equity issues would be placated by secrecy. The larger the faculty grew, the more the individual salaries were amassed and cloaked in a single line-item of the budget. Pique was overcome by not knowing and not being tempted to know. As poet Thomas Gray suggested: ignorance triumphed over folly—the choice of bliss in lieu of being wise. Modernly, don't ask or tell.

## FACULTY HIRING:

Finding a dean was not our only hunt. We had to track and find two more full-time faculty members to start the 1973-74 academic year. One position had been opened by the Wren departure, now filled by Fagg, thus leaving the Fagg vacancy. The other spot was the empty "clinic lawyer" office created in the previous year but not yet plugged. [See ch. 11, "Clinic Program"]

At the AALS convention in New York City in December 1972, we garnered six prospects even though the Fagg vacancy and deanship were not yet made official. Faced with so many missions in a single time space, we were so hectic that we found ourselves *ahead of beginning* just as often as we were *behind ending*. By the time the Fagg vacancy was formalized, we had lost three of the prospects for want of follow-up. It was the "woodworker lesson": Don't carve the pegs before drilling the holes.

John C. Barrett, a local attorney at the Multnomah County legal aid office, was hired to fill the litigator spot at our downtown Portland clinic. Our two clinician directors (Folberg and Snouffer) spoke highly of him. Barrett was enticed to academia by his interest in research and development of Native American law and history. Accordingly, he was assigned the first Indian law course in our curriculum and was given an office on the law campus and an assistant professor status. John left NWLC after a two-year stay to become the Director of Legal Aid in Iowa.

As for the remaining faculty position, the names of two potential faculty candidates appear of record in the February 21, 1973, faculty meeting: James L. Huffman and Steven Kanter. Steve, an M.I.T. and Yale Law School graduate, was working locally as one of the first four lawyers in the newly organized Oregon Public Defender office. His commitments, however, precluded him from joining us in the 1973-74

**TWO NEW PROFESSORS (1973)**

John Barrett and Jim Huffman

year. He would become a full-time professor at NWLC four years later.

Jim Huffman had a fellowship position at his alma mater, Chicago University Law School. He came to the campus in March for interviews and was also looking at three other law schools. He chose us. As he would later write, two reasons were foremost in his decision: For one, he was Montana raised, and those "western roots tugged"; it was "comforting to know that there were mountains" on Portland's horizon, "even though you couldn't see them most of the time." His other reason was a personal touch: dinner at Ed Belsheim's home. "The intimacy and generosity of that dinner had more to do with my deciding... than anything else."

In future decades, Kanter and Huffman would each become NWLC deans—the fifth and sixth under whom I would serve—the ninth and tenth in the law school's history.

### Staff Hiring:

It follows from the nature of a growing service enterprise that those who tend to the *business* will eventually exceed the count of those who serve the patrons—while, of course, those customers will outnumber all the custodians. Throughout my early years with NWLC, the sizes of faculty and staff had numbered about the same. But in the period through 1972-73 and the beginning months of 1973-74, staff numbers for the first time began to exceed full-time faculty size. With the addition of a fully operating clinic office and the need for library assistance and secretarial support, staff growth (from about 11 to 27) outstripped professorial increase (from 12 to 19). That would continue to be the pattern. As of this writing in the twenty-first century, administrators and staff [approximately 80] are double the size of faculty [approximately 40].

Escalation in management hiring had a start with the employment of Ann Kendrick. [See ch. 10, "Staff Hiring"] It took a further step in the summer of 1972 when then Acting Dean Fagg made a strong case for hiring a law school business manager. Growth in bodies and dollars had taken us out of the "departmental" category and into an operational venture well removed from college business officiating. We had an annual budget now in excess of $1 million [more than a $6 million inflationary equivalency as of this writing]. We had law buildings valued at $1.5 million in 1972 [more than $50 million today, based on expansions plus exploding real estate values]. We had a student body a quarter the size of the college student body. Great was the need for someone to be stationed on our Tryon Forest campus to manage the budgets, capital, and accounts of our fiscal status.

The faculty wasted no time backing the move toward management of our own business. President Howard was likewise convinced. The college business office, under Bill Malinson, would continue, however, to be the cashier and banker of monies. In big business, a separation will always evolve between those who direct and those who handle the flow of money. Like at a well, efficiency commands that some must prime and pump while others must catch, carry, and pour. Although a line was now drawn between law school and college fiscal handlings, we were destined to see times when Malinson's office would seek both to prime and to direct the flow.

At Acting Dean Fagg's insistence, the faculty interviewed and approved James Vandegrift as NWLC's first business manager. He was pirated away from the Oregon State Bar office where he had been an administrative officer. Before that, he had been a colonel (retired) in the U.S. Air Force. He assumed his duties with NWLC on October 16, 1972.

**JIM VANDEGRIFT**

Although Jim did not have a law degree, the acting dean nevertheless gave him the title of "Assistant Dean for Finance" instead of "Assistant *to the* Dean." When it was pointed out that Ann Kendrick's title remained as "Assistant *to the* Dean," Fred changed her title as well to "Assistant Dean of *Student Affairs*." Soon, they would have to be re-titled again. Fred was unaware that without law degrees, they simply could not be called "Deans." [See ch. 10, "Staff Hiring"] So, they were dubbed "Directors." In the process they were also accorded appellations more vast and vague: "Director of Administrative Services Vandegrift" and "Director of Ancillary Services Kendrick." Tasks sometimes change with new titles but often are left intact. Hence, in the latter case, the tinkering is no more than a change of clothes—re-dressing without reorganizing.

## REORGANIZATION:

Fred Fagg III was given to order and structure. Organization became reorganization and then re-reorganization. As already observed, he took pains with administrators' titles and with a re-vamping of faculty committees. Late in the evening, when most others were loosening the day's knots, Fred with pen and note pad would be knotting loose ends together. He was noted for last minute epiphany. Those who were then made to work overtime called it "procrastination."

Fred increased the number of faculty meetings. His record for frequent callings topped his predecessor's record—a feat that I did not think was possible. [See ch. 6, "Meetings . . ."] We met often in the summer of 1972, a season not within professors' terms of employment. Likewise, Saturdays were not free from Fred's schedulings. Somewhere in the fall semester, Fred responded to a rash of complaints about over-administration and too many meetings. He reduced faculty "regular" meetings to just one per month but then created faculty "administrative" meetings—also set separately at once a month. To streamline the meeting times, both kinds were conducted under parliamentary procedure. We became all too familiar with Roberts Rules of Order, which then, in the hands of law-trained strategists, became tools as well as rules.

The tighter that formality becomes on the surface, the more certain it is that unceremonious informality will develop beneath it. Unbending orderliness can stifle and thereby uncork the caucusing that really decides matters. So, in addition to the "regular" and "administrative" convenings, there developed rump sessions, which Fred would call "get-togethers." They were short on notice—almost spontaneous. A November 2 memo from Fred brought us together the next day at 1:15 p.m. to de-brief on the Ruud inspection. A November 13 notice "scheduled" a get-together at noon the same day. A January 18 memo announced a gathering the next day at noon to discuss tuition raising to meet unexpected library needs. These notices meant deliveries that hastened Doris McCroskey up and down the hallway knocking on professors' doors. E-mail and voice mail were but dreams of such curriers.

All of this reorganization was perpetuated back in the fall of 1972 by one who had been recently made interim dean, not fully robed as boss—an assumption of power that to some was well beyond the role of a caretaker. But then, Fred and the disgruntled were both aware that our assemblies, after all, were prompted by flurries of tasking. We were moving along a fast train on quick pursuits: ABA accreditation, AALS overtures, dean search, fiscal development, personnel hires, budget modifications, and an array of emergency business. In such melee, we needed organizing.

## SCOLS-FACULTY RELATIONS:

The hectic pacing was further prodded by (some said "encumbered by") the need to coordinate with SCOLS. Between faculty at one side and the president and trustees on the other, Fred's middle management style leaned toward the upper side as represented by SCOLS—a trustee standing committee. Where Fred's predecessors (Deans Stevens and Wren) had come up through faculty ranks, Fred, the "MBA," was fresh out of the business world, and had been raised in the family of a college administrator. Relatively new to the faculty world, he emphasized the need of faculty to pay greater deference to the hierarchy. With the newly created SCOLS budget and admissions sub-committees and with Fred as liaison, the line between advising and supervising grew hazy. [See ch. 10, "Administration"] To be sure, we were all headed in the same direction, and most often, there was cooperation. But sometimes SCOLS and faculty met at crossroads. When we did, some professors saw it as a rivalry and were never quite sure where our dean's loyalties lay.

One such crossing occurred at the March 14, 1973, "Ninth *Administrative* Faculty Meeting," also labeled the "Fourteenth *Regular* Faculty Meeting." The two were combined either for the sake of expediency or because recorders were no longer able to tell the difference. This time Professor Bross did not prepare the minutes, but secretary Doris McCroskey kept a rough transcript bordering between verbatim and summary. She recorded that Professor Vail unleashed this issue: "A number of students are interested in soliciting [on their own] scholarship funds for our minority students."

Dean Fagg sought to arrest any discussion of the issue. He said that any fund raising "had to be coordinated with other campaigns"—something for the college development office. He urged curtailing the matter. The plea was ignored.

Professor Hughey spelled out the dire need for some sort of outside soliciting of moneys, because our students receive "no funds from CLEO" as other law schools do. CLEO was the non-profit Council on Legal Education Opportunities that began in 1968 and was designed to improve racial diversity in law schooling by providing financial and other aide to under-privileged and disadvantaged students of CLEO member law schools. NWLC was not a member. Some argued we ought to be. But that was an issue different from whether we should endorse students doing money campaigning.

Dean Fagg argued that the SCOLS' budget subcommittee, headed by Oregon Supreme Court Justice Ralph Holman, an alumnus of our law school, had already considered the general issue and felt that "we were not in a financial position" to raise money for minority enrollees at this time. As an alternative to outside fund raising, the dean suggested that "tuition waiver" might be a different approach; but to do so, he "would like to meet with [SCOLS]... to get preliminary approval."

The necessity for SCOLS consent was not greeted warmly by the faculty. Professor Folberg had a motion: "The students are interested.... I have agreed to work with them. I move that we vote faculty approval of an intensive student effort to solicit funds for minority programs."

> The dean repeated his point: "It needs to go to [the SCOLS Budget Sub-Committee]. I will raise... with Holman that we proceed in the CLEO program and make assistance available."
>
> Folberg persisted, "I move the first question."
>
> The dean sought to re-phrase Folberg's motion in these words: "[Moved] that we allow our students *to cooperate with the development office* to attempt to raise funds to attract... racial minority students."
>
> McCrosky's transcript simply reports: "Folberg motion passed," making it unclear as to whose version was approved.
>
> Professor Hughey then urged that we also become CLEO members in order to come under its opportunity program. To do that, we had to "make a contribution that CLEO requires." Hughey was referring to a membership initiation fee.
>
> The dean wanted to know from where that contribution would come.
>
> Hughey was indifferent. He moved that "we support CLEO program to the extent of... $3,000... either inside the budget or money that we could raise ourselves . . . ." That motion carried.

It did not sit well with the dean. Money raised and expended outside of our budget was a fiscal operation that by-passed the business in which we were engaged and the hierarchy to which we were beholden. He then asserted, "This must be approved by the Standing Committee [SCOLS]." And there the record ends.

The situation was typical of the clash occurring whenever enthusiasts seek to circumvent what processors endear. The latter see an operating budget as the fiscal blueprint for how to build and deploy the entity's energy and resources. All activity must stay within those confines. If contingents of the entity go outside of those parameters, it is taken as competition, not loyalty.

Dean Fagg did not oppose advancing the underprivileged and disadvantaged, but he was opposed to going outside the box to do it.

Academicians occupy a role unique from employees in other businesses. Those at the front line of schooling—the teachers and scholars—are more than just orderlies who do biddings. They do more than render up education; they tend to it. Seeing themselves as such, they are difficult to fit into any reorganized, dutiful boxes.

As for the faculty's allowing student solicitation of funds for minority enrollment and for CLEO membership, no such soliciting or funding ever took place—either because of a failure in the follow-up or a hitch in the higher-up. The March 14 faculty meeting wranglings were another case of contest transcending content.

## STUDENT INVOLVEMENT:

Student bodies throughout the nation continued to be riled by disturbing current events—arousals that could last for years. The Attica incident back in 1971 reached across the continent from New York. Inmate protest against prison conditions had turned to mob uprising in New York's Attica penitentiary and ended in over thirty prisoners and ten guards being killed, followed by criminal indictments of sixty black prisoners and no prison guards. That ignited national indignation. A wave of public dissent against violent suppression of dissent ensued. "Attica!" became a shibboleth shout in support of protestors anywhere for any reason—fertile soil in which mobs could grow. That potential plus the 1970 Kent State campus killings and the 1968 clash between the Chicago police force and Vietnam protestors at the Democratic convention, were lessons that cautioned demonstration organizers to maintain order. *Peaceful* protest in the spirit of Ghandi and Martin Luther King was emphasized.

In April 1973, ripples of the 1971 Attica incident still disturbed as far away as NWLC. Our law student newspaper printed a national appeal for an "Attica Summer." It was a calling to citizens to come to Attica in upstate New York "to help." The report announced, "volunteers cannot be paid.... [There will be] tight discipline.... All drugs (including pot) and weapons are barred. Anyone breaching... will be required to leave." The forebodings in that appeal told of the tender balance between peaceful shout and belligerent resistance of that day.

Meanwhile, our student body was also having trouble within. It had no by-laws, no honor code, no duly elected representatives—in short no formally adopted organization. Nevertheless, that disarray did not stop students from contesting faculty proposals. A couple of faculty ideas proved to be particularly troublesome: (1) canceling "**dead week**" and (2) mandating a "**senior thesis**." Editors of the student newspaper reported that students were "jolted by the proposals."

"Dead week" was the week preceding final exams in which no classes were scheduled. Some called it "cram week" or "procrastination week." It was traditional, but the faculty proposed to start exams immediately after the last day of classes. The "senior thesis" proposal would require seniors to research and write a paper of publishable quality as a requirement for graduation. Students did not want a thesis, but did want dead week.

Both issues were scheduled for the February 28, 1973, faculty meeting. The session was heavily attended by student spectators—a practice that had been allowed to proliferate. The agenda list was lengthy. A motion to put the two student items at the top of the list passed, and the "dead week" issue came first. Dean Fagg allowed student spectators to speak in opposition—a deviation from his usual penchant for order. Bross's minutes labeled the student say, "considerable discussion"—a label that others called "gross understatement."

Perhaps succumbing to the length rather than the weight of argument, the faculty voted to leave the dead week alone. Canceling dead week would not die, however. Like so many issues, it would simply nap. Compromise was the only way to kill it—albeit hard to image how one can kill a week labeled "dead." In the future, the compromise became a "dead half-week."

The senior thesis issue took much longer to resolve. Protracted comment again ensued from the gallery of spectators. In spite of the breadth, length, and strength against it, the faculty voted in favor of the thesis. Predictably, the two items took all of the meeting time. We postponed the rest of the agenda and agreed to return in two days.

The two day hiatus was time enough to allow the students to reconnoiter. They were there again on March 2, where they succeeded in reviving the senior thesis issue. Four days after that meeting, Editor Larry Wilson commented in the student newspaper: "Students invaded the meeting *en masse*; and faculty allowed student discussion." Wilson was disturbed at his fellow students conduct. "I trust in the future students will be organized,... otherwise the only alternative for the faculty will be to hold meetings behind closed doors."

Student Tom Gordon was even more critical: "...to blame are the students.... Faculty meetings can't possibly function efficiently when one is turned into an all-school debating society." Gordon praised fellow student Dennis Odman for having "competently voiced all of the opinions.... [H]is presentation... was far more persuasive than fifty repetitive individual opinions,... and it took one-fiftieth the time."

Gordon did not lay all of the blame on the students, however. He proclaimed a "discouraging lack of organization on the part of both faculty and students.... Administrative planning and organization leave something to be desired.... One gets the feeling that the professors themselves dread these meetings and it is easy to understand when they spend one meeting deciding issues and the next meeting undeciding them."

Professor Newell wished never "to see the carnival repeated" and predicted that "unless some kind of procedure is developed, we will have the same kind of mess repeated." Student Gordon also had a somewhat more hopeful prediction. "When the emotion and the hard feelings of last week die down, something will come out of all this."

Indeed, a number of effects "came out." The most direct result was faculty abandonment of its previously authorized senior thesis. The issue was sent back to the Curriculum Committee, where it remained unresolved for the rest of the year. That student success, however, came at a price. The faculty adopted a formal structure for faculty meetings—among which was limiting meeting discussion to faculty, administrators, and duly elected student representatives and closing the doors to spectators—thus ending the short experiment with open faculty meetings at NWLC.

Another effect was the revival within the student body of the value and need for organization. Eight students were somehow "elected" to look into the adoption of organic by-laws for student association.

A more distant result was an eventual legal writing requirement that called upon each student to complete, not one, but two types of research papers of scholarly quality as a condition to deserving the advanced degree of Doctor of Jurisprudence.

### PROJECTING STUDENT BODY SIZE:

We began the 1972-73 year with 630 enrolled students (333 day and 297 evening). In just three years time, enrollment almost tripled in size—a 186 percent increase! Size became a concern.

The first-year entering class was far more than anticipated. The 119 day "first-years" were as projected, but the 110 evening enrollees were 30 more than expected. [See ch. 10, "Future Admissions"] In the fall semester, "then-Acting Dean" Fagg bemoaned the fact that "our average full-time professor would now be grading 380 exams per year"—twice as many as at other law schools. Even granting leeway for decanal exaggeration, it was more than fair standards ought to tolerate.

By the end of the 1972-73 year, "now-Dean" Fagg was boasting that we had received 8,400 inquiries from law school aspirants. Those inquiries, he wrote, were reduced to seven to eight applications for each open seat in our freshman entry for 1973-74. The publicity was good, but beneath the promotion lay growing cautions. Beyond the law academic world and the host of those seeking it, were the practitioners, the profession, and the public. In those quarters the influx of lawyers was now being greeted with alarm. Some urged that, while a flood of demand may be good economics for the educational system, the flood of supply was not so good economics for judicial administration and law business.

So, at the start of the 1972-73 year, the faculty vowed to bring our student body numbers for next year (1973-74) down to a maximum of 600 by simply admitting fewer first-year enrollees. But then the ideals of education came back to the realities of finance. To arrive at a 1973-74 student size of 600, we could enroll a maximum of just 140 day and evening students. We would be losing about 170 upperclass students to graduation and other attrition. The 140 new tuitions versus the 170 lost tuitions would bring income far short of our ambitious $1.3 million in projected expenditures so necessary for accreditation. Like the "mice and men" of poet Burns, our "best laid schemes" were "gang aft agley."

## BUDGET BALANCING:

A September 1972 faculty meeting lasted two days concerning our 1973-74 projected budget. In those sessions we ran into fiscal maneuvering that foiled the Budget Committee desire for fewer enrollees. A faculty consensus directed its Budget Committee to balance the future budget by projecting additional first year admittees instead of increasing tuition dollars. To get money, we thought it better to get more customers than to raise prices. Not many businesses can project the future by dictating customer size. But, the legal education business was in a unique position to do so; it had a booming customer market.

While it may have been necessary fiscal maneuvering to spend and then draw freely upon plentiful customer demand, was it sound educational policy? An unbridled acceptance of students was a danger that threatened to dilute the quality of our service rendered. So, we had these choices: (1) take on more customers, (2) cut expenses or (3) price our services higher. A fourth choice, of course, was to do some of each. But, the trend nationally was to emphasize the third choice—raising tuition. That was the opening salvo on what would become a phenomenal rise in the nation's cost for higher law education—a cost that over time would far surpass inflation in general.

But in 1972-73, the NWLC faculty decided to go against the national trend. We had raised tuition in the previous years and that was enough for now. Rather, we resorted to balance expenses by gingerly dipping into the plentiful demand for our services. It was contrary to initial desires. And as it turned out, contrary to our trustees' desires.

## TUITION:

A November 8, 1972, memo from Acting Dean Fagg to the faculty glowed with the report that SCOLS had unanimously approved the faculty's 1973-74 operating budget proposal with "no modifications whatsoever." He reported it triumphantly, but then, in a casual aside, mentioned that the SCOLS budget sub-committee, chaired by Justice Ralph Holman, was not entirely satisfied with the low tuition amounts and, in the future, would initiate "a recommendation with respect to the 1974-75 budget tuition" (two years hence), particularly as to the "relationship between day and evening tuition." The faculty suspected a return to the evening tuition issues that seemingly had been laid to rest back in 1971-72. [See ch. 10, "Tuition"]

Almost immediately, suspicion came to fruition. Shortly after Fred's memo, the Board of Trustees ordered SCOLS to take another look at tuition, not two years from now, but rather for next year. Although SCOLS had already recommended approval of the faculty's 1973-74 budget, they were now required to reconsider the absence of tuition raises particularly in the evening division. A January 18, 1973, memo from the acting dean to the faculty stated, "As you all know, the faculty previously voted to hold the line in both day and evening divisions next year on tuition." Fred called for a faculty "get-together" tomorrow afternoon... "to try to shape our position."

Once again, sparring lines were drawn between faculty and higher authority over a province the professors believed was theirs. Skirmish on the evening tuition issue had begun one year before when the faculty proposed a $150 raise (from $800 to $950) but President Howard felt it should be a $300 raise. The trustees had compromised and made it a $200 raise.

Now here in January 1973, contrary to the faculty proposal, the need to raise evening tuition was based on the need for more library volumes and was propelled by haste in having a committed plan to do so in order to achieve accreditation at the ABA meetings just three weeks away. The price increase for just the evening students was made all the more inviting by a nod from Justice Holman, an alumnus of the night school who saw the raised evening payment as an opportunity for night students to take the lead in the final push that would inch the school into ABA recognition.

Nevertheless, the evening alumni, the old Northwestern trustees, and, of course, the law faculty were astonished at the backtracking on the previous course chosen. None of it mattered, however. The raise was on a foregone course set by those with the power to do so. In poker terms, opposition was "drawing to a dead hand." The 1973-74 annual evening tuition would be $1,100 instead of $1,000, just as President Howard felt it should have been one year before.

Today, $100 may seem much ado over nothing. But under the surface, more than dollars were involved—beneath were tussles over dominion and vindication.

## BUILDING:

During our busy 1972-73 year, pressure was building for a fourth structure on our campus. Originally, four buildings had been contemplated for the law complex, but only three received "go-ahead" due to a lack of funds and an uncertainty about the future of accreditation. Now that faculty, library, and budget had each doubled in size, plus a student body that had tripled, buried fourth building plans were exhumed.

Professor Doug Newell was designated a committee-of-one to put plans into motion. One of his first suggestions was to remove Paul Thiry from any future building design. Thiry had been the architect of our original complex, which included the bunker-look of the classrooms, the steep ramp, the concrete acoustics, the fountains, the joining of library and offices under the same ceiling, and the hyperbolic paraboloid roofs. Doug's ideas were much more functional than Thiry's aesthetics. Where Thiry saw law schooling as inspirational and in need of edifice, Doug saw it as industrious and in need of workshop.

It did not matter to Doug that Thiry was nationally known—the principal architect of the 1957-62 Seattle World Fair and one who had played a large role in preservation of the nation's Capitol Building. When it came to authority figures, Doug was never one to shrink. At the November 29, 1972 faculty meeting, the faculty agreed with Doug. And in December, the Board of Trustees approved plans for a fourth building with a different architect.

A survey of professors and staff listed essentials for the new housing. Most of it had to do with separations. A cafeteria headed the list, thus separating law and college eating spots. Professors' offices, lounge, and reading room called for space away from the student library and study areas. Also set apart were a bookstore, a staff lounge, a duplicating room, and suites for the registrar, admissions, development, business, and career placement services. Such dispersals were a far cry from the compacted quarters of business on Huddleston Lane just a few years before.

In probing for the functions that the new facility would serve, Professor Newell emphasized the importance of foreseeing all future needs, because this would be our last structure. He said that our projections "would have to be *far-fetched* enough to make due indefinitely." But alas, try as we may, our anticipations were not far enough fetched to deal with what destiny had in store for us. The fourth building would not be the last. Down the road, a fifth extension would prove that the prime architectural planner is really Time.

Now here in 1972-73, there was no fourth building; much less a fifth; we were still under just three roofs. The fourth was simply a vision coming into focus—yet another dream in this decade of Cardozo's "endless becoming."

## MISCELLANEOUS FIRSTS:

Listing a cornucopia of infinite, in-house labors and events is often capped by a tag line such as: "...and other things." What follows here are *"et ceteras"* that may seem today mundane, but in 1972-73 were "firsts":

*Bar Exam Results:* Our 1972 passage rate on the Oregon exam grew ten percent. We were the only school that ascended. In 1970, we were 44 percentage points behind the front running school. [See ch. 9, "Bar Exam Results"] In 1971, we had closed the gap to 19 points. Now, here in 1972, we trailed by only seven. "An astonishing display of competence," boasted Dean Fagg. What was for the individual examinees simply a matter of getting a license, was for the alma maters an intermural rivalry. NWLC could not yet claim first but could claim breathing on the neck of first. Like its students, a school needed grading in order to know how it was doing.

*Board of Visitors:* Back in the winter of 1970-71, Dean Wren had instituted the idea of having a group of outside law professionals visit the law campus to observe what we were doing and to suggest what more we could do. At first Wren called them "the Fellows." That title, of course, lost favor with the growing distaff side of our student body. And so, they became the "Visitors." Now, here in the spring of 1973, for the first time they *visited* in an all-day session on campus. Their inspection was coupled with NWLC's first "Alumni Day," which was capped by a banquet at which ABA President Chesterfield Smith was the main speaker.

*Summer School:* Success in the 1972 first summer semester [72 enrollees and a $3,000 surplus] prompted the faculty to do it again. Professor Ed Brunet was assigned to oversee the 1973 summer session.

*Student Teaching Assistants:* The "T.A." concept [teacher assistants] was adopted for the first time in the school's history. At the beginning, only the legal writing program was furnished student aides. The experiment would eventually blossom into T.A.'s for moot court, tutorials, and professorial research. As previously reported [see ch. 11, "Student Graders"], I was using them to grade exams—a use that lasted about seven years before the faculty decided that, while students could do research for teachers and could tutor each other, they could not grade for teachers nor grade each other.

*Grade Reporting and Posting:* The old issues of deadlines as to when professors had to finish exam grading and when they could publish their grades—so hotly contested in previous years [see ch. 11, "Grade Deadlines"]—were now quickly resolved without contest. For the first time, fall semester grades were due at the Registrar's office no later than the end of January. For the first time, individual professors could post their grades any time they chose. What had seemed so major in the past was minor by comparison to major issues now confronting us. The issues of deadline were now dead.

*First Year Elective:* For the first time we scheduled an elective choice in the first-year course offerings. In their spring semester, newly admitted enrollees would enter a two-credit hour course of their own choosing. That would put them with upper-class students. The choice was limited to day students. It was an experiment that lasted just a few years before shelving. Shifting the building blocks of course offerings, especially in the first-year curriculum, was to be one of those tinkerings that would resurrect every several years—much like the penchant of some (my mother, for instance) to constantly re-arrange the living room furniture—an obsession not born of seeing things wrong but rather a craving to see them differently. One first-year student saw the tinkering from a different perspective. The "new" way was not different when the "old" way was brand-new for him. He pleaded with the academicians to mandate the *whole* first-year course schedule: "How could I, a babe in the law woods, do better. You know best. I just got here. I trust you. That's why you are the teachers. Do your job." Had that been an exam answer in a test of good advocacy, I would have given it an "A" for articulation and "B+" for substance.

*Clinical Program:* In 1973, AALS finally got around to joining the ABA in encouraging law schools to provide street learning along with book learning. Furthermore, CLEPR grant money and its emphasis on in-the-field practical education was still a growing stimulant in legal education. [See ch. 11, "Clinic Program"] Although enthusiasm was exploding on the outside, inside at NWLC there was imploding. Low student sign-ups for the clinical semester gave Professors Folberg and Snouffer extra time to help Professor DuBoff in the Legal Writing course. But as the saying goes, small packaging can bring big gifts. In that small 1973 NWLC clinic operation was our first law student to become a teacher of lessons learned there. Student J. P. "Sandy" Ogilvy is a nationally known clinical director and professor of law at The Catholic University of America.

Back in 1969-70, the clinical program was but a seed newly planted to show accreditors our good intentions. [See ch. 6, "The Clinic"] Many years of stumbling along would pass before the clinic would succeed in the capable hands of future director and professor, Richard Slottee. For a number of years, I remained a member of the Board of Clinic Directors of the Lewis & Clark Services Program, Inc. When at first the clinic had moved to downtown Portland offices, it was still tied to the apron. But, like a child through adolescence to adulthood, the drift away would widen and result in periodic efforts to make our clinicians visit home with their alma mater, and, more so, vice versa.

My personal experience in early clinic years served to teach me a cardinal lesson about "hands-on" learning: Schooling is not just tested by practice; it is enjoyed by practice. In the classroom, learning is motivated by self-help, peer-competition, and fictional challenges. In the clinic, however, learning is motivated by helping others. In writing my 1980 novel, *Skylarks & Lecterns: A Law School Charter*, the final denouement concerns a clinic law student who found purpose when helping an Hispanic *abuela* and her grandson with a car repossession problem. The fiction was inspired by a true case from the Valley Migrant League experience. It was a final chapter that served to resolve why students ("skylarks") were learners, why schools ("lecterns") were teachers, why lawyers were servants, and why Law was a calling.

*The Computer:* A new baby contraption in the business office was already showing signs of its need to be fed and diapered. We were in the market for our first computer maintenance nanny. The search ended with a candidate for admission to law study. His application had a perfect credential: a background in computer programming and analysis. It was a small matter, but one that made payroll equal to tuition. But we were looking at the tip of a tiny pyramid whose immense base was buried deep within future sands. One day, computers would be personal in every office and with every student. Three new long-range dynamics were giving us signs of what would one day be impacting all of education: (1) a new technology, (2) a new generation infused with it, and (3) a new language that networked the former two in world-wide communication. But for now in 1972, we simply had a first in need of nursing.

*Student Advancement Petitioning:* The summer of 1972 produced another first—a shift away from past practice. A last vestige of Gantenbein leniency was the routine, annual entertainment of student petitions and hearings seeking re-admission, probation, credit hour allowances, and other pleas for exception to the rules. [See ch. 6 and ch. 9, "Student Petitions"] In mid-summer 1972, the faculty met to hear twenty pleadings that took all of that Saturday. Some of the decisions made there carried over into September meetings. Shortly after that succession of hearings, a "fed-up" faculty could take no more of it. New procedures were adopted. Precise and detailed rules were promulgated with instruction to administrators and the faculty Advancement Committee to apply the rules strictly. Rules should rule. A student's academic standing must be fixed by norms, not by anomaly. But just three months later, at our November 29 faculty meeting, three student petitions concerning advancement managed to reach the full faculty agenda even though their pleas had been denied by the Advancement Committee. Not only did the faculty allow hearings on the appeals, the faculty voted to overturn the committee's decision on one of the pleas. Adamant about its self-imposed order, faculty mind-set was nonetheless tugged by heartstrings—"something that does not love a wall."

*"Beauty Contest":* At the January 24, 1973, faculty meeting, a proposal suggested that there be an annual selection of "the best educator" from our full-time faculty. This was a first that ran into a brick wall. In the minds of academic colleagues, trophies were for beauty contests and the entertainment and sports worlds. A motion was made "to flush the idea down an appropriate receptacle." The whimsical Bross minutes recorded, "The *movement* carried." But it did not go away. In a few more years, the students would take up the contest and make it a permanent fixture that today has blossomed into the Levinson Award for teacher of the year, as selected by the graduating seniors. Leo Levinson was a 1926 alumnus and part-time teacher at old Northwestern throughout the 1950s and early 1960s. I had shared a banquet table with him once and knew of his reputation as a powerful teacher. That was merit enough to deserve the legacy bearing his name. The honor might have gone to Thomas H. Tongue or John B. Cleland, two other strong teachers in old Northwestern history; but the former's name already graced one of our classrooms, and the latter had a statuary bust of himself now gracing our library. The search for titles is rather like the journalist's search for news. Author Dorothy M. Johnson wrote of a newspaper editor's advice: "When the legend becomes a fact, print the legend."

*Obituary:* All "firsts" must entail "lasts." A beginning must be the ending of something. And so, too, the reverse. On September 8, 1972. Judge James W. Crawford came to his end. He had been a member of the part-time faculty of the Northwestern College of Law for some thirty years and served as its dean from 1946 to the 1965 merger. He had been a fellow fly-fisherman with ex-U.S. President Herbert Hoover. Our law school courtroom was commemorated with a plaque in his name. [See ch. 8] The courtroom too was destined to die—a victim of remodeling in a future decade. Crawford's death would leave John Flint Gantenbein as a last remaining guardian of the vintage Northwestern heritage. It was Gantenbein who had opened the door to my law teaching career. On Pearl Harbor Day and the bicentennial year of the

**GANTENBEIN & CRAWFORD**
Two towers of Old Northwestern

Declaration of Independence (December 7, 1976), he too would die. Their dusks were at the dawn of what their school was to become.

## GRADUATION DAY:

Once again, in June 1973, we approached our annual finale. Once again I looked forward to a commencement filled with backward feelings. Once again the law school had to participate in an all-school graduation that included seniors herded together for arts, science, music, education, and law degrees. Once again it was destined to be a tediously long ceremony with a list of speakers not always meaningful to law careers. Once again professors and students had tried to convince President Howard and the Board of Trustees to have a separate law school graduation.

But once again President Howard stood on ceremony. He was, after all, the one whose wings sheltered all. He saw school, not schools, took a strong hand in pomp and circumstance, and had a deep attachment to the symbolic, culminating assembly. He wrote:

> "The single ceremony has served to symbolize the solidarity of the entire school, to focus public attention at one time upon the collective achievements of our whole academic community, and to challenge each of us to look beyond the strict borders of our particular discipline, outward to the general society where we also serve the public, hopefully with wide vision and broad human concern."

"Solidarity," "collective achievement," a "look beyond the strict borders of our particular discipline" were all noble insights indicative of another broader issue that had risen from time to time since the merger of the law school and liberal arts college: Should we change the college name to "Lewis & Clark University?" As aforesaid [see ch. 11, "End of the Year"], "college" denotes an undergraduate school engaged in a liberal arts and sciences education - - one given to an overview of collective knowledge often preparatory to, but not offering, specific career training. A "university" is that and more; it's a college that has additional graduate schools and separate faculties usually focused on technological or professional learning. A "university" is universal and diversified, while a "college" is collegial and unified.

So much for denotations, but connotations in some minds meant the difference between *open* and *closed*, between *out-going* and *cloistered*, between *ecumenical* and *parochial*, between searching *horizons* and crouching in *huddles*. With its strong international studies program and now its law school, Lewis & Clark College was worldly, yet it clung to hearth and family when it came to how it shall be called.

Then, too, it was all just semantics. Lewis & Clark was a place of higher learning, and it made little difference if we were called college, university, school, lyceum, academy, institute, or gymnasium. The real wisdom was not in what our name makes of us, but rather what we could make of our name.

Nevertheless, the name-change contentions insinuated themselves into the annual graduation ceremony. Should the doings be "all-school" or separated? Segregating commencements was resisted by the notion of family. But now in 1973, sheer numbers were becoming a drag on that solidarity. This year the law school would be graduating its first daytime seniors. Whereas in previous year there were only 37 Juris Doctor degrees to be conferred, now there would be 125 doctor candidates to cross the stage for hooding and handshaking along with hundreds of others seeking their Bachelors of Arts, Bachelors of Science, Bachelors of Music, Bachelors of Education, Masters of Music, Masters of Music Education, Masters of Education, and Masters of Arts in Teaching—each with separate invocation and sometimes with separate honors inscribed *cum laude, magna cum laude,* and *summa cum laude.* And 1973 would not be the apex in law degree numbers. In following years we would have law graduates approaching 200. The case for separate ceremonies was gradually being made by the simple weight of mathematics.

Nonetheless, as of 1973, the weight had not yet torn loose the grasp on solidarity. The graduation would be "all-school." Separatists would have to try again next year.

One piece of solidifying, however, served the law seniors well: The Doctor of Jurisprudence certificates were identical for the new day and old night graduates. Whatever differences the two divisions may have struggled with during their education, graduation was a time of coming together alphabetically to be handed a degree with the same words, same signatures, same calligraphy, same meaning, same alma mater, same suitability for framing—an identical ticket stub for exiting education and entering the profession. Henceforth the line between day and night faded in the twilight that joined the two.

# 14
# THE FAGG REGIME: PART TWO
*1973-74*

## SIDE ORDERS

At the beginning of the 1973-74 academic year, NWLC had been on the education accreditation climb for eight years and was about to enter the ninth. The
ascent had been a trudge at first and then, last year, it swept skyward in thicker labor
and thinner air. We had been breathing hard, to say the least.

To give some idea of the energies we each expended in the previous year, my
personal list in this memoir, is but an example. There was a lot of bouncing around
in committee chores. Throughout the year I was at one time or another a member
of the faculty Budget, Curriculum, and Advancement Committees, plus chair of the
Promotion and Tenure Committee and faculty representative to the trustees' Standing Committee on the Operation of the Law School [SCOLS]. My basic teaching
assignments in Torts and Evidence courses carried a load of seventeen contact hours
per year, which involved grading about 500 exams.

In addition to those school tasks, my list had included community, government,
and Bar duties. For the last two years, I had been co-editing an Oregon State Bar,
two-volume publication on Damages. I also served on the Lawyers Committee of the
Oregon Civil Liberties Union; was a member of the Oregon Bar Committee on Press
and Broadcasting; was a member of Portland School Board's Citizens Committee on
School Finance; was a legal advisor and Bill drafter to the 1973 Oregon State Legislature; and continued work as the founding executive secretary for Oregon's Judicial
Fitness Commission.

Then too, back at the school house, I had staggered through the chore of leading
a national dean search, the first such faculty involvement in the history of the school.

It had commanded a lot of negotiating between SCOLS and the law professors. Hard feelings developed and had to be placated in order to keep a divided faculty together. Professor Williamson's memo of January 16, 1973, threatened many faculty leaving if a wrong choice of dean was made. [See ch. 12, "Dean Search"] Likewise, trustees had been concerned about too many faculty exits over the last several years. Stevens, Runkel, Walker, Cairns, Gerhardt, Lenoir, Bloomenthal, Jurkins, and Wren had all departed. Two "no-shows"—Broeder and Jagiello—added to the list of farewells. Jumping ship was not the sign of smooth sailing.

Once the choice of a dean was done, all professors stayed aboard. The 1972-73 year had been the first year since the merger that the faculty held ranks. Not only had we maintained, we also gained; new professors Barrett and Huffman raised the faculty roster to nineteen. What most schools would see as normal operations, was for us achievement.

My work load had been typical—just an example of what others too could claim as demands upon their time. The largest work order that engulfed all of us in the previous year, had been the gaining of permanent recognition from the nation's law practitioners. That task and the feast that follows dwarfed all others. But, now here in September 1973, one huge serving at our table was yet to come: gaining recognition from the nation's law educators. Before that dessert, however, was still the day to day operation of schooling to consider—just items. In large imbibing, small orders go unnoticed. Each item in its own way was a piece of who we were and of what we were up against. The sum of all little done tells as much about core values as does a major singularity. Here served are side orders that made our plate throughout the 1973-74 academic year:

ITEM—THE CATALOG:

The content and layout of our 1973-74 catalog received an extreme compliment from Fred Franklin, the Assistant Director of the ABA in Chicago, who went out of his way to write:

> "I receive catalogues from all ABA approved law schools [and]... was so impressed with your 1973/74 catalogue that I felt impelled to write.... It is the most attractive, well presented catalogue I have seen."

Law school publications in those days were typically and deliberately drab and dull in keep with academic dignity and appeal to the intellect. Now that customers and the competition for the best of them had skyrocketed, we were among the first to make our presentation with eye-candy. Today, hawking higher education wares in "Madison Avenue" vogue is commonplace.

### Item—The Ramp:

We rebuilt the ramp—the one with the decline so steep that it threatened drowning in our fountain pool. [See ch. 8] The previous eight-foot slide was replaced by a much longer ninety-foot slope. The remodeling was allegorical—indicative of a more puzzling introspection: Had our past accreditation inclinations been too short and hurried? Was our present correction now too long and sluggard? On a graph, which is worse: a sudden slide down or a slow slope up?

### Item—Bar Exam Passage:

Almost eighty percent of our recent graduates passed the 1973 Oregon Bar Exam— the highest passage rate in the history of NWLC as of then. That luster may be dulled by the fact that the overall passage rate of all examinees from all schools was also the highest ever—an influx that many Oregon Bar members called too generous.

### Item—A Faculty Lounge:

Although plans and fund raising were well underway for a fourth building that included a faculty lounge, eight faculty members could not wait. They wanted a temporary structure for the lounge and proposed the purchase of a trailer home. Opposition to that transience centered on aesthetics and finance. Student representatives warned that students would be "damn mad if there is a faculty lounge and tuition goes up." Nevertheless, the temporary-trailer-lounge motion was passed by a vote of 8 to 7; two absent; three abstainers plus Dean Fagg, who only voted in case of ties. Such one-vote margins were frequent in those years, making it difficult to abide the democratic principle of majority-rule. Fortunately, trustees were not impressed by the impatience, the eyesore, the one-vote margin, and the cost. They overruled. Faculty would have to temporarily endure instead of temporarily indulge.

### Item—Black Butte Ranch Retreat:

Another case for faculty over-exuberance was the scheduling of a weekend retreat at the Black Butte Ranch, a rather plush resort almost 150 miles away on the other side of the Cascade Mountains. Some justified it as more than a vacation inasmuch as the agenda included all-day curriculum study sessions. Four condominiums and a house were reserved in mid-September 1973 for the occasion. Budget dollars were involved. For that reason and others, as we neared the time, a poll of the faculty showed that many of the professors would not make the trip. So, the site was cancelled in favor of conducting our curriculum business on campus. The lesson of over-indulging, however, was not learned. Just a little over three months later, we were destined to try extravagance again on an even grander scale. This time we would plan a faculty trip to New Orleans. There was "hell-to-pay" when that mission would be accomplished.

## ITEM—FACULTY SESSIONS:

Our faculty meetings under Dean Fagg continued to be long and frequent. Some sessions took almost two full work days. Agendas were now beginning to retrace old issues. A Friday curriculum meeting lasted into Saturday, where we rehashed items on electives, course sectioning, senior thesis, seminar enrollment, clinical program, summer school, graduation requisites, and other matters that brushed upon a canvas previously colored but were now in need of re-touching due to the ever-changing landscape and its new artists. The baton of minute-taker at those lengthy meetings had been passed from Professor Bross to our newest faculty member, Assistant Professor Jim Huffman, whose two-day-long grasp and record of faculty ways was no doubt impaired by his desire to be in the picture rather than to paint it.

## ITEM—INTERNATIONAL LAW SOCIETY:

Scribe Huffman's detailed minutes of the October 18, 1973, faculty meeting provide a peek into the ways of academician contest. Professor Hughey proposed that the law school spend $1,000 to establish a chapter of the International Law Society at NWLC. Dean Fagg sought to expedite discussion, by reminding everyone that last year we had already approved the Society's establishment. So, the only question now was the matter of funding it. Our catalog and other publications currently represented the existence of the chapter. The discussion that followed led to two tight pinches: a squeeze on money and another on voting margins.

Some felt that we should not give money from student tuition for support of social groups. To which others argued that $1,000 was but one peanut from our $1,000,000 budget jar. But some felt that more than $1,000 was at stake; it marked precedent for other internal "societies" to rise and put a hand out.

From there, the discussion took a turn when it was suggested that money should not be awarded until the society chapter was a "going concern." To which, others countered that money was needed to make it a going concern. Dean Fagg noted that "going concern" meant *established* and that we had already agreed to *establish* a chapter. One cannot establish something and then leave it penniless.

Then someone cautioned that at least some muster of student interest had to precede the seeding of money. To which, Professor Hughey informed that thirteen students had met at his home to discuss formation of the chapter. Professor Dente wondered if thirteen was evidence of sufficient interest in a student body of hundreds. The dean had to interrupt again to remind that funding, not establishment, was the only issue at hand.

Student representative Haley observed that the society should first try to operate without finance and seek support later. Hughey announced that that course would "guarantee failure."

Professor Williamson then moved to amend Hughey's original motion by deleting the "$1,000 funding" request. Haley seconded. The dean tried again: If the amendment were to pass, then all that was left of the main motion would be no more than an approval of what was already established. Nevertheless, a vote was taken on the amendment and it passed by the narrow vote of 9 to 8, with 3 abstaining, the dean wanting to vote but not allowed.

Professor Belsheim then moved to fund $500 for the existing Society chapter. Some felt the motion was out of order in view of defeat of the previous amendment. But others were quick to point out that that vote simply defeated a $1,000 funding, not something less. That's when Williamson said that he intended his amendment to strike funding of any size. To which someone retorted that, if intentions counted, then he cast his vote with the intent of striking "$1,000," not "funding." After further discussion (some of it parliamentary and some playful), a vote was taken and Belsheim's motion was narrowly defeated 9 to 10, one abstaining. Seemingly then, someone could have moved to fund at $400, then $300 and so on. But the "so on's" gave up at the $500 attempt.

One-vote margins on niggling quantums were pinches instead of punches. The session was just a window into the parlor, parley, and parliamentary doings at business sessions anywhere.


ITEM—CONFERENCES AND EVENTS:

The 1973-74 academic year saw NWLC plunge deeply into the national academic practice of conference and event presentations. In addition to our annual Board of Visitors Day and our annual Alumni Day, NWLC staged an Estate Planning Conference for February 1974. Into that schedule, we crammed still more. Two years ago Dean Hal Wren had committed us to hosting an AALS Regional Conference of all the western law schools in the United States and Canada. Now at the start of the 1973-74 year, we were left with preparation for that event set in April. Professor Belsheim noted that planning an event of that size would involve a lot of hard work and questioned the wisdom of doing so. At a time when there was so much else to do, others also felt we should cancel. But there was no escape. We were in no position to break a promise with AALS—the accreditor we were about to curry. Indeed, the conference would not only have to take place, it would have to be outstanding.

That's when Professor DuBoff proposed a Law and Visual Arts Conference for the month of March. Invitations would be extended to law educators from all over the nation. It would be co-sponsored by the American Society of International Law. At first the idea of taking on another conference seemed out of the question. Ann Kendrick, Director of Programs, wondered why the faculty would squeeze another event into an already crowded spring schedule: the February 3 Estates Planning Conference; the March 1 Alumni Day; the April 5 and 6 Western Law School Conference; the April 18 and 19 Board of Visitors visit; and now a March 16 Law and the Arts conference.

Nevertheless, on September 5, 1973, the faculty approved a go-ahead on DuBoff's conference. September was a long way from March and willingness came easy when work was so far ahead. Hectic would follow such antics.

Professor Folberg was assigned the job of coordinating the AALS Western Regional Conference. It turned out to be a crowning event. Its theme would be "Lawyers in Watergate—an Ethical Leak in Legal Education?" The conference was one of the first in the nation to respond to the recent Watergate exposure and to the misguided actions of President Nixon's staff, most of them having law degrees. Those ethical failings aroused self-guilt within law education. All across the nation, the cover-ups and "dirty tricks" had prompted law schools to intensify professional responsibility schooling.

Aside from the primary purpose of serving education, conferences also provide the opportunity to showcase the organizing institution and its personnel. Folberg's Conference was a leading effort in that direction. It drew national attention, and NWLC crested on the wave of Watergate upheaval. Our ambitious display of events led wag Bross to call it our entry into "conferencology."


ITEM—PROGRAMS:

Closely aligned with conferences and events were a flurry of proposals for perpetual programs focusing on specialty. As aforesaid, Professor Hughey urged an International Law Society; Professor Huffman sought a Natural Resources Law Institute. Professors Folberg and Bross pressed for a Neighborhood Law Institute. The latter was a cry for another echelon of government—one less distant than national or state government, smaller than county, and smaller still than city—a part in governance for united neighbors. The law school needed programs focused on law vicinities as wide as the transcontinental and as narrow as city blocks. Or so it was argued.

As for programs of any and all kinds, it was true that, in order to profess, one had to have a soap box, bull horn, attendants, and attention. A professor without a program was a chassis in need of wheels.

## Item—Dignitaries:

During the year, we were visited by a host of notables. Retired U.S. Supreme Court Justice Thomas Clark led that list. He was the second Supreme Court Justice to take the NWLC rostrum. Justice William O. Douglas had been the first. [See ch. 9, "Nader-Douglas Visits"] Other dignitaries in 1973-74 included ex-U.S. Senator Wayne Morse, Samuel Dash (the lead Special Counsel in the Watergate investigations), Professor Andrew Watson (the nationally prominent law psychotherapist on Michigan University's law faculty), and Betty Roberts (NWLC alumna, candidate for Oregon Governor, and soon to be Oregon's first woman justice on the Oregon Supreme Court).

## Item—JFC and Moonlighting:

The spring issue of the third volume of *Environmental Law* published excerpts from my Second Biennial Report to the Oregon Legislative Assembly and from my address to the Oregon Judicial Conference, both of which concerned my work as Executive Secretary to the Judicial Fitness Commission, a state agency. That issue marked the beginning of *Environmental Law*'s inclusion in the nationally published *Index to Legal Periodicals*. The recognition was a major step forward for our law review. How judicial fitness fit into ecological fitness was certainly a wonder to know. Nevertheless, I was thanked "for helping *Environmental Law* through its struggling existence," and the article was flattered with the claim [whimsically, of course] to "be the reason our journal was included in the *Index*."

The article also drew faculty attention to the matter of "moonlighting." Colleagues and accreditors both frowned on full-time professors engaged in work separate from their academic job. And so, there was inquiry from some colleagues about my separate duties. Were they conflicting? My JFC work took an average of about twenty hours a month of my time, for which Oregon paid me a small annual salary of about $2,200. My investigations of complaints about allegedly wayward judges were confidential. Therefore, under no circumstances, could my work include law student assistance. In short, the work did not connect to schooling even though officed at the law school address with one of the law school secretaries serving as a part-time JFC clerical assistant (Pauline Kallenbach followed by Betty Lou Johnson).

Often there would be weeks in which there was no judicial fitness work to do.

But other times, it took a couple of days in a week to go to some distant courthouse in Oregon. Usually, the cases were simple claims from a citizen or lawyer reporting an isolated incident. A complaint might concern injudicious decorum like unruly temper, insult, or bad language toward a witness, juror, or lawyer. Or it might also concern an incompetent law ruling by a judge—a matter for appellate courts, not the JFC. On few occasions, the charges went beyond a single incident and into chronic misbehavior. Those took more time and travel. For example, one judge was said to have the habit of bringing his cat with him when he was on the bench during court sessions. Another eastern Oregon judge had a continuing argument with his county commissioners because they would not install a men's room on the second floor of the courthouse where the judge's chambers were located, thus forcing the judge to walk down to the first floor public restroom—a situation unbecoming court dignity. That much was of no concern to the JFC. When the judge took matters into his own hands and "installed" a coffee can in his chambers, it was still of no matter to the JFC. But when it became commonplace to see him emptying the can out of his second story window into the public courtyard below, I was called to verify.

A couple of times, charges were even more serious and warranted more extensive detective work. Public drunkenness was an example. Those investigations took me away from campus at classroom times, and that stirred faculty involvement. Placating those concerns, however, was not difficult. The JFC commissioners needed an investigator within the law discipline but not someone who might one day have to appear before judges as a client representative. That ruled out practicing litigators. Furthermore, someone with detached perspective could better engage in the delicate handling of an executive and legislative branch intrusion into the third branch of government. Indeed, it took an amendment of the Oregon Constitution to create the Judicial Fitness Commission, inasmuch as its work was a crossing of the separation of powers.

By the same token it was why the name "secretary" was chosen for my job. If the emissary of the Commission was going to approach a member of the judiciary about matters as delicate as alleged unfitness in the office, that prober ought not be anything as threatening as a "director" or "investigator." A "secretary," however, had the diplomatic advantage of subordination. Today, judges have come to accept the idea of government probing into judicial fitness. Accordingly, the title of "Executive Director" is now official—a label not so wise when judges were adapting to new-fangled scrutiny.

And so, back in 1973-74, just as judges had to be convinced of the Commission's connection to judicial work so too did my colleagues have to be convinced of the connection to school work. The faculty came to understand that Academe was not just there as a law school; it was also a law *center*—a hub where a crucial beneficiary of the place was society and where essential pupils in the place included the teachers themselves.

After about seven years of service as the first Executive Director, I handed the baton to Professor Bill Snouffer, who eventually passed it on to Professor Williamson, who would pass it to Professor Bernie Vail, who handed it to Professor Paula Abrams in the mid-1980s. While JFC work passed muster, other moonlighting engagements would not. *E.g.*, opening a law office or catering to a clientele were clearly cause for breach. The distinction was often worded as the difference between "consulting" and "practicing." A professor could consult but not practice—fuzzy words for a fuzzier division separating them. Nevertheless, the distinction was critical to accreditors and to school employment. Indeed, in the future, there were occasions for separating professors who did not observe the separation.

### ITEM—PROMOTION AND TENURE:

Late in 1973-74, I was appointed to draft a more detailed set of rules on promotion and tenure of full-time professors. Why it was handed to me, I do not know; my attitude against the promoting and "tenuring" of bodies was well known. I submitted my innovative proposal at the April 4 faculty meeting. The draft was a bold departure from long-held, well-honored tradition. For example, I proposed to do away with professorial rank. The echelons of "assistant," "associate," and "full" professorships were meaningless signs of seniority. As for tenure, I disparaged it as nothing more than a badge that no longer carried its once useful function. Bold stances, to be sure. Opponents argued that tenure gave academic freedom—like as though without tenure, professors had no freedom to profess controversial issues and like as though those with tenure could not be fired for ethical impropriety, incompetence, business cutbacks, or failures of duty. On the contrary, neither the tenured nor those on track for tenure would ever be made to leave except for the good causes of morality, ability, economics, or dereliction. I granted that there would have to be an initial period of a few years in which academic performances of new hires would be subject to evaluation. But the title of "professor" was information enough. Vested rank was not more than a trophy for the mantle. In the Wizard of Oz, the lion, the tin man, and the scarecrow were not given courage, compassion, and intelligence by the awards of a medal of honor, a heart-shaped ticker, or a college diploma. Those bestowals were but tokens of what was there all along. A faculty of mature scholars did not need adornments. Why is it that higher educators saunter so, while primary and secondary teachers do not?

My proposal (as I knew it would) died quietly. It was itself a token. As long as everyone understood that rank and tenure, like the hoods and gowns we wore at graduation ceremonies, were no more than pomp and circumstance, I had no quarrel with the fun of those who needed costume and rites.

That's how I felt in 1973-74 when I was in my early forties. Older now as an "emeritus" professor (another rank) and as something of an antique myself, I confess to seeing antiquity with more respect.

### ITEM—SABBATICAL POLICY:

The academic year of 1973-74 was my seventh year as a full-time professor—my eighth year in service to NWLC when my part-time teaching as a practicing lawyer was included. Higher education everywhere follows the *Genesis* schedule: The sabbath seventh year should be a time of rest, but NWLC had no sabbatical policy. I was the first to take that leave. It would not happen until the fall of 1981-82, my fifteenth year on the job. In those early energetic years of creation, there was simply no time for recreation.

### ITEM—LIBRARY HIRES:

In 1973-74, the caliber of our law library was expanding, not only in shelves and pages, but also in tenders. Librarian Walt Brown's staff now included Virginia Kelsh, Penny Hazelton, and Dorothy MacPherson. Virginia and Penny also enrolled as evening law students while engaged in their full-time library jobs. As alumnae of our law school they went on to profound careers in law librarianship. Virginia became the head librarian at the University of San Francisco Law School and served there for

**LIBRARY TENDERS**
Virginia Kelsh, Penny Hazelton, Dorothy MacPherson

some twenty-two years, retiring in 2005. Penny serves as Associate Dean and head librarian at the University of Washington law library having fitted into the big shoes left by the nationally noted Marion Gould Gallagher. At one time in Penny's career she was the Acting Director of the United States Supreme Court Library in Washington, D.C. and President of the American Association of Law Libraries. In future years, other staff members in the NWLC library have also gone on to careers in our nation's law libraries. George Pike is the Library Director at the University of Pittsburgh Law School. Christopher Simoni is the Director and Professor at the Drexel Law School library. Joseph Stephens is the chief librarian at the Oregon State Law Library. Our feed of shepherds into the nation's law athenaeums has been proud.

ITEM—FEMININISTS:

As our student body size grew to record numbers, even more impressive was the growth of female enrollees. In August 1973, they more than doubled in size from 47 in the previous year. Two of ten of our first year students were women. One year later, in the fall of 1974, women students would number 139 and would constitute three of ten of our entering first year class.

The matrimonial support group for law students, called "Law Wives" [see ch. 1], had to change its name to "Law Wives and Husbands." That title lasted only a short time. As society shifted to acceptance of couples living together without matrimony, the organization called itself "Law Wives and Partners." Same sex partners, however, were not contemplated in the 1970s. Dawning had not yet come to that far horizon.

While Law Wives and Partners had widened its membership, it was still led by its distaff side and its agendas continued to be domestic. At its March 13, 1974, meeting, the guest speaker was a representative of a seed company, who gave a talk on home gardening.

Just as the word "feminist" had replaced "feminine," so too at the opposite end, the word "chauvinist" was being coined for male antagonists. The chauvinists openly argued that women by their gentle nature were not equipped to be lawyers. Sometimes that male derision exceeded argument and became menacing rage. One such occasion was downright ugly. Our law student newspaper published this hate mail directed at the editors:

> "Do not print no more of that feminist nonsense in your paper or you will be shot. If you think I am not kidding, just try to test out this threat."

Ironically, it was signed simply "A Friend"—rather like signing a Declaration of War with "Cordially Yours." The anonymity and grammar gave faculty investigators an excuse to say that a law student must not have written such disturbing trash.

Counter to the chauvinism that argued against female capacity to handle law work, there was this: At the 1974 graduation, NWLC would bestow a *summa cum laude* degree—the highest scholastic award that can be given a graduate and the first time in history of the law school that a student's grades had ever reached that high level. It went to student Karen Creason—just as the first *magna cum laude* degree three years before, went to Ann Morgenstern.

### ITEM—RACIAL INTEGRATION AND DIVERSITY:

While female enrollment was showing rapid growth, the enrolling of racial minority students was not so successful even in the face of efforts at recruiting. We had about seventeen minority students in a total student body approaching 700. Many reasons were given for the inadequate showing, among which were: lack of scholarship or aid monies, a relatively small minority population in the Pacific northwest, and the U.S. Supreme Court dictates in the *DeFunis* and *Bakke* decisions. [See ch. 11, "Racial Affirmative Action"]

Aside from our internal efforts to overcome the lack of diversity within our own walls, outside of our walls racial discrimination landed at our front door. Somehow a law school soiree for our alumni at the September 1973 Oregon State Bar Convention got scheduled at a clubhouse of a fraternal lodge that denied entry to certain races and ethnic cultures. Fortunately, the faculty acted in time to change the location in spite of disgruntlement from out our walls.

### ITEM—GRADUATION CEREMONY:

Once again we tried to get President Howard and the Board of Trustees to have two separate commencements—one for the college and one for the law graduates. [See ch. 13, "Graduation Day"] Although it would not happen in 1974, the turmoil that struck the 1974 ceremony, made it all too clear that it would happen soon. Bad weather drove the ceremony indoors. The bleacher seating in the gymnasium was simply not large enough to handle all the guests and some had to attend in the hallway. Throng paved the way for future change.

But the change would not be abrupt. A middle ground between one and two ceremonies would first be tried. So, next year in 1975, the law school would be given its own so-called "special function;" it could not be called a "graduation ceremony." The latter would follow one week later where graduation would continue to be an "all-college" affair. At the "special function" for the law seniors and guests, the gowns, hoods, oration, music, processional, pomp, and all the circumstance of a graduation could be employed, including the bestowal of a "faculty scroll." The scroll would not be the official Juris Doctor diploma, however. That sheepskin had to be conferred at the official commencement one week later—a ceremony that a law candidate did not have to attend; the doctorate degree could be mailed or picked up.

Needless to say, in the following year (1976), the nonsense of the "special function" label would succumb to the force of "the duck-wisdom:" If it quacks and preaches like a commencement, waddles and parades like a commencement, preens and robes like a commencement, then it's a commencement.

Just as a yawn begets a yawn, so too does nonsense infect. Professor Bill Williamson, in his own inimical and inimitable way, seized the commencement separation as an opportunity for further distancing. Billy proposed removal of the Lewis & Clark College colors (black and orange) and the adoption of a different color scheme for the law school's graduation hoods.

*Rotor Mortar Board*

As a further dress whimsy, someone proposed that Registrar Dorothy Cornelius be given a special hat for graduation—a beanie with a spinner on top. Because Dorothy had no college degree whatsoever, she was not permitted by protocol and decorum to wear a tassel on top of her mortar board hat. She could wear the gown and hat board, but not the tassel. Out of all that parade of garb and paraphernalia, the only item that signified successful, academic completion was a tiny, inconspicuous dangle atop each head. So, in playful defiance, the faculty passed a motion allowing her to wear a propellor instead. The mid 1970s was still a day when graduations were rigged with colorful additions such as bubbles, balloons, ribbons, flowers, and other signs of individuality, all welcome and jubilant. A spinner would fit in. But Dorothy was annoyed and wanted to know if the spinner had something to do with her being a spinster. Furthermore, unlike Billy, or the graduates, Dorothy had no mischief and plenty of propriety in her. She had been with the law school since the mid-1950s and had seen more law graduations than anyone else. Respect—ours for her and hers for graduations—was all it took. There would be no new coloration or whirligig to mar the tradition of the alma mater's final ceremonial good-bye.

Even though I favored the separate ceremonies, there were drawbacks. The ever-widening breach between the law school and its adopting parent, was troubling. I, for one, regretted casting off all ropes and going adrift from pre-law shores. Law was, after all, a servant of civilization; and civilized progress hinged on its beauty and truth—its art and science. I was the only law professor who attended both ceremonies. Perhaps that says something about me; I just don't know what it is.

All of the foregoing "items" were just that—pieces and parts of what scattered throughout our time in 1973-74—all testaments to C. Northcote Parkinson's famed insight about the work of organizations and the human nature that controls them:

> "Work expands so as to fill the time available for its completion.... The thing to be done swells in importance and complexity in a direct ratio with the time to be spent."

We did not set a lot of time for completion of the foregoing and so they were merely "items." There was another issue in 1973-74 for which greater *time was made available for completion* and, therefore, was *swelled in importance and complexity*. AALS Accreditation was the main course by which the menu would be defined, making all side orders seem like leftovers. But, indeed, the routine of dealing with scraps was what told us we had moved out of just *learning* to be like a law school and had shifted into being one.

# 1973: TIME CONTEXT

A Watergate burglar pleads guilty and reveals White House instigation. Top White House officials are investigated and resign. Senate hearings begin.

Attorney General John Mitchell, indicted for perjury and obstruction, resigns.

Former White House assistant, James Dean, implicates Nixon in the Watergate calamities. Senate subpoenas Presidential tapes and Nixon refuses to turn over all of them. Talk of impeachment begins.

Vice-President Agnew resigns and pleads no contest to income tax evasion. House Speaker Gerald Ford becomes Vice-President.

U.S. Supreme Court rules in *Roe* v. *Wade* that there is a constitutional right to abortion during the first two trimesters.

Paris Peace Accords nominally end the Vietnam War.

Fighting breaks out again between Arabs and Israelis.

Militant Native Americans take over South Dakota village of Wounded Knee for 70 days.

Violence continues in North Ireland between the Irish and English.

Congress enacts the Endangered Species Act.

Oregon legislature creates the Land Control Development Commission with broad powers over land use.

Competing with Playboy and Penthouse magazines, Hustler magazine becomes the most pornographic of them all.

Oregon becomes the first state to decriminalize marijuana possession.

Billie Jean King defeats Bobby Riggs (three straight sets) in a much publicized tennis "battle of the sexes."

# 15
# THE ENDLESS BECOMING
*1973-74*

"All is fluid and changing.
There is an endless becoming"
–Benjamin Nathan Cardozo

H igh above the current law school's three-story, reading room, screwed to the ceiling rafters is a wood carving I had made of Cardozo's foregoing quote. I applied it to the sojourn NWLC had been taking these past years—an insight that says: the dusk of one feat simply puts us at the dawn of another. The final piece in our accreditation quest, a pursuit that began seven years ago, was to gain membership in the Association of American Law Schools [AALS]. Having been approved permanently by the ABA in February 1973, the faculty assumed that the bridge to AALS was now a clear one. But like all of the spans in that era, our crossing was strewn with obstacles.

## APPLICATION TO AALS:

The first impasse was unexpected; it rose within our own ranks. Some trustees, a few college administrators, and a contingent of undergrad faculty assumed (or at least hoped) that once ABA permanent accreditation was achieved that would be an end of pampering the newly merged law school, now living a block away from the main campus. Throughout past years, the Board of Trustees had been obliged to make commitments to the law school on account of dictates forced by ABA conditions, such as the purchase of land, the raising of structure, the hiring of expensive cadre, the enormous buildup of books, the mounting expense of travel, support, consultation , development, preparation and just plain consumption of time and money, all keyed to satisfying national minimums and medians. Chasing those dictates produced pent-up expectations that begged for release and snatched at fulfillment. Our success with the ABA warranted, not just achievement, but also finish. Done. Over!

And so, in the months following the ABA bestowal back in February 1973, a few were surprised to learn that there was more to do. Others were mildly aware of another law accreditor. They had heard Dean Wren back in the fall of 1971 boast that we would be members of AALS by December 1972. They knew that President Howard had made the trip to the AALS Convention in New York City to make those overtures. [See ch. 12, "ABA Accreditation] Nevertheless, they saw no immediate reason for a second recognition.

The questioners wondered if pursuing AALS was simply joining a "club," not gaining a license. They pointed to the fact that there were many ABA approved law schools who were not members of AALS. Of approximately 150 ABA schools, only 120 were AALS schools as of summer 1973. The difference between ABA and AALS was compared to the difference between a state's Department of Motor Vehicle and the American Automobile Association [AAA], respectively.

The disinclined also cited the 1965 Merger Agreement wherein the terms made AALS attainment optional:

> "The express purpose of the merger is to provide [education]... upon a basis fully accredited by the American Bar Association.... [The college] may desire also to attain accreditation by the American Association of Law Schools."

That optional status was further bolstered by the Law School Admissions Council [LSAC], a separate organization that aided its member schools with testing [the LSAT] and assessing law application qualifications. LSAC had recently amended its by-laws to allow an ABA accredited law school into its ranks even though the school was not an AALS member

Factions within the ABA itself also felt that the ABA ought to be the sole accreditor. They argued that it was more suitable for the law profession, not the law educators, to judge law education. After all, the professional organization was more encompassing than the professorial organization. And a certain nettling arose from the fact that professors could belong to the ABA but lawyers per se could not play a part in AALS.

All of these deterrents had surfaced for the first time within the months following our ABA acceptance. Consequently, trustee William Swindells, chairman of SCOLS, in conference with President Howard and trustee Paul Boley, created a new SCOLS Accreditation Subcommittee to be chaired by Justice Arno Denecke of the Oregon Supreme Court.

Under constitutional separation of powers and far above accrediting agencies, the Oregon Supreme Court had the ultimate authority to order who could and could not be a lawyer in Oregon courtrooms—the domain of the judicial branch of government. It was the court who threatened to no longer let graduates of NWLC or any other unaccredited school to enter the Bar as advocates. In that way and in various other ways throughout the accreditation era, members of the supreme court interacted with NWLC. Beginning in the early 1960s, then Chief Justice William McAllister had nudged downtown Northwestern College of Law to get accredited. Oddly, that happened to be at a time when I was clerking for the chief justice. Justice Thomas Tongue (a long-time teacher at Northwestern) was a Northwestern trustee who had negotiated and signed the Merger Agreement. As the successor to the chief justice seat, Kenneth O'Connell had been the keynote dedicator of our new Tryon Forest law campus. [See ch. 8] Justice Ralph Holman, a Northwestern alumnus, played an active role in accreditation matters, as seen in these pages. Justice Dean Bryson was another Northwestern graduate. Now, here in 1973, Justice Arno Denecke was assigned to lead the study of the AALS accreditation issue. Three classrooms on the law campus are named for Justices Tongue, Holman, and Denecke.

The Denecke subcommittee met on March 28, 1973, and swiftly recommended application to AALS for membership. At the April 10 meeting of SCOLS, the subcommittee recommendation was considered. Swindells, a non-lawyer and highly successful, no nonsense, businessman, went to the bottom-line: What *benefits* were there to be gained from AALS joinder and at what *cost*?

The benefits were largely prestige and association—honor and sharing. Having

**OREGON SUPREME COURT (MID-1970s)**

[Standing l. to r.]: Associate Justices Ed Howell, Ralph Holman, Tom Tongue III, Dean Bryson. [Seated l. to r.]: former Chief Justice Bill McAllister, Chief Justice Ken O'Connell, future Chief Justice Arno Denecke

established our own law faculty was groundwork; but connecting nationwide with all law faculties would be the unity from which edifice arises. Dean Fagg called AALS "the preeminent agency." Boley said that acceptance into the nation's alliance of law schools was "the supreme accolade." Justice Denecke reported that the Oregon Supreme Court considered AALS acceptance as more than just a dues-paying membership like joining the AAA; it was a credit—a credential—an accreditation. Indeed, AALS itself labeled its screeners an "Accreditation Committee." Then too, assurances had been given throughout the years to our students. E.g., The 1965 Howard letter to prospective students also promised that their law school would meet the "standards acceptible to the ABA and to the AALS."

As for cost, Dean Fagg saw "no great expense." True, we would have to pay yearly membership dues. There would be room, board, and travel expense for a three-person inspection team to come here and for our emissaries to go there. Our 1973-74 proposed budget (already approved by the trustees) listed $6,000 for those initial costs. Aside from some needed library build-up, there ought not be any major capital expense. And, oh yes, by the way, we would also need to hire a consultant.

That final expenditure perked ears and raised eyebrows. Why would we need our own consultant? In gaining ABA approval, the ABA furnished its own consultant; he worked for and was paid by the ABA. While we did reimburse some of his expenses, we did not have to pay him a fee. But AALS membership procedures worked differently. Michael Cardozo, AALS Executive Director, had told us that where the ABA employed a permanent investigator called a "Consultant," AALS simply had an "Inspection Team" composed of three educators from different schools temporarily chosen on a one-time basis. There was no one to provide an applicant school with mentoring. Cardozo advised that we would be wise to get someone with experience in the subtleties of AALS scrutiny. AALS academicians would have a different perspective from ABA practitioners. Someone had to be paid to pilot us through AALS waters.

Having exhausted the pros and cons, the April SCOLS meeting minutes state that Justice Denecke asked for SCOLS' "wishes" on whether to seek AALS membership, and SCOLS gave the request a "vote of confidence." Thus, a mere "wish" and " confidence" were the record's *tepid* way of putting what needed to be a *hot* pursuit.

Most notably, the launch was missing faculty input. To be sure, the law faculty position could have been taken for granted. Throughout the last seven years, four law deans and some twenty-five law professors had worn their desire for AALS membership on their sleeves, but never was it formalized. The nation's law educators would want to see in the record that formalizing an application to an educator association had come from educators. So, to set the record straight, a June 4, 1973, law faculty meeting was called at 1:30 p.m., where it was moved and unanimously passed that the law professors recommended seeking AALS membership. That was then hastily followed at 4:00 p.m. on the same day by a SCOLS meeting where the faculty idea was unanimously accepted. Thus, a sensitive handling of the record showed this sequence: SCOLS first *wished*; then the faculty *launched*; then SCOLS *accepted* faculty initiative. This would assure the nation's law professors the petition to AALS stemmed from the conductors of education: the professors.

## HIRING A CONSULTANT:

The faculty's next step on the destination was to choose a consultant. Back in the Wren regime, Professor Daniel Dykstra of the University of California (Berkeley) had been mentioned for that role. But his potential was outshined by another. Ideally, our best mentor would be someone we knew and who was already familiar with our operations. One name jumped to mind. Who better than Millard Ruud.

Was he amenable? Yes, he was. Was AALS comfortable with using an ABA consultant as our advisor? Professor Ronan Degnan, chair of the AALS Accreditation Committee, saw no problem; after all, Ruud was also a half-time law professor at the University of Texas. Were SCOLS members in agreement? Although SCOLS membership had its divisions, there was no difficulty there. Millard made no enemies; he made friends.

President Howard, SCOLS, the alumni association, the Board of Trustees, AALS, the faculty, and Millard himself were all in accord. In the summer of 1973, we got a consultant—the man who wrote that a "consultant is someone who looks at your watch and tells you what time it is."

But in spite of that self-effacement, he did not toy with consulting; rather, he toiled at it. He wrote, "The most satisfying aspect of the job was helping a new law school... to change its program so that it was eligible...." That was a totally different attitude from his ABA predecessor John Hervey, who emphasized "pruning away weak schools and strengthening those that remained." He favored weeding instead of seeding. In June 1969, Hervey wrote, "Legal education might be strengthened by the elimination of some schools." Hervey took pride in listing ten schools that, during his term, the ABA had either kicked out or turned away or in his words: "closed," "denied," "disaffiliated," "discontinued," rendered "extinct." In Ruud, we went from hindrance to help. Ruud liked us; he wanted us to succeed.

Since the take-over from Hervey five years ago, Ruud focused on ABA accreditation, yet kept one eye on AALS accreditation as well. From what he could see, the two accreditors needed to work together. Although sometimes their paths crossed, most of the time they ran parallel and in the same direction. He felt their inspections could be joined. At Ruud's urgings, leaders in both camps warmed to the idea and quietly behind the scenes set the prospect in motion. When in September 1973, Michael Cardozo decided to retire from the AALS Executive Director post, the door opened to the joinder. Millard was hired as the new AALS Director. Meanwhile, the ABA agreed to continue Ruud as the ABA Consultant until the end of December, 1973.

Thus, for four months from September through December, Millard held both positions: ABA Consultant and AALS Executive Director. In his own words, he was "a double-agent." Then too, during some of that time, he was also NWLC's consultant. When we learned of that serendipitous trinity, we were elated to say the least. How now could we miss! So, at the start of the 1973-74 academic year, a cocky law faculty strutted to the starting line. We were so confident that we set a time and place for celebrating the win before opening the race. When AALS certainly would grant us membership at the convention in New Orleans in the last week of December 1973, we should all be there. Minutes of the September 1973 faculty meeting recorded, "In a spirit of general frivolity, a motion that we all go to the... convention... was passed." There was even talk of chartering a private plane for an air flight to get us all there for "supreme accolade"—the bestowal of membership.

*Triple Agent Ruud*

As much as I longed for that expectancy, I had been with the wait between nesting and hatch long enough to learn two contradictory lessons about eggs and time: *lots of time* to lay an egg yet *no time* to count chicks.

### THE QUESTIONNAIRE:

Annual faculty contracts of employment do not include eleven summer weeks—a time without duties or pay. Nevertheless, the summer of 1973, not covered by contract, found many of us preparing for NWLC's joinder with AALS. Our formal application to AALS had to be put in the form of a response to a detailed "AALS Questionnaire," consisting of 54 questions. Our answers covered almost 100 pages (65 pages of text plus 31 pages of charts, tabulations, breakdowns, schedules, rules, rosters, agreements, and other counts and accountings which were accompanied by samples of our faculty meeting minutes, our quarterly news bulletins, student newspapers, admission materials, operating budgets, and such. Once again our *qualifications* were made known by such *quantification*—value by sizing.

As she did with the ABA Questionnaire, Secretary Doris McCroskey was of profound assistance in conducting and arranging the final packet in the last hours before a deadline imposed by AALS. The whole of it went out under an August 10, 1973, eleven-page cover letter signed by President Howard and Dean Fagg.

Arrangements with AALS put our application on a short schedule insofar as it aimed for a bestowal at the AALS convention in the last week of 1973, just a little over four months away. Between now and then, there were a lot of steps to climb. Speed in the processing caused many to complain—not the least of which could have been Doris whose hurried labors were further tightened by the dean's well-known eleventh-hour epiphanies. Those in the law discipline were accustomed to many deadlines: *e.g.*, court dockets, client appointments, statutory time limits, and other expediencies. Whenever that is the case, procrastination would infect even the most organized person. Doris had to work late hours to meet the final posting of the Questionnaire. And with that mailing, our application was underway.

## THE INSPECTION TEAM AND TIME TABLE:

Copies of our application went to four California law professors: Ronan E. Degnan of the University of California (Berkeley), John A Bauman of the University of California (Los Angeles), Mortimer D. Schwartz of the University of California (Davis), and Jan Vetter of the University of California (Berkeley). Degnan was the chair of the AALS Accreditation Committee. Bauman would lead an Inspection Team that included Schwartz and Vetter. Thus, well in advance of our formal application, inspectors and preliminaries had been set in order to speed the process. It was a rush job that troubled many AALS officials as well as us. Not only were we put on track, trackers were posted along the rails waiting for us—posts that had to be reached before the end of the calendar year. Our timetable was this: The three-person Inspection Team would visit our campus on September 17 and 18. They would make a detailed written report and recommendation to the AALS Accreditation Committee by the last week in October. That Committee's recommendation had to be put to the AALS Executive Committee in the first week of November. The recommendations of the inspectors, accreditors, and executives would then all be relayed to the delegates of all law school members for their vote at the annual convention of law schools in New Orleans between Christmas and New Year holidays.

## AALS—ABA INTEREST AREAS:

By the time the Inspection Team was due to arrive, our consultant Ruud had to withdraw from that role. He had now become the Executive Director of AALS. But before that departure, he gave us a number of forecasts, one of which was to point out some differences in the way ABA and AALS saw matters—differences that centered on street savvy versus book learning—different facets, but of the same diamond—differences nonetheless. Specifically, *e.g.*, it meant that where ABA might emphasize the new clinical skills learning, AALS would be more interested in library size and quality. Where ABA might seek the education of law rules, AALS might look for the education of law principles. Where the ABA might admire a curriculum enriched by practical specialty courses, AALS might be more impressed with a curriculum given to theoretical research and innovation. Where ABA was more attentive to the attorney-client relationship (i.e., the profession's connection to the public), AALS was more directed toward the teacher-student relationship (i.e., education's duty to aspirants).

The approaches were not incompatible, but they were attitudinal—tweaks of difference between *the arena* of law and *the garden* of Academe. Ruud was the first to recognize that the advice was, perhaps, too vague to be of much value in life's discourses, but he emphasized it in dealing with an inspection by academicians and with judgments about education.

## AALS GUIDELINES:

AALS *Guideline Statement of Establishment of New Law Schools* was a pamphlet and good exemplar of Ruud's advice. My assignment was to familiarize myself with and fully comprehend that *Guideline Statement* to see how it might differ from the ABA "Standards" which we had recently met and passed. Right from those opening titles, a distinction was clear: Where "standards" were rules, "guidelines" were considerations—the difference between formality that was mandated and formation that was urged, between attitudes that imposed and those that implored. At one point AALS Guidelines warned that a "law student not become a statistic and the law school not become a processing center."

Our budget for the current 1973-74 year at $1,450,000 income, called for $470,000 academics, $600,000 administration/maintenance, $240,000 library, and $37,000 scholarships. One may observe we were administratively top heavy. AALS Guidelines urged that almost two-thirds of operating dollars should go to academics; whereas we were allocating only about one-third. We were also considerably short on money returns to students. We also budgeted $100,000 surplus income. Dean Fagg liked to call that excess a "Reserve." That reserve-surplus was in addition to the budget item for "Contingencies." Although schools are non-profit organizations, an MBA graduate knew full well it would please a governing board from the business world to know that income exceeded expense—thus, profitable enterprise. How better to measure a "going concern?"

But AALS cautioned that ciphering was not the heart of education. A school's failure to reach thresholds would not bar membership if reaching them was the mission. The whole of AALS *Guideline Statement* emphasized that the grant of membership focused on future course of action where the school's currency and history are but clues. Promise, not past, was the key.

On reading the AALS guidelines, I was reminded once again of my favorite words of Oliver Wendell Holmes, Jr. which I doodled into the margins of my copy of the *Guidelines*: "Life is more the painting of a picture, than the doing of a sum." Thus, were I to paint the picture, my seven years of dealing with accreditation told me that the heart of accreditor inspection came down to these four inquiries: (1) Are the *teachers* vigorous and smart?; (2) Are the *students* motivated and smart?; (3) Are the *tools* handy and smart?; (4) Are the *supporters* dedicated and smart? Everything else in the painting was form, not substance. How much of this and how much of that? How many of these and of those? How large and how small? The sizes of place, dollars, and bodies? The quantums of color, line, accent, brush stroke, and frame? All are but sums, not the picture.

In some minds, this approach seems too amorphous—too much leeway and not enough precision. But until we learn how to see the picture, the danger in sums is that, instead of hints, they become mechanical detours around tough decision-making.

## NWLC REPUTATION:

Ruud also told us that we might have to deal with our image—not just what we were inside, but how we looked outside. Professor accreditors were a much smaller, tighter-knit group than the ABA accreditors. The closer the group the more it bred familiarity and with that came gossip, caste, and elitism all fertile grounds for the swift spread of reputation. In the vast, but inner circle of legal education, NWLC likely had already gained a face—features that we might capitalize on or features that we might have to cover cosmetically.

What Ruud meant became clear when at gatherings we mixed with academicians from around the country. At those conversations, we would eventually be asked: *Aren't you the ones with that new environmental program? Aren't you the ones with the big student body there in the Pacific Northwest? Aren't you the ones with the name that gets confused with Northwestern University Law School in Illinois? Aren't you the ones with the fountains we saw on the cover of the ABA Annual Law School Review?* [See ch. 8] The queries would also connect us with Oregon: *Aren't you in Oregon where they've gone wild with bottle bills and public beaches? Don't you have that maverick Senator Wayne Morse who voted against the Vietnam War? Weren't you Oregonians the first to make Labor Day a holiday? Wasn't the Communist John Reed an Oregonian—the guy who's the only American buried in the Kremlin? Isn't Oregon that place where Hollywood filmed that hippy, toga-party Animal House movie? Aren't you the ones with the governor who urges people to come visit Oregon but not to stay? Isn't Oregon the place where that new NIKE company makes those new, crazy, waffle-soled running shoes?*

Foremost among such rumor there smoldered the embers of the Dean Stevens dismissal during the 1967 AALS Convention. That impact was still alive within AALS in 1973-74. A hint of it surfaced in the November 1973 minutes of an AALS Accreditation Committee meeting where it was stated that the NWLC dean "is supported by a president who was once not very supportive." The minutes went on to wonder if "a change in critical personnel might signal a change in direction."

On account of that spectre in our closet, Millard took me aside and urged me to talk to John Bauman, the AALS Inspection Team leader, about what lessons and transformations had occurred since that time in 1967. "Give him the same background that you gave me a year ago," Ruud said. [See ch. 12, "ABA Accreditation"] AALS, even more then the ABA, would want that update.

## LAW LIBRARY:

Before Ruud had to step away from consultation with us, he also cautioned us to be ready for some probable Inspection Team probes into soft-spots in our library. AALS placed great emphasis on quantity and quality of library collections, access, facility, and personnel—an emphasis far more meticulous than ABA demands.

Accordingly, almost one-half of the pages in our 96-page "Response to the AALS Questionnaire" concerned library information. The 1967 AALS guidelines had called for 40,000 volumes as a minimum goal in a member's library. In the summer of 1972, we had only about 32,500 volumes. One year later, pulled by ABA accreditation and pushed by our alumni association's successful book campaign, we were able to report a book count of 62,500. That amassing was profound. Equally profound was the intensive labor of librarians who made the 30,000 new volumes accessible. It's one thing to possess a book and quite another to make it handy when lost among its kind. AALS pressed for that a research library having both source and recourse. Recourse meant that books must be delivered, carted, catalogued, and shelved. In 250 working days in 1972-73, 30,000 books (that's 120 books per day) had been moved, identified, indexed, and placed. Librarian Walt Brown passed the credit along to his staff—principally Virginia Kelsh, Penny Hazelton, and Dorothy McPherson. President Howard recognized it as a "truly remarkable achievement." Marion Gallager, a nationally recognized and celebrated head librarian at the University of Washington law library was brought in to assess our collection and its appointment. In her three-day July 1973 scrutiny she found little deficiency and had the best of things to say.

Oddly enough, while we were able to report a book count of 62,500—far more than the AALS 1967 minimum of 40,000—it still fell a tad short of AALS new guidelines. The recommended AALS book count had been rising year by year and had grown faster than we had. In September 1973, Ruud told us that AALS library standards now called for 65,000 volumes. No doubt we could reach that level by December. Iin fact, we actually reached 72,000 by that time and went to 85,000 by March 1974. Nevertheless, the AALS changes indicated that we were not grasping, but rather chasing an elusive rabbit.

### STUDENT BODY RELATIONS:

As Ruud had forewarned, AALS inspectors would also be concerned about the disorder afflicting most schools of higher education throughout the land: How was NWLC connecting with its student body? Unrest, upset, and protest from activist students were still afoot nationally. While the war in Vietnam had reached a cease-fire agreement, that cool-down was countered by a firing-up in Congress over suspicious doings in the White House. The suspicions grew into Senate investigations, indictments, White House resignations, and a House Judiciary recommendation in favor of Presidential impeachment.

Internationally, war and violence erupted in the Mid-East and in North Ireland. Insurrection and assassination took place in Spain, Chile, and Greece. Back in the U.S., seeds of future unrest had been sown by a U.S. Supreme Court decision ruling it unconstitutional to criminalize abortion in the first two trimesters of pregnancy.

That was the world beyond NWLC's cloister in 1973-74—the world into which our students would be released. Was it any wonder then that students across the nation looked at the world and their education with anxiety and suspicion? And was it any wonder that accreditors would want to know how a school and its customers were doing?

Accordingly, the AALS inspectors would certainly meet with student groups and examine student newspapers and petitions in order to gain some sense of the rifts and bridges in our landscape. If they became aware of some tiffs and tempers within our student body, the record would not have always shown the faculty's best handling of those frictions. For example, a student memo to our faculty Judicial Committee claimed violations of the faculty's newly administered *Meeting Structure and Procedure Act*. Charges were made that the student representatives were not given adequate notice of meeting times and agendas and that reports of faculty action "have not been filed with the student newspaper or posted for review by all of the students." Typical of aggressive style in those days and in mimic of Watergate investigations, the student critic urged the Judiciary Committee

> "...to investigate the circumstances; to subpoena... Dean Fagg... and all perti-
> nent notes, letters, memoranda, and tapes; and to receive an explanation... and
> assurances that the regulations... shall be honored."

The written response from Professor Bob Myers, the Chair of the faculty Judiciary Committee, called upon the student to provide the committee with details. But
it was more ridicule than request; it sought to know:

> "Does violation... render the action void? Voidable? Criminal? Just plain sneaky?

> "Who might be the designated violators against whom some sanctions might
> be imposed? ...professors? administrative personnel? the day custodian? The
> night custodian? Alex DuBoff, etc.? [The latter was Professor DuBoff's seeing-
> eye dog.]

> "Does a violation... permit the sanction of removal from office? Suspension?
> Fine? Imprisonment in the bookstore...?"

The most that might be said for that exchange was that it was at least an "exchange"—
conversing, not confronting; dialogue, not demonstration.

Day student representatives submitted another memo seeking "improved student
involvement in school decision-making and policy formation." They wanted more
"identity" and wrote of "emotional barriers that separate us." They listed: "manifes-
tations of the problem: last year's senior thesis proposal, faculty hiring procedures,
clandestine budget decisions, and faculty travel expenditures."

Mostly, however, the complaint emphasized the disproportionate size of the
student voice—nineteen professor votes to just two student representative votes.
Just three years ago students were accorded two votes when the faculty vote was
eight. [See ch. 9, "Student Representatives and Voting Power"] Now both the faculty
and the student population had each more than doubled in size, yet the student
vote was stuck at two—a fall from a twenty percent student block to less than a ten
percent block. Accordingly, the day students argued for two more student votes to
bring it to the former ratio.

Some professors calculated that four student representatives would come danger-
ously close to giving the students a veto power on the hiring of new professors,
inasmuch as an affirmative hire called for an eighty percent vote. Noting that most
schools do not allow student votes, some of our professors frowned on complaints of
not having enough of what others had none.

Dean Fagg scheduled a special Saturday morning get-together with students to discuss "problems of communication and representation... which we are all anxious to remedy." In an effort to head-off fervor and promote cooperation, the dean was careful with his words. To keep the gathering, "educational" and not confrontational, he called it a "Seminar"; feelings were called "concerns" and not demands; problems needed to be "identified" and not argued; proposals needed "considerations" and not ultimatums. And, oh yes, "coffee and doughnuts will be supplied"; but "bring along a brown bag lunch."

The "Seminar" was attended by thirty-five students, eight faculty, and five administrators. After airing everyone's say-so, the final solution was to create still another committee for still further study. The new committee's composition would give the students a super majority: nine students, two faculty, and two administrators. Furthermore the committee would be chaired by student Bill Cox. Professors DuBoff, Hughey, Knudsen, Myers and Newell declined to serve on the two faculty positions. Professors Folberg and Huffman accepted the call. Their step forward was indicative of an interest in school governance that would lead them both to become law school deans one day.

As far as the record shows, nothing more came from that committee study. Delegation to a committee is a delay maneuver—not just a tool for an answer but also a test of the question. Some questions will simply die in the cold of their own lost heat if given the time to do so.

Another matter struck us near a time when it did us no good. The student news pamphlet published an editorial that mentioned, "Some professors here can't teach and should be fired." It was not anonymous, but the author shall go unnamed here. For unexplained reasons, Professor Hughey was outraged and took it personally, even though his name did not appear. Hughey's letter of response was published in the next issue. He demanded of the student author:

> "...please be candid and name names; if I am on your... undisclosed list, I'd like to know.... I for one would like the chance to disabuse you of the notion.... Meanwhile stop using such unfair devices as injurious charges respecting unnamed individuals."

To say the least, when it came to student affairs, Professor Hughey was not our most appropriate emissary. The student's published response to Hughey stated simply: "You missed the point."

Indeed, there were points being missed. But we were learning, and the learning eventually paid off. As time would show, important lessons were taken from those early 1970's struggles between student activism and school officialism. What follows is how the lesson developed:

Northwestern College of Law in downtown Portland had provided night education to primarily mature adults with families who held daytime, non-law occupations. Their desires focused on the practicality of learning about a new career from practicing lawyers and judges. Students and teachers came from different lives to gather at evening hours and then depart. The classroom was the only rendezvous. The relationship was across the lecterns of learning. Beyond that pale, they were in their separate worlds. The link was based on trust and respect and "just show me how."

But the incredible flood of day-time young folk in the accreditation era brought a mood of concern about global instability and brought a choice of law career as the best promise for a saner world. That new generation wanted to know "why," not "how." After an adjustment phase in those accreditation years, NWLC professors would gradually begin an open door, more personable approach to student relationships—a bond that remains today as one of NWLC's distinct assets. Cooperative spirit developed out of full respect for what the school had been in order to find and to found what it needed to become. But as of the early 1970's, professors were just beginning to learn that a first step in teaching was connecting.

Professors' accessibility and willingness to communicate, together with generous budgetary allotments for student affairs, have expanded student participation in their schooling. Accordingly, our student body has become more satisfied by greater voice than vote. And when it comes to counting, the question is: Who has the better clout in solution? The voice or the vote? The persuader or the chooser? The advocate or the jury?

But back in 1973-74, students wanted more vote and the faculty was still learning. The only good fortune that befell us was that the AALS Inspection Team was on a rushed schedule that brought them to campus in September 1973, long before the foregoing trouble surfaced.

## TUITION:

Prior to the AALS Inspectors visit, our consultant Ruud gave us another piece of advice. He was aware of our in-house squabbling over discrepancy between day and evening tuitions. [See ch. 13, "Tuition"] It was an open wound in faculty-alumni-trustee relationships. Dissension, not the discrepancy, was what the inspectors would note. "Fix it," Ruud said.

The annual quarrel over how much to charge our students for schooling in the next year came earlier than usual. President Howard wanted the faculty's proposed 1974-75 operating budget for 1974-75 submitted to SCOLS no later than the end

**CONNECTING**

Student Access and Approachable Faculty

of October 1973. That up-dated deadline put budget labors side by side with our accreditation toils. It gave us just two months in which to make financial predictions for an academic year that would be ten months away—a lead time that was bound to put projections on greater guesswork than in previous faculty proposals. "Hit the target, but don't worry about bulls-eyes," was the admonition that guided hurried work. Budgets, we were told, would be honed by SCOLS and its budget subcommittee. The faculty knew too well that tuition would be a central focus in that honing.

The faculty Budget Committee, chaired by Professor Knudsen and officiated by Dean Fagg, after study in August and September of 1973, presented the law faculty with a proposal in mid-October. In an intense two-day session on October 17-18, the full faculty met and tackled the allocations, including next year's tuitions. Here follows a summary account of the manipulations and maneuvers of the passage of key issues in that day. Like a steeplechase, the 1974-75 proposed tuition scale had to snake its way through sessions of the faculty, SCOLS, and the Board of Trustees while leaping mathematical, parliamentary, and policy hurdles.

Dean Fagg and his Administrative Director, Jim Vandegrift, estimated a need for an annual $200 increase in day tuition and a $350 increase in evening tuition. It would take the day schooling price from $1,900 to $2,100 [a 10.5 percent increase] and the evening price from $1,100 to $1,450 [a 31.8 percent increase]. Thus, as some would put it, the evening tuition percentage raise was three times greater than the day tuition raise. It took no wizardry to know that the disparity was glaring and would be trouble.

The dean justified the proposed range as a step toward equalizing the pay for a three-year day education and a four-year evening education. Professor Knudsen agreed that "it was time that the day division stopped subsidizing the evening division," but he argued that this should be done gradually by a "uniform increase," meaning the same dollar amount raise. Professor Jensen concurred and moved "equivalent day and evening increases at $275 each." Uniform increase gave the appearance of parity while cloaking the percentage disparity. Under the Jensen motion, the evening tuition would be raised 25 percent and the day division raised about 15 percent.

The evening student representative opposed the motion because it was "not consistent with the Merger Agreement," which called for fees lower in the evening than in the day. [See ch. 10, "Tuition"] Equal *percentage* amounts, not equal *dollar* amounts, was more in keep with the promises.

The day student representative, on the other hand, supported the Jensen motion and observed that evening students would still be paying $800 less annually ($1,375) than day students ($2,175). Furthermore, he argued, "Evening students are working students who can afford tuition increases more than day."

That, of course, triggered a flurry of response, capped by Professor Folberg's observation that we are maintaining a fiction about day and night schooling being equal. Education between 6:00 and 10:00 p.m., three or four nights a week after faculty office hours was not the same opportunity as daylight hours between 9:00 a.m. and 5:00 p.m., five days a week during faculty hours.

Then, aside from the tuition disparity issue, someone suggested that $275 was simply too much for either day or night; it ought to be a $200 increase. Knudsen and Fagg strenuously opposed, because a $200 raise would not be enough to cover needed expenses.

Mixed discussion then ensued on both issues—size and inequality of tuition dollars. At some point when the discourse reached no sign of togetherness, a motion to table any further tuition talk was made. Parliamentary rules made that motion non-debatable. So, without discussion, the motion passed. Whereupon debate on the passed motion ensued after, not before, the vote. That allowed the tuition issue to wiggle its way off the table and back onto the floor. The resurrection happened like this: Professor Newell moved to appoint the evening student representative and me to the faculty Budget Committee for a re-examination of the tuition proposal. Budget chair Knudsen expressed no limit of disgruntlement over the lack of respect given to his committee's proposal. That then reminded us that we had to submit a faculty budget proposal in less than two weeks, which led to defeat of Newell's motion and along with it a disregard of the table.

Knudsen then moved to make a uniform day-evening raise of $270; that was his "middle-ground" between the tabled $275 and $200 proposals. A brief skirmish ensued over the motion being out of order in view of the issue having been tabled. But Roberts Rules of Order gave way to expediency. The $270 motion passed, whereas just minutes before the $275 motion had been passed over. The vote margin on $270 was squeaky: nine "ayes" to eight "nays." Grumbling from the naysayers was joined by a rumbling from Roberts, turning over in his grave.

The SCOLS budget subcommittee chaired by Justice Holman, reviewed the faculty budget proposal and rolled back the recommended tuition raise from $270 to $250 for both divisions. Holman was a 1937 graduate from downtown Northwestern College of Law. He estimated his entire evening education over four years to be only $440 including books but not including approximately forty miles of nightly travel costs. That view of tuition was coupled with thanks for the chance in 1933 to gain law schooling without ever having to attend an undergraduate college and having no more than a high school diploma. Now as one of seven justices on Oregon's highest tribunal, he was keenly sensitive to the values of low cost and evening opportunity at NWLC.

Due to lack of quorums, at two consecutive meetings of SCOLS, no official action was taken on its budget subcommittee proposal. SCOLS then hastened to take an unofficial telephone and letter poll of their membership. The count was reported at 21 in favor of and six opposed to a uniform $250 tuition hike. By my recollection and surmise, five of the six opposed were undoubtedly the remaining four Northwestern trustees who had signed the Merger Agreement plus tax lawyer David Patullo. The sixth dissenter could have been me. I cannot be certain. A dissent would have been my personal choice; but as a faculty representative to SCOLS, I would have been obliged to vote the faculty's disposition, which seemed to lean toward a uniform raise. My quandary, however, was that the leaning came from a 9 to 8 vote on a $270 raise, not $250, and was taken contrary to parliamentary order under time pressure that was now being ignored by SCOLS' quorum failures and unofficial polling. In that mess what was my duty as the emissary?

The dubious 21- 6 SCOLS vote then went to the Board of Trustees, where they wanted to know how an equal tuition hike for both divisions was in good faith with the Merger promises that demanded, "Fees charged... in the evening... shall be lower than the fees charged to [the] day..."

Dean Fagg's responsive memo made the case with numbers:

"The [proposed] ratio of Evening tuition [$1,350]... to Day tuition [$2,150] will be 63 percent for next year. In other words, on an annual basis, an Evening Division student will pay only 63 percent of that paid by a Day student for his tuition and fees."

Dean Fagg then compared that ratio to ratios existent at forty-five other law schools having evening divisions. His tabulations showed that on average those schools had evening tuition at 72 percent of day schooling.

Then, someone noted that those ratios were based on *annual* tuition rates; but what about *total* tuition payment where evening students had an extra year of tuition charges? The dean's statistical tabulation was ready. He labeled it "Degree Tuition" as opposed to "Annual Tuition:"

"An evening division degree at Northwestern... will cost only 84.3 percent of a Day Division degree, [whereas] in America... the average cost of an Evening Division degree is 98 percent of a Day Division degree."

As for the contention that evening and day education were not in reality the same, the dean argued that, nevertheless, the juris doctor degree bestowed must reflect the ideal that lawyerly readiness is the same, whether garnered in the night or the light. The Board was convinced that an across-the-board equal tuition hike for day and evening was justified.

The dust having settled on that battle, a clearer view now opened on the other aspect of that raise: How much should it be? Was $250 too much or not enough? Surprisingly, no major objections came from the students. Students, faculty, SCOLS and Board all succumbed to the fact that NWLC's tuitions and fees were currently far below charges at other law schools. The Board approved the $250 annual tuition jump.

Shaping up and whittling down evening tuition numbers had gone from $350, to $275, then down to $200, back up to $270, and now down to $250. While the numbers may seem paltry in today's world, it was in those times combative. Granting the deviousness of maneuvering in percentages, the $250 ended up the largest tuition *percentage* raise in the school's history.

Over the next decades with gradually higher percentage increases in the night tuition, the two tuitions have reached a ratio wherein annual evening tuition is 75 percent of the day tuition. Thus, evening students over a four-year period and day students over a three-year period, pay the same cumulative total.

Today, the total cost at NWLC for a legal education, whether day or night education, is approximately $96,000 and rising—an amount in keep with the law schooling market throughout the nation. The kernel has certainly grown into a field, causing some to regret the inevitable passing of an evening education cost "which can be afforded by those in need" and which is "lower than the fee charged to day law students." Whatever was lost in the Merger Agreement attempt, is now sought to be remedied by scholarships, grants, and loans instead of by a bifurcation drawn at sundown.

As Ruud had advised us, AALS inspectors, accreditors, and other law school delegates put a watchful eye on our tuition encounters with particular heed to: (1) how much credence the college gave to its law faculty's price evaluations, and (2) how much attention the whole institution was willing to give to prices set at all of the nation's law schools.

ENROLLMENT PROJECTIONS:

The total money pool to be raised by tuition involved how many as well as how much. The former was principally a question of admissions: What should be our target number of new, first year enrollees? More than money was implicated in that decision. Sound schooling—the "quid" for tuition's "quo"—was an even greater consideration in setting the number of those to be taught. On that matter AALS inspection would go beyond mere scrutiny and become involvement.

Our student body size was enlarging rapidly. At the start of the 1973-74 year, we had 687 law students (364 day and 323 evening)—a nine percent growth over the previous year. Just four years before in September 1969 [the last year without a law campus or day division or accreditation], we enrolled only 220 students. Since then we had more than tripled in size. By March 1974, Dean Fagg would report that the NWLC Admissions Office "was buried by 13,000 inquiries" and that our applications were 83 percent ahead of last year, whereas nationally most law schools were experiencing merely a five percent increase. Granting leeway for the usual embroidery of deans and the weaving of spells by percentage pictures, the past, present, and projected fabric of NWLC was looking quite fashionable.

But in September 1973, we grew wary: Was our quantity measurement pulling wool over our eyes on quality assessment? So, in projecting a budget for 1974-75, the faculty aimed for a total student body of no more than 656. That would be 31 fewer students than the current year and meant a maximum of 210 new first year admittees (120 day and 90 evening). The faculty and AALS were not the only ones interested in that entering class, so were President Howard, SCOLS, the alumni, and the Oregon Bar—albeit each had different reasons. Some components of the Bar and alumni were concerned about the flood of new attorneys and would like to have seen fewer enrollees. When Northwestern and Lewis & Clark merged in 1965, there were about 2,500 lawyers in the Oregon State Bar. Now here in the fall of 1973, there were about 3,700—a one-third increase in just eight years. "Litigious" was a word increasingly used in U.S. parlance.

On the other hand, elements of the college hierarchy wanted to see more tuition payers. AALS was attentive to the public need for increasing legal representation, while at the same being concerned with the caliber of educational service.

From the faculty's target number of 210 first-year enrollees, the SCOLS budget subcommittee upped the total to 225 (120 day and 105 evening). President Howard suggested an even higher number. Figures of 240 new admittees were mentioned (160 day and 80 evening). These higher reaches were prompted by the notion that we ought to "take advantage of" the market's mounting interest in our law school. I noted that, in a non-profit charity, "advantage" was something to be *given*, not "taken."

The thought of 30 more first-year students than the faculty had initiated, did not set well. A memo from Professors Jensen and Newell voiced strong opposition:

> "[Enrollment] is a faculty decision and not one for the Standing Committee
> [SCOLS] or any of its subcommittees. While they may have the right to tell us of
> a need to increase revenues or cut expenses, we feel that the size of enrollment
> should be within our control.... We believe the faculty decisions re: enrollment

were not made lightly and should not be discarded without even permitting us to consider the issue."

An unexpected reaction to the memo came from Professor Knudsen. He was indignant. As chair of the faculty Budget Committee, he was responsible for overseeing and apprising the faculty of the progress of the faculty's budget proposal in SCOLS. He took umbrage with an implication in the Newell-Jensen memo that the faculty had not been "permitted to consider the issue," Jensen and Newell wrote that they had to learn about the SCOLS tamperings "through the grapevine." The latter triggered a Knudsen reaction. He pointed out that his colleagues did not need a "grapevine" to get the message. All professors had been sent his memo forty days prior to the Newell-Jensen memo telling the faculty about the SCOLS doings and urging professors to:

> Let me know in writing [within two weeks]... why you feel we should limit the entering day and evening classes to [210]... in the coming school year."

Accordingly, said Knudsen, the Newell-Jensen memo came too late to be of much good. Newell may not have cherished Knudsen's indignity, but he would have empathized with Knudsen's forceful way of putting it. Both of these colleagues shared a disposition for vigor and passion in driving home a point.

Once the detour of alleged dereliction had straightened out, the faculty turned to the substance of the tardy Newell-Jensen complaint. A slumbering faculty had not set its alarm but now was fully awake. Belated or not, Newell did not slow down. At an April 3, 1974 faculty meeting, he moved that, henceforth, SCOLS recommendations (particularly on admissions numbers) should be subject to faculty approval and not vice-versa. The motion passed with no dissent.

Dean Fagg then sought to clarify the effect of the motion. He suggested this chain of deliberations: First, the faculty would initiate budget enrollment numbers. Then the SCOLS subcommittee "would join in." Then the "whole matter would go before the faculty, then to President Howard *before final presentation to the entire Standing Committee [SCOLS]*; and then the trustees."

There was a hitch in the dean's sequencing. The problem was with the second SCOLS step on the assent. Process was now the bigger issue and dwarfed the issue of enrollment size. The faculty was getting tired of SCOLS and its subcommittee interventions. It would seem, from lack of quorums and phone voting, that SCOLS was also getting tired of its role.

That's when AALS became involved. The straightening of protocols and provinces, took the diplomacy of Millard Ruud, now AALS Executive Director. He pointed out that AALS required the faculty to be in complete charge of admissions policy. The size of individual tuition dollars was a business aspect and, therefore, a matter eventually for trustee governance. But the numbers and caliber of tuition payers more directly affected curriculum, classroom numbers, student-faculty ratio and relationship, and other educational service, and was therefore a matter for academicians. Many of the law schools who were accredited by the ABA but not AALS, were schools that did not wish to relinquish academic policy to law professors. Ruud's admonitions, tactfully put, were the beginnings of the law faculty's tighter grip on education policy.

Eventually, the faculty's originally desired 656 enrollment, including 210 new admittees, was finalized in the projected 1974-75 budget. But our actual enrollment in September 1974 would end up with fifteen more first year enrollees than we had planned (121 day and 104 evening).

Rising above all that finagling over projected numbers, was the revelation of how vitally interested AALS was (compared to the ABA) in the balance of authority in the administration of legal education and especially in the position of the law faculty in that balancing. Quantums predicted, projected, and produced were secondary. Primarily was: Where were the paths and where were they headed, and, foremost, who was walking them?

## ENVIRONMENTAL IMAGE:

As Ruud predicted, AALS inspectors would be curious to know about our environmental curriculum and its cornerstone periodical: *Environmental Law*. How was that program being received by scholars? By lawmakers? By the press? By students and would-be students? And especially by our college hierarchy?

Two of the AALS Inspection Team, Professors Degnan and Vetter, were on the faculty of the University of California (Berkeley) Law School. That school had recently begun an environmental emphasis of its own. They were well aware of the impact that the environmental surge was having on private business, public policies, and the nation's campuses. Each year a mounting crunch of controversy surround that movement. NWLC felt the pressure in an early incident. Assistant Professor Jim Huffman, in his maiden year on the law faculty, was brash enough to turn his reserved car spot in the law school parking lot into a garden. He hauled in dirt atop the asphalt, boxed it off, and planted seeds and seedlings. Converting that islet back to its vegetative nature, was his playful statement against the concreting of America to accommodate the stationing of internal combustion machines.

The demonstration, however, got much wider play than expected. It made national news. A local television reporter saw it as a good visual that pitted agriculture against car culture. The local broadcast armed with pictures, pleased the national news service and its television viewers.

But back on the NWLC campus, Huffman meant nothing so strenuous by it. It came at a time when he sought Dean Fagg's signature on a grant petition proposal to the Hill Foundation. The dean wanted the garden removed from the parking lot because "important folks" were unhappy with the publicity. The dean turned Jim's "request" into an exchange. He would sign the petition if Jim would rid the parking lot of its botany.

The deal was struck. It was not a difficult decision. After all, the garden was not doing so well in the shade of its forest benefactors. Of greater weight, Jim was not an "environmentalist" in the growing connotation of that word. Rather, he was given to the libertarian notion of free market and commercial resolution of problems, not the government regulation that the environmental movement was spawning. In spite of the intellectual sparring of laissez-faire versus regulation, I have always felt that the real Jim Huffman was the playful rascal who ventured gardens in parking lots.

Be that as it may, in September 1973, we were alert to the murmurs of environmental discontent. In November, the rumblings found voice in the SCOLS budget subcommittee chaired by Justice Ralph Holman. As an alumnus of old Northwestern College of Law in downtown Portland and as a trustee of Lewis & Clark College, Holman urged that it was time for our law review to come away from its topical specialty and to change the *Environmental Law* name. The periodical needed a "format with a broader base," he said. *Environmental Law* was a title and perspective "too narrow for a first-class law review."

A few weeks later, the SCOLS budget subcommittee sought the law faculty's reactions to that revamping. The faculty simply ignored the solicitation, just as it had done in Spring 1973. Then in May 1974 the Holman idea was formally embraced by the entire SCOLS membership, particularly by SCOLS chairman Bill Swindells and by trustee Paul Boley, two of the law school's biggest supporters. That triumvirate of friends of the law school had been powerful in the accreditation pursuit. Their clout was not to be taken lightly.

SCOLS formally asked the faculty (for a third time) to take up the matter of name change and direction of our law school periodical. This time the "request" was put in the form of specific action. SCOLS wanted the faculty to "empanel a committee to study whether or not it would be desirable" to make the change. It was put gently, yet with relentless purpose. SCOLS gave two reasons: The current name "tends to limit its subject matter and also identifies it in some minds with controversial issues." Backing up its "request," SCOLS designated five of its high-powered members to serve on that joint committee: Swindells, Boley, General Chester McCarty, law school alumni president Judge Phil Roth, and Oregon's U.S. Attorney Sid Lezak.

While Dean Fagg favored the study, he was the head of the faculty and knew the faculty's head. He could not let his leaning interfere with his leading. But he was involved in the Rocky Mountain Legal Foundation and would one day become an executive in that Denver organization—a composition of property owners given to resource development and thus generally at odds with environmental regulation. And so, in that delicate role, the dean took a step forward without crossing the line. He sent a memo to the faculty reporting the formation of a SCOLS-faculty joint committee to explore the advisability of changing our periodical's course. The memo reported that Professor Williamson had agreed to serve on that committee and that student editors of the law review would also be asked. He also wrote that he intended to ask me, as faculty representative of SCOLS, to join. His memo ended by asking for faculty reactions.

Within two hours, he got Billy's written "reaction." It was hasty and not happy. Billy began by dispelling the notion that his agreement to be on the committee meant that he approved of its formation. "Quite the opposite is the case," he wrote. Then he went on to call the committee:

> "...another unnecessary attempt to create animosity and division between the faculty and students on the one hand, and the trustees on the other.... [O]ur time can be better spent...than in constant self-defeating bitching and criticism on what earlier has been agreed upon.... [The committee] would make a decision that is only appropriate for the Board of Editors and the faculty to make... and would create further unnecessary hostility between a school and student body that is setting standards of excellence...."

Billy also objected to my serving on the committee. While he had nothing but

> "... the greatest respect for Ron, I have never explored his views about the law journal in any depth.... For all I know,... the Dean and Ron are opposed to the law review's present orientation.... The opposite may also be true."

Billy's ambivalence about my views may have been taken from the previously reported, long ago conference that he and I had with Millard Ruud and Dean Wren back in the summer of 1969 in my living room office on Huddleston Lane. [See ch. 6, "Law Periodical Project"] It was there that we first decided to found an environmental law review. I had initially proposed a general law review but eventually conceded the wisdom of a topical specialty. Since that time (almost five years before), much had changed, not the least of which was the magnitude of the environmental field itself and also the magnificence that *Environmental Law* was having on our image. I assured Billy that while my hopes for a general law review publication were still alive, they were on hold until the day when the two publications could stand together. *Environmental Law*'s success had solidified its seat. I further assured him that "any change in NWLC's environmental headway would have to be over our two dead bodies."

Billy then said he had nothing against my membership on the committee. He explained that he simply objected to my appointment by the administration instead of by the faculty. "The person who represents the faculty should be chosen by the faculty," he wrote. Other faculty members agreed with Billy's point, albeit not necessarily with his bluntness.

It would not be pleasant for us to reject a request from friendly supporters like the Swindells-Boley-Holman trio, but that was what we did. Not only did the faculty oppose any change, it did not want to talk about it. The faculty refused to empanel any committee. The overwhelming vote was sixteen in favor of no need to study the issue, two opposed (Knudsen and a student representative) and one abstained (Folberg). Dean Fagg as presider cast no vote. Had he been called upon to vote, he would certainly have chosen to explore the matter further rather than take the tactless course of abrupt rejection.

The faculty's brusque behavior did not end there. A following motion put the faculty position in no uncertain terms: Moved that SCOLS "shall not *consider or recommend* on this matter because it infringes on academic freedom." I moved to change the words "consider or recommend" to the word "decide." We were being bold enough to cast refusal and admonition at a trustee committee, but we did not want to turn boldness into brashness by dictating that they could not so much as ponder or suggest. The motion as amended also passed by the same 16 to 2 count.

Our strong message was another step in the staking of turf and a waning of the need for a trustee committee to oversee academic operations. As of 1973-74, the eighty-year history of the downtown Portland evening law school and now its eight-year history with Lewis and Clark College, had been controlled by proprietorship in the form of Gantenbein owners and college trustees and officers. Now, however, a permanent career faculty had matured enough to start taking charge of schooling. It was what AALS accreditors wanted to see.

All of that environmental development, however, was not there for the AALS Inspection Team in September 1973. But it waited in the shadows. What was clear to some SCOLS members, probed by AALS inspectors, and eschewed by the faculty was: Had our environmental image become one-sided. Now that the environment had become a battleground, how could we deflect the false image that our schooling was partisan instead of scholarly detached? Had we gone back to nature like the earlier conservationist movement? Had we gone too green?

Professor Huffman, in his maiden year on the faculty, proposed a solution. Taking time away from the building of gardens in parking spaces, he pressed for the creation of a Natural Resources Law Institute [NRLI], whose emphasis would be on resource appropriation, which he said was the focus on the *over* and *under* utilization of the environment. Huffman pitched it in a written grant proposal:

> "Natural Resource law is both part of and a prerequisite to a complete environmental program. Environmental law, as it has developed in recent years, is primarily that area of law devoted to *correcting the abuse* of our natural and human environment. Natural Resource law... comprehends the social *rules under which we develop and utilize* water, oil and gas, minerals, public lands, and our other natural resources."

In short, while granting that the two programs were joined at the hip, Huffman distinguished the two by use and abuse. Natural Resource law would approach concerns from the perspective of how to employ resources, whereas environmental law had come to mean an approach from the perspective of how to preserve resources.

One might have ridiculed the distinction by likening it to the puzzle: at which rope end shall the noose be tied? But beneath the scoffing laid serious policy issues about opportunity, commerce, and agenda played out between those who seek to take nature's bounties and those who seek to caretake them.

The NRLI proposal gained attention from both education and business. Both were in search of weight to counter the energy that was growing against mankind's appropriation or pollution of water, air, ores, trees, oil, wildlife, wilderness, and other earth rewards. Like dual advocacy at trials (a method with which lawyers were quite familiar) the tug of opposing forces was the better way to arrive at the truth that lay somewhere between unbridled misuse and an unproductive non-use. The faculty gave Huffman's proposal a go-ahead. Initially, the school specialty would be labeled the "Natural Resources and Environmental Law Program." But that title was destined to flip. It became the "Environmental and Natural Resources Program" Titles sometimes deliver their own message.

And so, on our way to AALS, we were trying to keep our wheels on the rails: balances between faculty and hierarchy and likewise between developers and preservers of environment. Tucked away in that equipose, there was still another need for

WILLIAMSON—FAGG ASUNDER

equilibrium. Two opposing players were moving too fast in opposite directions to be of ballast for one another. A split in personnel begged mending. Just four years ago, I had been the sole emissary of the law school on hand to greet, interview, and sell both Billy Williamson and Fred Fagg III on the bib and tucker of NWLC. [See ch. 6, "Two Walk-ons"] Both donned NWLC raiment and became key and devoted hires. As the once garment salesman and now the tailor, I felt the need to hem a rip widening between the two.

## FACULTY HIRING AND LEGAL WRITING:

Training college graduates in the skills of legal writing, research, and analysis was an assignment wrought with intense labor. The *writing* portion of that training was the main headache. It was a hands-on job that called for one-on-one evaluation and consultation. Beginning in the primary school grades, writing is one of the fundamentals of the educational trinity: "reading, *writing*, and arithmetic." The emphasis continues on up through higher education. Every professional, scientific, technological, vocational, or office discipline has its own peculiarities; and cardinal among these ways are grammar, diction, phrasing, and jargon. It is especially so in legal education where words and wording are a lawyer's tools. After all of their varied pre-law study, law students had to re-learn how to do what they already thought they knew. Like walking, talking, and breathing, writing skills had been ingrained. Consequently, re-adaptation was met by frustration for both learners at one end and teachers at the other.

In the fall semester of 1973-74, in the midst of the AALS accreditation quest, our legal writing program was crippled. Professor DuBoff served notice that he was no longer interested in leading that program. He said that, when Dean Wren hired him as the head writing instructor, he had not committed himself to that position. The arrangement had never been reduced to formal contract, and Wren was no longer with us. DuBoff had been the writing teacher for just one year. The abandonment was not at an opportune time. A law school without a well-organized writing plan would not set well with AALS accreditors.

Our newest faculty member, Professor Huffman, had also been hired as a legal writing assistant. But now that he was on line to develop a natural resources institute, he too opted out of the writing assignment. Professor John Barrett and Librarian Walt Brown, who had shared in legal writing chores, also declined to head the program. In prior years, the entire faculty was involved in legal writing chores, but professors wanted no more of that extra load. No professor would deny the import of writing skills in the schooling of lawyers. But just as surely as that import was not doubted, so too it was ducked.

AALS inspectors were aware of and sympathetic with that problem. All law schools from time to time were challenged by "the writing course dilemma": essentiality on one hand yet avoidance on the other. AALS needed to know how and when we would do something about a new legal writing and research director. We needed someone with both commitment and ability. Those two aims were not necessarily linked. Did we want continuity or talent in that position? Some emphasized dedication to the task, others effectiveness in the task. Once everyone had their say, the poles, like so many issues, melded. It was not an "either-or" proposition. We needed both, and the balance between the two was left up to Professor Ed Belsheim's faculty Appointments Committee.

Belsheim was not confident. As former dean at Nebraska's law school, he said he had "struggled with legal writing for twenty years." Finding the right combination of talent and commitment would be difficult. The committee lined up fourteen potential candidates to be interviewed at the December 1973 AALS Convention in New Orleans. Nine of them were women. Since Jacqui Jurkins left the faculty, we had no female teachers, neither full-time nor part-time. Our growing feminine student body signaled a growing demand for role models. That made a third criterion for our new hire: we sought a capable, committed woman. "Affirmative action" would not be a problem here. We were a private school hiring an employee; we were not a public school choosing customers.

Results of the New Orleans interviews culled the interviewees down to just one possibility: an instructor at UCLA, who shall go by the name "Ms. Grammar." At a January 16, 1974, faculty meeting, our interviewing professors spoke for and against her. Professor Newell said he had "mixed reactions" and was "concerned about her as a colleague," as evidenced in a "friction" that developed during her interview. He wanted to bring her to the campus for further interviews.

Professor Huffman expressed similar reservations. Professor Bob Myers joined with Huffman and Newell. Professor Knudsen said "she was somewhat neurotic, and

I found her writing to be somewhat pedestrian." Dean Fagg reported that we "could do better" and that "he could not recommend her." One of her UCLA professors wrote that she was "more of an advocate than a scholar"; that she had proposed a strange seminar for UCLA, which she labeled, "Women and the Law"; that she had written about "how awful it is to be a woman."

With so much opposition, I was confused: How come Ms. Grammar was chosen as the one possibility out of nine? The reason: Just as she annoyed some, so too she was enjoyed by others. Professor Hughey was "favorably impressed" and called her a "dynamo" with whom he had "no personal conflict." Professor DuBoff said "she was the best we interviewed." He wondered, however, if she would stick with the program; but that may have been more the product of his own personal abandonment than with candidate assessment. Professor Vail was "tremendously impressed" and thought she was a "remarkable woman." Two letters from other UCLA professors were read, one was "favorable" and the other was "ecstatic' about her.

Our two student representatives on the faculty mirrored the faculty split; the day student was "yea;" the evening student was "nay." All of it was a stereotypical slice of what blocked or budged attitudes of that day. In 1973, the new aggressiveness of women was still a work in progress—a work that shocked tradition.

Grammar's competition for the job was Diane Spies, a local attorney who had surfaced among Portland prospects. Accordingly, it was decided that both should be brought to the campus for comparison. Then, just one week later, the faculty decided to call four additional candidates to the law school for interviews. Thus, we had started with fourteen prospects, narrowed it down to nine, then one, then two, and now back up to six.

Thereafter, the record is blank and my memory is clouded. What is clear, however, is that the time sequence of events that followed was this: Ms. Grammar was the student body's overwhelming choice; but it was Spies who was hired without record of any eighty percent faculty vote. Thence, came a flurry of student complaints about process and a faculty motion to reconsider, which was rejected.

Spies would not begin on the faculty roster until well after our December 1973 pitch to AALS had come and gone. She was NWLC's twenty-ninth full-time, tenure-tracked professor. Almost one-third of that roster had departed. Now there would be twenty at the start of the 1974-75 year. By the end of that year, it would drop back to nineteen. Spies lasted just one year—destined to fall short of task and commitment. She had been only the second woman professor at NWLC. Both of them were no longer here.

In future years, the writing program came under a chain of other czars that included David Patterson. He had the bizarre honor of being the only academician I ever knew to receive benefits under Oregon's Workers Compensation Law. He was injured when he crashed into a cyclone fence chasing a foul ball while playing in a faculty-student softball game. He was successful in proving that such contest was "work-related." Apparently chasing what was "foul" had legal implications.

After Patterson came Jack Landau, a recent graduate of NWLC—our first alumnus legacy to become a full-time faculty member. He took the lead and finally put the legal writing program on a path of success. But then his career in education detoured. He went on to become a respected member of Oregon's judiciary—a Court of Appeals judge and Supreme Court justice. He was replaced with our first, firmly seated, legal writing leader Judith Miller. She accelerated the progress made in research and writing instruction. Eventually, the Legal Analysis and Writing program came under the leadership of Professor Steve Johansen who, with commitment, skill, and a cadre of assistant instructors from topnotch law alumni, made what is now among the top law writing programs in the nation. It was, indeed, a far cry from what we offered the AALS Inspection Team in September of 1973. We had no other course but to present a program that tried to stand upon a wobbly chain of limp links and lame ducks.

This then was the face on which we readied ourselves for presentation to AALS in the fall semester of 1973. In the mirror we saw what we were and also what we wanted others to see of us. There, in the reflection were our books, our students, our faculty, our leadership, our costs, our income, our reputation, our commitment. In the looking glass, we primped, donned adornments, powdered our blemishes, rechecked our buttons, and stood ready for inspection. Prepared but tired, we drew a deep breath in hope that this would be the last of it.

# 16
# THE LAST LAP
*Fall 1973*

## DUM FERVET OPUS

In the evening of September 16, 1973, Professors Bauman, Schwartz, and Vetter—the Inspection Team—flew in from California. From the beginning of their stay, urgency propelled them. The time schedule given them was tight. Their report had to be delivered to Chairman Degnan and the AALS Accreditation Committee in 40 days. Aside from our written answers to the Inspection Questionnaire, they knew little about us. They had three nights and days to learn everything.

Some of us met with them on the evening of their arrival at the airport. I recall one of them likening their visit to Clement Moore's Saint Nicholas: they would speak "not a word" and go "straight to work." They were there to listen, to watch, and to read and then would have plenty to say in their written report.

They were not pleased to be in such hurry. Later their report would say, "This is a somewhat unusual if not downright awkward procedure... necessitated by the severe time restrictions imposed upon us." In order to arrive at the final AALS vote at the end of December, just one hundred days away, the process had to pass through two other votes, one at the Accreditation Committee and the other at the Executive Council. Likely it was the new AALS Executive Director, Millard Ruud, who had managed to set up that schedule—a time line met by disgruntlement at each leg of its fast track.

As I recall, the reason for the rush was the notion that we ought to capitalize on our recent victory with the ABA. Ruud felt we were geared up, ready to go, and headed with momentum in that direction. The notion was fueled by an old Latin expression about when to strike: *dum fervet opus*—"while the work glows."

Still, a slap-dash, full-tilt, headlong action worried me. A hurried look by disgusted people might miss the merit beneath a facade hurriedly erected.

GROWTH:

While the inspectors were impressed by our rapid and enormous growth, it was that very growth in which they found most of what troubled them.

Among the first things they noted was our packed house. They witnessed one of our regularly scheduled faculty meetings which at that time was held in our campus Jury Room—a room just large enough for a table to seat twelve. We had twenty-four in attendance. We did not use one of our four classrooms because they were being used for schooling. We could not use the faculty lounge because it shared the same paraboloid ceiling with library studiers. We could not use seminar rooms because we had none.

Inspection went right to the heart of our fiscal problems. "Substantially, all of the income of the School of Law is generated by fees and tuition," they observed, and that rendered us "vulnerable to precipitous drops in enrollments." We rode the crest of a high tide of law applicants, but could we survive the ebbs?

The inspectors were right to caution us about our woeful lack of endowment—not so much because we needed it for a rainy day, but rather because we needed "nest eggs." The term comes to us from the fact that early chicken farmers, when collecting eggs, would leave one egg in the nest. That egg was what encouraged the hen to continue laying. The chicken farmer knew what the hen knew: Without an egg, a nest is not a nest and would be abandoned. Would donors prefer to give money directly to the needy or to the well-endowed charity that donates its largess? Endowment was not for rainy days; it was mainly for egg laying.

The inspectors saw another trouble with our growth—a problem of placement. It was not enough for a nation of law schools to educate aspirants for careers in law; law educators had a duty to assist graduates in locating career jobs. While Professor Belsheim, the ex-law dean, had preached the same lesson, the inspectors were aware that we had dodged that responsibility on at least one occasion. The team heard of our refusal back in 1970 to join an AALS scheme for Pacific northwest law schools to share placement information and to jointly participate in job prospecting. We had politely excused ourselves from that cooperation because we were in one of the Pacific northwest's few populous centers where opportunity was more generous. In short, it was not so much that we were in need, as it was that we did not want to give need. Our hoarding did not earn us heart. Compatriots in legal education and the association that united them, including the association's inspectors, were critical.

Growth was another source of trouble in the library. Books, like bodies and buildings had been a rapid escalation that brought pitfalls along with blessings. Notwithstanding significant progress and glowing reports, Inspector Schwartz, an experienced law school librarian, detected some shortcomings missed by other scrutinizers. He suggested that the library was understaffed and recommended five more clerks and some student help. As for facilities, he listed at least ten other deficiencies, not the least of which was the lack of air conditioning. The latter was for the sake of books, as well as their readers. For bibliophiles, however, it was a loving thought: Books and bodies share prickly heat in common.

But rapid growth might also have a saving grace—at least I hoped so. Extreme progress may have wiped clear all AALS bad memory of us. But, alas it did not. Just as Millard Ruud had warned me one year prior, the AALS Inspection Team expressed concern about the Howard-Stevens rift that happened years ago. Five annual AALS conferences had passed between then and now, yet still it lingered. I gave the team my assessment just as I had with Ruud. [See ch. 12, "ABA Accreditation"] Our swift river had not totally cleared itself; at bottom it still kicked up muddy waters.

## THE INSPECTION REPORT:

In spite of the foregoing scrutinies, the Inspection Team's written report was generally heartening for two reasons. Not only was its substance encouraging, so too was its process. Before submitting their report to higher-ups, they first gave us their draft for our suggestions. It was extraordinary and also a good sign. Including us in their drafting meant they liked us. And if they liked us, they would not likely hurt us. The signs proved true: While targeting our crowded condition, it also gave us credit for a future promise: our capital campaign to raise money for a fourth building in our Tryon Forest site—a ground breaking destined for the start of 1976.

As for our placement troubles, we satisfied inspection by our change in direction. NWLC had already joined inter-school discussions of mutual job-finding problems for the flood of law graduates in the marketplace. Our Director of Programs Ann Kendrick had just been elected President of the National Association of Law Placement Officers. As for in-house career service endeavors, Professor Belsheim continued to urge the fair notion that diligence in finding our students jobs after their schooling had to equal the diligence in recruiting them in the first place. Getting them in meant helping them out. In Belsheim there lived the Gantenbein spirit that had graced the Northwestern halls for over sixty years prior to merger.

Our ambitious scheduling of future conferences and events [See ch. 14, "Conferences and Events"] also impressed the inspectors. Such programming showed a willingness of NWLC to join the national family of legal education not just by seeking from it but also by giving to it.

As for the danger of no fiscal reserves for future enrollment drops, the inspectors were satisfied with the pledge of President Howard and key trustees that, should rainy days arise, they were prepared to meet and overcome them. They also assured that future endowment funding would be raised to alleviate some of the law schools' dependence on tuition. Citing the 1965 Merger Agreement and its Amendment, the inspectors applauded the fact that:

"The Law School shall be self-sustaining, but Lewis & Clark College accepts responsibility for financially assisting the Law School in its efforts to comply with the standards for accreditation. The effect of these agreements is to deny to the College any claim to funds generated by the School of Law while permitting the School of Law to look to the College for financial assistance when needed."

While Inspector Schwartz had listed a number of needs in our library, the Inspection Team's report was quick to add that the listing "was not intended as criticism" but rather as "evaluation that will be of use in planning for the future." It was future potential, not current weakness, that moved the inspectors to write:

"[T]his library can well develop into a major research center in the Pacific Northwest, second only to the University of Washington with a potential to be first."

Decades ahead, our future librarian, Peter Nycum, would lead the NWLC library to just those heights.

## THE AALS FORWARD LOOK:

The inspectors' look toward the future was a theme that ran throughout their report. It marked a subtle difference between the ABA and AALS approaches to the bestowal of accreditation. [See ch. 15, "AALS Guidelines"] The ABA had withheld permanent approval until fulfillment of standards. Thresholds had to be crossed, not just promised. AALS, on the other hand, saw us as a moving picture, not a snapshot. AALS was concerned with our direction, not our status. We were not just what we were; we were what we could be. The *AALS Guideline Statement* put it this way:

"[N]orms should be achieved within a reasonable period following initial accreditation.... [Inspection must reveal] satisfactory assurance that the law school within a reasonable time [will] conform to the higher standards set forth in this statement."

So, where the ABA looked for present impasses, AALS looked for future passageways. The difference may not seem like much, but the one gave deserts instead of daunting, instilled cooperation instead of opposition. Folks pull for those who trust them and are pushed by those who task them. Both incentives can succeed, but the former boosts up, while the latter lets down. Entrusting a school with approval allowed the school to use that award as a report to donors, recruits, and the public in gaining their esteem, and perhaps most importantly in gaining self-esteem. Dealing with the lawyer association (the ABA), especially under the Hervey regime, we had received its cold shoulder many times before gaining its wholeheart. The first AALS Inspection Report recommended our immediate, unconditional membership.

The October 11, 1973, draft of that report was thirty pages long plus exhibits. As aforementioned, the NWLC professors were asked for suggested edits of the report. We dared not change a single word, for fear that it might incline the inspectors to inspect their own inspection, which ended with a favorable recommendation in glowing terms.

We were now in the spotlight and that brought the lessons of both awe and caution. The awe was: Light is *brighter* to those in it than to those who shine it from darkness. The caution was: *Bright* is just as blinding as darkness.

## CLIMBING AALS STEPS:

We had reached just the first landing. The AALS process had four landings—four successful votes, one each from the Inspection Team, the Accreditation Committee, the Executive Council, and the House Delegates. The next three landings were far from our turf: Washington, D.C.; Montreal, Canada; and finally New Orleans—a succession, now on a time limit of only eighty remaining days.

The Accreditation Committee, chaired by Professor Ronan Degnan, met on October 27, 1973, in D.C. The committee members did not receive the Inspection Team report until "a few days before the meeting." The late arriving report also included Millard Ruud's written observations. Committee members were aware of the crash basis under which the Team had acted and were bothered by the urgency in which they themselves were being asked to act.

Prompt dispatch made their conference with us telephonic—a hook-up from D.C. with President Howard and Dean Fagg "who had held themselves available [in Portland] for that purpose." I remember that Professor Knudsen, Belsheim, and I were there in the President's office as listeners. Perhaps there were others. The technology of the "conference call" was something new to business in 1973.

After the phone conference, we were furnished a copy of minutes of what further transpired in their closed meeting. The minutes show that some committee members were particularly troubled by three items, one of which was our "faculty-student ratio projections." The other two were somewhat new to us. The committee wondered about the fact that our full-time professors were teaching only 67 percent of evening division course hours. Their third concern was a needed change from the "older form of *teaching* institution to teaching *and research*" institution—just another way of saying that professors needed *to profess*. These were the first inklings from accreditors of the need for more academic publishing. Indeed, in the eight-year existence of a NWLC full-time faculty, I can remember only two law publications emanating from our faculty. We had been simply too busy. Throughout the accrediting quest, no sooner had we resolved an issue, than a new one would pop up to challenge us—just as it did now.

They also wondered about our lack of law teaching experience. Of the nineteen NWLC professors only six of us had more than three years of law teaching. Seven had but one or no years of prior professorship. Almost half were assistant professors—the lowest rank on the promotion scale.

The AALS accreditation minutes also alluded to that suspicious incident in NWLC history: the 1967 Howard-Stevens collapse. The committee minutes acknowledged that the matter now seemed rectified: "At present, a strong and determined dean is supported with enthusiasm... by a president who was once not very supportive...." The committee, however, was still leery:

> But deanship tenures are not as long as they used to be, and a change in critical personnel might signal change in direction.

Indeed, the best evidence of the potential for change is the history of change. Change changes.

Having made its observations, the Accreditation Committee voted unanimously to recommend that NWLC be granted membership. Professor Myron Jacobstein, Stanford Law School's Librarian, abstained from the vote because of "inadequate time to make a judgment satisfactory to him." In his view, the whole process had been too rushed. We were fast learning that librarians were the toughest scrutinizers.

Our application for membership was then passed upward to the AALS Executive Council who met just six days later (November 2 and 3) in Montreal, Canada. Chairman Degnan was there to present the recommendations of the Inspection Team and his committee. The Executive Council was composed of AALS President Maurice Rosenberg of Columbia University School of Law and all AALS officers, including Executive Director Millard Ruud. This time the conference would not be wired. President Howard and Dean Fagg were advised to appear in person before the Council in Canada.

The hearing was extensive. Informed by two recommendations, Ruud's encouragements and president-dean assurances, the Executive Council unanimously added a third recommendation of approval. The Council embellished its approval with this observation: NWLC has had phenomenal growths that "meet or exceed all of the current standards—a high order of overall quality." Furthermore, in keeping with the AALS penchant for forward-look, the executives recognized that we were "capable of sustaining that high level of performance and improving on it in the future."

While the AALS House of Delegates vote was to be the official dubbing, the Executive Council's vote was taken by us as the guaranty. Accordingly, we made attainment of what should have been anticipation. At our November 28 faculty meeting, it was moved to "give appropriate accolades to those responsible for AALS accreditation." Applause. Special appreciation was extended to President Howard. Applause. Then, at our next faculty meeting on December 19, Dean Fagg announced formal plans were underway for a banquet celebration on January 26 at the Benson Hotel in downtown Portland. It was also suggested that we charter a plane to take all professors and spouses to the AALS Convention to cheer the House of Delegates bestowal.

All of the hurrah was premature. But we had picked up strong headwinds, were in sight of port, and were anxious to go ashore—all in spite of some wading still ahead.

Fortunately, disappointment did not come. On December 28, 1973, the House of Delegates unanimously approved our membership. Of almost 200 law schools in the nation, less than two-thirds of them were doubly annointed. NWLC, the 152nd ABA accredited school now became the 128th AALS accredited school.

## THE CONVENTION FIASCO:

As token to the "up's" and "downs" of our eight year quest, however, our success was capped by one last vainglorious trip-and-fall—a bad decision on our part. Even though we had been convinced that the House vote was simply a matter of routine, we were still anxious to present a full faculty front in attendance at the delegate meeting in New Orleans in order to assure what was no more than rubber stamping. But Dean Fagg wrote that "strong faculty attendance... would enhance our chances for early accreditation." We should all be there. It was more rationalization than reason. We had already applauded ourselves and fixed a banquet and celebration weeks in advance of the official dubbing. No one seriously considered the chance of failure. The New Orleans and Bourbon Street trip was more dancing than "enhancing."

We did one thing right, however; we dismissed the idea of chartering a plane. When Professor Knudsen observed that we could not afford to lose an entire faculty in a single airplane crash, Professor Bross's faculty meeting minutes noted that student representative Haley "refrained discretely from making comment."

Of course, there was nothing remiss about professors going to an educational convention and sharing with their national peers. Our mistake was in authorizing an expense paid trip for professors' spouses as well. If there were qualms about such expense, they were muffled by the harbingers that herald final victory.

At least ten wives made the trip. My wife Jewel did not go, mainly because, as a prospective elected Multnomah County Auditor, as the treasurer of the Betty Roberts for Governor campaign, and as a CPA, she balked at the fiscal connection between law education and her presence in New Orleans. A few other colleagues and wives likewise made that decision. The convention lasted five days and four nights (December 26-30). Board and room expenses for wives were $3,647.41, paid out of the dean's $6,000 contingency budget. The expense by today's inflationary calculations would exceed $15,000.

When students informed themselves, they saw it this way: The wives' expense was paid from the tuitions of almost two day students or slightly more than three evening students. Student representative John Geil's January 22, 1974, memo to the faculty exposed the matter.

> "Many students have approached me with questions concerning the recent expenditures for the trip to the AALS Convention in New Orleans. I would like to obtain an accounting... along with explanations and assurances that such large amount will not be expended... in the future."

The issue continued to fester. Student representatives complained to the SCOLS Budget Subcommittee at its February 12 meeting. At that meeting Professor Knudsen explained that the expense was important "as a material assistance in overcoming past reputation impediments to achieving accreditation"—presumably, a reference to the Howard-Stevens episode that surfaced at the 1967 AALS convention. That incident, so long ago interred, would simply not stay buried. Usually, it resurrected as fault to be excused; now it rose as excuse for a fault.

In a memo to SCOLS, I made a sentimental plea for moderation and offered the lyrics of an old song to help explain (not necessarily to defend) the need for spousal sharing in triumph long sought:

> "If no one shares,
> If no one cares,
> Where's the good of a job well done.
> Or a prize you've won?"

The SCOLS subcommittee's attempt at resolution bounced back and forth across ambivalence. The expense was "within lawful authority" but was "judgmentally questionable"; was "made in good faith" but, was "not intended as precedent"; was made "in the conviction that such would materially aid the accreditation" but was now in need of "procedure in order to insure... cooperation and communication." Of necessity, it was the kind of solution that fled, rather than fixed. At its February 26 meeting, SCOLS construed its budget subcommittee's recommendation to mean that wives attendance at AALS was a "good public relations effort."

Somewhere between the meetings of SCOLS and its subcommittee, Dean Fagg had made a written statement titled "Dean's Comments on New Orleans." It was principally addressed to the student body in an attempt to assuage and to detour any further publication of the matter. The opening sentence described the depth of the issue:

> When an action of the law school meets with as much student and community outcry as met the decision on... wives expenses..., no one can seriously contend that it was a good decision."

And he was contrite:

> "Frankly, both the Dean and the faculty made a mistake in this one..., and pledge ourselves to work even harder to achieve the sense of community, cooperation, and common commitment essential... to reach the levels that we all seek."

He went on to offer "to repay the wives expenses personally," but also noted that the SCOLS subcommittee "did not believe that the Dean should cover the expenses or that the faculty should."

The dean also reported that "some students... were threatening to sue the law school." He warned that "we have worked far too hard building up this school to have a round of bad publicity even temporarily set us back." Accordingly, he advised the disputes "ought to be given a chance to be worked out inside... before... publicly aired.... Surely we... can devise procedures to resolve our own disagreements."

The situation was at the cusp between celebration on the one hand and fiasco on the other. Eventually, the outcry became a whimper that died away for many reasons among which were the dean's importunings, student complacency, and the drag of time.

## AFTERMATH:

Gaining that final accreditation pulled a cap that released a flood of ambitions held in wait. Dean Fagg became an AALS Inspector and member of the AALS Accreditation

Committee. Librarian Brown was elected to the Oregon State Senate (a move that greatly troubled President Howard and eventually led to Brown's resignation). Doris McCroskey would leave NWLC in order to return to her main love of writing, as a published author in major magazines and newspapers: *Christian Science Monitor*, *Readers Digest*, *Ladies Home Journal*, and *Sunset*. I began a series of teaching lectures in Iowa, Montana, South Carolina, Reno, and Stanford on Evidence Law for the American Judicial Academy. NWLC entered its first inter-school moot court venture, where students Linda Triplett and Larry Wobbrock won an upper division first place. It was a feat that began decades of NWLC moot court success.

But all such movement and acclaim could not dim our final December 1973 accreditation victory. That success began a parade of publicity that moved us out of Portland's shadows and into its limelight. A host of press conferences ensued, complete with battery of reporters, mikes, and cameras from radio, television, and newspapers. The Oregon Journal newspaper headline read "Law School Goes Big Time." The story reported in part:

"What many probably do not realize is that a Portland law school born in the

**MIKES, CAMERA, ACTION**

Press conference in Boley Library on gaining full accreditation: President Howard, Dean Fagg, and Alumni President Keith Burns (chief assistant to Oregon governor).

dark of night and destined to struggle..., has moved into the front rank of legal training.... Portland's only law school has come of age."

## CELEBRATION:

On such emergence, there was, indeed, reason to put on the dog, sound the horn, raise the colors, and paint our town red. Festivities took place on Saturday, January 26, 1974, in the Crystal Room of the swank Benson Hotel—an inn almost as old as the law school. Much had changed since the late 1880s when school and hotel made the Portland scene. Over a half century ago, the two had come together when Northwestern College of Law held its graduation dinner-dance at the Benson. At that 1922 fete, one of the graduates and her family were turned away at the hotel lobby door. She was not allowed to enter and participate with her classmates at the celebration of their four years together. Beatrice Cannady and her family were black.

Now here in 1974, we were celebrating in the same place, but this time with no bigoted impasses. Rather, crystal bright light blazed with color and good cheer unshadowed by the dark of ignorance and hate.

The dinner was fancy. The printed program read: "Champagne, Consommé, Chef Salad, Gourmet Dressing, Prime Rib of Beef, Peas Bourgeoises, Fresh Fruit Chantilly Tart," and more champagne—all in capital letters and finesse. Attire was gown and black tie optional. I opted out of the tuxedo—a rental cost that this author found too elite for his parsimonious, Great Depression, blue-collar upbringing. I had rented a tux for a college prom once and vowed never to do so again. I rationalized that the rental money better fit the empty pocket of needed student loans or grants. I did not preach that attitude; it suited only me.

The program treated the diners to remarks from President Howard and Dean Fagg, who both delivered the usual cordialities and expected gratitudes. Key addresses were presented by Professor Maurice Rosenberg, President of AALS, and by Justice Ralph Holman. Their texts were wide apart in tenor and style. They bridged the gap between the old and the new law school. Holman was *the old*—a 1937 graduate of the downtown Northwestern night law school. Rosenberg was *the new*—figurehead of the nation's legal education family in which we were now its newborn.

Rosenberg's comments were standard praise. He characterized our college and president and dean as having "dignity, charm, and sincerity," just as he (Rosenberg) abounded in dignity, charm and sincerity. As for the 128th member of AALS, he said NWLC had "well exceeded minimum standards" and had shown "unmistakable signs of forward movement,... vibrant, forceful support of alumni and friends,... superb setting and physical plant." He capped his praise with the prediction that we were "destined for the front ranks among law schools of America."

In contrast to Rosenburg's customary, appropriate, and congratulatory welcome to the fold, Holman's comments were challenging—even upsetting to some. His speech called for two name changes; one of which managed to disturb the older crowd of his fellow alumni and the other managed to irk the younger crowd of alumni. He urged that "Northwestern" be dropped from the law school name and that "Environmental" be dropped from the law review periodical name. That took the words "name dropping" to new and astonishing impact. When it comes to the trauma of sudden shifting from old to new, the changing of names has to be the most violent of disruptions. I'm certain that if Congress should ever propose dropping, "United States" from "The United States of America," there would be so many secessions that no Civil War and no number of Lincolns could ever succeed in holding our borders together.

RALPH HOLMAN

Nevertheless, Holman used the ceremonial banquet as an opportunity to urge removing "Northwestern" and "Environmental" from our store window. Had we not

**CRYSTAL ROOM FESTIVITY**

Benson Hotel Victory Party (January 1974). Identifiable celebrants (l. to r.): the author, AALS President Maurice Rosenberg, Ruth Howard, Justice Holman (background), Mrs. Rosenberg, Judge Charles Crookham (background).

been in a dignified, celebratory mood for cheers, there might have been jeers. It would have made no difference; Holman had never been one to shy from candor or distraction. One could never be sure about his tongue. Where was it—in his heart or in his cheek? His arguments for re-naming school and law review proceeded much as previously detailed. [See ch. 15, "Environmental Image"]

But this was a red-letter day; and nothing, not even elocutions too blunt as in dull or too blunt as in brusque, could overcome the spirit of laughter, dance, balloons, toasts, and whatever else it was that sent everyone home with lucky stars to sleep on.


Quite early the next morning, Sunday, January 27, the day following the celebration and the day before my 42nd birthday, I ran an errand back to the Crystal Room of the Benson Hotel. I had forgotten my promise to Dorothy Cornelius to retrieve the college's podium logo plaque. I arrived before the hotel clean-up crew and found the plaque still draped with serpentine and a deflated balloon.

In the quiet and shadows, midst stale champagne glasses, confetti-ridden floors, and unlit crystal, I remembered something that had not dawned on me the festive night before. Just one hundred yards away, on a straight line through the walls of the hotel and into the walls of the next door building, I first taught a law school class as a practicing lawyer. It was a class in Code Pleading in a dingy room on the upstairs floors of the Giesy Building, now razed and replaced.

Here, seven and one half years later I had returned nearby to an elegant crystal ballroom. At that scene, we had capped a quest that turned a dim-lit classroom one hundred yards away into this opulence and national cognizance. The short distance through those walls had been a long tunneling.

While sitting alone with memory of what had brought us to this crystallization, someone flicked on the lights and the chandeliers and sconces blazed again, as workers arrived to tidy the room and empty it of my ghosts. Sparkle and glimmer shined upon the clean-up that made ready for tomorrows.

The era was over now, and a new day had begun.

# 1974: TIME CONTEXT

U.S. Supreme Court unanimously rules that Nixon must relinquish to the special prosecutor all of his tapes.

The House Judiciary Committee recommends Presidential impeachment.

Nixon resigns the Presidency.

Gerald Ford becomes the 39th U.S. President.

Ford pardons Nixon for any potential crimes and grants amnesty to all Vietnam draft dodgers and military deserters.

Muhammad Ali regains heavyweight title.

Streaking becomes a fad.

Hank Aaron breaks Babe Ruth's home run record.

Little League Baseball, Inc., allows girls to play on its teams.

Northwestern School of Law of Lewis & Clark College begins its first academic year as a nationally recognized place for educating those who embrace a nation formed by the People and governed by their Law.

# EPILOGUE

## EDDIES, HALLMARKS, AND LEGACIES

Below is a chart of some of NWLC statistical growth in rough numbers during and beyond the accreditation era:

| Statistical Category | Near the Start of the Era | At the End of the Era (Fall 1973) | Modernly (2009 - 2010) |
|---|---|---|---|
| Annual Operating Budget | $110,000 (1966-67) | $1,340,000 | $27,000,000 |
| Evening Tuition | $500 | $1,100 | $24,000 |
| Day Tuition | [None] | $1,900 | $32,000 |
| Library Volumes | 7,000 | 62,500 | 500,000 plus |
| Student Body (Day & Eve) | 230 (Fall 1967 | 690 | 740 |
| Women Enrollment | 14 (Fall 1967) | 97 | 340 |
| Ethnic Diversity Enrollment (Minorities) | 10 | 18 | 135 (in 2008) |
| Faculty (Tenured or Tenure-tracked) | 5 | 19 | 40 |

| Statistical Category | Near the Start of the Era | At the End of the Era (Fall 1973) | Modernly (2009 - 2010) |
|---|---|---|---|
| Staff (including non-tenure-tracked Legal Writing and Clinical Professors | 3 | 27 | 110 approx. |
| Student-Faculty Ratio* | 44 to 1 | 30 to 1 | 10 to 1 approx. |
| Author Lansing's Salary | $12,000 (1967-69) | $25,000 | $121,500 (in 1999-2000) |

*Caveat: Standards for interpretation of faculty-student, full-time-equivalency [FTE] numbers have changed over the years*

And so it is that growth is customarily measured in ciphers arranged in charts of either columns or pies or in graphs marked by numerical peaks and pits. The rise of the spikes tends to obscure the dips, and Portland's law school has had its share of those bottoms—depressions that cannot be truly fathomed by mere numbers. Here's a different way of sounding those depths:

THE EDDIES:

Law schooling in Portland began in 1884 with a mere handful of students taught in faculty living rooms and rented quarters. The school nearly died in World War I and World War II. It was abandoned in Portland in 1915. It was taken up by new parentage twice—once in 1915 and again in 1965. It had to change its name twice and then again a third time following the accreditation era.

In that stormy accreditation era, the deanship changed four times; almost one-third of its faculty departed; and the struggle to enter national acceptance was denied admittance four times.

The school's effort to rise met setbacks from many directions on many occasions, among which were: ambivalence about seeking AALS membership; accrued indebtedness for past deficit spending; attempts to withdraw from an environmental image; national indignation at the ouster of a respected dean; bad publicity at poor bar exam passage; encounters with a trustee standing committee directed to manage faculty decisions; and resentment within the college family about fostering its new and needy law school ward.

Thus, there were times when the NWLC current circled backward. An optimistic

Edison would not have called those ebbs and eddies failures—each being a success in learning. But even Edison would have to admit that it is punishing to be schooled in that way.

But, whether disappointments or lessons, they were challenges and were made all the more so by the whirlwinds outside our doors—movements seeking peace, civil rights, gender equality, and safe environment. Those dynamics widened gaps between dove and hawk, distaff and spearside, trees and jobs, black and white, protest and police, young and old—all riled by the anxieties and angst of threatened cold and hot war, atomic annihilation, assassinations, White House criminality, pollution, over-population, defiance of integration, sexual revolution, drug abuse, and growing distrust of established authority by a new age.

The era began with five full-time professors and went through the comings and goings of twenty-eight professors, ending with nineteen remaining. Only one lasted through the whole struggle. That loner fancied himself a co-captain refusing to abandon a sinking ship or was in fact merely a passenger trapped in steerage or a stowaway hiding in predicament. I have never been able to figure out which.

Likewise, the law school itself was in something of a refusal, a trap, or a predicament. For a time it wavered between attitudes. On the one hand was the tug of a venerable, proven, provincial past with its independent mind. On the other, was the yearning to become a nationally recognized school with a mind willing to extend itself and its values into cooperation with the national union of legal education.

THE HALLMARKS:

When accreditation was eventually achieved, Professor Maurice Rosenberg, President of AALS, foretold that NWLC was "destined for the front ranks among law schools in America." Since then the school has reached many plateaus true to that prediction. Out of the foregoing ashes, the new born Lewis & Clark Law School has risen to these accolades and milestones:

From a place with virtually no interscholastic **moot court** efforts, the school now has participated in eleven different annual court competitions in categories ranging through negotiations to trial to appellate practices; from specialities ranging from immigration to taxation to Native American Law; on regional, national, and international levels. The contests have shown remarkable success. E.g., In the twenty years of National *Environmental* Moot Court competition, with some seventy law schools participating, Lewis & Clark teams have placed in the top three finalist spots twelve times and have been first seven times, including first in the last three years as of this writing. In the Animal Law Moot Court, Lewis & Clark has won the competition in two out of the last three years, having had the advantage of a coach in only the last few years of the seven years in which there has been such contest. In the 2009 Jessup International Law Moot Court competition, the brief of the Lewis & Clark team placed fourth among 400 law schools from 90 countries and was first among the 145 U.S. law schools competing. Early in the 1990s, the NWLC Client Counseling Moot Court Team rivaled with teams from Scotland, Wales, England, Australia, Canada, and the U.S., and won that competition in Canada. By 2007, the contest grew internationally, and the Lewis & Clark team had the highest score among fifteen semi-finalists and then went on to place in the final six. In 2008, it won third place out of 143 schools contesting. In short, numerous cups and plaques now adorn our trophy case.

From a sole **clinical operation** that began with no quarters of its own and weekly visits to the Valley Migrant League offices, Lewis & Clark Law School now has not one, but six clinics available for student training: three officed on campus (Pacific Environmental Advocacy Center; International Environmental Law Project; and Animal Law Clinic); and three with downtown offices (National Crime Victim Law Institute [NCVLI]; Small Business Legal Clinic; and the granddad of them all, the Lewis & Clark Legal Clinic). Students have researched and written briefs, have argued, and have won numerous cases before appellate courts, including the Supreme Court of the United States.

Since a maiden **externship** idea that placed a few students at law offices in the Portland vicinity, Lewis & Clark Law School now supports an expanded placement of twenty students on average per year in semester-long apprenticing in supreme courts, trial courts, the U.S. Congress, state legislatures, the United Nations, federal and state agencies, prosecutor and public defender offices, and other law-related positions in workplaces from Oregon to Washington, D.C., to Hong Kong.

From dim and dingy, upstairs rentals and from make-do living room, bedroom and kitchen quarters, and since the accreditation era's three building complex, the law school's **Tryon Forest campus** has further expanded with a fourth, three-storied building (the Swindells Research Center) and an elaborate, three-storied, "Wood Hall" extension of the library building.

As of 2009, the size of the Lewis & Clark **law library** (well over a half million volumes) reportedly makes it the 64th largest law library in the nation—the second largest in the Pacific northwest, and the largest in Oregon. Beyond mere size, it has been rated in the top twenty percent of *the all-around best* law school libraries.

Prior to the merger and accreditation, the law school could claim only one **book publication** by its law faculty, and that was way back in 1893. The school's co-founder and first professor, Richard Hopwood Thornton, had published his first edition of *Principles of Commercial Law*. The third edition was published in Portland in 1897. Since the accreditation era and as of 2009, the law school's professors have authored

115 published books. And that does not include a large number of volumes in which professors contributed chapters in books or edited books. Nor does it include the vast amount of law articles printed in the nation's law reviews or periodicals from Lewis & Clark pens. Aside from publications of faculty, the school itself now publishes not one, but three academic periodicals. In addition to *Environmental Law* (begun during the accreditation era and the first of its kind in the nation), the school now produces *Animal Law* (also the first of its kind in the nation) and *Lewis & Clark Law Review* (a traditional law school publication).

As for the meager **endowment** at the end of the accreditation era, the school now has five endowed Professorships and five endowed Faculty Scholars. Additionally, many funds are earmarked for student scholarships, dignitary visits, and annual events. Among those dignitary events, seven U.S. Supreme Court Justices have graced NWLC halls. As reported in the text, Justices Douglas and Clark visited during the era. Since then Justices Ruth Ginsberg, Lewis Powell, Anthony Scalia, Sandra Day O'Conner, and Anthony Kennedy have also come to the campus. Many other celebrities were visitors, some more star than dignitary, e.g., Erin Brockovich and Robert Redford.

The sheer number of hopefuls who continue to deluge the **Admissions** Office for entry as first-year students, shows more and more the growing reputation of the school. In 2009, the school received well over 3,000 applications from law career aspirants. Inquiry prospects exceeded 6,000. The numbers advance, not just in quantity, but also in quality. The LSAT and undergraduate grade point medians of first year enrollees placed the school in the top quartile of U.S. law schools. Another indication of a school's rise competitively is the company it keeps. Somewhere in the 1980s, applicants to Lewis & Clark Law School began listing, as alternative choices, top-ranked, elitist schools in the east and around the nation. We were rubbing shoulders in the national and international market place.

Modernly, from those who indulge in **ranking** the nation's two hundred law schools, Lewis & Clark Law School has been highly placed in certain categories. Its Environmental Program annually leads at the first or second place. Consistent with such renown, the ABA awarded the program with its Distinguished Achievement Award—the first time that honor was ever given. The Legal Writing program is regularly slotted among the top twenty in the nation. The Public Interest Law program has been ranked third in the nation.

Nothing speaks better of an alma mater's hallmarks than does the success of its **alumni**. Since merger and accreditation, the graduates of NWLC include U.S. Ambassadors, U.S. Congressmen, state legislators, trial and appellate judges, White House aides, district attorneys, public defenders, federal and state agency officers, city and county commissioners, eminent lawyers, law professors, and business leaders. All of these have added to the rich heritage of Oregon's top public servants in the past: governors, secretarys of state, speakers of the House of Representatives, and Supreme Court justices.

## THE LEGACIES:

Like the moment of a baby's birth—after conception, gestation, and parturition—accreditors will count to make sure a school has ten fingers and ten toes. From thereon, just as a person will grow its own personality, so too a school will form its own character. The foregoing lessons, milestones, accolades, and victories are but the seeds of that character. History is not heritage. History comes and goes, leaving heritage for now and hereafter.

So, what is inherited from the 1965-74 accreditation struggle and its lessons learned? And how much of that tradition is unique? Answers are surmise bordering on fancy. Singling out a legacy from years of growth and a mass of dissemination is a task no different than the search for the tree where a forest began. And when found, one must distinguish legacy from legend.

*Environmental Legacy:* One inheritance is obvious and certain. Lewis & Clark Law School maintains strong attention to the use or the abuse of this planet's air, water, and land resources—an emphasis that has now been joined by the nation as a whole. And that legacy has also seeded similar respect for animals, which once again has put this school on lead nationally in animal law programming.

*Student Involvement Legacy:* Born out of student body activism in the 1960s and supported by a young faculty, there came an early recognition that students at the graduate level are not just *objects* of schooling, they are key *subjects* in the development of their schooling. Accordingly, the law school placed unique value on student representation and initiative, backed by voice and vote, on important educational issues. That student involvement has also developed into close and open-door, faculty-student relations. Modernly, the value of student input has given rise to faculty respect for and use of detailed student evaluations of professor performance—a fair exchange for teacher grading of students.

In September 1968, it was a handful of evening students, not the dean or faculty, who first petitioned for the start of a NWLC law review publication. The idea was not then accepted. When Dean Wren arrived, in the following year, he knew the value and made the student idea happen. That legacy of student initiative was alive again in the 21st century when a handful of students, without law school sponsorship, set in motion the nation's first Animal Law periodical that today is fully embraced by its school and by national following.

Another example of strong student initiative (so characteristic of origins in the accreditation era) is today's student-operated Public Interest Law Project [PILP] among the first to organize in the nation's law schools.

*Faculty Management Legacy:* During the accreditation era, the law school also developed a somewhat uncommon characteristic for faculty involvement in administrative business—an alertness that, of course, had to concern educational policy but that developed a tendency to go beyond policy and into implementation. Such scrutiny had been a necessary task for professors when administrators were but a handful, when gaining threshold accreditation was the primary task, and when situations arose for wresting reins from higher commands yet welcoming their counsel.

Today, that legacy is still evident. Unlike many law schools, Lewis & Clark professors not only tend to teaching, writing, and serving the community, they also have kept a keen watch on internal operations. To that end, job placement, fiscal matters, financial development, admissions procedure, alumni affairs, and other administration (including deans' offices) are not free from professorial scrutiny and chores. In short, it has been said that one of the legacies born of seeking national recognition is the image of Lewis & Clark Law School as faculty operated.

*Diversity Legacy:* All law schools in those 1960-70 years developed a pronounced awareness of the need for diverse race and gender backgrounds. But at NWLC diversity had been advanced in still other ways. From its parent college came attention to international and cultural mix in enrollment and study. Then too, most distinctively, diversity was wrought from old Northwestern and its evening enrollees—a joinder of occupations and ages—a cross-generational study atmosphere. Today, what with a mixed body of day and night schooling, a sizeable portion of students in their early twenties, fresh from collegiate life, are joined with many in their thirties and forties who come from family and other work careers. On average one out of every three students are married. They bring to the common focus on law study diverse color, class, gender, and age in backgrounds ranging from chemist to carpenter, politician to police, teacher to technician, surgeon to seller, mechanic to musician.

*Teaching Legacy:* Another theme engrained in the law school's character is more subtle. It traces back eight decades before the merger and was kept alive in the accreditation era. For want of a better name, I have taken the label for the legacy from its evening origins. The word "Practical" first came to mind, but unfortunately, that word puts what is meant here in contrast to "Theory"—an antithesis which is simply not the case. Law itself, in a democracy, is at one and the same time, practiced and principled.

Late in the 1800s, night school and its focus on sound law practice began in Portland and grew out of the desire for part-time and handy law learning in preparation for career opportunity. That convenience found its place at night in order to accommodate family, work, and other day time obligations. Taught by professional practitioners and active judges, the teaching went directly to the core of law analysis at work after hours. It was an emphasis and still is a reminder that "Living Law" is not just an art viewed from towers; it is an applied science tested in streets. Thus, classroom teaching became the central focus and forum for learning, where teaching before bedtime had to awaken minds and befit folk learning.

While other schools share a regard for classroom teaching and skill learning, Northwestern College of Law night schooling accentuated that healthy combination of pedagogical and vocational proficiencies—a legacy still evident today in the classroom and the curriculum. Course scheduling shows study in legal-research and writing skills, trial practicums, appellate advocacy, moot courts, externships, clinical offerings, and pro bono work.

"Street Law" was a project that emphasized the need to bring Law to the public and to primary and secondary schools. Originating here at this law school, as led by Marilyn Cover, it now has its own separate organization called "Classroom Law Project" and has joined others to reach national and international scope.

As for the classroom, the school continues to honor its teaching identity with an annual, best teacher award, with academic chairs and faculty scholarships expressly targeted on teaching ability, with a pool of thirty to forty part-time teachers taken from the top ranks of Bench and Bar. The latter have included Oregon Supreme Court justices, U.S. Judicial Circuit Court appellate judges, federal and state trial judges, noted law teachers visiting from the nation's leading law schools, and a host of Oregon's best lawyers.

*Name Legacy:* Throughout these pages, there has been agonizing over titles and name changes. E.g. "University" or "College"? "Assistant Dean" or "Assistant to the Dean"? "Northwestern" or "Lewis & Clark"? The struggle to find the right use of words is something that lawyers and poets have in common, albeit for different motives—technical meaning (denotative) vis-a-vis passionate feeling (connotative). The word for the debate that often ensues is "logomachy".

At the law school, the most significant contention has surrounded the name of the school. That title has changed so many times that evolution has become part of the legacy. In 1884, it began as the "University of Oregon Law Department" (a christening). In 1915, it became "Northwestern College of Law" (an orphaning), soon followed by just "Northwestern" (a nicknaming). In 1965, it changed to "Northwestern School of Law of Lewis and Clark College" (a wedding), here narrowed to "NWLC" (a space saver). Modernly, somewhere near the turn into the 21st century, it settled into "Lewis & Clark Law School" (an adaptation to national and international usage). All were inevitable.

So, who knows? Perhaps, the school banner is not yet ready for permanent staking. Perhaps, it is not at the end of the trail forged. After all, "Lewis and Clark" refers to a band of explorers led by two white men, and served by an Indian woman, a black slave, and a Newfoundland dog. Like Meriwether, William, Sacagawea, York, Seaman, and others, this law school searched and found a passage into new ground— a *Northwestern* frontier—environment for pioneering.

As the last of the downtown, night-time, part-time law teachers, I rued the fading of the "Northwestern" name but was relieved to know it is only language that evolves. Heritage never changes. The legend and legacy remain.

*Oregon Legacy:* One cannot escape the fact that place is bred into soul. This law school was born just twenty-five years after Oregon statehood. Oregon Country was the "Land of Empire Builders," so sings its state anthem. Indeed, at one time, in the mid-1800s, it was its own nation. Its flag differs from other state flags in that its opposite sides unfurl two different patterns. The Oregon motto is: "She Flies with Her Own Wings"—a grand tradition that gives to its own a reason to soar.

This has been but some of the outer garments of a school since its accreditation era. Other fabric undoubtedly lies unseen and untold. Sometimes texture may be so finely woven that only the unraveling of time will reveal its threads.

# Appendix A
# THE DEANS

## FOUR ACCREDITATION ERA DEANS

As of 2009, the 125 year history of Portland's law school has had eleven permanent dean regimes and six interim doyen or doyenne. It is difficult to know where to place temporary deans in a dean regime progression. Where the one must show progress, the other must maintain—a difference between venturing forth and taking care. Over the decades, some of those caretakers have included Robert S. Miller, John Flint Gantenbein, and Lydia Loren. Others went on to become fully appointed, e.g., Steve Kanter and Fred Fagg.

As for the accreditation era, four decanal regimes were spread across almost nine years. Deans George Neff Stevens, Harold Wren, and Fred Fagg III and interim Dean Jack Cairns brought unique attributes needed in the circumstances: the experience of Stevens, the devotion of Cairns, the energy of Wren, and the finesse of Fagg.

Dean Stevens, with his many years as a law educator and administrator, faced an undergraduate college that had never had a professional graduate school. Lessons from his tenure, punctuated by forceful confrontation and publicized departure, provided a sober reminder that law schools were no longer to be treated as just another "department" in the undergraduate list of arts and sciences, as once they were in decades past.

Dean Cairns stepped into abrupt vacancy with a legal education background limited to student and part-time teacher at his alma mater. Yet, as a committed alumnus of old Northwestern night schooling, and as a trustee who had helped negotiate the merger, he met the caretaking challenge with a term that stuck to the promises in the merger agreement by commencing a huge building fund campaign and the purchase of land for construction of a law campus.

Dean Wren brought a much needed exuberance that energized his regime with the start of a day division, the hiring of nineteen professors, the advent of many events and conferences, the building of a Tryon Forest law complex, and the award of temporary accreditation from the ABA.

Dean Fagg cemented a stronger link between the parent college and its adolescent law school, while at the same time juggling a growing independence in a law faculty bent upon control. His tact and maneuvering were high among the reasons that produced permanent accreditation from both the ABA and AALS.

# Appendix B
# THE PROFESSORS

## WHERE NOW?

As previously stated, twenty-eight full-time, tenure-tracked professors reached the NWLC faculty roster during the accreditation era [1965-74]. Nine of those 28 exited during the era ["The Departers"]. Nineteen were left at the end of the era ["The Remainders"]. At present, four of the 28 are still active on the faculty: Ed Brunet, Jim Huffman, Doug Newell, and Bernie Vail. The other 24 bade farewell for various reasons:

Seven **retired** from their law careers. The first to part was Jim Lenoir in 1970 after just one semester with NWLC. After the era, Jim Dente was the next to leave in 1988 at age 61 after 16 years with NWLC. Then Bill Knudsen went emeritus in 1989 at age 67 after 19 years. Bob Myers departed in 1991 at age 65 after 19 years. Billy Williamson left on or about year 2000 at age 62 after 31 years. This author retired in January 2009 at age 76 after almost 43 years at NWLC and continues to be officed on campus and carried on faculty rolls as an emeritus professor. Leading the list of retirees should be Ed Belsheim. He had been a law teacher for over sixty years—the last twenty-two of those years at NWLC. When he stopped teaching in 1994, he was almost ninety years old and died just months later.

Five of the departers **returned to the practice** of law: Jack Cairns and Paul Gerhardt were, in 1970, the first to leave academia for the profession. Then Hal Bloomenthal left in 1972. Three years after the era, John Barrett and Alan Jensen departed in 1977 for law practices in Florida and Portland, respectively.

Five went on **to other law schools.** In 1969, Ross Runkel went to the faculty of Willamette University College of Law, and Wayne Walker joined the Ohio State

University Law School. Then in 1972, Hal Wren went to the Richmond Law School. Three years after the era, in 1977, Jim Bross went to Chicago-Kent College of Law and on to Georgia State University College of Law. Jay Folberg became the dean of the University of San Francisco School of Law in 1990.

Four went **to other endeavors**: Jacqui Jurkins departed in 1972 to become the Multnomah County Law Librarian. Two years after the era in 1976, Bill Snouffer left the classroom for the bench as an Oregon District Court and Circuit Court trial judge. In 1979, Walt Brown exited for a career as an Oregon State Senator and Socialist politician, being that party's candidate for U.S. President in the 2004 election. Fred Fagg took leave in 1984 to become the President of the Mountain States Legal Foundation (a group dedicated to "individual liberty and the right to own and use property"), and then became "of counsel" in a Portland law firm as well as co-founder of a law software computer business. Three of the 28 accreditation era professors **resigned**. George Neff Stevens in 1967; Jerry Hughey in 1974-75; and Len DuBoff in 1994-95.

**Necrology**: Six of the above who desisted are now deceased; Ed Belsheim [d. 1994]. Fred Fagg [d. 2002]. Paul Gerhardt [d. 2002]. Jerry Hughey [d. mid-1980s]. Jim Lenoir [d. mid-1980s], and George Neff Stevens [d. 1998]. There may be others—those whose whereabouts are lost in the fog that shrouds endings.


Over the years, the faculty story has not been just departure. Indeed, a faculty breathes—exhales and inhales—lives on. In the few years immediately following the era, the faculty received four new acquisitions. Mindful of the fact that all but one of the foregoing were men, the new recruits were all women: Diane Spies, Elizabeth Madsen, Patricia Watson, and Barbara Safriet. Only Safriet stayed around long enough to leave an imprint. She left in 1988 to become a chief administrator and lecturer at Yale Law School.

The trafficking of professors to and from the NWLC faculty has thus continued throughout the decades. As of this printing, there have been a total of 74, full-time, tenure-tracked law professors. After account taken of defections (for any of the foregoing reasons), the current faculty roster lists about forty members—one-quarter of whom are women professors.

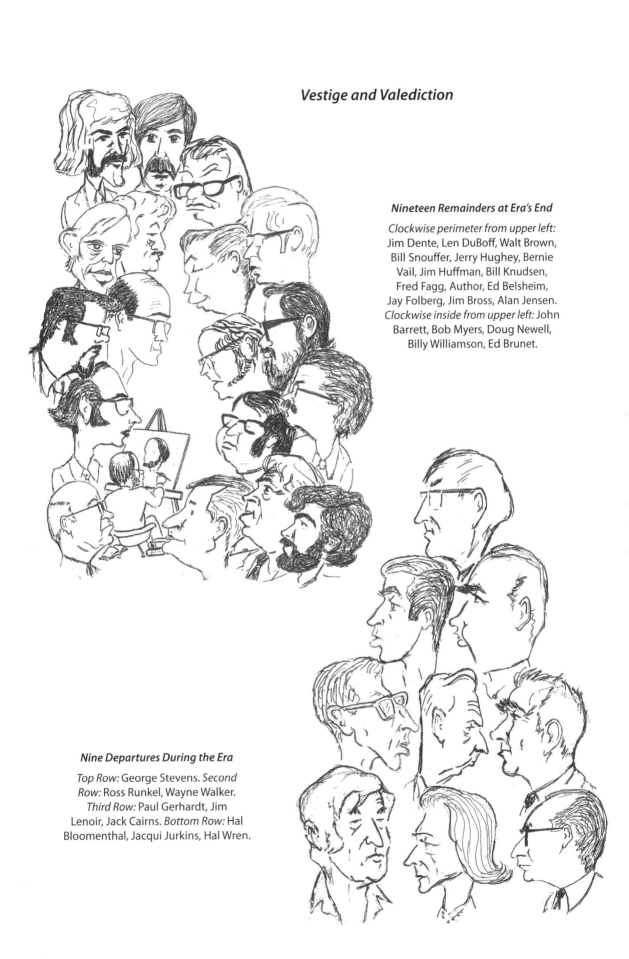

# Vestige and Valediction

### Nineteen Remainders at Era's End

*Clockwise perimeter from upper left:* Jim Dente, Len DuBoff, Walt Brown, Bill Snouffer, Jerry Hughey, Bernie Vail, Jim Huffman, Bill Knudsen, Fred Fagg, Author, Ed Belsheim, Jay Folberg, Jim Bross, Alan Jensen. *Clockwise inside from upper left:* John Barrett, Bob Myers, Doug Newell, Billy Williamson, Ed Brunet.

### Nine Departures During the Era

*Top Row:* George Stevens. *Second Row:* Ross Runkel, Wayne Walker. *Third Row:* Paul Gerhardt, Jim Lenoir, Jack Cairns. *Bottom Row:* Hal Bloomenthal, Jacqui Jurkins, Hal Wren.

# Appendix C
# PRIME MOVERS

Reviewers of this manuscript longed to know my opinion as to who, beyond the law faculty, were other key contributors to our accreditation success. A host of helpful trustees, alumni, administrators, donors, friends, and students could fill pages. Indeed, only some of their names are spread throughout the pages of this book. Listing all of them is a task too horrendous to undertake and a risk too prone to mistake. Recognizing the massive teamwork will have to suffice as the only homage given.

However, aside from law deans and professors, four men stand out and were highly instrumental throughout that era: President John Howard; trustee William Swindells, Sr.; trustee Paul Boley, and ABA Consultant and AALS Director Millard Ruud. Ruud's career and ours seemed to follow parallel paths as he too began when we did and grew as we did into national recognition.

President Howard was the one who fought to have this law school merged with his college. He may not have always been endeared in his times, but in retrospect, the respect now given him is deserved. His firm leadership against strong resistance to the law school's development may not have been noticed up close; but from this distance, it was monumental.

Notably missing from the list of contributors thus far noted is the absence of female names—an absence born of attitudes inherent in the past, not of present neglect. But in spite of suppression, there were distaff staff whose work effort and dedication went beyond the call to buoy our ascendancy. Among them were those who led: Dorothy Cornelius, Virginia Hughes, Ann Kendrick, Grace Kralovec, Doris McCroskey, and Mary Ann Normandin.

Without the efforts of key contributors, stalwart workers, and the vast array of movers in between, there would have been no accreditation as it were. That others would have accomplished the quest sooner or later had we not, is to say no more than humankind would have also learned to fly without the Wright brothers and would have invented the electric light bulb without Edison or baseball without Doubleday. But others did not, and they did. And history, perforce, toasts and boasts what was real, not what can be fancied.

Clockwise from upper left: John Howard, Millard Ruud, William Swindells, Sr., and Paul Boley.

# Appendix D
# THE DOWAGER AND I

Like many in this world, I have always wanted two goals: to write a book and to be a star. A memoir is an ideal place to satisfy both penchants. But this reminiscence was equally about a dignified dowager. Born in 1884, she is reportedly the fourth oldest evening law school in America, the seventy-fifth law school in the nation, and tied for the second law school in the West. As of this publication, she is 126 years old.

This memorialist is almost 79 years old as of this wet ink drying. I began teaching law at the school when I was 34 and when she was still known in common parlance as simply "Northwestern." I am the last of that old cadre of lawyers and judges who taught part-time in downtown Portland. I have been on the faculty rolls ever since the name changed to "Northwestern School of Law of Lewis and Clark College" [NWLC]. And I was on those rolls through the national and international evolution into "Lewis & Clark Law School."

Thus, I have been with her for 45 years—more than half of my existence. And she has accepted me for more than one-third of hers. Those years in attendance have been longer than any other courtiers—*e.g.*, co-founder Richard Hopwood Thornton (about 20 years), Proprietor John Flint Gantenbein (about 35 years); Dean James W. Crawford (about 40 years).

I mark this connection, not with a star for me, but rather in fond admiration of her. I age. She evolves—grows younger. And therein lies another benefit of the memoir and the legendary: Both outlast and humble us.

# ACKNOWLEDGMENTS

Diaries are always the effort of a single author. Lecture notes and grocery lists are usually the same. Novels are principally so. But this story has been more than a private journal, note reminder, or work of fiction. It is a memoir marked for publication, meant for accuracy, preserved for posterity, and linked to school history. Accordingly, the assembly and input of many went into the product for which this author is given all the credit—some of which must now be shared:

Here are the advisors who reviewed early drafts of the manuscript and gave extensive consultation and encouragement: John Bates (former Chair of the College Board of Trustees), Barnes Ellis (lawyer and Honorary Alumni of the law school), Michael Blumm (Professor of Law), John Parry (Professor of Law), Joanne Nordling (author and friend), and Jewel Lansing (author and wife). Others who furnished insights (much appreciated) were Professor Steve Johansen, Professor Craig Johnston, and Professor Lydia Loren.

Fact informants appeared along the path of research. Here are but a few who had patience with my pester: Shannon Davis (admissions office), Susan Galyen (registrar), David Kelley (business office), Peter Nycum (law librarian), Janice Weiss (environmental office), Lynn Williams (assistant librarian), Doug Erickson and Jeremy Skinner (college archivists), and Martha Spence (Associate Dean of Academic Affairs and Admissions).

The diligence of digitizing and duplicating and the patience of packaging and processing through five years and more than twenty drafts, is what made these pages possible. Here then, are some of the workers whose inkings made my ink well read: Brienne Carpenter, Shirley Johansen, Sue Page, Andy Marion, and Duane Wheeler.

# REFERENCE SOURCES

Ordinarily, this would be called "Bibliography." But the prefix "biblio" refers to books, and books are not a cardinal source of a memoir where recall is the keepsake core. While author memory is central, sometimes the recollection of others who shared the times, served as mind joggers: Jim Huffman, Jack Kennedy, Bill Knudsen, Doug Newell, Bill Snouffer, and Hal Wren. Numerous other old-timers (mostly alumni) reminisced with me in correspondence or at soirees, banquets, reunions, and other encounters. But, alas, although treasures of the mind are sources for the researcher, they are not readily "re-sourced"—imprinted, but not in print.

With that caveat in mind, some written materials were mined, nevertheless:

## BOOKS:

Grun, Bernard, *Timetables of History*. (N.Y. 1979).

Hall, Kermit, *Magic Mirror: Law in American History*. (Oxford U. Press, 1989).

Leeson, Fred, *Rose City Justice*. (Or. Hist. Soc., 1998).

Reed, Albert, *Training for the Public Profession of the Law*. (N.Y. 1921).

Stevens, Robert, *Legal Education in America from 1850s to 1980s*. (Chapel Hill, N.C., 1987).

## ARTICLES:

Charnquist, C.H., "Northwestern School of Law," *Portland Commerce*, pp. 18-21 [July 1972].

Feldman, Stephen, "Transformation of an Academic Discipline: Law Professors in the Past and Future." *J. Leg. Educ.* 54: 471 (Dec. 2004).

Geil, John C., "Lewis and Clark Law School: Northwestern School of Law, 1884-1973," *Or. Hist. Soc. Q.* 84:389 (Winter 1983).

Stevens, Robert, "Aging Mistress: The Law School in America," *Change* (Jan-Feb 1970, pp. 32-34).

Thompson, Lindsay, "Richard Hopwood Thornton 1846-1925," *The Advocate* (NWLC, 1984).

Articles and essays of this author may furnish insights into the memorialist's perspective of the school and into the law school's imprint on the memorialist: Lansing, "Cast of Caricatures," *The Advocate* 29:38 (NWLC, Fall 2009); "A Song of Sixpence." *The Advocate* 28:35 (NWLC, Fall 2008); "Alice in Law School Land." *Or. St. Bar Bulletin* (January 2005); "School, Bench, and Bar." *"Advocate Abridged p. 33,* (NWLC, Summer 2005); "Who's First." *Or. St. Bar Bulletin* (Aug-Sept 2003); "History of the Law School: A Dream Realized." *The Advocate* 22:13 (NWLC, Fall 2002); "Law School Genesis" and "Teacher," *Chalkings* (an audio tape, bands 2 and 17) (Monkey Tree Studio, March 2001); "Bryson and I," *The Advocate,* 21:20 (NWLC, Fall 2001); "Classrooms—Phalanx and Chalk.," *The Journal* 67:11 (Lewis & Clark College, Spring 1987).

## NEWSPAPERS:

What would the events of history be without benefit of current and daily publication?—which is to say, without newspapers. Pertinent articles in *The Oregonian,* the now defunct *Oregon Journal,* and the *Daily Journal of Commerce* are cited in the text. While there was also television and radio coverage of law school episodes, forty-year-old air-time has been exactly that: air—lost in time—not a convenient source for resourcing.

## ACCREDITOR PUBLICATIONS:

*ABA Standards for Legal Education* (1969 version)

*AALS Guideline Statement on the Establishment of New Law Schools* (1967 version)

*ABA Review of Legal Education,* Annual series from Fall 1967 through 1974.

Ruud, Millard, "Chairpersons' Reflections," 1969-93 (formerly posted at the ABA website).

## NWLC IN-HOUSE PUBLICATIONS

Modernly, Lewis & Clark Law School's alumni publication is a multi-paged, magazine called *The Advocate*. It's predecessor in the accreditation era was NWLC's quarterly *Bulletin* (originally called the *Newsletter*—a four to six page pamphlet to alumni and friends). The law school's second major publication is its *Catalog*—another customary, photo-filled, multi-paged, annual designed for prospective students, pre-law advisers, and interested public. Its predecessor in the era was NWLC's student brochure—a 24 page handbook called "Announcements."

Helpful in gleaning the student voice was a stream of various student newspapers throughout the era, beginning with the *Demurrer* in 1969; followed by the *SBA Newsletter*, later in 1969; then the *Nightowl* in 1970; the *Law School News* in 1972; and finally the *Legal Beagle* in 1974. Some other titlings would follow in post-accreditation years: e.g., *In Re*; *Forum*; and *Letters of Law*. Their turnover was almost as frequent as graduates. Most appropriately, one was named *Disappearing Inc*.

## DOCUMENTS:

Most research for the accreditation era came from unpublished records. Principal among these writings was the merger contract that marked the beginning of the era: the "Agreement between Lewis and Clark College and Northwestern College of Law," dated 13 September 1965; plus its "Amendment Resolution of the Lewis and Clark Board of Trustees," dated 2 June 1969.

From that origin sprang a vast stream of paper: correspondence, memoranda, directives, budgets, proposals, reports, schedules, rosters, questionnaires, and minutes of trustee and SCOLS meetings. Most helpful were the minutes of the law faculty meetings as recorded by faculty scribes Jim Bross, Jim Huffman, this author, and sometimes by secretary Doris McCroskey.

Typical of many organizations, assemblies, and collectives, NWLC records were not always organized, assembled, or collected. Much documentation lies fallow in warehouse boxes, on storage shelves, or in scattered offices—piled but not compiled. A fair portion of these materials have been garnered by this memorialist—a collector, albeit a lame custodian and far from a much needed professional archivist. And so, as an alternative to an official archive, here now is this memoir that seeks to amass and crystallize what happened once upon a time to a school that journeyed through the vast grove of Academe and is now living happily ever after.

# APOLOGIA

No memory is safe from forget. And no omit is safe from offense taken. If there has been omission, I pray that my neglect will not boomerang—that the offended will not come back at me, will not do what I did, and will not forget forgiveness.

# INDEX

# ABOUT THE AUTHOR

Ronald B. Lansing is a Professor of Law Emeritus at Lewis & Clark Law School—formerly Northwestern School of Law of Lewis and Clark College—formerly Northwestern College of Law—formerly a Law Department of the University of Oregon. Lansing taught at that Portland based law school for forty-three years. He has been a law clerk for the Chief Justice of the Oregon Supreme Court, a pro-tem trial judge, a law review editor-in-chief, a practicing lawyer, a published author of three books and various law articles, a national chair of all tort law teachers, a chair of civic research studies, a faculty member of the American Judicial Academy, the original executive director of Oregon's Judicial Fitness Commission, and most appropriately here, the last surviving faculty member who worked throughout all the accreditation era that is the focus of this book.

## Other Books by the Author

*Skylarks & Lecterns: A Law School Charter* [N.Y., 1983]

*Juggernaut: The Whitman Massacre Trial* [Ninth Jud. Circ. Hist. Soc., 1993]

*Nimrod: Courts, Claims, and Killing on the Oregon Frontier* [Wash. St. Univ. Press, 2005]